Why Is America Different?

American Jewry on Its 350th Anniversary

Edited by
Steven T. Katz

UNIVERSITY PRESS OF AMERICA,® INC.
Lanham • Boulder • New York • Toronto • Plymouth, UK

Copyright © 2010 by
University Press of America,® **Inc.**
4501 Forbes Boulevard
Suite 200
Lanham, Maryland 20706
UPA Acquisitions Department (301) 459-3366

Estover Road
Plymouth PL6 7PY
United Kingdom

Library of Congress Control Number: 2009931860
ISBN: 978-0-7618-4768-7 (clothbound : alk. paper)
ISBN: 978-0-7618-4769-4 (paperback : alk. paper)
eISBN: 978-0-7618-4770-0

Contents

Preface

This volume is the second work to be published under the sponsorship of the Elie Wiesel Center for Judaic Studies at Boston University. As with our first publication—*The Shtetl: New Evaluations* (New York University Press, New York, 2007)—the subject of this present collection of essays reflects the Center's interest in the entire range of the Jewish experience, past and present. The particular event that acted as a catalyst for the focused conversation embodied in this collection was the 350th anniversary of the American Jewish community in 2004.

As the Director of the Elie Wiesel Center and the editor of this volume I have the pleasure of thanking a number of people whose help and hard work made this publication a reality. First, I need to note that the conference at which the papers in this collection were first presented was made possible by a gift to the Center from the Mike and Marilyn Grossman Endowment. In working on this manuscript I have felt, once more, the real absence created by Mike Grossman's death two years. Second, I am again indebted to Professor Elie Wiesel who supported the conference in every way possible and participated in it by giving a public lecture, the written version of which appears in this volume. Third, I need to thank all the individuals who participated in the conference and whose important research and reflections appears in the studies here being published. Grateful acknowledgement is also given to Eric Goldman for permission to print "Reflections on the Jewish Experience through American Cinema."

As regards the individual presentations I would add two further comments. First, there was no single model suggested to the presenters that they should seek to emulate. There is, therefore, some variety in the style of

presentation, for example, as to the length of the presentations and regarding such matters as whether or not to include footnotes. Most essays follow
a conventional academic format and do include notes, but not all do so.
Second, there were two presentations at the conference on the role of Jews
in American politics. These were presented by Congressman Barney Frank
and by Mr. Steve Grossman, former national Chairman of the Democratic
Party. Both gave interesting and informative talks but neither wanted to
put their views into print. (I would also note that we tried very hard to get
some Republican political figures, for example, Senator Orrin Hatch, to
participate but, in the end, were not successful in doing so.)

Lastly, no one organizes a conference and produces a publication by
himself. I am fortunate to have wonderful support and help at the Wiesel
Center from several individuals. First amongst these is the Center's Administrative Assistant, Ms. Pagiel Czoka. Ms. Czoka worked tirelessly to make
sure our original conference was a success and has continued to assure that
all the steps that needed to be taken to produce this book were done effi-
ciently, with a minimum of stress and a maximum of good humor. I would
also like to thank Ingrid Anderson, a graduate student in the Judaic Studies
Program, for help in checking the notes for each contribution. A thank you
is also due to Mrs. Judy Rothman and Ms. Samantha M. Kirk, our editors at
the University Press of America, whose help and many courtesies are greatly
appreciated. Finally, a public expression of gratitude to my wife Rebecca
who, as usual, helped in a variety of ways with this project.

Steven T. Katz
Editor

In Place of an Introduction: Some Thoughts on American Jewish Exceptionalism

Steven T. Katz, Boston University

Scholars, and others, interested in Jewish and American history, when reflecting on Jewish life in the United States, often ask whether the American Jewish experience represents a singular communal circumstance or whether it repeats, with obvious and unavoidable variation, the older European pattern of Jewish existence. In 2004, on the occasion of the 350th anniversary of the establishment of the American Jewish community, this question seemed well worth revisiting. To explore it more fully, the Elie Wiesel Center for Judaic Studies at Boston University brought together a distinguished group of scholars expert on the main areas of American Jewish life, stretching from the colonial Jewish experience to the image of Jews in contemporary films. The present volume represents the fruit of this collective reflection and interrogation.

With the publication of this rich and diverse set of essays, readers will be able to think along with the contributors to this collection about many of the major subjects that need to be considered in evaluating the American Jewish experience and come to their own conclusions about whether, and in what ways if any, this lived reality represents a departure from previous Jewish history. Thus, rather than attempt to briefly summarize the individual contributions to this volume, as is often done by volume editors, I would like to offer some reflections of my own on the topic of American Jewish exceptionalism.

Without being unduly pollyannish about the history of Jews in America, this now over 350 years-long tale appears to me, even already in the colonial era, to represent a significant deviation from prior historical Jewish experience. To explain why this is the case I would begin with the most

1

obvious as well as the most fundamental fact about America—that it was a new creation brought about by colonial conquest of the New World. As a consequence of this conquest, the majority of the land's original inhabitants were killed, primarily by unfamiliar imported pathogens against which the indigenous peoples had no immunity, and secondarily by war and the other destructive factors that flowed from colonial expansion and subjugation. In their place, and the place of their native societies, a novel socio-political reality came into being as a result of the migration of a variety of European peoples to the nascent American colonies. These peoples, together, constructed a socio-political order built not on primordial and material factors such as common ancestry, ethnicity, a common language and religion—as was the case with almost all of the world's previous cultures—but on ideological beliefs that were brought from the Old World to the New and which were then transmuted by the immigrants' experience as conquerors and settlers in a wholly different geographical space. Though some of these foundational doctrines and tenets continued to be colored by classical anti-Jewish elements, the core of the emerging colonial ideology, at least in the English colonies, carried, if largely unintentionally, positive implications for Jews and the first Jewish communities in these areas.

This fledgling core ideology included at least four fundamental beliefs. First among these was the idea of America as the "New Israel," i.e., America as a land of refuge, especially favored by Divine Providence. Just as God had protected the biblical Israel and brought it from bondage in Egypt, across the sea, to the "promised land," so too God was working to guide and protect those who now crossed the Atlantic in search of a new land of freedom. Accordingly, America had a special salvific role to play in human history. This theo-political belief is most often associated with the Puritans of New England who saw John Winthrop as their Moses and who gave their towns and geographical markers biblical names like Canaan and Bethlehem, but they were not alone in advancing this theological understanding. One has, as always, to be cautious in generalizing and to recognize that this paradigmatic vision was not universal, but elements of this typological reading of colonial settlement were at work in varying degrees in most of the colonies.

The second principle shared by the emerging American community was a belief in the value of immigration from many places as essential to its mission. To populate the land and subdue it required the welcoming of peoples from all quarters of (mainly Christian) Europe. This passage was justified primarily in theological terms. Christians were to come to America, first and foremost, to proselytize the Native Americans. America's salvific role in history required an authentic conversionary outreach to the indigenous population. Thus, in Virginia, William Symonds, in his *Virginia, A Sermon Preached at White-Chappel in 1609Virginia, A Sermon Preached at White-Chap-*

pel in 1609, challenged his audience thus: "Can there be any doubt, but that our Lord that called Abraham into another country, doeth also by the same holy hand, call you [the colonists of Virginia] to goe and carry the gospel to a Nation that never heard of Christ." And the King's Preamble to the Virginia Charter of 1606, speaks of "propagating the Christian religion to such people, as yet live in darkness and miserable ignorance of the true knowledge and worship of God." There was, of course, more than a smidgeon on self-deception, false consciousness, and the rationalization of injustice in these doctrinal pronouncements but they were not only this. Early immigrants—and the issue of immigration—were authentically framed in these dogmatic terms by many. It was certainly a central belief in the earlier Spanish colonial enterprise—note the work of the Franciscans and Jesuits in particular—and though less manifest in English colonization—the English, as Protestants, lacked missionary clerical orders—it was not marginal to the *Weltanschauung* of the Puritans, Quakers, Mennonites and other Protestant groups.

Third, reflecting the advanced intellectual opinion of the day among European thinkers such as Locke and Montesquieu—indeed America was, in practice, the laboratory for implementing their ideas—the American colonies supported the value of individualism and individual rights. For Jews, this represented a dramatic change in their historic sojourn among the nations. Previously Jews, like all members of traditional societies, had been defined by their group identity. Everyone, including Jews, had rights, privileges, and imposed limitations based on the political and religious group(s) to which each person belonged. Thus, no matter how talented or extraordinary a Jew might be, he or she, by definition, was limited in what he/she could do and how he/she could do it. So, for example, Jews could not be members of guilds, or regular students at universities, and were often, particularly after the creation of official ghettos as part of the tactics of the mid-sixteenth century Catholic Counter-Reformation, unable to live where they chose. They had to pay special taxes and wear special clothes, both in Muslim and Christian countries, and in Muslim lands were not allowed to ride horses, being limited to riding donkeys. Only through conversion could a Jew alter this circumstance. Now, with the emergence of modernity, the unprecedented idea was coming into being—both in Europe and, more rapidly, in the colonies which were less hindered by tradition and entrenched privilege—that one could "separate a Jew from his (or her) Judaism" and value him or her as one valued all human beings,[1] that is, as an individual.

Already in the colonial era this fertile idea began to create heretofore impossible and unprecedented opportunities for Jews. One does not want to exaggerate here for Jews still faced restrictions on voting and office holding, among other limitations, in some of the colonies. However, the signs of a novel relationship between Jews and the political order were becoming visible. Later this revolutionary idea—that Jews as individuals were, in their human essence, just like everyone else and therefore deserving of equal rights—was given expression in the words of the Declaration of Independence, "*All* men are born free and independent." This radical notion was not a mere political slogan but rather an essential belief and, therefore, Jews were included as full citizens from the time of American independence. A few reactionary state governments, for example, that in New Hampshire, tried to resist and delay the implications of this equality, but the decisive issue had been settled at the time of the Revolution. Jews in the new republic did not have to wait while this repercussive matter was debated over the course of two years, as occurred in the National Assembly after the French Revolution in 1789—and at the end of which debate only Sephardic Jews were granted citizenship while the struggle of Ashkenazic Jews for full and equal inclusion in the body-politic would take several more years. Nor did they have to wait for nearly a century, as many Jews did in the various countries of Western Europe between 1789 and 1881. It was only in 1881 that the process of Jewish emancipation in western Europe was finally completed when the Jews of Switzerland were granted that country's citizenship.[2] (Conversely, this separation of "Jews from their Judaism" also had the effect of making one's involvement in, and commitment to, Judaism, the Jewish Community, and the Jewish people *voluntary*. One was no longer required by the civic authorities to remain a Jew and to support Jewish life simply because one was born a Jew. This is a fundamental, often problematic, issue in modern Jewish life to which I shall return at the end of this essay.)

Fourth, this commitment to individualism entailed a number of separate but inseparable corollaries. These included: a commitment to economic individualism that encouraged competitive capitalism rooted in self-interest; a belief in the sufficiency of the individual; support of the freedom to pursue private happiness; a determination to limit government power; a resolute confidence in the will of the people; endorsement of the Lockean idea of the 'Natural Right' to acquire, protect and dispose of property as one chose; an appreciation of the need to respect and value human autonomy; and a conviction regarding the inherent value of hard work. It was also understood to favor a republican form of government that fostered the idea of citizenship and encouraged individuals to be concerned with virtue and the public good.

In addition to these "benign" ideological commitments that provide the bedrock of the nation's political and legal traditions, it is essential to recognize that America, as a political, social and economic reality, was an "open society." That is, it was an environment in which opportunities existed in all spheres of life that Jews could avail themselves of without immediately evoking negative responses from the state or from their non-Jewish neighbors. Indeed, this condition of "openness"—or its absence—has defined much of the Jewish historical experience over the centuries throughout the diaspora. Where the political, social and economic order has been "open" Jews have settled and succeeded. This was the case, for example, in early Islamic Spain where the newly dominant Muslim overlords saw the Jews as allies against Christians and Christianity, as well as valuable subjects possessing political and economic skills that could be put at the service of the incipient Muslim state. So, too, in sixteenth-century Poland where a series of kings, recognizing their nation's economic backwardness, welcomed Jews in order to bring needed economic energy to their kingdom. This perception of Jews as a valuable economic community, as an economic leavening agent, also motivated Suleiman the Great and his Ottoman heirs to open the borders of their empire to Jews, especially the gifted exiles expelled from Spain in 1492 and from Portugal in 1497.

Alternatively, as societies that were once open become increasingly "closed," Jewish opportunities—and hence Jewish individual and communal life—have declined. So, for example, the fate of Spanish Jewry after 1391, finally resulting in the expulsion from Spain in 1492. In this instance, Ferdinand and Isabella sought to unify and homogenize their newly united kingdom through a common religious and cultural identity. Accordingly, Jews, in this now closed state, were no longer valued or welcome. Jews could convert to Catholicism and become part of the Spanish nation, but as a separate community they were seen as a danger to national unification and therefore had to be expelled. Where Spain once prided itself on its multi-culturalism, on what is known in medieval Spanish sources as "convivivencia," it now prided itself on its harsh, monolithic, religious ideals. Again, as Poland became increasingly Catholic and nationalistic in the seventeenth and eighteenth centuries Jewish life became more and more difficult. Jews were increasingly seen as ruthless economic competitors, alien exploiters of the peasantry, and religious adversaries who employed diabolic rituals such as "the desecration of the host" and the murder of Christian children to express their unlimited hatred for Christianity.

More recently, the sort of open access of which I here speak, and the many possibilities it creates, has existed in Canada, South Africa and Australia, as well as America. Given their openness—if in different ways and to different degrees—all of these societies have welcomed Jews and have permitted their individual advancement. And not surprisingly, Jews welcomed these chances to create a new life, both in order to escape pogroms and so as to capitalize on the economic, social and political opportunities they afforded. In this they have replicated a pattern already in evidence in the American colonies before the revolution. So, for example, in the early colonies there were Jewish office holders, something that was unheard of in Europe for centuries to come. In 1655 Asher Levy won the right to stand guard in New Amsterdam; in 1718 two Jews were elected constables in New York; and in 1774 Francis Salvador represented South Carolina in the provincial congress. Also to be noted is the fact that when Brown University opened its doors in 1770 it admitted Jews, as Jews, to the university.

Importantly, in America, almost from the first, what was true socially and politically was also true in the economic realm. Jews could start with push-carts and as peddlers and end up owning department store chains. One has only to think of Bloomingdales, Goldwaters, Macy's, Neiman Marcus, and Filenes. This economic openness continued, even accelerated, in the twentieth century with the success of Jews in innovative industries such as the making of motion pictures; in the world of professional sports, so central to our contemporary culture, where many of the teams are owned by Jews and the professional sports leagues are often overseen by Jewish commissioners; in modern medicine—(where one thinks immediately of Jonas Salk and the Salk Polio vaccine, among many others); in the business of television both in front of and behind the cameras; in the ownership of corporations devoted to all things connected to computers and information technology; in bio-technology; in the domain of money management and related services on Wall Street; and in the ownership of newspapers such as the *Washington Post* and the *New York Times*.[3] (Not to mention the disproportionate number of influential Jewish journalists and newspaper editors, a fact not ignored by antisemites.) And, of course, in clothes manufacturing. (At one time the Jewish garment industry—both as workers and entrepreneurs, as well as Union organizers—clothed nearly the whole of America.) Fortunately, intellectual curiosity and the free flow of capital to support fresh ideas (and further profits) continue to be two of the pre-eminent identifying markers of American society. One therefore has reasonable grounds for believing that this crucial pattern of economic openness—that carries with it fundamental consequences in the social and political realms—will continue and that as a result so, too, will Jewish achievement.

Another unusual element of real import in America was that Jews were not (and are not) the largest minority in the country. The largest minority by the eighteenth century were Blacks who, brought to the American colonies and then later the United States as slaves, have been the main targets of bigots and the primary victims of a pernicious, deep rooted, racial bigotry. This prejudice was propagated and encouraged by the desire, rooted in the economic interests of the master class, to maintain and defend the "peculiar institution" of Black chattel bondage. Why this fact is relevant to an understanding of American Jewish history is explained by noting a more general historical phenomenon, namely, that it is usually the largest minority that bears the main brunt of a nation's prejudice because it is this minority that usually represents the most pressing and dangerous "threat" to those who hold the reigns of power. So, for example, Jews were the only real minority in Christian Europe. Armenians (who were Christians) were the main minority in the Muslim Ottoman Empire. Ukrainians were the main national enemy of Stalin. All of these sub-groups, for religious and/or nationalistic reasons, generated "anxiety" on the part of those in control of the state who, in turn, responded to what they perceived as a lethal threat through political violence intended to assure the maintenance of their hold on power. But in America, for the first time in their residence in a Christian country, Jews were not the largest minority. Thus they were not, as a rule, seen as threatening and as a result they could be ignored. They could be allowed to just get on with their lives.

The hateful, negative stereotypes that were regularly applied to "aliens" and "foreigners" in the press and other cultural and political venues were not created to stigmatize and did not apply primarily to, or only to, Jews, as had occurred in the past and would occur again in modern Europe. In America during the colonial era there was fear of and prejudice against Native Americans and Blacks, while after 1850 such prejudice continued to apply to Blacks—both slave and free—and to be leveled, in the public arena, primarily at Irish and Italian immigrants (who were Catholic). This is not to say that there was no anti-Jewish prejudice, or that caricatures and stereotypes of Jews could not easily be found in the cultural artifacts of the nineteenth century. The circulation of these demeaning images was, however, limited and more muted than ever before. Put another way, European antisemitism, both in its depth and its extent, was not replicated in America.

Then, too, as already implied in my comment about anti-Black prejudice, Jews were the right color. There may have been some resistance to this idea in certain nativist and racist circles[4] but, on the whole, based on simple sense-perception as well as cultural norms, Jews were seen as, understood as, and classified as, white. Given the importance of color, of racial animus predicated on color, and of all sorts of cultural and pseudo scientific theorizing based on color in the history of America, the fact that Jews were white was important to their inclusion as equals and citizens.

Here one needs to recall explicitly that color was a, if not *the*, defining factor in the lives of individuals and groups in American history from the early colonial era onwards. Though it was undoubtedly the case that economic motives led to and sustained the creation of New World slavery, anti-Black racial theories were early and continually used to legitimate this evil institution. While white men and women had been enslaved in the medieval era, in the modern world this role was primarily, overwhelmingly, almost uniquely—recognizing some early Spanish and Portuguese, and other,[5] efforts to enslave Native Americans—allotted to men, women and children of African descent. The need for labor in America (and the

Americas and Caribbean) was distinctively met by targeting Africans. Racism, in the form of a pervasive ideology, provided the colonizing European peoples with the rationale, the rationalizations, they sought for creating and maintaining a system of subjugation so apparently at odds—especially in Anglo-America—with their own cultural and ethical presuppositions. Now African men, women and children were identified not only as "outsiders" and of a different color but also as racially, i.e., inherently and therefore necessarily and permanently, "inferior." Accordingly, in America from the early seventeenth century on, color, that is, the consequences of one's skin pigmentation, meant being "naturally" superior or inferior; having rights versus being denied all rights; being protected by the state as compared to having no state protection; and, ultimately, being free rather than being enslaved. Because Jews were white there was rarely any restriction on the daily activity of Jews, or on Jews being included in the community that was defined as having "natural rights," or on Jews being seen as entitled to state and legal protections.

In reflecting on the issue of minorities in America—and of Jews as a minority—we remember, too, that America, from the first, was a country of minorities. Unlike the countries of Europe in which Jews were, as already observed, usually the only significant non-Christian sub segment of the population, in America every ethnic and religious group was, in a real sense, a minority. This unprecedented circumstance, in which every group was weak, gave rise to the notion of political checks and balances and allowed, even required, each community to organize in its own self-interest. Accordingly, consistent with this understanding and the politics it spawned, Jews, like others, actively came (and still come) together in self-defense. Now it was acceptable for Jews, as a collective, to advance their case in the media, to hold public protests, to seek legal redress, to lobby their government representatives, and to use the ballot box to reject antisemitic candidates.

This unique political-demographic situation also gave *factions* a new and legitimate role. In comparison to the criticism of factions that was prominent among European political elites, who saw such segmentation as a corrosive and divisive phenomenon within a theoretically (and practically) unified state and culture, the Founders believed in the existence and value of a balance of "factions." This was based, at least in part, on the notion that all aims and motives of individuals and groups were equally self-interested (and perhaps even equally irrational) and therefore equally indifferent to the "general good." Thus, the object of political institutions should be to render all denominations and factions equally important or, perhaps more accurately put, equally impotent. Madison and Hamilton in the *Federalist Papers*, no. 1 (see also 6 and 51) wrote: "In a free government the security of civil rights must be the same as that for religious rights. It consists in the one place in the multiplication of interests, and in the other in the multiplication of sects." In effect, the Founding Fathers, skeptical of dogmatism and authoritarianism, both religious and political, held that factions acting from "self-interest" were safer than fanatical men acting on principle. Furthermore, factions, being only factions, need to acquire supporters—and/or voters—to achieve their ends and therefore understand the need to make coalitions (which come into being and pass away based on changing interests and circumstances) with many groups, including Jews.

I would add in this context that the two-party political system, that has been a defining feature of American life, leads in the same direction. Its salience as a Jewish issue lies in the fact that the competing parties, in order to get elected, appeal to, and seek to include in the electoral process, all substantial ethnic and religious blocs. Each party needs votes and Jews can vote. Thus, one seeks to include them, not offend them. Two party politics thus fosters a politics of outreach, compromise, negotiation, and inclusion. It also tends, because of the need for compromise and negotiation, to reduce the ideological content of American politics while, at the same time, increasing the push for pragmatic solutions to local and national (and even international) problems.

I would also note two other factors, little commented on by scholars, that have been influential in American Jewish history. The first is the Common Law tradition, imported from England, which allowed judicial decisions to sanction social and political change even without formal legislative enactments. The second is the influence of *Marranos*[6] on Jewish political behavior in early America. These Sephardic Jews, who had lived as *conversos* (converts) and who, as Christians, had been able to participate in public life in the same way that all Christians did, were more used to involving themselves in national (and local) economic and political affairs than the *shtetl* Jews of Eastern Europe.[7] Thus, after having crossed the Atlantic, these Spanish and Portuguese Jews (and their descendents from Amsterdam and Antwerp) continued this pattern of behavior in the new republic (and earlier during the colonial era). Thus began the tradition of overt, unapologetic, Jewish involvement in the political life of America.

I would immediately add, however, that this last phenomenon should not be exaggerated. The much later, highly consequential, weakness of the American Jewish community during the 1920s, '30s and '40s—that were years of growing antisemitism, the passage of crucial anti-immigration laws that would eventually trap millions of Jews in Nazi Europe, and the overall inability to alter the inhumanity of the Roosevelt administration during the Holocaust—is proof enough of this. Nor should this active participation as citizens, like other citizens, in political debate and party politics be confused with the myth of Jewish political power emphasized by antisemites from Henry Ford to Pat Buchanan and more recently by critics of American support for Israel whose antisemitism is couched, expressed, and justified in terms of the need for political debate over American foreign policy in the Middle East.

When making a list of the innovations that effected Jews in American society the most important factor was, without doubt, the elimination of an official state religion. This was a revolutionary idea without historical precedent. It was crucial for the Jews now coming to settle in America because, for the first time since the Christianization of the Roman Empire by Constantine in the early fourth century, it gave Jews the same legal and political status as Christians in the polity. This crucial separation of church and state came about in early America due to the unique circumstance in which *all* the religious groups found themselves. No denomination, no religious communion, was large enough to be dominant and therefore, out of a common weakness, all (or almost all) religious communities sought to protect themselves through the dis-establishment of religion. The 1st amendment of the Constitution regarding the establishment of religion—that entailed the separation of church and state which itself is not mentioned in the Constitution—is, historically, based on the fear shared by all denominations that were one religion to become "official" those of other theological persuasions would be coerced and controlled by a religion not their own.

By 1640 there were 20,000 Englishmen of differing religious opinions in the colonies, almost all of whom were religious and political dissenters who were fearful of state power and authority. There were Catholics, who had fled and feared Protestant domination, in Maryland. There were Puritans, who were dissenters from the Anglican Church and the authority of the King and who had been persecuted in England, in New England. There was Roger Williams, who was banished from Massachusetts for challenging Puritan claims to authority—he believed in church-state separation and the freedom of conscience—who started the colony of Rhode Island where dissenters were welcomed. And there was Thomas Hooker, who was active in opposing the Puritan theology dominant in Massachusetts, who helped to create the Congregational Church in Connecticut. Furthermore, despite the theocratic views of the Puritans, they and many other dissenters did not believe in a Pope or centralized religious authority. This credo was concretely expressed in 1705 when John Wise of Ipswich opposed Cotton Mather's attempt to tie the churches more closely together under one ruling authority. Instead, as both a pragmatic and theological compromise, each local Puritan (and Congregational) congregation governed itself. And more generally, the Congregationalist Church covenant model, that emphasized the centrality of decisions of conscience, voluntary consent, and individual freedom, was applied not only to internal church affairs but also to the functioning of civil society.

Ongoing events in Europe further complicated the early religious and political situation in the American colonies. Thus when Cromwell and the

Puritans gained power in Parliament between 1648 and 1660, Royalists and Anglicans came to Virginia, Maryland and the Carolinas. These parties, which had now experienced political opposition, were very different in their politics and theology from the Puritans of New England. In addition, other small, outsider, sectarian offshoots also came seeking refuge and opportunity. For example, the Quakers, who were bitterly persecuted in England because they refused to pay tithes or take an oath in court, came to and became prominent in Pennsylvania; Scotch and Irish Presbyterians came from Catholic Ulster; Hutterites and Mennonites (a breakaway Lutheran group from Germany) came to Pennsylvania; as did Anabaptists, Amish and Dunkers (from Germany and Holland). Then again, French Huguenots (Protestants) came to New York and Virginia, especially after the revocation of the Edict of Nantes in 1685. Thus America became the land of religious pluralism. However, and this is the decisive issue, none of these communities was strong enough to force its will and beliefs on others, and all feared that others might force their will—and beliefs—on them.

Amongst these many diverse religious groups, Judaism and Jews were just another small, very marginal, community, that did not provoke the type of demonization common in Europe. The potent, denigrating and accusatory *Adversus Judaeus* tradition, that traces itself back to the Apostle Paul, the Gospels of *Matthew* and *John*, and the Church Fathers, never gained much traction in the theological-cultural climate of Anglo-America. Jews were certainly objects of curiosity, and there was anti-Jewish prejudice, but the sort of ferocious, paranoid, collective anti-Judaism—and the deadly violence that it spawned—that was, and had been for centuries, entrenched in Europe was largely absent from the American scene. This is evidenced by the fact that, among other things, American Christians and the American government never changed public policies relative to religion in order to decrease the impact or relevance of Judaism in America. In America Jews were just another "faith," not a foreign people nor an alien nation.

One should furthermore take note of the fact that this tradition of separation of church and state also had very substantial consequences within the Jewish community. In comparison to European countries, where there were officially appointed Chief Rabbis and where Orthodox Judaism was established as the official version of Judaism, in America there was no Chief Rabbi and no one accepted version of Judaism. In consequence, a variety of Jewish denominations (or traditions) were established and flourished. First it was Sephardic Orthodoxy with its toleration of religious moderation, brought by Jews from Holland (and elsewhere) in the colonial era. Then, in the nineteenth century, Reform Judaism, imported from Germany in the middle of the century, (particularly after the failed European revolution of 1848), took root. Indeed, though the Reform movement is historically linked by origin to Germany it was actually in the United States that it really grew and flourished. In 1880 there were approximately 225,000 Jews in the United States, the majority of whom came from Germany and for whom American Reform Judaism as championed by R. Isaac Mayer Wise—who spoke of and created a prayerbook entitled *Minhag America (American Custom)*—seemed the appropriate religious position. Then with the mass immigration of Eastern European Jews after 1880, when two million Jews arrived in the United States, Eastern European Ashkenazic Orthodoxy, with its more stringent observance, became a presence on the American scene. The early twentieth century saw the start of the Conservative movement (which was, likewise, rooted among the newly arriving Polish and Russian immigrants who found the practices and ideology of Reform to be too radical). In the 1930s a new denomination known as Reconstructionism emerged, based on the teachings of Mordechai Kaplan (who was the son of an Orthodox rabbi and a student and teacher at the Conservative Jewish Theological Seminary (JTS) in New York City). In the 1940s, primarily as a result of the Holocaust, hasidic sects and their charismatic leaders *(zaddikim)* arrived from Poland and Hungary, and the remnants of the non-hasidic Ultra-Orthodox world came from Lithuania. Finally, the last half-century has witnessed the burgeoning of modern neo-Orthodoxy which is based on the nineteenth century teachings of Rabbi Samson Raphael Hirsch (of 19th Frankfurt) and others—especially Rabbi Joseph Soloveitchik who was descended from a great Lithuanian rabbinic family. Today the ideology of the neo-Orthodox community is exemplified in the important *Torah-U'Mesorah* Day School movement, whose schools educate most children from modern Orthodox families, and in the culture and religious paradigm manifest by Yeshiva University in New York City. Though Yeshiva University opened its doors in 1928 it has only been since the 1950s that it has exerted substantial influence on American Jewry.

Though a subject of considerable controversy both within and without the borders of the Jewish community, Jews, at the beginning of the twenty-first century, wisely continue to be among the chief defenders of the separation of church and state in America. They correctly argue that America has not been, is not now, and should not in the future become, a "Christian country." America has had, and continues to have, a majority of Christians among its population but this means only that it is a nation with many Christians not, as is often erroneously asserted, that it is a "Christian country," i.e., a country that should be organized and managed on the basis of Christian doctrine. Thus the national census, sponsored by the government, has never collected statistics based on the religion of its citizens, and no public declaration of religion was or is required in order to become a citizen. (Yet despite—or perhaps because of—this church-state separation, religion, including Judaism, was and is seen as promoting civic virtue. So the oft repeated and true tale of Haym Salomon's financial support for the

Revolution. For those who do not know the story, Haym Solomon was a successful Jewish trader in Philadelphia who gave much of his fortune to support the cause of American independence and worked tirelessly to sell bonds being issued by the new, unproven, nation.)

Lastly, I would cautiously argue that American and Jewish values have been able to form a sympathetic symbiotic relationship. By this I mean that Americans came to appreciate, as Jews have and do, the centrality of cities *contra* Thomas Jefferson's vision of a nation of gentlemen farmers, to value the importance of education, to care about families, to advocate the giving of charity and philanthropy, and to admire hard work. Reciprocally, Jews, in the main, have embraced American values such as liberalism, autonomy, self-reliance, and pluralism. They chose not to create a central, organized, religious hierarchy as exists among Catholics and Mormons. They accepted the notion that religious affiliation must be based on a free choice. And, in general, they appreciate and endorse capitalism, thrift, ambition, and enterprise. In addition, Jews and the Jewish community have adopted a broad view of self-interest that entails working for social, economic, and political justice and equality for all individuals and communities within the body-politic. They have understood that an unjust society will eventually be unjust to Jews.

As a result of all these inter-related and repercussive factors American Jewry, almost from its inception, was, if not yet fully, what would later be called a post-emancipation Jewry, just as America, even in the colonial era, was, though not yet completely, a post-emancipation country. The principle elements that one thinks of as defining modernity—i.e., liberal, secular, pluralistic politics, diversity in matters of culture and religion, and a competitive capitalist economic system with open and free markets—were, from the colonial era onwards, salient factors in America. What this has meant is that the place of Jews in America, and in the "mind" of America, has been very different, almost since the first Jewish immigrants arrived from Recife (Brazil) in 1654,[8] from what it had been (and continued to be) in Christian Europe and the Muslim world. For this reason, among others, in the United States, unlike in Europe, no special legislation was needed at the time of the American Revolution to give Jews equality and citizenship. Similarly, no special efforts have been needed since 1776 to protect this precious franchise. Jews, like all white Americans, were citizens from the first days of American independence on general constitutional grounds. In effect, there was no "Jewish Problem," no *Judenfrage*, in America. Jews were given, without significant protest, equality by the Bill of Rights and the Constitution.

Furthermore, and an issue of great significance, since 1776 all groups in America applaud the Revolution. This is at the core of what has been called America's "civil religion." In consequence, there is no major group in America that defines itself on the basis of a hoped for return to a mythic pre-modern, non-democratic, non-republican reality that excludes and per-secutes Jews. To appreciate the profound significance of this universal em-brace of the Revolution within the United States one has only to compare the situation in America vis-à-vis the American Revolution with the debate in France over the meaning, and merits, of the French Revolution, a debate that has gone on for over two centuries. Here one needs to understand that in France (and Europe more generally) since 1789 there have been major groups that opposed the French Revolution and what it stood for. In part at least, some of these groups have been critical of the French Revolution because it led to the end of the era of Jewish exclusion and the extension of political rights to Jews. Thus their antisemitism reinforces their anti-revolu-tionary views, and their anti-revolutionary views are driven, in part, by their antisemitism. Criticism of the Revolution is inextricably intertwined with the reactionary hope for Jewish dis-emancipation and the exclusion of Jews from the mainstream of national social and economic life.

This backward-looking call for rejection of the possibility of Jews as full citizens has been heard in many conservative and reactionary circles ever since the Revolution itself. After Napoleon's conquest of Germany, and his emancipation of the Jews of Germany, the French Revolution and Jewish freedom were viewed as the inseparable enemies of German reactionaries and antisemites. After Napoleon's final defeat in 1814, conservative factions in Austria and elsewhere sought to retard Jewish rights. In nineteenth century Catholic and intellectual circles there was undisguised revulsion of the French Revolution and unceasing fear of Jewish emancipation. Then there was the outpouring of hate both for Jews and the Revolution spawned by the Dreyfus Trial in Paris in 1893. This "affair" provided the context for the expression of both radical an-tisemitism and anti-republicanism in France and elsewhere in Europe. And nearly everywhere, throughout the nineteenth and early twentieth centuries, most European aristocrats saw the French revolution and the acquisition of Jewish political rights as signs of an unmistakable decline within European civilization. In the twentieth century this illiberal ideo-logical fixation was essential to Hitler's Europe and in more recent times has found support among the followers of La Pen in France, neo-Nazis in Austria and Germany, and reactionaries in post-Soviet Poland and Russia. In contrast, no similar anti-Jewish project, that would involve and be predicated on the overturning of the American Revolution, has ever existed in mainstream America. There have been, and are, antisem-ites and antisemitic groups in the United States who would support a program of Jewish dis-emancipation but, after reviewing the historical record, one can say with confidence that this odious sentiment has been manifest only at the margins of American political life.

The ideological, demographic, economic, and socio-cultural elements just described have produced, in the form of the current American Jewish community, the wealthiest, best educated, and most charitable community in history. In *per capita* income the Jewish community surpasses all other American communities by a significant margin. In terms of education the American Jewish community is remarkable. It produces three times the number of doctors, four times the number of lawyers, and many times the number of Ph.D.s *per capita* as the community at large. Over ninety percent of Jewish children go to college, and they are very heavily over-represented in Ivy League and other prestige universities. And the rates and size of charitable and philanthropic giving to both Jewish and non-Jewish causes—universities, hospitals, museums, symphonies, and the arts—is both laudable and unprecedented. I note that according to recent statistics compiled by the *Chronicle of Philanthropy*, twenty-one of the largest sixty donors to charitable causes in the country in 2005 were Jewish.[9]

In Jewish cultural and religious terms, despite real problems and deficiencies, the community has also achieved considerable success. There are a substantial number of rabbinical seminaries and close to four thousand rabbis have been produced by the various denominations. There are major Judaica and Hebraica collections in university libraries as well as in public libraries, and hundreds of books of Jewish interest are published each year, many by the most prestigious university and commercial publishers. The Association of Jewish Studies, the professional society of academics teaching Judaic studies—a significant number of whom are not Jewish—has approximately two thousand members. College Judaica courses are proliferating and over five hundred colleges teach Hebrew.

The American Jewish community has also taken its international responsibilities very seriously, and to good effect. Its support of Zionism and the State of Israel is, and has been, remarkable. So, too, its involvement in the liberation of Soviet Jewry, its concern with the *Falashas*[10] of Ethiopia, its long-standing support of the life-saving work of the American Joint Distribution Committee in many parts of the world, its financing of HIAS (Hebrew Immigrant Aid Society) that helps Jewish (and non-Jewish) immigrants to America and elsewhere, and more recently, its creation of the American Jewish World Service which is active in Latin America and Africa, among other locations. All of these efforts speak to the compassion and very deep moral sensibilities that are active and influential in the American Jewish community. (And this list of worthy causes is just the tip of a large iceberg as I have not even mentioned any of the charitable and educational programs sponsored by the main religious denominations.)

There has also been, if the opinion polls and other forms of research are to be trusted, a marked decline in antisemitism. Today, just about all corporate boardrooms, political offices and educational opportunities are fully open to Jews. This is especially notable in Washington where, in 2000, Senator Joseph Lieberman was selected as the Vice Presidential candidate on the Democratic ticket (and came within a few Florida votes of winning), and where, after the 2006 mid-term elections, there were thirteen Jewish senators and thirty Jewish congressmen. (To fully appreciate what these numbers mean one needs to remember that Jews make up only about two percent—or less—of the present American population.)

At the same time, however, there are darker clouds on the horizon, related to three phenomena of real consequence. The first is the rise and spread of Islamic radicalism, which has reached the shores of America. Second are the several demographic factors effecting the size and maintenance of the Jewish population in America. Declining Jewish birth rates, approximately fifty percent intermarriage rates, the high percentage of children born to intermarried families not being raised as Jews, the late age of marriage by young Jews (that effects the size of their families), and the unprecedented rate of Jews not marrying at all, plus a seemingly disproportionate homosexual population, all point to a significant contraction in the overall size of the future American Jewish community. Third, the rate of non-affiliation by Jews with the organized Jewish community is, allowing for variations by geographical location, at an all-time high. During a recent lecture tour in California I was told by community professionals that there are 600,000 Jews in the greater Los Angeles area seventy percent of whom—some 420,000 individuals—are unaffiliated with the community. In Orange County and the greater San Diego area, where there are an estimated 175,000 to 200,000 Jews, the rate of non-affiliation is, or so it was reported to me, over eighty percent. At the same time, one recognizes that all of these undesirable, internal, communal phenomena (with perhaps the exception of homosexuality) are the result of free choices—and the voluntary nature of contemporary Jewish life mentioned above—made by Jews. As such they reflect, if now in a discordant way from the perspective of Jewish collective continuity, the openness of American and American Jewish society. Moreover, and a fact of importance that must not be neglected, different choices could alter, or reverse, these present corrosive conditions. The future is open.

These last mentioned issues are not inconsequential matters. They raise serious difficulties and dilemmas that need to be puzzled over and addressed by those interested in the future of the American Jewish community and the Jewish People. Furthermore, it is not a given that the individual and communal successes of the past will be replicated in the future. Yet given its past, and the principles on the basis of which it conducts its present—that have broken most of the basic "rules" governing Jewish existence in the diaspora—it seems reasonable to judge that, for the foreseeable future, the American Jewish Community will continue to prosper and flourish.[11]

NOTES

1. The complex issue of Black Slavery and its ideological justifications is, of course, the great exception to this rule in the American colonies and then in America until, and in many ways even long after, the Civil War.

2. I am referring here to national political rights and freedoms. A few American states after independence, under the principle of states' rights, continued to bar or limit Jewish participation in the political process. Thus, for example, it was only in 1877 that Jews got full voting rights in New Hampshire.

3. I am told that the present owner of the New York Times, Mr. Sulzberger, likes to stress he is a Protestant. But this does not change the historical fact that the Sulzbergers who made the Times the paper of record were Jews.

4. For more on this see Eric Goldstein, *The Price of Whiteness: Jews, Race, and American Identity* (Princeton, 2006).

5. For example, Native Americans, especially Native American girls and women, were enslaved in California during the gold Rush, i.e., from 1849 to 1860.

6. Marrano, which means swine in Spanish, was the pejorative term used by Christians to describe Jews who had converted to Catholicism in Spain (and Portugal). The correct, non-pejorative terms that were applied to these individuals were New Christians or Conversos. I use the term Marrano here because this is the more usual way to refer to them.

7. One must be careful not to suggest that the Jews of Eastern Europe were overly passive in the political sphere as this would be a serious historical error. But their political culture, and the way they participated in, and tried to influence, the more general political realities of Poland and Russia was very different from the manner in which Conversos joined in political life in Spain and Portugal—and later in Holland, Belgium and the Ottoman Empire—or the way their "returning" descendents involved themselves in political activity in the American colonies and early post-revolutionary America.

8. The Jews fled Recife in 1654 when the Portugeuse reconquered it from the Dutch.

9. Printed in the *Forward* (March 2, 2007).

10. Falashas is the term most often used for the Black Jews of Ethiopia. It was originally, like the word Marrano, a pejorative epithet but now it is the most widely used and easily recognized term used to refer to this group.

11. I would like to thank Professor Jonathan Sarna of Brandeis University who kindly read this essay and made helpful comments on its contents.

1

Enlightenment, Statesmen and the Jews in Europe and the United States, 1776–1820

Allan Arkush

There has been a great deal of scholarly work in recent years on the European Enlightenment and the Jews. European, American and Israeli historians have shed much new light on a whole variety of subjects, including the attitudes of Enlightenment thinkers toward the Jews and Judaism, the influence of the Enlightenment on the attitudes of European statesmen toward the Jews, the relationship between the Enlightenment in general and the Haskalah (its Jewish branch), and the character of the Haskalah in places other than Central Europe, such as Italy and England.[1] If there has been no comparable efflorescence of scholarship on the American Enlightenment and the Jews, one ought not to be surprised. Eighteenth-century American thinkers and statesmen showed much less interest in the Jews than many of their European counterparts. And there was no significant American Jewish literary activity whatsoever prior to 1820, indeed scarcely any noteworthy writings at all by American Jews. This can no doubt be explained, for the most part, by the very small size of the American Jewish community at the time. But the easier it is to account for the lack of early American concern with "the Jewish problem," the harder it is to justify any comparison of the situation in Europe and America during the late eighteenth and early nineteenth centuries.

It is doubtful that anyone would even think of making such a comparison were it not for the subsequent emergence in the United States of the Diaspora's largest, most prosperous, and most successfully integrated Jewish community. American Jewry's later achievements retroactively render its rather paltry beginnings vastly more interesting than they would have been if they had led to less impressive results. It is hard not to look at them and ask whether there was not, from the very beginning, something different about this country, something that made it a much more hospitable setting for Jewish life than modern Europe.

I have never given any careful thought to this question, prior to the preparation of this paper. My own academic work has focused to some extent, however, on the ways in which thinkers of the European Enlightenment and late eighteenth-century European statesmen influenced by them regarded and treated the Jews. Whether I can draw upon this research in ways that might illuminate the rather different American experience is something that I will have to leave it to the reader to judge.

If one had to summarize the attitude of the European Enlightenment toward the Jews while standing on one foot, the best way to do so, in my opinion, would be to point to the Enlightenment's acknowledgement that "the Jew is even more man than Jew." I have taken these words from the famous, epoch-making treatise by the Prussian official Christian Wilhelm von Dohm, *On the Improvement of the Civic Status of the Jews*, but they epitomize, I believe, the basic standpoint from which virtually all of the Enlightenment thinkers regarded the Jewish people.[2] In their eyes, Jews were at bottom human beings different in no essential respect from other human beings and fully deserving of recognition as such. This did not necessarily mean that they were worthy of receiving completely equal rights immediately, but only that they were *potentially* capable of full participation in society—without first having to cease to be Jews and become Christians. It might be necessary, as Dohm himself believed, for governments to wait for the Jews to improve themselves before placing them on precisely the same plane as their gentile fellow citizens.[3]

What I have said so far might seem to amount to an unduly benign characterization of the fundamental stance of the European Enlightenment toward the Jews. One could accuse me of overlooking the unsavory side, the ways in which the Enlightenment revived older, pre-Christian strands of anti-Semitism and continued to reflect longstanding Christian antipathy toward the Jews and Judaism. Everyone conversant with this subject is undoubtedly familiar with Arthur Hertzberg's identification of Voltaire as "the major link in Western intellectual history between the anti-Semitism of classic paganism and the modern age" and his description of him as someone who "ruled the Jew to be outside society and... hopelessly alien even to the future age of enlightened men."[4] And, in the nearly forty years that have passed since Hertzberg wrote these words, quite a few other scholars have sought to show how intolerant many Enlightenment thinkers were of Jewish "otherness."

I would not deny that Voltaire's writings were full of what George Eliot called anti-Jewish fulminations. Yet Hertzberg's highly influential reading of his work is, in my opinion, deeply flawed.[5] I cannot take the time here to review all of its questionable aspects, but I would like to point to the more balanced portrayal of Voltaire in Ronald Schechter's recent book, *Obstinate Hebrews.* Schechter shows how Voltaire concluded that there was "living proof that Jews, like other people, could cast off their superstitions and depart radically from the condition of their contemporaries and their forebears."[6] There was, for Voltaire, no denying that a Jew could become a *philosophe.* Voltaire, to be sure, as well as many others, believed that the process of becoming one involved the sloughing off of the Jewish religion (which they regarded as a set of pernicious superstitions). But the very fact that they believed Jews to be capable of such a move demonstrates how much they were in agreement with Dohm, and with what I consider a fundamental tenet of the Enlightenment, that "the Jew is even more man than Jew." For all of them, becoming a better man definitely entailed becoming less of a Jew, but it did not necessitate ceasing altogether to be a Jew and becoming a Christian. Of course, they did not believe that there was any harm, either, in the abandonment of Jewishness. For Dohm, in particular, a man who has gone down in history as a great friend of the Jews, it apparently made no difference whether the descendants of the people he was attempting to liberate became less Jewish or, in the end, non-Jewish. What was important was that they improve themselves in the truly decisive respects.

This new attitude toward the Jews would have a major impact on the lives of most of them only after it passed beyond the confines of intellectual circles and began to inform the policies of European statesmen toward the Jewish inhabitants of their countries. In the continental autocracies, this process occurred somewhat slowly and unevenly. Not every crowned devotee of the Enlightenment became a benefactor of the Jews. Frederick the Great of Prussia, a friend of Voltaire (at least for a time), Maupertuis, and other avatars of the Enlightenment, developed no new appreciation of the Jews' capacities and in no way altered Prussia's oppressive policies toward them. Another friend of Voltaire's, Catherine the Great of Russia, did make an effort to expand the opportunities open to her Jewish subjects, but retreated quickly in the face of internal opposition.[7] Of the eighteenth-century European monarchs influenced by the Enlightenment only Joseph II of Austria took significant steps to reduce the disabilities under which the Jews labored and to integrate them, with some measure of coercion, into the general society.

The impact of Enlightenment ideas on state policies toward the Jews was, of course, much more abrupt and much greater in France. The ministers of Louis XVI had indeed toyed with the idea of improving the Jews' situation, but the French National Assembly, after some initial hesitation, went far beyond anything that had previously been contemplated in the halls of power and granted all the Jews of France fully equal rights. That this measure was the product of Enlightenment thinking scarcely needs to be underlined. But this does not mean that all subsequent efforts to curtail the rights of French Jews constituted a reaction against the ideas of the Enlightenment. When Napoleon Bonaparte promulgated special, discriminatory legislation to regulate Jewish affairs in the first decade of the nineteenth century, he stood squarely within the earlier, tutelary tradition of the Enlightenment. Napoleon's plans for the reorganization of French Jewish life and even his "infamous" decrees were designed, after all, not to exclude the Jews from society but mostly to facilitate their acculturation and assimilation.

When one looks away from Europe and considers the situation in the United States at this time, the picture seems much simpler. Here the Enlightenment did not produce two different brands of policies toward the Jews, one concentrating on the utilization of government power to improve them and prepare them for closer integration with non-Jews, and the other treating them as people who were *already* fully deserving of equal rights. In the early days of the United States, the main thrust of public thought automatically included the Jews among the religious minorities that were entitled to enjoy full American citizenship. None of our Founding Fathers thought otherwise. Jews obtained equal rights in America, as Jonathan Sarna has put it, through the work of Revolutionary-era thinkers "inspired by the ideas of Enlightenment rationalism."

"Classical Enlightenment texts—among them the works of Locke, Rousseau, Grotius, Montesquieu, Harrington, and Voltaire—found many readers in America." The "leading patriots" influenced by these works were often Deists themselves, disinclined to regard Christianity in any form as a prerequisite of good citizenship. Through them, the "Enlightenment view of religious liberty eventually gained the upper hand in America."[8]

What Sarna has said is no doubt true. The thinkers he names did provide the inspiration for much of what the American Founders undertook. But we should note that their liberalism only went so far. There is nothing in Grotius, Montesquieu, Harrington or Voltaire that affirms the rights of practitioners of all religions at all times to complete political equality. Of those Sarna names, only John Locke explicitly called for the recognition of the Jews' equal rights. But in America, of course, that was quite enough of an inspiration (on the federal level, at any rate).[9]

Locke was unequivocal on the subject of the Jews' rights, but he was also unimpassioned. All he said was that "neither Pagan, nor Mahometan nor Jew ought to be excluded from the civil rights of the commonwealth because of his religion."[10] In tune with Locke, (really, more consistently than Locke, who was less generous to Catholics than he was to many non-Christians), the U.S. Constitution prohibits the use of religious tests as qualifications for any federal office. And it guarantees freedom of religion to all. These measures incorporating the Jews into the body politic made no special mention of them and provoked very little opposition. Such few critics as there were of the extension of equal rights to non-Christians were not cautious gradualists or "conditionalists," in the manner of Dohm, but old-fashioned Christians who feared the inundation of the United States by Jews and pagans. These people, as Frederick Jaher has trenchantly observed, "were barely visible compared to the many" others who feared, prior to the adoption of the Bill of Rights, that the new constitution provided "an insufficient support of freedom."[11]

A few of the Founding Fathers had some favorable words to say about the Jews in their correspondence and other writings, but only George Washington addressed an American Jewish community directly and memorably. I am referring, of course, to his reply to a letter sent to him in 1790 by the Hebrew congregation at Newport, Rhode Island. Echoing the language that his Jewish correspondents had utilized in greeting him, Washington expressed his pride in leading a country in which "all possess alike liberty of conscience and immunities of citizenship." Again, using almost the same words that the Newport Jews themselves had employed, Washington went on to speak, famously, of the Government of the United States as one "which gives to bigotry no sanction, to persecution no assistance," and "requires only that they who live under its protection should demean themselves as good citizens in giving it on all occasions their effectual support." Where Washington went beyond a reiteration of what had been said to him was at the end of his letter. "May the children of the stock of Abraham who dwell in this land continue to merit and enjoy the good will of the other inhabitants; while every one shall sit in safety under his own vine and fig tree and there shall be none to make him afraid."[12]

No European statesman at this time, not even in France, indeed, to the best of my knowledge, no Gentile leader since King Cyrus of Persia ever sent a more respectful, warmer letter to a Jewish community. All by itself it shows very clearly that America was, from its inception, a different sort of place for the Jews, a better place than Europe. But we should not allow our gratitude for this letter to impel us to overestimate its significance. Before we conclude that Washington and the other Founding Fathers were particularly pleased to have Jews around, it might be wise to pose some other questions.

Was their acceptance of religious diversity in their new nation accompanied by a genuine appreciation of it as a positive good? If so, what benefits did they think that it would bring with it? Or did they look forward to a time when diversity would give way to uniformity? Did they, in short, regard the presence of Jews and other religious minorities on the American scene as something that enhanced or detracted from what they called "the general welfare?"

Let us consider George Washington himself first. A man without formal education, but a man of the Enlightenment nonetheless, Washington never betrayed any signs of real attachment to Christianity. But he consistently emphasized the social utility of religion in general. He did so most memorably in his famous Farewell Address. "Of all the dispositions and habits which lead to political prosperity," he wrote, "Religion and morality are indispensable supports. In vain would that man claim the tribute of Patriotism, who should labor to subvert these great Pillars of human happiness, these firmest props of the duties of Men and citizens. The mere Politician, equally with the pious man ought to respect and to cherish them. . . . And let us with caution indulge the supposition, that morality can be maintained without religion. Whatever may be conceded to the influence of refined education on minds of peculiar structure, reason and experience both forbid us to expect that National morality can prevail in exclusion of religious principle."[13]

But what kind of religious principle? Any kind at all, it would seem, as long as it inspired the proper sort of behavior. Judaism, in Washington's eyes, clearly fell into the category of acceptable religions, but there is no reason to believe that he took any special delight in its presence on the national scene.

George Washington presided over the Constitutional Convention in 1787, but he did not play a large part in designing the document that it produced. For deeper reflection on the significance of religious diversity in the United States, we need to turn to one of the men who did, the great architects of religious freedom in our country, James Madison. There is, I am sure, no need for me to elucidate his role in upholding the individual's right to liberty of conscience and erecting a wall of separation between church and state. But we do need to consider his somewhat less well known reasons for believing that the United States was better off for being a country where a multiplicity of religions flourished.

We cannot overlook some of the things that he said in the *Memorial and Remonstrance* he wrote in 1779 in opposition to Patrick Henry and other Virginia legislators who were promoting a "Bill to establish a provision for teachers of the Christian religion." While Madison opposed this bill primarily because it illegitimately granted privileges to one religion that it denied to others, he also contended that it was "adverse to the diffusion of the light of Christianity." Those already basking in this light, he said, ought to have no greater desire than to see it "imparted to the whole race of mankind." But, he commands his readers, "Compare the number of those who have yet received it with the number still remaining under the dominion of false religions; and how small is the former!" One of the problems with the bill proposed by Patrick Henry was that it "discourages those who are strangers to the light of [revelation] from coming into the Region of it."[14]

Governmental support for Christianity is a bad thing, in other words, because it scares off people who might otherwise immigrate to this country, live among Christians, see the light, and convert to the true religion!

Madison made this argument, but he did not really take it to heart. He himself placed his faith not in the God of Christian revelation but in nature's distant God, and certainly didn't care how many of the earth's inhabitants "saw the light."[15] It does indeed tell us something about the world in which he lived that he sought to fortify his principled arguments for liberty of conscience with this more pragmatic one, tailored to the views of many of his fellow citizens who were not exactly like-minded. But we learn more about his real ideas concerning the utility of religious diversity when we consider what he says in one of his most famous writings, the tenth of the Federalist Papers (and one of the most famous of them, if not *the* most famous).

Federalist 10 focuses on developing a remedy for the problems caused by *faction*, which Madison defines as "a number of citizens, whether amounting to a majority or a minority of the whole, who are united and actuated by some common impulse of passion, or of interest, *adverse* to the rights of other citizens, or to the permanent and aggregate interests of the community."[16] A faction does not cause too much of a problem if it makes up less than a majority of the population. In that case, "relief is supplied by the republican principle, which enables the majority to defeat its sinister views, by regular vote." When a faction becomes a majority, however, the same principle enables it to "sacrifice to its ruling passion or interest, both the public good and the rights of other citizens."[17] Madison has in mind many different kinds of factions, but at the top of his list he places groups that are motivated by "zeal for different opinions concerning religion."[18] Among other things, he fears the formation of a zealous religious majority that would persecute and oppress those who were not in agreement with it.

One conceivable cure for the problems caused by factions, Madison says, would be to give "to every citizen the same opinions, the same passions, and the same interests."[19] But this is "impracticable." Curiously, he does not say that diversity ought to be preserved for its own sake. "Perhaps," as David Epstein has written in a book on *The Federalist*, he "refrains from a more direct defense of diversity because of the possibility of true opinions, and enlightened and permanent interests, which would be desirable for all men if they could be discovered."[20] In any case, for Madison diversity is an intractable reality, not something that he identifies as an optimum state of affairs.

Still, it is a reality that can be turned to everyone's advantage. In fact, the more of it there is, the better. If you "extend the sphere," i.e., enlarge the country, "and you take in a greater variety of parties and interests; you make it less probable that a majority of the whole will have a common motive to invade the rights of other citizen." And even if such a majority does exist, it will be more difficult for its members to "discover their own strength, and to act in unison with each other."[21] The best way to avoid the formation of a majority faction actuated by religious zeal is, accordingly, to create a large republic in which there is a "multiplicity of sects."[22] Madison does not mention the Jews explicitly—he did not need to—but this is where they come into the picture. They are welcome not because diversity in itself is such a good thing, but because by their mere presence alongside other minorities they "increase the variety of sects dispersed over the entire face of the nation" and thereby reduce the likelihood of the formation of an oppressive majority faction.

In its fundamental assessment of the Jews, then, the Enlightenment was the same everywhere, in Europe and in the United States: The Jew was "even more man than Jew," and fully capable of being integrated into the general society, sooner or later. Comparing the situation in Europe and in the United States, we see, above all, that in the United States enlightened thinking pointed in only one of the two directions mapped out by enlightened European thinkers: completely equal rights for the Jews, immediately. There was nobody in the newly established United States arguing that the Jews (or for that matter, anyone else) must first be trained for full citizenship before it could be granted to them. With respect to what the Jews might do with their new freedom, we do not find anyone (not among the enlightened, anyhow) ardently looking forward to their abandonment of their ancestral religion and their assimilation into the general the population. But neither do we find among the authors of our Constitution anything like an enthusiastic affirmation of their presence as a group that by its very existence contributes to some kind of "gorgeous mosaic," to borrow a phrase from a recent mayor of New York, David Dinkins. At least in the case of James Madison, "the father of the Constitution," the welcome extended to them is less admiring than calculating. Just by being themselves, by being different, they can play a part in staving off the danger of any religious "tyranny of the majority."

This may be less edifying than some anachronistic readings of early American history would have it. It would be more gratifying, perhaps, to look back on our country's foundational period and discover everywhere a strong endorsement of diversity for its own sake, one that inspired a whole-hearted appreciation of the Jews' presence. There is, indeed, some evidence of such sentiments in the early years of this country. One recalls, for instance, the parade held in Philadelphia on July 4, 1788 marking the ratification of the U.S. Constitution. Marching together, in one division, one observer reported, were "the clergy of the different christian denominations with the rabbi of the Jews [really, a communal leader mistakenly identified as such], walking arm in arm." As Jonathan Sarna relates in his new book, *American Judaism*, "the famed physician, Dr. Benjamin Rush, who witnessed the unprecedented spectacle, wrote that this first-ever ecumenical parade "was a most delightful sight." Rush went on to say that "there could not have been a more happy emblem of that section of the new constitution, which opens all its powers and offices alike, not only to every sect of christians, but to worthy men of *every* religion."[23]

No less than James Madison, Benjamin Rush was an enlightened man, even if he was also, as Henry F. May has described him, "a lifelong believer in original sin, divine grace, and the Christian millenium."[24] Among other things, he taught chemistry at the University of Pennsylvania and belonged to the American Philosophical Association.[25] And while he was not a member of the Constitutional Convention, he was a signer of the Declaration of Independence.

To contemporary ears, I am sure, his views on religious diversity sound a lot better than those of James Madison. But which of these two men better reflects the impact of the Enlightenment on early American statesmens' attitudes toward religious diversity? It seems to me that Madison's calculations were more characteristic of the times than Rush's enthusiasms. Nevertheless, I think that it is safe to say that the regime designed by the American Founders, whatever their intentions and expectations may have been, established a more solid and secure basis for Jewish life than anything undertaken by their contemporaries in other nations touched by the Enlightenment.

NOTES

1. Among the more notable works to appear in just the past few years are *The Jewish Enlightenment* by Shmuel Feiner (Philadelphia, 2003), *Judaism and Enlightenment* by Adam Sutcliffe (Cambridge, 2003), and *Jewish Enlightenment in an English Key* by David Ruderman (Princeton, 2000).

2. Paul Mendes-Flohr and Jehuda Reinharz, eds., *The Jew in the Modern World* (New York, 1995), p. 30.

3. Ibid., 33. In her recent biography of the Abbé Grégoire, Alyssa Sepinwall has usefully characterized Dohm as well as her subject as "conditionalists," contrasting them with "unconditionalists," who "argued that Jews should be incorporated into society with no conditions other than those demanded of other citizens." See *The Abbé Grégoire and The French Revolution:The Making of Modern Univeralism* (Berkeley, 2005), p. 62.

4. Arthur Hertzberg, *The French Enlightenment and the Jews* (New York, 1968), p. 10.

5. For further analysis of Hertzberg's views see my article"Voltaire on Judaism and Christianity," in *AJS Review*, vol. 18, no. 2 (1993) pp. 223–245. For a related analysis of Hertzberg's views on Montesquieu see my article "Montesquieu: A Precursor of Jewish Emancipation?," in *L'Antisémitisme Éclairé:* Inclusion and Exclusion:

Perspectives on Jews from the Enlightenment to the Dreyfus Affair, Ilana Y. Zinguer and Sam W. Bloom, eds., (Leiden, 2003), pp. 45–60.

6. Ronald Schechter, *Obstinate Hebrews: Representations of Jews in France, 1715–1815* (Berkeley, 2003), p. 53.

7. Richard Pipes, "Catherine II and the Jews: The Origins of the Pale of Settlement," Soviet Jewish Affairs vol. 5 (1975), pp. 3–20.

8. Jonathan Sarna, "The Impact of the American Revolution on American Jew," *Modern Judaism*, vol. 1, no. 2 (September 1981), p. 153.

9. For a documentary history of lingering discrimination against Jews in various states, see Jonathan Sarna and David Dalin, *Religiion and State in the American Jewish Experience* (Chicago, 2000).

10. Jacob Katz, *Out of the Ghetto: The Social Background of Jewish Emancipation, 1770–1870* (Cambridge, MA., 1973), p. 38.

11. Frederic Cople Jaher, *The Jews and the Nation: Revolution, Emancipation, State Formation and the Liberal Paradigm in America and France* (Princeton, 2002), p. 144.

12. *The Jew in the Modern World*, p. 459.

13. George Washington, *Writings* (New York, 1997), p. 971.

14. Marvin Meyers, ed., *The Mind of the Founder: Sources of the Political Thought of James Madison* (Hanover, 1981), p. 12.

15. See Frank Lambert, *The Founding Fathers and the Place of Religion in America* (Princeton, 2003), pp. 159–79.

16. Thomas Jefferson, James Madison and John Jay, *The Federalist Papers*, ed. Isaac Kramnick (London, 1987), p. 123.

17. Ibid., p. 125.

18. Ibid., p. 124.

19. Ibid., p. 123.

20. David Epstein, *The Political Theory of the Federalist* (Chicago, 1984), p. 68.

21. *The Federalist Papers*, p. 127.

22. Ibid., p. 321.

23. Jonathan Sarna, *American Judaism* (New Haven, 2004), p. 38.

24. Henry May, *The Enlightenment in America* (Oxford, 1976), p. 211.

25. See Donald J. D'Elia, *Benjamin Rush, Philosopher of the American Revolution* (Philadelphia, 1974).

2

American Exceptionalism: The Case of the Jews, 1750–1850

Frederic Cople Jaher

In reviewing the Jewish experience in modern western society one development immediately compels attention. The great revolutions of the West, the Puritan, American, French, and Russian, profoundly transformed society and/or helped create nation-states. Hence, it would be expected that these upheavals had a huge impact upon the Jews living in these countries. Such was the case in England, where Jews were readmitted shortly after the Puritan triumph, and in France and Russia, where Jews respectively were officially emancipated in 1791 and 1918. America, however, was an exception. Neither revolution nor formation of the United States evoked major changes in the status of Jews. This difference reflects aspects of American exceptionalism in general and, as a ramification, significant variance in the Jewish experience here from that in Europe.

Revolutionary emancipation of Jews, in France and the Soviet Union for example, was declarative; civic equality derived from abstract principles of natural rights or socialist comradeship. Liberation was embedded in modern nation-building; it was a *de jure* conferral that abruptly transited Jews from semi-autonomous corporate communities to members of the national community, from outcasts to citizens. This process was memorably inscribed by Stanislas Comte de Clermont-Tonnerre when, on December 23, 1789, he urged emancipation during the first great debate on that subject in the National Constituent Assembly:

> The Jews should be denied everything as a nation, but granted everything as individuals. They must be citizens . . . they cannot be a nation within another

nation. . . . It is intolerable that the Jews should become a separate political formation or class in the country. Every one of them must individually become a citizen; if they do not want this, they must inform us and we shall then be compelled to expel them. The existence of a nation within a nation is unacceptable to our country.[1]

Jews would forfeit their historical existence as a corporation ("a nation within another nation") for equal rights (citizenship in the new nation emerging from the Revolution).[2]

Political equality for American Jewry developed differently: it was organic, not abstract, de facto, not declarative, gradual, not abrupt, and not as embedded in larger processes like a revolutionary transformation of society or the emergence of a modern state. America in this, as in other respects, resembled its primary progenitor. Indeed, it is possible to suggest an Anglo/American model of Jewish emancipation, as in the emancipation of slaves and women, in contrast to a European/continental model.[3] In common with America, Jewish equality in Britain was a gradual, incremental and organic process. Jews in these countries shared historical developments that differentiated them from European Jewry: They lived in nations with greater denominational variety and pluralism. Catholics for long stretches of time were deemed the most dangerous religious enemy. British and American Protestantism was more philosemitic than French Catholicism, German Lutheranism, or the Russian Orthodox Church. Neither America nor the United Kingdom (since the Jews returned in the seventeenth century) had enforced ghettoes and semi-independent, legally recognized communities, trade restrictions, special tolls and taxes on Jews, and anti-Semitic movements or political parties. Finally, American and British Jews entered their respective national cultures earlier than did Jews on the Continent, with the possible exception of the Jews of Holland. Equally, if not more important, was the broader national context. The United States and the United Kingdom historically have encountered weaker *völkish* urges and political tribulations than in European countries. Comparatively free of foreign invasions and conquests, insurrections, constitutional crises, and governmental turnovers, their stability is mutually related to a sturdier national identity.[4]

Two events in colonial America early indicate the American way. In 1654, twenty-three Jews landed in New Amsterdam from Brazil; the first Jewish settlement in this country. Governor Peter Stuyvesant, an anti-Semite, urged removal of this group upon the Dutch West India Company. The directors refused his request because the colony needed settlers and trade to survive and Dutch Jews had vital commercial connections and were among the principal shareholders in the nearly bankrupt Company. Over the governor's objections, the Company permitted the Jews to trade, and, contrary to prevailing practice in Europe, to own real estate and live where they

pleased. Within two years after their arrival, the Jews of New Amsterdam became burghers, another dramatic departure from their European brethren.
While the freedoms conferred did not amount to total equality, civically,
as well as geographically, these Jews had come a long way in a short time.[5]

Limited liberation in New Netherland was not a reification of concepts
of natural rights or of theories of citizenship associated with nation building. Instead, it was organic and concrete, deriving from the interests of the
West India Company shareholders in Amsterdam. They needed capital to
sustain their company and colony, Jews were large investors, and therefore
Jewish settlers must be admitted and accorded certain rights regardless of
the aversions of the other settlers and probably of the directors themselves.
Moreover, Jews were admitted at the founding of the colony; they were
present at the creation and, unlike their usual existence, present as semi-
emancipated burghers not as ghettoized subjects of the king or some other
form of feudal lordship.

Another dispute about Jewish settlement occurred in Georgia in 1733.
This time, however, it was the Governor who wanted Jews and the charter
company who did not. The founding trustees urged deportation of Jews
from Savannah, fearing their presence would discourage immigration.
Governor James Oglethorpe had a different view of the imperatives of
settlement. He felt that arrival of the Jews would address the desperate need
for inhabitants and not inhibit other newcomers. Accordingly, Oglethorpe
gave Jews plots of land at a time when Jewish landholding in Europe was
generally forbidden. Reconsidering their earlier protest, the trustees in 1737
gave a Jew a large loan to grow grapes. The need for a staple commodity
that might lead to profitable trade overcame the trustees' traditional hostility not only to Jewish residents but to Jews engaging in landed pursuits.[6]
As in New Netherland, Jews had obtained rights rarely or never received
across the Atlantic because of practical necessities rather than concepts of
nationhood or the rights of man. And once again the Jews were present in
palpable if not total equality at the incipience of what would become part
of the United States.

Three of the four great modern revolutions wrought significant change
for Jews. On this side of the Atlantic the combustible combination of
abrupt and violent social change and state formation or modification
did not radically alter the status of Jews. Before 1775 America's Jews
had embarked on the process of realizing the utopian universalisms,
the emancipatory and egalitarian yearnings that helped impel (though,
imperfectly and in the end unsuccessfully) these and other western insur-
gencies. What had transpired for American Jews before 1775, in contrast
to their coreligionists in England before 1640, France in 1789 and Russia
in 1917, conditioned the different subsequent trajectories of the Jewish
experience in these nations.

Plotting the course of this country's Jews begins with contextualizing it as a variety of what has become a truism, American exceptionalism (the consensus liberal paradigm), originally conceptualized by Alexis de Tocqueville in *Democracy in America* (1835, 1840) and further elaborated by Louis Hartz in *The Liberal Tradition in America* (1955). Unlike other western nations, the initial settlements of what became the United States emerged in the modern era, i.e. after the passing of the Middle Ages and at the conclusion of the wars of the Reformation and Counter Reformation. Hence American Jews were largely exempted from demonization, ghettoization, exclusion, submission, and other persecutions that tormented them in the Old World.[7] Conditions in the New World, the absence of a feudal past and a legally enshrined nobility and corporate organization of society and a unitary intercolonial church establishment, and the imperative for attracting settlers, promoted a political, cultural, and ethnic diversity (American pluralism, currently called multi-culturalism), that eventuated in an inclusive nationalism, a cardinal tenet of the American creed. These ideological and situational developments early enhanced the integration of Jews in American society and differentiated them their counterparts elsewhere.

Egalitarian impulses were additionally fortified on both sides of the Atlantic by Enlightenment doctrines of natural rights and the faculty of reason as interrelated and inherent in all men and, indeed, the qualities that distinguished them from other species. These principles were expressed in the Declaration of Independence and its partial derivative, the Declaration of the Rights of Man and the Citizen, the definitive documents of the rebellions of 1776 and 1789. Thomas Jefferson, America's leading *philosophe*, drafted the American declaration and Benjamin Franklin, another Deist, was on the Continental Congress committee that prepared the document. A decade later Jefferson wrote the Virginia Bill for Religious Freedom, America's most uncompromising defense of liberty of conscience, an act he wanted inscribed on his tombstone. James Madison, likewise an advocate of liberty of belief, maneuvered it through the state legislature.

American principles and practices, conventions and exigencies, by the late provincial and revolutionary periods yielded for Jews a unique magnitude of acceptance in modern western society. At various times and in various colonies during the eighteenth century, Catholics, Presbyterians, Baptists, and Moravians were officially persecuted; after 1680 such mistreatment never befell Jews.[8] Avoidance of negative encounters was not the only measure of progress toward parity. Jews participated in American life in ways that were rare or non-extant across the Atlantic. They attended colleges and Rhode Island College in 1770 (later Brown University) acknowledged the generosity of Jewish donors by amending its charter to permit freedom of worship, exemption from chapel attendance, a Jewish tutor if justified by the number of Jewish students (none came before the Revolution), and permission for Jews to fund their own chair in Hebrew and fill it with a member of their own creed.[9] In the 1740s and 50s Jews were among the founders and members of elite cultural and charitable organizations in Savannah Georgia, Philadelphia, Newport, Rhode Island, and other places. In 1781 a Jew became grand master of a Masonic lodge and deputy inspector general of Masonry. Rhode Island Lopezes and the Levy-Franks clan in New York and Philadelphia belonged to the urban gentry and daughters of affluent Jewish families married well, as in the union between Phila Franks and New York aristocrat Oliver DeLancey. A significant marker of progress toward equal rights was the service of Jews as Revolutionary army or militia officers up to the rank of colonel at a time when European Jews were generally excluded from the military.[10]

Although formally barred from public posts by the requirement of swearing to the divinity of the New Testament, a number of Jews held office despite this apparent prohibition. In the seventeenth and early eighteenth centuries they were constables in New Amsterdam and Boston and in Charleston one became what would later be called chief of police. Higher office beckoned later in the provincial period. In 1731 Rodrigo Pacheco became New York's colonial agent to Parliament; a generation later Moses Lindo, the South's leading Jewish merchant, was inspector general of indigo for South Carolina, another Jewish trader was inspector for tanned leather at the port of Savannah, and Jews served as justices of the peace in Georgia. By the Revolution, Jews held offices of greater power and prestige and of political rather than economic jurisdiction. This development reflected a Jewish preference for the patriotic cause due to lesser prejudice in America than England and to the fact that most Jews had few ties to the mother country or the imperial establishment. Appreciation for siding with the rebels, along with their own social and economic distinction, enabled a few Jews, particularly in the South, to attain political prominence. Whig merchant Mordecai Sheftall in 1774–75 headed the most important Georgia county government as chairman of the parochial committee of Christ Church Parish (Savannah and its environ). During the war he was colonel of a Georgia brigade and commissary general for South Carolina and Georgia. A newly arrived Jew from London sat in the First and Second South Carolina Provincial Congress, and after independence, when the Provincial Congress became the General Assembly, he was the first Jew in an American state legislature.[11]

Suffrage, like office holding, was a function of citizenship inconsistently exercised by Jews. In an age where bureaucracy was limited and interest and privilege often surmounted legality, informal arrangements afforded intermittent political opportunities. In provincial New York, North and South Carolina, Massachusetts, New Hampshire, and New Jersey Jews sometimes went to the polls and at other times were disenfranchised. In Rhode Island, rich merchants like the Lopezes probably voted in local elections, and Jews seemed to have had uninterrupted suffrage in Georgia. Conversely, in colonial Connecticut, Pennsylvania, Delaware, Maryland, and Virginia, Jews never voted or were eligible for government positions. The New York Constitution of 1777 gave Jews *de jure* political equality, but even in an age of revolutionary republicanism this was a unique conferral. The South Carolina Constitution of 1778, for example, excluded non-Protestants from the Assembly despite Jews in the 1760s and 70s having regained voting and office holding rights they lost in 1716.[12] As with so much else concerning American Jewry in the colonial and revolutionary epochs, the assumption of civic rights was an incomplete process with advances and withdrawals dependent upon intra-colonial conflicts and other circumstances. Nevertheless, Jews engaged in political activities of a type and on a scale denied them in other western countries.

One colony wide endeavor illustrates the advancement toward, and ambivalence about, making Jews citizens. The British Parliament mandated in the Plantation Act of 1740 that Jews and Protestants in the empire, but not in England, were eligible for naturalization. Catholics were excluded and Jews did not have to take the otherwise required Christian oath. When Parliament in 1753 legislated this procedure for the homeland this extension aroused such hostility that it was revoked within a year. The Plantation Act aimed to strengthen the settlements by attracting Protestant and Jewish immigrants. Naturalization granted full economic but not political rights and was a middle ground between denization (already given Jews in several seventeenth-century colonies) and citizenship. Resistance in some provinces and previous exercise of these rights meant that few Jews (under sixty—mostly in New York and Pennsylvania) became naturalized. Outside Massachusetts, New York, Pennsylvania, the Carolinas, New Jersey, Delaware, and possibly Maryland, objections obviated implementation. Recalcitrance was most notable in Rhode Island, where Aaron Lopez, the leading Jew in that colony, was denied naturalization because a 1663 Rhode Island laws restricted this status to Christians. Lopez and other Jews then transferred their legal residence to Massachusetts or New York.[13] Despite its limited application and colonial objections, London, in the Plantation Act, significantly advanced *de jure* legitimization of American Jewry.

Although the War for Independence did not radically alter the status of American Jewry, revolutionary republican utopianism quickened the quest for equality. Jews faced two impediments to full citizenship, sectarian establishments and hindrances to political activity. Starting in the Revolution and largely completed in the early national period, these disabilities gradually disappeared. Rhode Island, New Jersey, Pennsylvania, and Delaware never had an establishment in the provincial period and during the Revolution, New York, Virginia, and North Carolina terminated public taxes for sectarian purposes. Although half of the states still provided for public funds for religion, the trend was clear. Disestablishment was completed in South Carolina (1790) and Georgia (1798) after the Northwest Ordinance (1787), the U.S. Constitution, and the First Amendment of the Bill of Rights (1789) affirmed freedom of conscience. Other states (Vermont, 1807; Connecticut, 1818; New Hampshire, 1819; and Massachusetts, 1833) belatedly disestablished religion. Neither the federal government nor any states formed after the U.S. became a nation provided for funding any creed.[14]

The other state constitutional impingement on civic rights for Jews was swearing to belief in Christianity in order to hold government posts. Many states felt that membership in the body of Christ was vital to the spiritual and social health of the commonwealth, and therefore necessary for full membership in the body politic. They required test oaths for office holding, even when, as in the Pennsylvania, Delaware, and North Carolina Constitutions of 1776, no provision was made for public support of religion. Eleven of the thirteen original states limited officeholders to Christians or Protestants.[15] The influence of the Virginia Bill for Religious Freedom, Article VI of the federal constitution (". . . no religious test shall ever be required as a Qualification to any Office or public Trust under the United States"), the Northwest Ordinance, and the Bill of Rights helped ensure that new states did not require Christian oaths and that most of the older states dropped these tests. Within a decade of the Revolution, Delaware, Pennsylvania, South Carolina, and Vermont rescinded their abjurations, and Georgia did so in 1798. New York and New Jersey never required religious tests. Connecticut (1818), Massachusetts (1821), Maryland (1825), North Carolina (1868), and New Hampshire (1876) subsequently discarded test oaths.

Legal impositions upon full citizenship in the states were for the most part soon overcome and the momentum for civic rights for Jews owed much to Article VI in the U.S. Constitution. The provision that Jews did not have to meet a religious test for holding office made America the first nation to grant civic equality to this long oppressed people. This radical break with the past, however, did not evoke the passionate rhetoric, pro and con, that Jewish emancipation evoked in the French National Assembly. Article VI stirred little discussion or dissent in the Constitutional Convention of 1787, only the North Carolina delegation opposed and Maryland divided over its passage. Nor did it arouse controversy in the state ratifying conventions or the widespread debate over the Constitution.[16]

A similar affirmative, brief, and dispassionate congressional response greeted another momentous break with the past and other nations when that body passed the Bill of Rights (1789). The First Amendment stated: "Congress shall make no law respecting an establishment of religion, or prohibiting the free exercise thereof."[17] By 1791, when the states ratified the Bill of Rights, the national constitution made America's Jews unconditional

citizens. "Only in America," as later generations of Jews would say in prais-
ing their country, had Jews achieved this level of rights. *De jure* emancipation took place a few months later in France, but it was short-lived and less
complete.[18] In this respect the French and Soviet Revolutions resembled
each other and differed from their American counterpart. Ironically, one
reason for this variance was that religious sects in America did not oppose
the War for Independence, while organized religion was hostile to the
Communist uprising and to more radical stages of the French Revolution.
The Communists and the Jacobins persecuted all religions when they seized
power.

Ideology coalesced with policy to encourage emancipation. Renowned
figures of the Revolution and the Age of Reason, Benjamin Franklin, Benjamin Rush, Thomas Jefferson, and George Washington advocated religious
liberty and supported civic equality for Jews. John Adams and James Madison also defended Judaism and Jewish citizenship.[19] Whether Deists or not,
the foremost American leaders believed in natural rights and creedal diversity and freedom. The substance and timing of his actions and his fame
as *the* founding father made Washington the supreme model for religious
tolerance and affirmation of American Jewry. Replying to praise from several synagogues in 1790 he wrote the head of the Newport congregation:
"For happily the government of the United States, which gives to bigotry no
sanction, to persecution no assistance, requires only that they who live under its protection should demean themselves as good citizens." Like other
champions of tolerance, Washington linked interfaith equality with respect
for Jews. "May the children of the stock of Abraham who dwell in this land
continue to merit and enjoy the good will of the other inhabitants." These
sentiments took on added significance because they were publicly voiced
while Washington was president.[20]

What was established in the colonial, revolutionary, and early national
eras escalated in the nineteenth century. Jews could be found in ever-higher
political posts, first in municipal and state governments and by the 1840s
in both houses of congress. In this facet of equality, however, they lagged
behind their French brethren, who had two ministers in the Second Republic cabinet of 1848. Not until the Civil War would American Jews attain this
rank (in the Confederacy); a federal cabinet appointment awaited the next
century. When, in 1842, Rhode Island removed the test oath, only New
Hampshire and North Carolina disqualified professing Jews from public
office. Other conferrals of civic recognition were renewed or introduced.
Leading politicians, e.g. Henry Clay and President John Tyler, reiterated
their predecessors' respectful and non-discriminatory pledges to the Children of Abraham. Further realization of full citizenship, absorption of
Judaism in the American civil religion, surfaced in1829 when a Richmond
rabbi voiced the invocation at the Virginia Constitutional Convention and

twenty years later when a rabbi from the same congregation gave the opening prayer at a Virginia House of Delegates session, the first official blessing
of a Jewish spiritual leader over a state legislature.[21]

Ascendance in politics was rooted in a more comprehensive integration
in society, as exemplified in 1811 when New York's mayor DeWitt Clinton
memorialized the state legislature for a charity school run by Congregation
Shearith Israel. The legislature granted the Polonies Talmud Torah the same
privileges it accorded Protestant and Catholic parochial institutions, and
the city council made payments retroactive to the school's beginnings.[22]
Parity with other religious charities was an inclusive civic gesture that
transcended individual expressions of appreciation for Jews and Judaism.
Positive institutional interaction between Jewish and official Gentile-domi-
nated organizations endorsed Jews as citizens. Twenty-two years would pass
before the land that proclaimed liberty, equality, and fraternity gave Jewish
schools state funding equal to those of other denominations and many
French municipalities ignored this law.[23]

Gershom Mendes Seixas, spiritual leader of Shearith Israel, America's
oldest and largest Jewish congregation, virtually incarnated civil Judaism.
In the young Republic, he personified, as symbol and creator, the elevation
of his faith as a theological component of the bourgeoning American civic
cult. At the presidential inauguration in New York City on April 30, 1789
Hazzan (cantor) Seixas walked in the procession alongside twelve other
clergymen. David S. Franks, scion of an eminent colonial Jewish family,
was one of the three marshals in this memorable civic ceremony. When,
on March 28, 1798, President John Adams proclaimed a day of fasting,
prayer, and national humiliation at the prospect of conflict with Britain
and France, at the synagogue on Mill Street Seixas entreated God to rescue
America. He sermonized on days officially designated for thanksgiving and
prayer and consulted with ministers of other denomination to plan such
events, thus forging ties between Jewish and other sectarian communities, a
role acknowledged by his being called "Reverend" and "minister." In addition, he occasionally preached in St. Paul's Episcopal Chapel and served as
a Columbia College regent and trustee, a post unprecedented for a Jewish
clergyman.[24]

Promoted and personified by Seixas, amalgamation of Jews with the nation consolidated in ensuing decades. As the Civil War approached, they
had attained acceptance, even prominence, in important phases of American life. As general entrepreneurs in young, relatively undifferentiated communities like Santa Fe, San Francisco, and Los Angeles, they pioneered key
ventures in trade, transportation, manufacturing, real estate, and banking.
Even in older places like Baltimore, Richmond, Charleston, Philadelphia,
and New York, where social distinctions rigidified with time, Jews increased
their role as directors and officers of prestigious firms.[25] Correlated with

business and economic achievement Jews won renown in law and medicine and studied at prestigious colleges.[26]

Although social acceptance was a more elusive goal than political, professional, or economic advancement, Jews had yet to encounter massive exclusion from upper- and middle-class organizations, hotels, and neighborhoods. In this respect antebellum American Jewry regrettably faced the past not the future. Voluntary associations of varying status and function, as in previous generations, admitted Jews. In Philadelphia, Richmond, Charleston, Los Angeles, Milwaukee, and other cities they belonged to elite social clubs, charity, artistic, and scientific societies, and militia companies as well as to plebian volunteer fire companies.[27]

August Belmont embodied confluent currents of economic, political, and social prominence in American Jewry. As the American agent of the Rothschilds, the founder of August Belmont and Company made that firm an important Wall Street investment house in the 1840s. During the 1850s Belmont was an important Democratic Party financier and in 1860 became Chairman of the Democratic National Committee. He was admitted to New York's premier club, the Union Club in 1848, four years before Judah P. Benjamin, another non-practicing Jew. Belmont also celebrated the paramount intermarriage of the era (his wife was the daughter of blueblood Commodore Matthew C. Perry) with the most fashionable wedding of the 1849 New York social season.[28]

Affirmation of Jews more importantly registered itself in political policy and public opinion. In 1840 Jews of Damascus were charged with ritual murder, several were tortured and sentenced to death, and Jews in that city were mobbed. Mass protest meetings were held in Philadelphia and Charleston and eminent Catholic and Protestant clergy attended these meetings. The Charleston assemblage, with the mayor present, denounced the Damascus Affair, resolved that ritual murder was not a Judaic practice and sent this resolution to President Martin Van Buren and American ambassadors. Van Buren and his secretary of state instructed the consul in Alexandria and the minister to Turkey to seek a fair trial for the defendants and halt attacks on Jews in Damascus.[29]

Ten years later another international incident involving Jews evoked support from America. President Millard Fillmore objected to discrimination against American Jews in the 1850 commercial treaty with Switzerland and the Senate refused ratification. Newspapers in many cities protested against the treaty and subsequent exclusion of American Jews from trading in some cantons. When the exclusionary provision in the treaty was enforced in 1857 (an American Jew was prevented from trading in a Swiss canton), however, Buchanan's administration did not abrogate the agreement.[30] In this case economic interest outweighed the citizenship rights of American Jews.

The good repute of Jews was manifest in many areas of American life, including popular and high culture. Antebellum American tragedians Junius Brutus Booth and Edwin Forest acted Shylock compassionately. Lafcadio Hearn appreciated orthodox Jewish rituals and condemned offensive Jewish stereotypes on the French stage as encouraging anti-Semitism. William Cullen Bryant celebrated free America, where "the Jew worshipped unmolested in his synagogue." More intimately, Margaret Fuller in 1845 told her German Jewish lover that he "show[ed] me how the sun of today shines upon the ancient temple."[31]

ANTI-SEMITISM

A triumphalist assessment of American liberalism, in so far as it bears on the Jewish experience in this nation, is tempting—even plausible; though it may not be completely invalid it is certainly an exaggerated exercise in flag waving. Every comment and gesture of affirmation and integration of Jews could be matched with those of distance and negation, even if the magnitude of the former, at least in the pre-Civil War halcyon century of escalating acceptance, might outweigh the latter. Undoubtedly, factors trended toward a favorable response to America's Jews: need for settlers; open immigration and naturalization policy; ethnic, sectarian, and cultural diversity; absence of medieval baggage of demonization, exclusion, and isolation of Jews, and of massive, organized violence against that people; establishment of the colonies after the great religious wars of the early modern era and during the heyday of the Age of Reason; and an accompanying lower intensity of denominational passion. These conditions and forces created a culture of civil society, an emphasis on voluntary associations and inclusive nationalism, and a palpable, if imperfect commitment, to consensus liberalism. Combined, they are the facets that define American exceptionalism, and compared to Europe the Jewish destiny in America has been exceptionally edenic.

Jews in this country, however, also encountered constraints and aversions. Gradually waning until the Secession crisis these circumstances nevertheless made the Jewish existence problematic. American liberal exceptionalism was powerful, perhaps predominant, but not absolute. The United States may have been born free but it also sprung from European antecedents and was additionally shaped by Christian commitments; these progenitors of American culture and society exerted an ongoing influence over what they begot and that constantly renewed legacy included a baleful view of Jews. Relatively muted on this side of the Atlantic, the sinister regard of the Jew as unrepentant Christ killer, unscrupulous commercial competitor, unpatriotic parasite, and unredeemable sinner nonetheless made the passage from Old to New World. For Jews of this nation, grateful for opportunities offered them in their new homeland and eager to identify with it, the antagonistic, though subordinate, elements in their reception imposed an anxiety of ambivalence. Few Americans harbored unmitigated aversion against Jews but many subscribed to varying degrees of doubt and disfavor mediated though they were by positive currents of the American creed.

The confluence of affirmation and aversion played out amidst the advance of Jews toward full citizenship and de facto integration. The political, social, and economic climb to parity from the colonial through the antebellum epochs were dramatic gains precisely because they outpaced those in other countries and modified a discriminatory past. Jews were not ghettoized or forbidden to participate in various occupations, but in most colonies and some states in the young republic, they had to pay taxes to established Christian sects and their voting and office holding rights were circumscribed by test oaths and other injunctions. These prohibitions largely withered away in the early national period and never existed in the national government (palpable progress) but had to be overcome (residual bias).

Personal as well as civic ambivalence existed, even among those who professed friendship for Jews and allegiance to egalitarian principles. Rhode Island Congregationalist pastor and subsequent Yale President Ezra Stiles was fascinated by all things Hebrew; he learned the language, sought Jews as friends, sometimes visited the Newport Synagogue and praised the building, the services, and the congregation. Stiles was outraged when his friend Aaron Lopez's petition for naturalization was rejected by the Rhode Island Superior Court. Thinking like a member of the revolutionary French National Assembly, he felt that such action would "prevent their [Jews'] from incorporating into any Nation, that they may continue as a distinct people." In 1773 he told his Norfolk congregation that the "Seed of Jacob are a chosen and favorite people of the most high and the subjects of the peculiar care of heaven." Such sentiments, however, did not prevent him from singling out Jewish merchants as violating the 1770 non-importation agreement against Britain. During the Revolution he charged that a Jewish cabal collaborating with the imperial government organized "a secret *Intelligence office* [italics in original] in London." With "Correspondents" in Boston and Newport, paid by the "Ministry" for the colonies, "this office boasted of having Intelligence of every Occurrence of any consequence in America." After the outbreak of war, he again accused Newport "Jews" of "informing against the [patriotic] inhabitants."[32]

Renowned physician Benjamin Rush, a signer of the Declaration of Independence, was another American with mixed feelings. Watching a July 4, 1788 Philadelphia parade, for Rush, the sight of "The Rabbi of the Jews" (Jacob Raphael of Congregation Mikveh Israel) marching arm in arm with two Christian ministers was a "happy emblem contrived of that section of the new Constitution [Article VI] which opens all its power and offices alike not only to every sect of Christians but to worthy men of every religion." A defender of natural rights (he was also an abolitionist), Rush, like fellow Deists Voltaire, Denis Diderot, and Baron d'Holbach, sometimes disdained Jews. He "anticipated when this once-beloved race of men shall again be restored to divine favor through reunion with Christians" in a "universal savior." In this case Christian triumphalism trumped rational liberalism. Contrasting Jesus' grace with "Jewish infidelity," Rush "condemned the Jews" for denying "a spiritual kingdom in the Millennium."[33]

An even greater American champion of the Age of Reason held conflicting opinions of Jews. Thomas Jefferson proposed the act that forbade compulsory denominational attendance or support in Virginia and proclaimed while president and in retirement that choice of worship should be unimpeded by governmental interference. The sage of Monticello assured Jewish correspondents of his profound respect for their creed, regret for persecution by misguided Christians, and hope that religious equality would be inscribed in American hearts, as well as in national law.[34] America's foremost Deist also denied the divinity of Christ but, in a letter to Rush, derogated Judaism: Jews' "ideas of him [God] & of his attributes were degrading & injurious" and their "Ethics...often irreconcilable with the sound dictates of reason & morality" and "repulsive & anti-social, as respecting other nations." He wrote to Joseph B. Priestly that Judaic beliefs and morality "degraded" Jews and "presented" the "necessity" for their "reformation."[35]

Other critics expressed less doubtful hostility. Official attacks were virtually non-existent, but a host of individuals and voluntary associations hurled a variety of epithets. Some accusations aimed at character defects, especially in regard to commercial malfeasance. This type of prejudice may be termed secular anti-Semitism related to but distinguishable from sacred anti-Semitism. The latter concerned the role of Jews in the Christian drama of salvation, particularly allegations of Deicide, and even more importantly, Jewish refusal to repent that deed. Carried over from the provincial period and medieval antecedents' secular anti-Semitism had a biblical provenance that identified Jews with commercial avarice. Such sinister practices were associated in the New Testament with sacred (Christological) Jew hatred. The nefarious usurer of medieval infamy originated in the Gospels. Judas, the apostle possessed by Satan, who betrays Christ for "thirty piece of silver" (Matt. 26:14–16; John 12: 4–6), also handles the funds of Jesus and the apostles (John 12:6; 13:29). This archetypal disloyal sinner, whose name in Hebrew is Judah (Judea), the names of the southern kingdom of Israel and one of the twelve tribes, symbolizes his people. Twelfth- century Christians identified Judas with money, cupidity, Jewry, and betrayal of Jesus. In legends he was portrayed, sometimes grotesquely, as fratricidal, patricidal, and incestuous with his mother.[36]

Sacred and secular anti-Semitism also merged when the Jew as evil usurer was associated with another imagined Jewish ogre, the ritual murderer. The one devoured the resources of Christian communities the other the blood of Christian children. Here, too, demonization may be traced to the New Testament. "I have sinned in that I have betrayed the innocent blood," says Judas in bringing "the thirty pieces of silver to the chief priests and elders" (Matt. 27:3–4). The priests respond: "It is not lawful for to put them into the treasury, because it is the price of blood." Instead, they use the misbegotten gain to buy the potters' field, to bury strangers in. "Wherefore that field was called, the field of blood" (Matt. 27: 6–8). Judas dies in this field (Acts 1:18–19); an outcast from redeemed society lies eternally with other aliens, anticipating what will happen to his people. Biblical connection of betrayal, blood, greed, and money was resurrected in medieval blood libels instigated by borrowers to avoid paying debts to Jews. The related stereotype of the blood-sucking creditor, later epitomized by Shylock, also linked usury and ritual murder. The latter crime had a sacred source of diabolicization in that it was a reenactment of the killing of Christ, a sin that turned into the ultimate transgression when Hebrews showed no contrition for what they had done.[37]

Since the Jews betrayed the Savior and were punished by eviction from the Holy Land to wander and suffer in the diaspora until they finally accept Jesus at the End of Time, in western history after the triumph of Christianity they became the extreme evil other. Living in exile for remorselessly betraying God, Jews pray for return to their spiritual home ("Next year in Jerusalem"). Wherever they reside, they are inherently aloof from other citizens and care only for their own kind (a "nation within a nation").[38] Hence, many gentile Americans embraced an interrelated, traditional, trinitarian condemnation of Jews as economic parasites, Christ killers, and disloyal compatriots.

Carried over from the Old World were folktales, ballads, exorcisms, incantations, and charms blaming the Jews for slaying Jesus.[39] Crucifixion fantasies spawned blood libels. Narrated by whites and blacks in every colony, most versions were based on Hugh of Lincoln, whose murder in England in 1255 was falsely blamed on the Jews as a ritual killing. Hugh is lured into a Jew's garden by his daughter, who stabs the child and collects his blood for a Hebrew holy day (usually Passover) service. In Virginia alone sixteen texts and seven different melodies have depicted this blood libel,[40] which merges New Testament dogma of the Jew as archetypal betrayer and murderer, slave of sterile Mosaic law, and pernicious foe of Christianity with the medieval and modern myth of the Jew as sensual violator of Christian innocence.

Embedded in the popular mind as folk myth, the image of the nefarious Hebrew was supplemented by contemporary negations of Jews as unpatriotic commercial predators. These accusations mixed modern contempt with ancient condemnations. Scapegoating grew in frequency and intensity in the revolutionary era, as usual in periods of social crisis. The Tory James Rivington satirized the Continental cause in a 1774 issue of *Rivington's N-Y Gazetteer* by announcing a bogus work entitled "Disappointment or the Sure Way to make a Patriot: Exemplified in the History of a Polish Jew.": The *Pennsylvania Evening Post*, during the state constitutional debate of 1776, printed several letters advocating that Jews and other "enemies of Christ" be ineligible for public office lest Pennsylvania become a bridgehead "for Antichrist" and "unsafe for Christians." Henry Melchior Muhlenberg, the foremost German Lutheran pastor of his time, feared that if the state constitution did not ordain Christianity as the civic religion "a Christian people" might be degraded under "rule by the Jews." The drafters of that document heeded these imprecations by including a test oath disqualifying infields from holding office.[41]

Charges of commercial duplicity compounded civic degradation. A Charleston merchant wrote to the *Charlestown Gazette* in 1778 that the "Tribe of Israel" deserted Savannah "after taking every advantage in trade," when "it was attacked by the enemy." They "fled here for an asylum with their ill-got wealth, dastardly turning their backs upon" Georgia. "Thus it will be in this State if it should ever be assailed by our enemies." Six years earlier Rev. David McClure, an Anglican missionary educated at Yale and Dartmouth, grudgingly conceded that Jews might observe their laws and rituals, "but hesitate not to defraud when opportunity presents."[42]

Imputations of disloyalty and cupidity were under-girded by traditional Christological anti-Semitism. Prominent clergymen of the era, Muhlenberg, Massachusetts Baptist leader Isaac Backus, Jonathan Edwards, America's most profound theologian and a fiery brand of the Great Awakening, castigated Jews as blind followers of their arid laws while shunning God's grace and, worst of all, unrepentant crucifiers. Ezra Stiles, in other moods an admirer of Judaism, mused in 1770 at a New York synagogue service, "How melancholy to behold an Assembly of Worshippers of Jehovah. Open and professed enemies to a crucified Christ."[43]

Despite popular prejudice and theological animosity in the provincial and revolutionary periods, Jews, as noted above, incompletely but irreversibly progressed toward equality and acceptance. Liberal impulses in the American creed surmounted detractive influences in shaping the destiny of Jews in the United States. These impulses, however, did not eliminate bigotry, which generally persisted in the early national, Jacksonian, and antebellum eras along the same lines as in colonial times. Two additional nineteenth-century developments, evangelical Christianity, which surged after the Protestant Revival in the early 1800s, and the emergence of the stereotype of the rich Jew as *arriviste*, presented new problems for American Jewry.

Political anti-Semitism was on display in the political conflicts of the early republic and residual struggles to remove test oaths from the state constitutions. Although there was an occasional tendency for Democratic-Republicans to disapprove of Jews, Federalists were more likely to resort to this disparagement. According to David Hackett Fischer, a prominent historian of Federalism, "During the 1790s there had been a wide and fetid stream of anti-Semitism." Fischer and other students of that era noted that Republicans were appreciably less anti-Semitic and that Jews accordingly supported the party of Jefferson. One indication of the comparatively favorable Republican attitude was the publication in a New York Democratic journal of denunciations of Federalist Rivington's ravings about Jews.[44] In a prelude to later and more bitter and extensive criticism here and abroad, Jeffersonians nevertheless occasionally associated Jews with the moneyed speculators while their opponents identified Jews with radicalism, especially with French Revolutionary Jacobins. Both sides combined political animus with conventional deprecation of Jewish commercial corruption and sometimes expressed these sentiments by investing their culprits with absurd Yiddish accents.[45] Language ridicule spoke to the issue of how Jews could be citizens if they did not speak proper English.

Another venue for the expression of hostility against Jews was opposition to removing test oaths in the dwindling number of states that had retained these abjurations. North Carolina resisted the trend toward civic equality. The 1835 state constitutional convention broadened the original declaration by substituting a pledge of Christian for Protestant belief, thus leaving Jews even more isolated in deprivation of full citizenship. Subsequent attempts to make the oath nondenominational were voted down by about two to one.[46] Expungment of this prerequisite for holding office in the Massachusetts constitutional revision convention of 1820–21 narrowly won (13,782 to 12,480) in the state poll on the amendment and opponents voiced the usual objections to Jews as "enemies of Christianity" and therefore not "suitable members of a Christian state."[47]

The greatest antebellum controversy over granting Jews full citizenship took place in Maryland, where the original state constitution (1776) required a pledge of Christian faith for state office-holding. Maryland Jews unavailingly appealed to the legislature in 1797 and 1804 for repeal of the test oath. Not until 1818 was a "Jew bill" introduced, but it failed to pass. Similar legislation, defeated in 1822, finally became law in 1825. The power of the opposition was manifest in the election a year after the 1822 defeat. Jeffersonian Thomas Kennedy, the main sponsor of the "Jew bill," who represented a normally Democratic-Republican stronghold in western Maryland, was defeated by a Benjamin Galloway, who called himself the candidate of the "Christian ticket" and Kennedy the head of the "Jew ticket." However, Kennedy was reelected in 1824 and by 1826 a Jew presided over the Baltimore city council.[48]

Conditional not absolute, advance with ambivalence, characterizes American Jewry's move toward political equality. This same mixture of results characterized the career of Mordecai Noah, the most prominent Jewish politician in the Age of Jackson. Also a lawyer, playwright, and journalist, Noah was the best known American Jew until Judah P. Benjamin and August Belmont during the Civil War. As American consul to Tunis and appointed sheriff of New York (he lost an election to stay in that post), Noah was the victim of unceasing public pillory. He was called "Hook Nose" and "Mordecai Mammon Noah" and predicted to be a "Shylock" as sheriff. Campaigning to remain in that office, he was denounced as an "infidel" running against a Christian, a vengeful Jew who would delight in hanging Christians. His opponent notified voters that a Jew could not give absolute allegiance to America.[49]

Disdain for Judaism cascaded across the spectrum of Christianity. Whether evangelical, fundamentalist, mainline, or liberal, Protestant or Catholic, a fusion of Christian triumphalism and Christological dogma condemned Judaism as obsolete, displaced by Christianity, and spiritually barren, and Jews as remorseless Christ killers and foes of His followers. Disparagement ranged from moderate to extreme. While not dissenting from the sins of the Israelites, some critics sympathized with the prolonged sufferings of that benighted people. They reprimanded Christians for not honoring the children of Abraham who, despite their transgressions, had brought forth the Savior and for violating His commandments by their harshness toward God's chosen people. Other critics were less sympathetic. Impenitent deicide, in their view, was a perpetual depravity that corrupted all aspects of Jewish life.[50]

Theological anti-Semitism infested even the most liberal of Protestant sects. "The Worcester Catechism" (1815), published by recent graduates of Harvard Divinity School, including the future first president of the American Unitarian Association (1825), was read by youngsters in Unitarian Sunday schools and churches. Among the lessons that these pupils recited were that "Jews manifest[ed] their displeasure at the conduct of Jesus" by "waiting for opportunities to take his life;" and that "God punish[ed] the Jews for rejecting the Messiah and for their other crimes" by the Roman conquest of Jerusalem, the burning of the temple, and the death, enslavement, and continuing dispersion of the Jews.[51]

These charges were traditional but conveyed in a way that achieved unprecedented prominence in the nineteenth century. From the late colonial period until the nineteenth century, Americans displayed extensive indifference to religion. Doubts about Christianity were frequently uttered, requests for prayer and sermons went unheeded at the U.S. Constitutional Convention and God went unmentioned in the Constitution; a congressional chaplain in the Washington and Adams administrations attributed to free-thinking the usual absence of two-thirds of the congressmen at prayer meetings; and in 1800 less than 7 percent of the nation's inhabitants belonged to a denomination.[52] As the new century dawned an evangelical impulse reawakened, people flocked to the churches, and Deism faded. The religious revival did not halt the momentum for liberty of conscience and equality for Jews, but it did foster a conversionary impulse that presented problems for those who did not believe in the divinity of Christ.

The Second Great Awakening—a series of revivals from the 1790s to the 1830s spawned the American Society for Meliorating the Condition of the Jews (1820). The ASMCJ, modeled on its English sister organization, was founded by an apostate Jew, several college and seminary presidents, and professors, clergymen, and Federalist patricians, mostly from New York and New Jersey and of Presbyterian and Dutch Reformed affiliation. Clashes between sympathy and severity, respect and reproach, agitated would-be rescuers of those who denied Jesus. This ambivalence was expressed by Hannah Adams, president of the Female Society of Boston and Vicinity for Promoting Christianity Among the Jews, in an exceptionally appreciative history of the Jews, and Philip Milledoler, in an 1816 presidential address to the recently founded American Society for Evangelizing the Jews (forerunner to the ASCMJ). Jews were the chosen people and the Redeemer sprang from them, they persevered despite suffering mightily, Christians deserved rebuke for persecuting the parental faith, and at the end of days Jews would be restored to their place next to God. Nevertheless, they brought the miseries of death, destruction, and dispersions upon themselves for defiant Decide and persecution of Christians, and because their original sin has devolved and ramified into fraud, avarice, and infidelity.[53]

Debasing depictions of the Jew as crucifier and denier and desecrator of Christianity, rigid ritualist; unscrupulous and avaricious pursuer of wealth; and ugly and cowardly (often speaking a grotesque mixture of Yiddish and English malapropisms), clown, penetrated American culture through textbooks, religious pamphlets and theological treatises, newspaper and magazine articles and cartoons, folklore, stage plays, and novels and short stories.[54] Such stigmas, disparaging the ethnicity and creed of the Jews and reinforcing their alien and humiliating status, long before the mid-nineteenth century were hoary in provenance and routine in expression.

In the second quarter of the century a new conveyance of calumny surfaced. Originating in Europe, it featured the Jew as vulgar *arriviste*. The Potiphars in *Morton's Hope* (1839) epitomize this negative stereotype. The novel was written by John Lothrop Motley, better known as a diplomat and a historian, and was based on his student years in Germany after graduating Harvard. The upstart image of the Jews, unsurprising etched by this Boston aristocrat, emerged as gradual emancipation opened opportunities in politics, business, and society here and abroad. Vilified as peddlers, pawnbrokers, and petty shopkeepers, Jews would now be additionally reviled as rapacious lords of finance. Moses Potiphar, patriarch of a wealth Jewish family in Germany, is a "large greasy looking plebian, a fat vulgar looking man." Physically repulsive, Moses is a cowardly banker and speculator who, "with few scruples" amassed a fortune.[55]

Aspersion of Jews was extensive, even in the relatively halcyon period of 1750–1850. The French minister to the United States, a member of the Maryland Assembly speaking on behalf of the "Jew bill," and New York's *German Correspondent*, respectively in 1786, 1819, and 1820, reported that Jews were uniquely despised and that such abhorrence inhibited civic and social equality.[56] Anti-Semitism was formidable but not determinative. Pogroms, massive boycotts, and anti-Semitic demagogues, organizations, and political parties which plagued past and future generations of European Jews were absent in America. Even open invitation to discriminate did not inevitably bring adverse treatment. Jews sometimes held public office despite laws requiring test oaths; Noah lost an election in which animosity against his faith had an impact, but other Jews successfully ran for government office. The worst consequences of Jew hatred never befell American Jews, and even "normal" anti-Semitism was muted. Although Jews were not assaulted, they were insulted; they competed politically and commercially, but faced barriers and constraints not confronted by white Protestants. Lesser victims of deprivation, humiliation, and violence than were Blacks, Indians, Asians, and Catholics, Jews also suffered as an out-group. Nonetheless, this era was comparatively tranquil for American Jewry. Such good times would not come again for another century.

NOTES

1. Speech of Count Stanislaus de Clermont-Tonnerre to the National Assembly, 23 December 1789, *Archives Parlementaires de 1787 à 1860, Premier Série* (1789 à 1799) (Paris, 1878), vol. 10, pp. 754–56.

2. For a fuller discussion of these issues see Frederic Cople Jaher, *The Jews and the Nation: Revolution, Emancipation, State Formation, and the Liberal Paradigm in America and France* (Princeton, 2002), chs. 2–3.

3. For a discussion of these different models in abolition of slavery and the struggle for women's rights see *ibid.*, pp. 186–88, 215–16.

4. *Toward Modernity: The European Jewish Model*, ed. Jacob Katz (New Brunswick, NJ., 1987), pp. 226–42; Todd M. Endelman, *The Jews of Georgian England 1774–1830: Tradition and Change in a Liberal Society* (Philadelphia, 1979) and idem,

Radical Assimilation in English-Jewish History 1656–1945 (Bloomington, 1990), pp. 21–22; Israel Finestein, " Jewish Emancipationists in Victorian England: Self-Imposed Limits to Emancipation," in *Assimilation and Community: The Jews in Nineteenth-Century Europe*, eds. Jonathan Frankel and Steven Zipperstein (Cambridge, 1992), pp. 43–47; Geoffrey Alderman, "English Jews or Jews of English Persuasion? Reflections on the Emancipation of Anglo-Jewry," in *Paths of Emancipation: The Jews, States, and Citizenship*, eds. Pierre Birnbaum and Ira Katznelson (Princeton, 1991), pp. 128–37; M.C.N. Salbstein, *The Emancipation of the Jews in Britain: the Question of the Admission of the Jews to Parliament, 1828–1869* (Rutherford, NJ., 1982); and David Cesarini, "Changing Character," in *Citizenship, Nationality and Migration*, eds. David Cesarini and Mary Fulbrook (London, 1996), pp. 57, 60–61.

5. The correspondence between Peter Stuyvesant and the Jewish settlers and the Dutch West India Company is in *A Documentary History of the United States: 1654–1875*, ed. Morris U. Schappes (New York, 1971), pp. 1–14.; see also Jacob Rader Marcus, *The Colonial American Jews: 1492–1776* (Detroit, 1970, vol. 1, pp. 71–81, 175–79, 209–10, 218–43, Frederic Cople Jaher, *A Scapegoat in the New Wilderness: The Origins and Rise of Anti-Semitism in America* (Cambridge, MA., 1994), pp. 89–91.

6. *The Colonial Records of the State of Georgia*, ed. Allen D. Candler (Atlanta, 1904–16), vol. 1, pp. 98–99, 149–53; vol. 2, p. 62; "Journal of the Transactions of the Trustees for Establishing the Colony of George in America," Dec. 22, 1733; Jan. 5, 1734, in *Documentary History*, ed. Schappes, pp. 24–25; Malcolm Stern, "New Light on the Jewish Settlement of Savannah," in *The Jewish Experience in America*, ed. Albert Karp (New York, 1969), vol. 1, pp. 74, 84–85; Marcus, *Colonial American Jew*, vol. 1, p. 471; vol. 2, p. 888; vol. 3, p. 1130; and Jaher, *Scapegoat*, pp. 111–12.

7. A fuller discussion of these matters may be found in Jaher, *Jews and the Nation*, pp. 9–56.

8. "The Charter of Georgia" (1732), in *The Federal and State Constitutions, Colonial Charters and other Organic Laws of the United States of America*, ed. Francis N. Thorpe (Washington, D. C., 1909), vol. 7, p. 773; Abraham Goodman, *American Overture: Jewish Rights in Colonial Times* (Philadelphia: Jewish Publication Society of America, 1947), pp. 192–93, 195; Marcus, *Colonial American Jew*, vol. 1, pp. 421–22, 441, 443–47, 451, 454–55, 466–67, 485, 499–505, 507–08; Jacob Rader Marcus, *Early American Jewry: The Jews of Philadelphia and the South* (Philadelphia, 1951–53), vol. 2, pp.330–31; and *Jewish Experience*, ed. Karp, vol. 1, p. 74.

9. Goodman, *American Overture*, pp. 21, 108, 126–27; Marcus, *Colonial American Jew*, vol. 3, pp. 1199, 1206–07, and idem., *Early American Jewry*, vol. 2, pp. 8, 244, 246–48, 466–67, 495–98.

10. Goodman, *American Overture*, pp. 126–27; *Jewish Life in Philadelphia: 1830–1940*, ed. Marray Friedman (Philadelphia, 1983), pp. 5, 291–92, Leon Huhner, *Jews in America in Colonial and Revolutionary Times* (New York., 1959), pp. 145, 149; Albert Ehrenfield, " A Chronicle of Boston Jewry: From the Colonial Settlement to 1900" (mss., 1963, a copy is in the library of the University of Illinois, Champaign-Urbana), p. 150; Marcus, *Colonial American Jew*, vol. 3, 1148–52, 1206–07, 1307–09, and idem., *Early American Jewry*, vol.2, pp. 8, 81, 244, 265, 330, 348, 495–98, 511, and idem., *American Jewry: Documents, Eighteenth Century* (Cincinnati, 1959), p. 7; Leo Hershkowitz, "Some Aspects of the

New York Jewish Merchant Community," *American Jewish Historical Quarterly*, vol. 66 (Sept. 1976), pp. 12, 25–27.

11. "Minutes of the New York City Common Council," Oct.14, 1718, Sept. 17, 1766, in *Documentary History*, ed. Schappes, pp. 19, 41; Hershkowitz, "New York Jewish Merchant Community:" 13; Goodman, *American Overture*, pp. 20, 199–200; Marcus, *Colonial American Jew*, vol. 1, p. 463; vol. 3, pp. 1261–62, 1276, 1279–80, 1307–09, and idem., *Early American*, vol. 2, pp. 160, 165, 229, 245, 344–48, 518–19, 527, and idem., *American Jewry*, p. 80; Huhner, *Jews in America*, pp. 147–49; Richard B. Morris, "Civil Liberties in the Jewish Tradition in Early America," in *Jewish Experience*, ed. Karp, p. 415; Jaher, *Scapegoat*, pp. 102–03.

12. Marcus, *Colonial American Jew*, vol. 1, pp. 405, 408–10, 422, 424, 436–37, 441, 444, 446–67, 462–65, 470. 510, vol. 3, p. 1282, and idem., *Early American Jewry*, vol. 2, 154–56, 166, 229, 265, 330–31, 518–19, 522–26, 529–30; Goodman, *American Overture*, pp. 110–14; Morris, "Civil Liberties," p. 416; Hershkowitz, "New York Merchant Community:" 13; "The Constitution of South Carolina" (1778), in *Federal and State Constitutions*, vol. 6, p. 3250; "The Constitution of New York" (1777), in *ibid.*, vol. 5, pp. 2630, 2632, 2636–38; Jaher, *Scapegoat*, pp. 103–04.

13. Marcus, *Colonial Jew*, vol. 1, pp. 435–37, 444–45, 485–90, 514, and idem., *Early American Jewry*, vbol. 2, pp. 515–16, and idem., *American Jewry*, p. 200; Ehrenfield, "Boston Jewry," pp. 113, 138–40; Morris, "Civil Liberties," p. 416; Jaher, *Scapegoat*, pp. 101, 105–06; Lopez's petition for naturalization is in *Extracts from the Itineraries and Other Miscellanies of Ezra Stiles, D.D., L.L.D.: 1755–1794*, ed. Franklin Bowditch Dexter (New Haven, 1916), pp. 52–53.

14. Jaher, *Jews and the Nation*, pp.144–45; The best general analysis of established religion in America is Leonard Levy, *The Establishment Clause: Religion and the First Amendment* (New York, 1986), pp. 1–63. Colonial charters and states constitutions are in *Federal*, ed. Thorpe.

15. *Federal*, ed. Thorpe, vol. 1: 566, 568, 5: 2793, 3100; Jaher, *Jews and the Nation*, pp. 145–46, and idem. *Scapegoat*, p. 121.

16. A fuller discussion of Article VI may be found in Jaher, *Jews and the Nation*, pp. 141–44; for the vote in the constitutional convention see *The Records of the Federal Convention of 1787*, ed. Max Farrand (New Haven, CT., 1966), 4 vols., vol. 2, p. 468.

17. House of Representatives Debate, 15 August 1789 in Levy, *Establishment*, pp. 76–81. The Senate debate was not recorded.

18. Later in 1791 Jews were given political equality in France, but emancipation was short-lived and not complete, see Jaher, *Jews and the Nation*, pp. 66–102.

19. *The Autobiography of Benjamin Franklin* (New York, 1990), p. 78; Franklin to Joseph Priestly, 21 August 1784, in *The Writings of Benjamin Franklin*, ed. Albert Henry Smyth (New York, 1906–07), 9 vols. 9: 266; James Madison to Jacob De La Motta, August 1802, and to Mordicai [sic] Noah, 15 August 1818, in *James Madison on Religious Liberty*, ed. Robert S. Alley (Buffalo, 1985), pp. 80–81; Thomas Jefferson to Mordecai Noah, 28 May 1818, in *Jewish Experience*, ed. Karp, p. 359; John Adams to F.A. Vanderkemp, 16 February 1809, in *The Works of John Adams*, ed. Charles Francis Adams (Boston, 1854), 10 vols., vol. 9, p. 609; and to Mordecai Noah, 31 July 1808, in *Jewish Experience*, ed. Karp, p. 361; Jaher, *Scapegoat*, pp. 123–24, and idem., *Jews and the Nation*, pp. 165–67.

20. George Washington to the Hebrew Congregation in Newport, Rhode Island, 17 August 1790, in *Jews and the American Revolution: A Bicentennial Documentary*, ed. James Rader Marcus (Cincinnati, 1975), p. 244; Paul F. Boller, Jr., *George Washington & Religion* (Dallas, 1963), pp. 165, 167, 173, 175, 179–82, 192–94; Jaher, *Scapegoat*, p. 124, and idem., *Jews and the Nation*, pp. 167–68.

21. Jaher, *Scapegoat*, pp. 122, 125, 177, Henry Clay to Solomon Etting, 16 July 1832, in *The Jews of the United States, 1790–1840: A Documentary History*, ed. Joseph L. Blau and Salo W. Baron (New York, 1963), 3 vols., 1:58–59; John Tyler to Joseph Simpson, 10 July 1843, in *Publications of the American Jewish Historical Society*, 11 (1903): 158–59; Tyler to Jacob Ezekiel, 19 April 1841, in Herbert T. Ezekiel and Gaston Lichtenstein, *The History of the Jews of Richmond from 1769 to 1917* (Richmond, 1917), p. 118.

22. Memorial of the Trustees of the Congregation Shearith Israel to the New York State Legislature, drawn up by De Witt Clinton (1811), in *Jews of the United States*, ed. Blau and Baron, vol. 2, pp. 445–46; Jacob Hartstein, "The Polonies Talmud Torah of New York," in *Jewish Experience*, ed. Karp, vol. 2, pp. 45–63.

23. Jaher, *Jews and the Nation*, p. 133.

24. N. Taylor Phillips, "Unwritten History: Reminiscences of N. Taylor Phillips," *American Jewish Archives*, 6 ((June 1954): 99; Rev. G. Seixas, "Discourse Delivered In the Synagogue In New-York. On The Ninth of May, 1798, Observed As A Day of Humiliation, &c..&c., Conformably to a Recommendation Of The President Of The United States of America," facsimile in *Beginnings, Early American Judaica: a Collection of Ten Publications in Facsimile*, ed. Abraham J. Karp (Philadelphia, 1975); and Faber, *A Time for Planting: The First Migration 1654–1820* (Baltimore, 1992), pp. 118–20.

25. Frederic Cople Jaher, *The Urban Establishment: Upper Strata in Boston, New York, Charleston, Chicago, and Los Angeles* (Urbana, 1982), pp. 593–99, 601–03; Gunther Barth, *Instant Cities: Urbanization and the Rise of San Francisco and Denver* (New York, 1975), pp. 72–73; Peter Decker, *Fortunes and Failures: White Collar Mobility in Nineteenth-Century San Francisco* (Cambridge, MA., 1978), pp. 116–18, 238–39; Max Vorspan and Lloyd P. Gartner, *History of the Jews of Los Angeles* (San Marino, 1970), pp. 34–35; Bertram Wallace Korn, *The Early Jews of New Orleans* (Waltham, MA., 1969), pp. 96, 115–16, 125, 225–27; Isaac M. Fein, *The Making of a Jewish Community: The History of Baltimore Jewry from 1767 to 1820* (Philadelphia, 1971), p. 17; Myron Berman, *Richmond's Jewry, 1769–1976* (Charlottesville: University of Virginia Press, 1954), pp. 72, 127; Charles Reznikoff, *The Jews of Charleston: A History of an American Jewish Community* (Philadelphia, 1950), pp. 89–90; Barnett A. Elzas, *The Jews of South Carolina from the Earliest Times to the Present Day* (1902; Spartanburg, SC., 1972), pp. 185, 188, 192, 196–97, 204; Henry Samuel Morais, *The Jews of Philadelphia* (Philadelphia, 1894), p. 271.

26. Robert D. Meade, *Judah P. Benjamin: Confederate Statesman* (New York, 1943), pp. 107–23; Fein, *Making of a Jewish Community*. p. 107; Morais, *Jews of Philadelphia*, p. 417; Dan A. Oren, *Joining the Club: A History of Jews and Yale* (New Haven, 1985), p. 10.

27. Morais, *Jews of Philadelphia*, pp. 33, 41, 272, 286–89, 298, 417; *Jewish Life in Philadelphia: 1830–1940*, ed. Murray Friedman (Philadelphia, 1985), p. 5; Ezekiel and Lichtenstein, *Jews of Richmond*, pp. 35–36, 39–40, 62; Berman, *Richmond's Jewry*,

pp. 18, 84, 128; Leopold Mayer, "Reminiscences of Early Chicago," in *Memoirs of American Jews: 1775–1865*, ed. Jacob Rader Marcus (Philadelphia, 1955), vol. 3, pp. 281–86; Morris A. Gutstein, *A Priceless Heritage: The Epic Growth of Nineteenth-Century Chicago Jewry* (New York, 1953), pp. 61–64, 276–77, 312; Elzas, *Jews of South Carolina*, p. 243; Reznikoff, *Jews of Charleston*, pp. 94–97; Korn, *Jews of New Orleans*, pp. 96, 115–16, 125, 225–28; Louis J. Swichkow and Lloyd P. Gartner, *The History of the Jews of Milwaukee*, (Philadelphia, 1963), pp. 55, 58–60; W. Gunther Plaut, *The Jews in Minnesota: The First Seventy-Five Years* (New York, 1959), pp. 23–24; Harris Newmark, *Sixty Years in Southern California: 1853–1913* (New York, 1916), pp. 203, 283; Steven Hertzberg, *Strangers Within the Gate City: The Jews of Atlanta, 1845–1915* (Philadelphia, 1978), pp. 20, 68–69.

28. Irving Katz, *August Belmont: A Political Biography* (New York, 1968), pp. 1–2, 6–9, 91–115.

29. Joseph Buchler, "The Struggle for Unity: Attempts at Union in American Jewish Life, 1654–1858," in *Critical Studies in American Jewish History: Selected Articles from the American Jewish Archives*, ed. Jacob Rader Marcus (New York, 1971, 3 vols., 3: 108–09; Joseph Jacobs, "The Damascus Affair of 1840 and the Jews of America," in *Jewish Experience*, ed. Karp, pp. 271–80; *Documentary History*, ed. Schappes, pp. 201–03; and *Jews of the United States*, ed. Blau and Baron, vol. 3, pp. 928–29, 940–43. The last two references contain correspondence between the secretary of state and the consul in Alexandria and the minister to Turkey.

30. Buchler, "Struggle for Unity," pp. 109–10; Gutstein, *Priceless Heritage*, pp. 323–24; Solomon Strook, "Switzerland and the American Jews," in *Jewish Experience*, ed. Karp, vol.3, pp. 78, 80, 85, 87–88, 90. 93–94. 98–99; Jaher, *Scapegoat*, p. 182.

31. Toby Lelyveld, *Shylock on the Stage* (London, 1961), pp. 63–65; Thomas R. Gould, *The Tragedian: An Essay on the Historical Genius of Junius Brutus Booth* (New York, 1868), pp. 73–81; Lisbeth Jane Roman, "The Acting Style and Career of Junius Brutus Booth," (Ph.D diss., University of Illinois, 1968), pp. 138–42; Lafcadio Hearn, *Occidental Gleanings* (New York, 1925), vol. 2, pp. 179–80; *The Prose Writings of William Cullen Bryant*, ed. Parke Godwin (New York, 1901), vol. 2, p. 358; *Margaret Fuller, American Romantic: A Selection from Her Writings and Correspondence* (Ithaca, 1963), p. 202.

32. *The Literary Diary of Ezra Stiles*, ed. F. B. Dexter (New York, 1901), vol. 1, p. 6n, 53–54, 65; vol. 2, pp.. 151, 391; *Extracts*, ed. Bowditch, p. 53; George A. Kohut, *Ezra Stiles and the Jews: Selected Passages from His Literary Diary Concerning Jews and Judaism* (New York, 1902), pp. 32–33, 52–53.

33. Benjamin Rush to Elias Boudinot, July 9, 1788, in *The Letters of Benjamin Rush*, ed. Lyman H. Butterfield (Princeton, 1951), vol. 1, p. 470; Rush to Julia Rush, June 27, 1787, and to Elhanan Winchester, May 11, 1791, in *ibid.*, pp. 431, 581–82.

34. "Jefferson's Reply to the Address of the Danbury Baptist Association" (1802), in *Jews of the United States*, ed. Blau and Baron, vol. 1., p. 11; Jefferson to Joseph Marx, July 8, 1820, and to Jacob De La Motta, Sept. 9, 1820, *ibid.*, p. 13, and to Isaac Harby, Jan. 6, 1826, *ibid.*, vol. 3., pp. 704–05, and to Mordecai Noah, July 31, 1818, in *Jewish Experience*, ed., Karp, vol. 1., pp. 359–60.

35. Jefferson to Rush, April 21, 1803, "Syllabus of An Estimation of the Merit of the Doctrines of Jesus, Compared with Those of Others," in *The Writings of Thomas*

Jefferson, ed. Paul Leicester Ford (New York, 1892–99), vol. 8, p. 226, and to Joseph B. Priestly, April 9, 1803, *ibid.*, p. 229n. For other examples of Jefferson's views see: Jefferson to John Adams, Nov. 13, 1813,, in *The Writings of Thomas Jefferson*, ed. Albert E. Bergh (Washington D.C., 1903), vol. 13, pp. 388–89, and to Ezra Stiles, June 15, 1819, *ibid.*, vol. 15, p. 203.

36. Gavin I. Langmuir, *Toward a Definition of Antisemitism* (Berkeley, 1990), pp. 319–30; Hyam Maccoby, *The Sacred Executioner: Human Sacrifice and the Legacy of Guilt* (New York, 1982), pp. 131–33; Lester K. Little, *Religious Poverty and the Profit Motive in Medieval Europe* (Ithaca, 1978), pp. 52–53; Jaher, *Scapegoat*, pp. 51–54.

37. R.I. Moore, *The Formation of a Persecuting Society: Power and Deviance in Western Europe, 950–1250* (Oxford, 1986), pp. 117–21, Maccoby, *Sacred Executioner*, p. 166; Jaher, *Scapegoat*, pp. 54–57.

38. Jaher, *Jews and the Nation*, pp. 61–102.

39. Felix Grendon, "The Anglo-Saxon Charms," *Journal of American Folklore*, vol. 12 (1909), pp. 179, 185–87; Ellen Powell Thompson, "Folklore from Ireland, II," *ibid.*: 225; Rudolf Glanz, *The Jew in the Old American Folklore* ((New York, 1961), pp. 10–17; Thomas R. Brendle and Claude W. Unger, "Folk Medicine of the Pennsylvania Germans. The Non-Occult Cures," *Pennsylvania German Society Proceedings*, vol. 45 (1935), Part 2, p. 175; and Jaher, *Scapegoat*, pp. 96–97.

40. Arthur Kyle Davis, Jr., *Traditional Ballads of Virginia* (Cambridge, MA., 1929), pp. 400–15, and idem., *More Traditional Ballads of Virginia* (Chapel Hill, 1960), pp. 229–38; Helen Hartness and Marguerite Olney, *Ballads Migrant in New England* (1953; Freeport, NY., 1968), pp. 28–32; Florence H. Ridley, "A Tale Told Too Often," *Western Folklore*, 26 (July, 1967): 153–56; Marcus, *Colonial American Jew*, vol. 3, p. 1117; Glanz, *Old American Folklore*, pp. 9–29; Jaher, *Scapegoat*, pp. 97–98.

41. *Rivington's N-Y Gazetteer*, Sept. 8, 1774, in Marcus, *Colonial American Jew*, vol. 3, p. 1128; *Pennsylvania Evening Post*, Sept. 24, 1776, p. 476; Sept. 26, p. 379; Henry Melchoir Muhlenberg, Oct. 2., 1776, in *Pennsylvania Magazine of History and Biography*, 22 (1898), pp. 139–30; "The Constitution of Pennsylvania" (1776), in *Federal and State Constitutions*, ed. Thorpe, vol. 5, p. 3085.

42. Letters to *Charlestown Gazette*, Dec. 1, 3, 1778, in *Jews and the American Revolution: A Bicentennial Documentary*, ed. Jacob Rader Marcus (Cincinnati, 1978), pp. 149–50; David McClure quoted in "Lancaster in 1772," in *Papers Read before the Lancaster County Historical Society*, vol. 5 (1901): 109.

43. Jonathan Edwards, *Works of Jonathan Edwards*, ed. Stephen Stein (New Haven, 1977), vol. 5, pp. 11–12, 17, 40, 47, 135, 140, 195–97, 218, 287, 292–93, 295–96, 333–34, 337, 410–11, and idem., *The Works of President Edwards* (New York, 1968), pp. 406, 501–19; and idem., *The Great Christian Doctrine of Original Sin Defended* (1758), rpt. as *Original Sin*, ed. Clyde Holbrook (New Haven, CT., 1970), pp. 182, 293–305, 335–43; *Jonathan Edwards: Representative Selections*, ed. Clarence H. Faust and Thomas H. Johnson (New York: American Books, 1935), p. 155; *The Journals of Henry Melchoir Muhlenberg*, ed. Theodore G. Tappert and John W. Doberstein (Philadelphia, 1942, vol. 1, pp. 125–26; *Isaac Backus on Church, State and Calvinism: Pamphlets, 1754–1789*, ed. William G. McLoughlin (Cambridge, MA., 1968), pp. 137, 144, 146–47, 149–50, 152–53, 156–57, 172, 181, 263, 274, 364, 402; *Literary Diary of Ezra Stiles*, ed. Dexter, Sept. 1, 1770, vol. 1, p. 68; and Jaher, *Scapegoat*, pp. 107–09.

44. David Hackett Fischer, *The Revolution of American Conservatism: The Federalist Party in the Era of Jeffersonian Democracy* (New York, 1965), pp. 164–65, 225; Eugene Perry Link, *Democratic-Republican Societies, 1790–1800* (New York, 1942), p. 51n; Morris U. Schappes, "Anti-Semitism and Reaction, 1795–1800," in *Jewish Experience*, ed. Karp, vol. 1, pp. 369–70.

45. For Federalist anti-Semitic sentiments see: James Rivington, "Preface to the American Edition," Henry James Pye, *The Democrat; or, Intrigues and Adventures of Jean Le Noir* (New York, 1795), vol. 1, pp. v–viii; Schappes, "Anti-Semitism and Reaction," pp. 366–69, 386–89; "The Letters of Joseph Dennie: 1768–1812," ed. Laura Green Pedder, *University of Maine Studies* (Orono, 1936), 2nd ser., no. 36, pp. xiii–xvi, 127–28, 168, 171, 182, 185–86. For Democratic-Republican anti-Semitism see: Alfred D. Young, *The Democratic-Republicans of New York: The origins, 1763–1797* (Chapel Hill, 1967), pp. 179, 185, 335; John Malcolm to Horatio Gates, March 24, 1790, in *Documentary History*, ed. Schappes, p. 73; Nehemiah Dodge. *Discourse Delivered . . . In Honor of the Late Presidential of Thomas Jefferson* (Norwich, CT., 1805), pp. 5–6, 10. 12, 25–26.

46. *Journal of the Convention Called By the Freemen of North-Carolina to Amend the Constitution* (Raleigh: J. Gales and Son, 1835), pp. 47. 49–51; and Jaher, *Scapegoat*, p. 133.

47. *Journal of Debates and Proceedings in the Convention of Delegates Chosen to Revise the Constitution of Massachusetts: Begun and Holden at Boston, November 15, 1820, and continued by Adjournment to January 19, 1821* (Boston: Boston Daily Advertiser, 1853), pp. 169–71, 187, 205–07, 613–14, 623–24, 633.

48. Isaac M. Fein, *The Masking of a Jewish Community: The History of Baltimore Jewry from 1773 to 1920* (Philadelphia, 1971), pp. 25–36, 43–44; *Jews of the United States*, ed. Blau and Baron, vol. 1, pp. 33–43. 48–49. 52–55; Edward Eitches, "Maryland's Jew Bill," *American Jewish Historical Quarterly*, vol. 60 (March 1971), pp. 258–79.

49. [Pascal Strong], "Extracts from Strong's Sermon on the Plague," *Evangelical Witness*, 1 (Feb. 1823), pp. 311–12; Jonathan D. Sarna, *Jacksonian Jew: The Two Worlds of Mordecai Noah* (New York, 1981), pp. 13, 44–46, 53–54, 62n, 78, 99, 119, 178; Louis Harap, *The Image of the Jew in American Literature from Early Republic to Mass Immigration* (Philadelphia, 1974), pp. 264–66; *New York Herald*, Nov. 18, 1837, p. 2; and *Washington Globe*, Oct. 2, 1833, p. 2; Oct. 3, 1833, p. 2.

50. Jaher, *Scapegoat*, pp.. 140–50.

51. *Ibid.*, pp. 149–50; *The Worcester Catechism*, in *an American Reformation: A Documentary History of Unitarian Christianity*, ed. Sydney E. Ahlstrom and Jonathan Carey, (Middletown, CT., 1985), pp. 181, 192, 194–95, 197–99.

52. Jaher, *Jews and the Nation*, pp. 150, 170.

53. Jaher, *Scapegoat*, pp. 127, 43–46; Shalom Goldman, *God's Sacred Tongue: Hebrew & the American Imagination* (Chapel Hill, 2004), pp. 89–112; Hannah Adams, *The History of the Jews from the Destruction of Jerusalem to the Nineteenth Century* (Boston, 1812), vol. 1, pp. iii–iv, 22–30, 41–42, 206–09, 218–19, 223–24, 229–35, 269–89, 394, 297–304, 308, 315–16, 320–21, 326–34, 338, 348–52; vol. 2, pp. 47–48, 63–66, 88, 110–111, 142–44, 146, 149, 162–63, 169–70, 174–75, 178–83, 210, 214, 270, 295, 318–21, 325–32; Philip Milledoler, Presidential Address to the ASEJ, *Religious Intelligencer*, vol. 1 (Jan. 25, 1817), pp. 555–58.

54. Jaher, *Scapegoat*, pp. 140–69.

55. *Ibid.*, p. 165; and John Lothrop Motley, *Morton's Hope; or, The Memoirs of a Provincial* (New York, 1839), vol. 1, pp. 197–98.

56 M. Otto to the Comte de Vergennes, Jana. 2, 1786, in Anson Phelps Stokes, *Church and State in the United States* (New York, 1950), vol. 1, p. 296; H. M. Brackenridge, "Speech on the Maryland 'Jew Bill'," in *Cornerstones of Religious Freedom in America*, ed. Joseph L. Blau (Boston, 1950), pp. 103–04; *German Correspondent*, Jan. 31, 1820, p. 6; Jaher, *Scapegoat*, pp. 168–69.

3

Why and How
Are Americans Different?

Hasia Diner

Since the summer of 2004 the subject of American Jewish history has been examined in multiple and diverse venues and media, with programs of one kind or another springing forth around the country. Some of these presentations have focused on the "big picture"—that is, attempting to make sense of the full sweep of that history—while others have focused on particular aspects of it, conceptualized around specific time periods, certain themes, and distinctive places. Whether the programs took place in specifically Jewish settings or in more general gatherings, whether they targeted scholars alone or if they brought scholars into conversation with community audiences, whether they involved single speakers, multiple speaker lecture series, symposia, exhibitions, film projects, television documentaries, publications—books, articles, pamphlets, journalistic accounts—sermons, or oral history projects, these texts and events will someday be used by historians to explore how American Jews at the onset of the twenty-first century made sense of their history.

All of these presentations regardless of intended audience or preferred mode of communication, shared a basic view of the past, and no doubt of the present. We—the scholars who have participated in the endeavor—have all contended that America made possible, and its Jews created there, the largest, most elaborately organized, well endowed, least fettered, institutionally plastic and culturally pluralistic Jewish community in the world today and indeed in all of Jewish history.

These performances of American Jewish history, from the most scholarly to the most popular have emphasized that this state of affairs, with its high levels of accomplishment and acceptance, evolved over the course of time. It did not just begin that way. This development, both its internal and external conditions, had to be won, or achieved. Jews did not arrive in seventeenth century North America with anything like the bundle of rights and the communal élan which would develop over time. Our lectures and writings have emphasized several key trajectories that brought the Jews of America to their present state of integration and communal fullness.

We, the scholars of American Jewish history have demonstrated a process by which the Jews in America moved from being a numerically insignificant band of "23" who interacted with the larger American society devoid of any assumed entitlements to a point in their history now where they could claim utter privilege, chained down by no fetters as they enjoyed access to every "nook and cranny" of American life.

350th projects have likewise depicted the movement by which the Jewish women and men of America proceeded from a history where they affirmatively sought anonymity as Jews, occupying in their early history literally unmarked Jewish spaces, to ultimately boldly and assertively putting their particularistic stamp on the American landscape. That is, the trajectory which the programs, be they coolly analytic or boisterously celebratory, has depicted, involved showing an arc by which Jews came over time in America to feel comfortable and empowered to make their case (or better cases) in their own name. At some point in their history they felt able to state that as Jews they had a group-specific stake in the great public issues of the day.

Likewise much of the discourse of this year has sketched out the ways in which Jews, as demonstrated by the words and actions of their organizations, organs of public opinion, networks of communication, and brokers, moved from quietly asking the vastly larger Christian society to give to Judaism some of the same privileges which the Protestant denominations enjoyed to eventually standing up and demanding not only equal rights for Jews and Judaism, but pushing American society to change itself. From a population that figuratively pleaded that Judaism be considered a legitimate American faith community, Jews ultimately felt able to take on America, and demand that some of the nation's most fundamental institutions change.

Three examples should suffice here. By the late nineteenth century many American Jews began to chide America for its deep commitment to the idea of laissez-faire as the best way to structure relations between the classes. Many American Jews including the leaders of some of the most prestigious bodies came to demand that the state enter into the economic life of the nation not as an advocate for business but as an advocate for workers and for the poor. By the early twentieth century American Jewish organs of public opinion, in English and Yiddish, joined in an avant-garde assault on American race relations, lambasted the United States for the pervasiveness of racism and calling upon Americans to fully live up to the nation's rhetorical creed of equality. Finally Jews by the middle of the twentieth century willingly stood out and apart from the many times larger Christian population, in their critique of the persistence of cracks in the wall between church and state. They willingly told the overwhelmingly Christian population of the United States that they did not in fact have the right to claim America as a Christian nation. By laying out these profound changes in the ways in which American Jews interfaced with the larger society, historians associated with the 350th events have shown how the status of the Jews have changed, how America has changed, and how Jews played a crucial role in making that change possible.

Finally as we historians of the American Jewish past have engaged with our many audiences we have described how the Jewish people in America came to define and redefine Judaism and the nature of Jewish life as a malleable entity, as something which they, often quite ordinary and unlettered women and men, could mold to fit their various beliefs, sensibilities, and tastes. Over such deeply significant issues of language, ritual, governance, and structure, American Jews in their local communities—we have shown this year—created religious practices and institutions that worked for them.

No issue has been more central to this part of the discussion this year than that of gender and women's rights. The historians who have spoken and written about the distinctiveness of the American Jewish historical trajectory have repeatedly outlined the ways in which in America Jewish women moved from behind the curtains of public invisibility to the center stage of the leadership of American Judaism. "Only in America"—to invoke a hackneyed but still useful phrase—did Jewish women find ways to give themselves voice and make demands upon the male leadership of their community to decouple religious responsibilities and rights from gender. Women, they asserted, should literally count and that when it came to participating in the public manifestations of Judaism, biology should not be thought of as destiny.

In short, we the historians have spent this year, if we admitted it or not, detailing both the exceptionalism of America and the contributions of the Jews to America. The titles of our talks, the labels affixed to the exhibitions, and the basic assumptions which underlay our presentations have been that Jews brought something distinctive to America and that America had a particular—and particularly positive—impact upon the Jews.

By framing our public discussions around the distinctiveness of the American experience of the Jews, we have reflected a long held view in the field of Jewish history. America, and the history of its Jews, stood in a class by themselves. This certainly reflects the reality that the history of American Jewry has been largely built around the fact of the absence of a process of emancipation. American Jewry never went through this excruciating and excruciatingly long ordeal. Likewise however much American Jewish historians have documented instances of anti-Semitism, manifested in both rhetoric and deed, the giant shadows cast by European ghettoes, pogroms, expulsions, and ultimately the Holocaust on modern Jewish history, have made the American experience not only a basically upbeat one, but has forced us to think about it in its own terms and not as part of the larger "modern" narrative. As such, we have, even when we strove for dispassionate analysis, articulated our basically whiggish view of this history.

If the historians, committed as they are to "objectivity," have basically sketched out an upbeat narrative, how much more so the community "celebrations," as they have been generally described? Certainly on the popular level a good deal of the rhetoric has tended to valorize American Jewry, to celebrate its achievements and to assert that certain characteristics of an entity referred to as "Jewish culture" have made all of this possible. Hard work, a traditional commitment to education, strong families, grit, determination, courage, intellect, all somehow have figured in to these discussions as explanations for how the Jews "made it" in America. These sterling qualities tend to be posited as particularly Jewish and as particularly prominent in the Jews' unique cultural tool kit. Artists, scholars, scientists, entrepreneurs, fighters for social justice who counted themselves as Jews—reflected essential Jewish characteristics and not just those of all.

From the obverse side of the equation in these "celebrations" of American Jewish history, public programs have emphasized the special attributes of the place, the United States The phrase "America is different" has been repeatedly invoked and always in the most positive of terms. Because the United States, its government and its people, made room over time for Jews and Judaism to achieve what they did, it has emerged in the 350th drama as a "best supporting actor," of almost equal billing to the Jews themselves.

Let me here just cite some salient statements from the call to "Celebrate 350: An Invitation" which launched the year's festivities. The document which appears on the Celebrate 350 website stated quite boldly that "we," the coordinators of the year's events, "need to reaffirm the reverence for justice, freedom, equality and respect for diversity that has made America the haven it has been for us and all Americans." The invitation to celebrate continued in a similar vein, urging that the participants in this historic moment remember and venerate, "our commitment to sustaining America's role as the champion of freedom and democracy throughout the world." This document, as embodied in these two statements, typical of the text as a whole, captured the ethos of the 350th moment. American Jews saw themselves as grateful for and celebratory of the United States, both past and present. The historians who helped craft this text and those who lectured under its banner or consulted with the museum and film projects that it spawned participated then in a discourse about American history and its particular impact on the Jews. In all of this the overriding theme has been not only that America was different but a rhetorical question hovered above and below which posed the query: how is America different.

I would like to offer a slightly different question and ask instead, why is America different. To do so I would like to offer a set of contexts for exploring and explaining those conclusions. At least five overarching realities of American life, extending from the seventeenth century outward, provided the basic soil in which American Jewish communal life could take root and then flourish. Let me state them and then return to each one in some detail. Each one of these notably existed in conjunction with the others and in each case we could say that the confluence of these forces functioned as the matrix around which this singular history—that of American Jews— proceeded. The factors that I will be developing involved the nature of immigration to America, America's enduring obsession with color, American materialism and the degree to which the society's basic nature sprang from economic forces, the role of religion in America, and finally, the structure of America's political life. I cannot say with certainty that if any one of these had been different or absent that the history of the Jews would have taken a different course. I do not believe in the practice of counter-history, but suffice to it to say here that these factors did all exist and they did all pivot around each other. Therefore we should focus on them to understand how and why vis-à-vis the Jews, America did differ.

IMMIGRATION

That America, both before national independence and after, owed its basic character from the fact of constant flows, indeed floods, of voluntary immigration has been well documented by historians. While the size of those population movements into America waxed and waned, with the period after 1924 until the early 1970s representing the nadir due to congressional policy, American social and cultural life took much of its tone and shape from the fact that most Americans—native Americans, the descendants of African slaves, and residents of certain parts of the southwest excluded— stemmed from women and men who had with some degree of volition chosen to leave someplace else and to transplant themselves to America. At the high water period of European immigration, the late nineteenth into the early twentieth century, Jews differed little from most of their neighbors as a result of their overwhelmingly foreign birth, their accented and limited (or no) English, and the newness of their American experience. Likewise their American-born children resembled the children of other immigrants around them, who also stood between parents of non-American nativity and the larger expanses of American culture.

America was the western world's largest receiver of immigrants. In the great century of migration, from 1820 through 1924—again a coincidence between the experience of Jews and of all other European immigrants—three-fifths of all Europeans who shifted residence across national borders, chose the United States. While Americans, from a number of political perspectives, have generally overstated the degree to which the romance of America propelled the emigration and the uniqueness of America as an immigrant destination and have as such minimized the importance of immigration to the histories of Canada, Brazil, Argentina, Australia, and even Great Britain, the fact remained that immigration to the United States had certain distinctive characteristics which in turn left their mark on the Jews who participated in this historic transfer of population.

Immigration to the United States differed from all of the flows to all the other places by the sheer diversity of its immigrants. To Brazil and Argentina, for example, two places which immigration shaped, the vast majority came from the Italian peninsula, with Spain sending a sizable but decidedly smaller percentage. Of those who chose Canada and Australia, the British Isles sent an overwhelmingly large proportion.

Yet as to the United States, a vast variety of Europeans, with none dominating the flow, contributed to the "national character." While certain decades saw larger and then declining migrations from certain places, over time no one group could be held up as the core population or as the embodying the quintessential immigrant experience. Over the course of the century of migration Italians and Germans—both obviously complicated "national" groups to highlight here given the political ambiguities involved in naming those places—arrived in just about equal number and immigrants from eastern Europe more than doubled the number from the British Isles.

Additionally, the flow into the United States proceeded on a continuous basis. For sure, some years, those characterized by a vigorous economy, saw more immigrants than others, and other years, when the state of the economy went into a temporary decline, witnessed a dip in immigration. But over the course of the great century of migration, the steady and inexorable process of Europeans choosing America continued apace. Again this tended to distinguish immigration to the United States from the other immigrations in that those extended over more limited spans of time.

In this the Jews of America resembled their non-Jewish neighbors for their immigrant status and the immigrant nativity of their parents. Since no one group dominated the population, of the large cities in particular, Jews like all the other immigrants and their children learned to negotiate America from the reality of this on-the-ground diversity. That the official creed, however problematically operationalized, valorized immigration as central to the fulfilling of America's exceptional mission, gave Jews a claim to one key aspect of the nation's central narrative.

Furthermore in the discourse launched by nativists from the 1850s onward about the defects of "the immigrants" and in their crusades to limit the rights of immigrants, Jews did not figure centrally. Unlike the Irish of the pre-Civil War period and Italians of the late-nineteenth century, both of whom functioned as the chief European targets of xenophobic fantasies, Jews attracted relatively little negative attention. Without understating the degree to which anti-Jewish rhetoric flourished, the bulk of the discourse about Jews as immigrants tended to see them as hard-working, studious, adept when it came to entrepreneurship, and set on a course, albeit one a bit too rapid, toward economic mobility. In the United States, as such, words like "foreigner" or "alien" did not connote Jew. Jews might be included under those usually negative labels but they did not stand out prominently as embodying them.

Not so in many of the other destination points for central and east European Jews. In those countries, Australia and South Africa, which constituted colonial outposts of larger empires, the Lithuanian or Polish Jews who came to settle, stood out as distinctive for their language, citizenship, and relationship to the imperial project. For those Jews who opted for Argentina, the overwhelming predominance of Italians as the main immigrant group who quickly constituted the majority of the entire population, differences in religion and language, made them obtrusive "others" And finally, the Jews who moved westward to Germany, France, and Great Britain in the last half of the nineteenth century, found themselves relatively alone as occupying the immigrant category. In England, for example, except for colonials from Ireland whose right to residence in the metropole could not be changed, barring changing the structure of the empire, Jews made up the largest group of newcomers, the largest category of non-natives, non-English speakers. In the halls of parliament and in the press, the debate over passage of the Aliens Act at the start of the twentieth century amounted to primarily a debate about the Jews, their merits and mostly demerits. Jews there and in other non-American receiving societies, stood out as quintessential immigrants, foreigners, and as serious problems in the construction of a national "type."

RACE AND COLOR

When contemplating the broad contours of American history and trying to understand the points of intersection between it and the history of its Jews the issue of race and color cannot be ignored. Indeed no aspect of American history can be conceptualized without factoring in the deep, wide, and pervasive American obsession with color. The entire history of America has been a history of color and racial classifications. This has been the dominant motif of the national experience and the very existence of the nation grew out of the encounter of Europeans, native people, and Africans on the shores on North America. The history of its Jews must follow suit.

In this place, since the earliest moments of Europeans colonization, perceived color mattered greatly. In fact, historians can, and have, rightly postulated that no other factor mattered as much, including gender. Color, assumed and constructed as it was as a category, meant the difference between rights and no rights, control over one's body or no control, entitlement to the protection of the state or not. To be on the wrong side of the color equation, which obviously meant the non-white side, subjected individuals not only to the absence of the privileges which accrued from basic definitions of being human or being a citizen, but it exposed them to the full fury of the power of the state and society which served as agents of subjugation and violence.

Despite some recent assertions to the contrary, in every meaningful way, Jews in America always enjoyed the benefits of whiteness. At no time did the formal apparatus of the society, the state and its agents, declare them to be unable to acquire naturalization and citizenship because of their color. At no time did Jews, men in the main, not expect the protection of courts in which to press their claims, equal access to the ballot boxes to voice their opinions, and freedom of movement to go unimpeded wherever they chose. As white men they could enter contracts, hold office, serve on juries, and possessed all the other basic rights that came with being an American.

Certainly rhetoric, particularly by the last quarter of the nineteenth century, could be heard which questioned the whiteness of the Jews. With the rise of scientific racism and the respectable proliferation of biologized views of difference, some writers, thinkers, and others categorized Jews as something other than white. But these voices remained just that.

Even in the many places where Jews in America suffered limitations and discrimination, in particular in the housing field, in employment, access to higher education, and in entry to places of leisure like clubs and hotels, anti-Jewish practices came from private individuals. The state stood aloof from all these matters. It would take in fact almost the entire course of the 350 years before the state, the federal government, wiped away the distinction between discrimination perpetrated by private sources versus discrimination which came from the state. The 1964 and 1965 civil rights acts (and on a state by state basis the civil rights laws passed after 1945) made private acts of discrimination the business of the state.

Jews, unlike African Americans, Americans of Chinese and Japanese ancestry, and Native Americans, never needed to view government—the

formal apparatus of the society, its courts, its legislature, its elected leaders, and indeed even its key text, the Constitution—as the source of their
sorrows. In all matters relating to the fundamental and extensive formal
privileges which flowed from the state, the Jews in America benefited from
the fact that phenotypically other Americans saw them as white.

Having this privilege represented in some ways a unique moment in Jewish history. Here, in the United States, for probably the first time, they did
not have access to the fewest rights and the sparsest bundle of privileges the
society had to offer. Others stood many rungs below them in the scale of
entitlement. Here, in the United States, they could distinguish between their
enemies—particular colleges, particular hotels, particular companies—and
the state, the standard of the nation. The former, they condemned for their
hostility to the Jews, while the latter, they lauded for the privileges it gave
them. Keenly aware that they benefited from American realities, including
those which accrued to them from the right skin color, some American
Jews recognized that their entitlements came from the deep and profound
stigmatization endured others. That our subjects—American Jews of the
past—recognized that they fell on the other side of the color line means
that we historians should also be aware of this history of racial privileging.
Being seen as white made all the difference for Jews in the positive fit that
took place between them and America.

MAKING A LIVING: JEWS AND THE AMERICAN ECONOMY

So too, in a much less problematic context, but no less significant, we can
think about the synergy between Jews and America, in matters economic.
The massive transfer of Jewish population to America—about 85 percent
of Europe's cross-border migrating Jews chose the United States—brought
these millions of Jews from places of low productivity and stagnant development to the most dynamic economy in the world. America from its
earliest days until well into the twentieth century experienced a constant
and chronic labor shortage, set amidst the vast natural resources waiting to
be exploited.

This reality under-girded the entire European immigrant flood to
America, that of the Jews as well. Like all other Europeans Jews left
settled places where economic opportunities did not exist and opted
for America where they did. However much the American Jewish communal narrative has focused on the outbreaks of anti-Jewish violence of
life in Europe—the pogroms in particular—as the engines which drove
the population transfer, analytically the more mundane story of a group
of people, Jews, seeking out places to live better—and ultimately to live
well—has greater validity.

The American-Jewish economic fit also reflected the long history of Jews and commerce and the long-observed, and often deprecated, American proclivity towards material acquisition. In nearly every period of American Jewish history we can see a confluence between American material needs, or better wants, and Jewish economic skills. Let me briefly sketch out two eras in American Jewish history as they reveal this symbiotic relationship.

From the middle of the nineteenth century into the earliest years of the twentieth as the American white population moved westward to the remote and least settled areas, families and communities of "settlers" articulated a desire for cosmopolitan goods. The westward movement of Americans across the continent made it possible for the commercial interests to gain access to vast stretches of "uninhabited" land which could be farmed, mined, and logged. The nation's penetration of the hinterlands, romantically and jingoistically, described as "manifest destiny," required capital, and it required women and men willing to work the land, fell the forests, dig the mines, lay the railroad tracks, and the like. It also needed intermediaries to bring to these people the kinds of "stuff" that made it bearable for them to live in these undeveloped places.

Some central and east European Jews met America on the shifting peddlers' frontier. Tens of thousands of Jewish men, well-acquainted with itinerant merchandising after centuries of life in Europe, turned their long time economic niche into an American opportunity. The Jewish peddlers, many of whom became the owners of Jewish dry goods stores in the small towns which served the hinterlands, the Jewish retailers in the big cities who outfitted the peddlers, and the Jewish tailors who sewed the clothes which then traveled in the peddlers' wagons and ended up on the bodies of rural dwellers, made up a Jewish economy that served the basic needs of the expanding United States. While behind this historic drama lay many complicated economic and political relationships, on the surface what transpired involved a marriage between Americans' desire for consumer goods—buttons, thread, needles, curtains, eye glasses, pictures and picture frames, fabric and ready made clothing—and the willingness of Jews to pick up the familiar peddler's pack and venture out to pretty much anywhere they could find paying customers.

By the 1860s yet another match took place between American economic needs and Jewish history. The expansion of the garment industry which began with the invention of the sewing machine at nearly the same moment in time as the Civil War coincided with a series of linked, but independent developments, which transformed not just America but European Jewry. Late nineteenth century urbanization, the movement of young women into industrial and white collar jobs in the years before marriage, the rise of the advertising industry, the emergence of "style" as something within the reach of working class women, new sanitary standards, all lead to the reality that by the end of the nineteenth century the garment industry took off as one of the most dynamic sectors of the American economy. Factories, heavily although not exclusively housed in New York, sewed the garments which clothed women and men around the world. The ready-to-wear clothing industry spread its dresses and blouses, shirtwaists, hats, and undergarments around the nation and the world fueling American economic development.

In this sector Jews as employers and workers found, and helped create, a niche for themselves. Jews in Europe had long made a living by means of the needle, but in America, they could use that lowly skill to create a vast enterprise which did nothing less than clothe Americans and others, employ in massive numbers successive streams of Jewish immigrants, both women and men, and indeed show Jewish women who worked in factories side by side with their "brothers." that gender inequities mattered greatly and limited their options. In addition this field with its relatively low need for start up capital provided to Jews one of the few means by which immigrant industrial laborers could move into the ranks of the employing class.

These two convergences between Jewish history, the peddling and the garment making, and the needs of the American economy had tremendous implications for Jewish economic mobility. Here we can see writ large an example of being in the right place, at the right time, with the right skill set.

AMERICAN RELIGION AND THE JEWS

The Jewish encounter with America, an encounter that took place in a relatively harmonious manner, reflected the significance of religion as a factor in American history. Here at least three matters shaped that meeting, making it possible for the Jews to be helped by the fact of their particular religion rather than hindered by it, as they were elsewhere.

First among these reflected the reality that to the primarily Protestant population which dominated America from the colonial period well into the early twentieth century, Jews were not Catholics. Jews could, in America, breathe easily in that for much of American history anti-Catholicism functioned as a powerful force in public life. Catholicism had long been deemed unsuitable for a democratic, egalitarian nation which venerated personal freedom and individual choice. An aggressive strain of anti-"Papism" dominated the public discourse of the Protestant nation and spilled over from the churches to the political realm. One of the country's most successful third parties, the Know Nothings, made anti-Catholicism a core principle and with this it enjoyed a brief, but still notable, hour in the political spotlight.

Judaism, by contrast, while seen as overly legalistic, at times, medieval and retrograde, particularly vis-à-vis the status of its women in public ritual, enjoyed a place or respectability in the American setting. From a negative standpoint, antipathy to it spawned no political movements nor did its arrival and transplantation into America cause American Christians to re-define public policy in order to lessen Judaism's possible and pernicious impact.

From a positive perspective, from the middle of the nineteenth century onward the appearance of Christian—Protestant clergy—at the dedication of synagogues and the pulpit exchanges between rabbis and ministers in-dicated that Judaism found for itself a legitimate space on the American religious landscape. While a hint of exoticism can be discerned in the Christian discourse on Judaism as well as a note that signaled the desire of evangelicals to convert the Jews, by and large, Protestantism in America did not demonize the planting of Judaism on American shores.

This no doubt reflected the general valorization of religion in America. Americans, observed since the days of Alexis de Tocqueville's now storied visit to the relatively new nation, saw religion—in part because it had been decoupled from state power—as a benign force for promoting civic virtue. While historians of the American Jewish experience may debate the degree to which the veneration of religion in America pushed Jews to repackage themselves as a "faith community" as opposed to a people or a nation, the prevailing positive view of religion in America allowed Jews to argue for extending to their religion the benefits which all other denominations enjoyed. By being bound to each other through a "religion," a concept somewhat extraneous to normative Judaism, American Jews could stand under the protective umbrella of American culture.

Finally, no discussion of the harmonious relationship which evolved between the Jews and the United States would be complete without consid-ering the impact of religious diversity and the concomitant political com-mitment of the society to the constitutional principle of the separation of church and state. Obviously the complicated history of these two twinned phenomenon has been the subject of vast scholarly and legal analysis. To simplify in order to detail this crucial issue within the constraints of time and space here, the fact that even from before the creation of the Repub-lic, too many denominations had established themselves in British North America and its successor state—and states—to allow any one church to im-pose an iron grip on civic life. While many gray areas, such as Sunday clos-ings continued to vex groups of religious outsiders, most aspects of public life fell outside the gray zone. Even so simple a fact that the state did not collect statistics on the number of members of particular denominations meant that private beliefs, that is, matters of the spirit, did not require pub-lic declarations. No check-off boxes on census forms or on tax statements which demanded, or suggested, that individuals divulge to government officials their religious affiliations, made a world of difference.

In matters of faith and society, the decoupling of religion and government rendered the former powerless to control peoples' lives and slowly forced the latter to validate many religions rather than any one. Religion, without the strong backing of the state, lost its authority and essentially defanged it. Religious institutions either conformed to the demands of their dues paying members or they died out.

For Jews the divorce between state and church not only afforded them the possibility of participating, over time, in the polity as equals to Christians, but it gave them the freedom to mold Judaism to fit their wishes, tastes, and sensibilities. Jews like all others enjoyed the freedom to structure their institutions as they wanted and the state could do little, indeed nothing, to stymie creativity.

POLITICS

A final aspect of American history left an indelible mark on the Jews, facilitated their political integration, and should be included in this survey. This involves an analysis of the political sphere directly. In nearly all paeans to America and its ability to integrate (white, male) immigrants, stump speakers and historians alike have cited the ease of the naturalization process for those of foreign birth and the fact that the political realm did not exclude anyone because of their religion. Vis-à-vis politics and governance, for nearly all of American history, not only did religion not matter in matters of naturalization, acquisition of citizenship, voting, and office-holding, but neither did nativity. With the exception of the constitutional requirement that the president of the United States needed to be native born, no barriers to political participation needed to be overcome for white men (and later women), regardless of how (or if) they prayed and where they had been born. This obvious fact deserves to be stated here because of its tremendous impact.

But it does not represent the totality of the political context for understanding how the Jews "met" America and how America "met" the Jews. Rather in politics, on a more abstract yet equally formative level, the long reality of the two-party system facilitated the American-Jewish symbiosis. The United States, for reasons well beyond the scope of this presentation maintained a long tradition of living with two parties relatively evenly matched with each other. Third parties, for sure, developed and nearly all of them failed. While those parties, from the right and the left nudged the two giants in one direction or another, and as such cannot be dismissed analytically as having had no significance, they still died and since the 1850s the political scene has been dominated by the Republicans the Democrats alone.

Particularly since the end of the Civil War and the resolution of the issue of slavery, the two parties tended to converge ideologically. These two parties, which have functioned without formal membership and only the vaguest of platforms, have often been issueless and as such, have valorized pragmatic majoritarianism. What mattered over the course of much of American history in this kind of politics was simply who got the most votes. One political scientist, Daniel Bell offered a powerful image to think about this historic reality. American parties, he wrote, resembled giant bazaars, under whose canopies, multiple hucksters sold their wares. The same hucksters appeared in each of the big tent and peddled their "stuff."

The barkers in the twin bazaars represented the various interest groups: labor, farmers, manufacturers, ethnic groups and the like. While both parties essentially served the interests of business, under the shelter of the two tents, the parties brokered among these constituencies. The parties wanted votes and each group had a particular, and usually practical, agenda.

Compromise and accommodation ruled the parties and in all of this politics, like religion, became tamed. America saw no party of the aristocracy or the clergy, the peasants or the urban proletariat. Rather each party sought to claim as many constituency groups as possible and had little incentive to offend any identifiable block and as such write off any potential voters.

And here, Jews fit in. Neither party defined "the Jews" as a problem, but rather both wanted their votes. Neither party wrote them off as not potential voters, nor did either refuse to provide them with some tangible rewards for voting correctly. Even when Jews had by the late 1920s become comfortably ensconced in the ranks of the Democratic Party, the Republicans did not incorporate antipathy towards the Jews into their political rhetoric. They rather, actually, hoped to woo the Jews over to their camp. By functioning in this bazaar type setting, Jews could literally shop around and make their case to both parties on the local, state, and national levels. They—no differently than mid-western farmers, blue-collar workers, or "members" of nearly every ethnic and religious group—could see who would make them the best deal in exchange for showing up on election day. In this non-ideological political structure which quashed extremism, Jewish men since the middle of the nineteenth century (and then women as well by the end of the first quarter of the twentieth century) found ample space to join in the competition for the attention and rewards that accompanied political participation.

This non-ideological defanged political process may not have helped the Jews secure everything they wanted. Obviously the tragic history of their mighty efforts and limited results in the Hitler era to influence American policy stands as a great failure. But in this they functioned like other interest groups, particularly those which represented ethnic and immigrant communities. The hurly-burly of the political marketplace made it possible for them to get some of what they wanted, but clearly not everything. They got just enough to allow them to feel part of the civic whole and to believe in the basic goodness of the system.

And as a result of this system as well as the other overarching attributes of American history and the culture which evolved from it and in tandem with it, Jews arrived into an environment which synergistically worked well for them. They arrived in a large enough—but not too large—a number to be able to thrive, to build the communities that they wanted, to take advantage of fundamental realities which often worked to the disadvantage of others, and to apply their economic skills sharpened in very different environments to American material realities. In the process they helped make the history which we have spent all of 2004 thinking about.

These five factors may not, in the end, be the stuff of celebration, but hopefully they offer analysts a way to think about what this particular history involved. It may not facilitate celebration, but in the ideal it can help stimulate analysis, the activity which in fact represents the historian's project.

4

Immigrant Jews and the Challenge of American Athleticism

Jeffrey Gurock

The vaunted values of American athleticism—the belief in the transcendent worth of competitive, physical aggression, mitigated only by the rules of sportsmanship, all in the quest for immortality through victory at an "end of days," or maybe better said: when the clock runs out—did not play at all, in the nineteenth century East European shtetl. For starters, in that traditional society, reverence and concern for the head, for the intellect, far more than the cultivation of the body was where these Jews' emphases lay. While few in the community were rich and knowledgeable enough to engage in full-time study, most people looked up to these *Sheyneh Yidn*, these Jewish "beautiful people." With that ideal squarely in mind, parents hoped to raise their sons to be scholars, to work with their minds and not with their muscles, even if so many fathers were butchers, bakers, porters, coachmen etc. Such work-a-day pursuits may have built up a laborer's torso. But, in keeping with traditional culture, adults did not make it a point of flexing their biceps to admirers even when they stripped down to bathe, or to swim publicly, during warm summer days and nights. Moreover, while on their own some children played primitive forms of baseball called "Oina" and "Myatch," where balls and sticks were hit for distance, these youngsters did so without their elders' blessing. Whiling away time as an athlete was no way for a kid to move up in class. Rather, the super stars of the Jewish town were the sedentary types who stuck to their books. If anything, parents wanted to be immortalized through their youngsters' reputations in the classroom, not in some unimagined playground. Of course, in keeping with Jewish tradition, even the most committed students participated in outdoor games on Lag B'Omer—the Jewish field day. But, there was no social sanction for daily and violent pastimes—"fighting [was] 'un-Jewish' in the extreme." And, there certainly were neither organized competitions among shtetl youths nor any talk on the Jewish street of producing well-rounded scholar-athletes.[1]

Girls, for the most part, did not have access to that closed and stuffy shtetl educational system that did nothing to improve the physiques of its all male student bodies.[2] But, females were not left to run free either. Within that traditional world, especially among the few Jews who had some money, "extra-curricular" time was available to expose daughters to music, art and other softer subjects. Of course, poor girls did not have time on their hands for such refinements. They went to work. But, in the end, whether rich or poor, most girls were trained to assume traditional roles within their families and society. And no one spoke to them—or to their parents—about the value of physical training as part of a young women's life.[3]

There were real exceptions within and without the world of the Jewish shtetl who were handy with swords, brick-bats and maybe even with guns. There even might have been some Jewish sportsmen circling or jumping around the fringes of society. Yiddish literature, for example, is replete towards the late nineteenth century, with tales and images of the Jewish "tough guy"—the ba'al guf—who lived by his fists and who was there when other Jews were physically endangered. He appeared on the scene, most dramatically, when riots took place, as writer Sholem Asch once put it, "to take matters into [his] own hands . . . into the streets [where he would] give hooligans a lesson." But, as much as the Jewish community appreciated his rough and ready efforts, he was not held up as an ideal Jew. He might have been respected but he was never to be emulated, except, in a moment of crisis. No one really wanted his kid to be a muscle man, even if, as previously noted, some working class Jews could not avoid raising calluses on their own hands.[4]

Jewish physical specimens might also be found among those who took to the streets in organized fashion when their people were attacked during infamous pogroms of the early 1880s and their successor atrocities of the early twentieth century. And from all accounts, Jewish battlers more than held their own in these confrontations.[5]

But, again, these Jewish men on a mission, to defend Jewish lives and pride, were exceptional figures. In the 1880s, an Odessa-based crowd was made up mostly of gymnasium-secondary schools and university students, enlightened young men who had broken with the world and values of the shtetl. In the early decades of Czar Alexander II's regime [1855–1881], they and their families had dreamed the dream that there could be room within a secularized Russian society for modernizing Jews like themselves. The pogroms of the early 1880s shook up their lives and their sense of comradeship with the Russian people. To a great extent, it has been said, when they went into the streets, they were both literally and figuratively "returning to their people."[6]

It is not inconceivable that, in calmer times, some of these Jewish student activists might have taken an interest in sports. Modern sports were not totally unknown in East European lands of the nineteenth century. We can gather from the first shards of research in this area that, by 1867, there was a gymnastics society in Lvov. Two years later, a skating association was created in Lvov. By the mid-1880s, Warsaw, Cracow and Lvov also had cyclist, fencing and skating societies. And, "at this same time, independent sports activities began within workers' circles such as Silesia, Lodz and in War-saw." It is possible that a highly enlightened Jew who lived in one of these major Jewish cities or a *Bundist* from Lodz or Warsaw might have found his way towards the gyms, tracks or ponds that local athletes attended.[7]

However, these student and radical defenders-athletes did not inspire large numbers of fellow Jews to take up arms against their oppressors. And, similarly, in better times, their frequenting of the sports gym did not inspire any sort of cult of physicality to emerge within the larger Jewish population. The lives and many attitudes of the masses of Jews changed dramatically in the nineteenth century. Ten of thousands migrated from shtetls to urban centers, as the city increasingly became the locus of Jewish life. There, Jews were pushed through government decrees into productive forms of labor. Though surely not their intention, demands that Jews become workers ultimately resulted in that oppressed minority acquiring a range of rudi-mentary industrial skills that would hold them in good stead someday in America. And, as some of them became workers, they began to harbor an incipient class-conscious mentality. But with it all, even as their lives were altered in disparate ways, most Jews did not assume a new posture towards the value of their own physicality and aggressiveness towards the hostile outside world. They continued to remain on the side-lines. Meanwhile, most children were still not socialized to become what we might call today "stand up guys," even if they all no longer lived in shtetls.[8]

What is most important to us is that those who most wanted to change the world and themselves with their ideas—and maybe their fists—were not among the first, nor the most likely, Jews to seek out America. Either they stayed and sought to revolutionize Russia or they took their battles to Zion.[9]

Therefore, of all the attitude adjustments immigrant Jews had to make in their encounter with the new American world around them, coming to terms with this country's tight embrace of physicality as a social value proved to be among the most difficult. For them, to idealize and emulate, for example, a rough-riding chief executive who enjoyed striking pugilistic poses while stripped to the waist to display his fighting trim required a fun-damental change in their approach to life. And, it appears that even as Jews came on board, in so many ways, with other American values and mores, the newcomers neither looked, nor could they act, the part of the robust, athletic American. Theodore Roosevelt's concept that the "brawn," "spirit," "self-confidence," and "quickness of men," acquired in the pursuit of sports victory, was essential to American greatness was foreign to this generation. Nor, did these immigrants show any aptitude for change in this arena, even if they loved and respected T.R., a great friend and protector of the Jews.[10]

This lack of athleticism and absence of physicality was not lost on outsiders who constantly inventoried the immigrants' cultural baggage. Both those who generally praised Jewish industriousness or their potential to contribute to America, as well as those who loudly feared that these foreigners were overrunning and undermining America, concurred that Jewish men could use some time in the weight room if they ever hoped to make it as Americans. It was a pervasive point of emphasis that "training in athletics will bring about a coincidental mental development that will stand him in hand in the classroom or study, and in the practical affairs of life." No one said that back in the shtetl! Gymnastic training of a different type—befitting what was deemed appropriate for the "weaker sex"—was prescribed for Jewish women if they were to fit feminine roles. Critics, friendly and otherwise, all spoke of "puny" Jewish men, with "narrow chests" and "dwarf stature"—"the popular opposite of our pioneer breed"—and of immigrant women who were "poor in physical estate and . . . lack the physical well—being of . . . the well-bred American woman."[11]

For friends of immigrants, these characteristics were hardly irreversible. That is. If immigrant Jews would only show an interest in physical fitness and sports. The leaders of the Educational Alliance, that renowned downtown New York settlement house, believed that "physical training" will "effectively remove" the stigma that "our co-religionists . . . lack physical courage." As they saw it, these newcomers "have an idea that physical weakness is a virtue . . . for this reason it becomes essential to encourage athletics among immigrant Jews." Dr. Maurice Fishberg, Medical Examiner of the United Hebrew Charities, had a specific plan in mind to bulk up his patients. He preached, with certainty, that "outdoor life and participation in the national sports will help develop the chest, which is decidedly smaller in proportion in height than that of non-Jews." However, he was also dismayed to report "that systematic exercises," including "gymnastics" were "not at all in vogue among immigrants." By the way, Fishberg also suggested that Jews take up "billiards, golf, tennis and hunting" which suggests that he was more than a little out of touch with what might have been reasonably expected out of those he sought to influence.[12]

In any event, Fishberg's fellow Jews took in few of his, and others, concerns and criticisms. In keeping with their East European values, work was deemed essential. And study, now more often than not secular education, to achieve in America was very highly–valued. On the other hand, sports and recreation, physicality, even at its best and purest, remained a disrespected frivolity, even if it might be good for them. An on the scene observer, David Blaustein said as much when he complained that "the whole concept of play is foreign to immigrant [Jewish] people—a waste of time, frivolity." And, the *New York Herald Tribune* of his day fully concurred. "The rage [of athletics] is something incomprehensible to him. He has cultivated his mind so long at the expense of his body that the American maxim 'a sound mind in a sound body' is something he cannot understand."[13]

Raconteur of downtown Jewish life, Irving Howe, has explained first generation disinterest with the gym this way. "Suspicion of the physical, fear of hurt, anxiety over the sheer 'pointlessness' of play: all this went deep into the recesses of the Jewish psyche."[14] It is also true that Jews of the older generation were prepared to pay many prices to be deemed good Americans. From the very start, immigrant newcomers worked as their fellow citizens did. And, in time, they learned the language of their new country. But, they simply did not understand why and how athleticism contributed to becoming an American.

The immigrants' children, on the other hand, clearly understood that being physical was a fundamental American trait. They certainly were bombarded from all sides about the promise, possibilities and necessity of sports and athleticism. In the public school, participation in "physical training and athletics" was consistently encouraged to "inculcate the virtues of self-reliance and unselfish cooperation"—two good Rooseveltian qualities—in these young people. In New York, for example, "physical training and hygiene" were integral parts of the curriculum from elementary school days on. "Ideals of courage, honesty, courtesy and strength" were promoted within young Jews, and all others for that matter. The desired result was, hopefully, the emergence of "able men and women trained in body and soul, for their own happiness and the welfare of the State."[15]

Meanwhile, downtown-based settlement houses in Jewish immigrant quarter proffered their own versions of this transforming and patriotic message. Their creed was to build upon the "public schools in the transformation of the crude immigration material into the real citizens and citizenesses [sic]." Towards that end, gymnasium work was deemed "a good example of practical training for democracy." Among its virtues was the inculcation of "respect for success and a willingness to be governed by tried and proved leaders." So said the leaders of the Chicago Hebrew Institute who bragged that "we train boys and girls to be self-reliant, independent, and on square in everything."[16]

While it is uncertain how loudly and clearly Jewish youngsters heard these transformative messages, it is undeniable that they really liked these sports programs. And they quickly made their mark on these leveling playing fields. But, it was not just the natural physical attractiveness of working up a good sweat—a feeling which was now liberated for Jews in this new country—that brought these boys and girls to the gym. They also could get their endorphin-rush, without encouragement, diving off East Side docks and other unsupervised venues. Or they could dance up a storm at a local ragtime hang out. Rather, the school or settlement team afforded them the chance to be "chosen in" as American athletes. And when they excelled in competition, it rewarded them with the triumphal feeling that they truly belonged here.[17]

Indeed, by the mid-1910s, Jewish participation and acceptance in New York's non-Jewish sports clubs was so commonplace, that a proud local Jewish journalist paused to note an "exceedingly rare" occurrence where a sprinter named Shapiro, carrying the banner of a Jewish team, "showed his heels to a large representative field at a 'monster' benefit athletic carnival at Madison Square Garden." For that observer, "it is much more common to find the names of the star Jewish performers on the roster of the Irish–American Athletic Club." And he wondered whether it brought "joy to thousands of Irishmen when they [saw] the colors of the I.A.A.C. brought to the fore by such loyal sons of Erin" with Jewish and other ethnic surnames.[18]

A young Jewish athlete also felt a surge of palpable pride when he took to the streets and earned a reputation in types of sporting pursuits that school and settlement house sages disdained. In America, the *ba'al guf* was more than an occasional or imagined figure. The downtown tough guy was a hero of the ghetto, someone worthy of respect and emulation because he beat up the kids from other ethnic groups. He also was the person who might have provided his fellow Jews with safe passage within the no-man's lands that separated ethnic neighborhoods. And, if this "Pride of the Ghetto" took his skills to the next level and he became a successful prizefighter, he often emerged as a larger than life figure. As one downtown pundit put it: "if in your walks along the East Side you come across young men with flattened noses and cauliflower ears, remember that there is a new hero-type in Israel-the pugilist. Our race finds grotesque expression in him."[19]

For another East Side writer, a ring combatant, like his fictionalized "Slugger Cohen," embodied a not-so-secret-Jewish desire to get even with past enemies for the persecutions their forefathers had suffered. As this particular ghetto yarn has it, when Cohen entered the ring, he saw "before his eyes . . . childhood memories of Kiev flamed and . . . boyhood tales of Kishineff rang in his ears." Inspired by these recollections, he took out his people's anger through "a few sharp jabs, a stiff uppercut or two—then a murderous blow to the top of the head and the young Pole crumpled to the floor." With his opponent prostrate before him "the avenger . . . thundered 'Praise God' in purest Hebrew as he flung aloft his mittened hands." The story ends with the vanquished Gentile emitting from the ring floor "the same cry in weaker tones: 'Praise God, oh Israel'."[20]

None of these athletic pursuits—from the good clean fun of the settlement court or track to the down and dirty fight in the prize ring and to the ill-reputed dance hall—sat well with immigrant Jewish parents. The published laments range from the father's complaint in the Yiddish press that baseball is "this crazy game [where] the children can get crippled" to the *New York Tribune's* report that "there is nothing that disturbs the Jew so much as to see his boy, and still more his girl taking part in the athletics of the schools." And memoir literature has it that Jewish parents of all sorts berated their athletically inclined youngsters—be they baseball or basketball players and especially if they were boxers—as "loafers." That is, of course, when they were not defining the next generation's participation in sports activities, not to mention their frequenting smoke-filled dance floors for a night of ruckus recreation, as a *"charpah"* and a *"shandah"* (a source of disgrace and shame.")[21]

For the minority of parents who harbored strong religious values—and the many others who possessed traditional Orthodox sensitivities—their straying sturdy sons and less than demure daughters were not only becoming bums, but non-observant ones at that. Some Orthodox families were able to make a partial peace with their children's ambitions and proclivities. As early as the turn of the century, one Yiddish author evoked this accepting mind-set when he wrote of the comfort zone a fictional rabbi, "a rabbinical scholar of the old type" and his wife came to occupy toward their son, "the professional pugilist." Initially, they were "shocked . . . who ever heard of decent people fighting like peasants." But, eventually, they became "reconciled to his vocation," and actually felt a degree of pride when he was victorious against a Gentile fighter.[22] The saga of "Slugger Cohen" seems to have gotten around! Regrettably, our scribe does not tell us how such parents felt towards the non-religious training regimen that must have become central to their young man's life.

A few children of observant parents assuaged their own guilt, or mollified their parents somewhat, through appeals to a similar sense of ethnic pride. In the late 1910s, The Atlas Club of New Haven, Conn., whose "founders included sons of a rabbi, a *shammos* [sexton] and a *shochet* [ritual slaughterer]" pitched themselves "not simply as another team of players but as a group of goodwill representatives of the Jewish community" who garnered "respect for the Jewish people," even if their matches were on Friday night. We do not know whether their elders' applauded this secularized sanctification of their Jewishness.[23]

What is sure, however, is that for many families a child's unmitigated interest in the sports world was a troubling source of intergenerational pain and conflict. For unhappy elders, it was just another sad reality in a world wherein "[the] father follows ancient customs; [while] the boy is a breezy young Americanized product, scornful of the elder . . . a drifting particle in the modern world in the great city." Or, as one 1910s Jewish social worker observed more specifically, immigrant parents for whom "orthodoxy . . . [was] a type of life rather than a creed" took little pride in their "half-baked second generation" youngsters' knowledge "of batting averages to a 'T' " while their "cocksure" and "smart guy" sons were "indifferent to, if not ashamed of, Jewish life." Clearly, as another contemporary commentator put it, "the appeal of the practical life and even of sport combined to make attendance at synagogue . . . very much less frequent than in the preceding generation." As this critic saw it, "earnest, however well-intentioned, however eloquent" rabbis cannot even begin to make an impression upon the growing character of these adolescents because these "well-known products of the larger American city street corner" do not deign to step a sneakered foot into their sanctuaries. Or to put it one other way, youngsters came home from school and settlement house, or up from the streets, with new heroes—a coach and not a rabbi or rebbe—new interests and new aspirations.[24]

As historians, what this research, of course, suggests, is that no comprehensive understanding of the immigrant Jewish encounter with foreign-American cultural phenomena can be considered complete without addressing the challenge athleticism posed to that community. For example, any appreciation of renowned Socialist newspaper editor, Abraham Cahan's efforts to mediate America to his vast audience of newcomers must include recognition of his very special effort, in 1907, to explain "the fundamentals of baseball" to *Forward* subscribers who were "unfamiliar with sports." There, he presented to parents, who had trouble with their children and the world these kids brought home with them from the schools and streets to their tenements, a diagram of the Polo Grounds diamond. A few years earlier, he had reassured a worried father that his young man's interest in the national pastime would not necessarily make him into "a wild American runner." It probably was better for this immigrant to hear from one of his own kind that "while chess is good, but the body needs to develop also . . . Baseball develops the arms, legs and eyesight. It is played in the fresh air." (By the way, Cahan was far from sold on football with its "accidents and fights.")[25]

Similarly, for a full picture of American Judaism's difficulties with the decline of observance among those making it in this country must take stock not only of those who worked on the Sabbath or shopped on the holy day, but also those who preferred to play in the streets to praying in the synagogue. In this arena, discussions of how rabbis of that era undertook Jewish retrieval work among those who were drifting from the faith must take note of Solomon Schechter's sage advice: "unless you can play baseball" or "unless you know about baseball, you can never get to be a rabbi in America." Those sentiments would make abundant sense to generations of graduates of the Jewish Theological Seminary of America who would be particularly adept in championing a "shul with a pool" strategy for reaching young people.[26]

Ultimately, the serious and properly examine saga of what transpired to young Jews on and off the fields, tracks or pools of this country—and how their "successes" were received back in their home bases and communities—is a clear lens through which the larger dimensions of that group's life in a very different America can be understood and taught.

NOTES

1. For retrospective studies of the socialization and education of children in the shtetl, with emphases on idealizing the scholar, see Mark Zborowski and Elizabeth Herzog, *Life is with People: The Culture of the Shtetl* (New York, 1952), pp. 74–77, 341–43, 353, 391 and Emanuel Gamoran, *Changing Conceptions in Jewish Education* (New York, 1924), pp. 112–13. Diane K. Roskies and David G. Roskies, *The Shtetl Book* (New York, 1975), pp.150, 158, 211 and *passim*, notes that the games children played during their heder years were of the non-physical type, like tic-tac-toe, memorization games, "IT," etc. They do, however, note, p. 150, that sometimes in heder youngsters "yelled or fought with each other," we imagine outside the purview of their teachers. For another vision of Jews as non-sportsmen in East Europe, see Chaim Bermant, *The Jews* (New York, 1977), p. 180. See also Cary Goodman, "(Re) Creating Americans at the Educational Alliance," *Journal of Ethnic Studies*, vol. 6, no. 4 (Winter, 1979), pp. 19–20.

2. For the record, by the late nineteenth century, on the scene witnesses of the traditional heder scene, including young men who survived its regimens, were far-from-sold on how well this educational system did its job as a molder of great Jewish male minds. For a discussion of truly un-romanticized views of the heder experience, see Steven J. Zipperstein, *Imagining Russian Jewry: Memory, History, Identity* (Seattle, 1999), pp. 42–45.

3. See Zborowski and Herzog, pp. 124–28. For Mary Antin's comment see her, *The Promised Land* (Boston, 1908), p. 111 quoted in Sydney Stahl Weinberg, *The World of our Mothers: The Lives of Immigrant Jewish Women* (New York, 1988) p. 44.

4. David G. Roskies, *Against the Apocalypse: Responses to Catastrophe in Modern Jewish Cultures* (Cambridge, MA., 1984), pp. 141–49.

5. On Jewish defense efforts against pogroms in the early 1880s, see Jonathan Frankel, *Prophecy and Politics: Socialism, Nationalism, and the Russian Jews, 1862–1917* (Cambridge), pp. 54–5.

6. My reference to Jewish students returning to "their people" from periods of estrangement is derived from Frankel's conceptualization. See Frankel, pp. 49–53.

7. "Sports in Poland," *Nowa Encyklopedia Powszechna*, vol.5 (Warsaw: PWN, 1998).

8. For an analysis of the transformation of Russian Jewish masses in the nineteenth century and their acquisition of industrial skills as well as an incipient labor consciousness, see Ezra Mendelsohn, *Class Struggle in the Pale: The Formative Years of the Jewish Workers Movement in Tsarist Russia.* (Cambridge, 1970).

9. Matters changed somewhat after the failed Russian Revolution of 1905 that convinced an ever increasing number of *Bundist* types to take their lives and messages to the United States. They would prove to be more activist in so many ways within the American ghetto. However, even when they battled in the streets of this country, as men and women in search of social justice or economic equality, they did not fight with their fists. On the periodization of the arrival of more activist Bundist types and Socialist Zionists, see Will Herberg, "The Jewish Labor Movement in the United States, " *American Jewish Year Book*, vol. 53 (1952), pp. 695–96 and Gerald Sorin, *Tradition Transformed: The Jewish Experience in America* (Baltimore, 1997), p. 44. For a look at what transpired when Jewish "rioters" took to the streets, particularly the evidence that most of the violence emanated not from the Jewish protestors but from the cops who broke up the protest, see Paula E. Hyman, "Immigrant Women and Consumer Protest: The New York City Kosher Meat Boycott of 1902," *American Jewish History* vol. 7, no. 1 (September, 1980), pp. 92–4. Hyman's article suggests that Jewish violence consisted of breaking windows, not breaking heads.

10. For the quotation on Roosevelt's attitudes towards sports, see the citation in Benjamin G. Rader, *American Sports: From the Age of Folk Games to the Age of Televised Sports* (Englewood Cliffs, N.J., 1996), p. 100. For a sense of Jewish affection for Roosevelt see "Roosevelt and I," *American Hebrew*, vol. 103 [hereafter *A.H.*] (January 17, 1919), p. 260.

11. Henry Smith Williams, "The Educational and Health Giving Value of Athletics," *Harper's Weekly* (February 16, 1895), p. 166. See also, for comments about Jewish lack of physicality by both friends and foes of immigrants, Hutchins Hapgood, *The Spirit of the Ghetto: Studies of the Jewish Quarter of New York* (New York, 1902), p. 76; Madison Grant, *The Passing of the Great Race* (New York, 1916), p. 14; Edward A. Ross, *The Old World in the New: The Significance of Past and Present Immigration to the American People* (New York, 1914), pp. 189–90 noted in Riess, "Sport, Race and Ethnicity in the American City, 1870–1950," in *Immigration and Ethnicity: American Society—"Melting Pot" or "Salad Bowl,"*, Michael D'Innocenzo and Josef P. Sirefman, eds. (Westport, CT., 1992), p. 215, n.15; Charles S. Bernheimer, *Half a Century in Community Service* (New York, 1948), p. 44.

12. Cary Goodman, *Choosing Sides: Playground and Street Life on the Lower East Side* (New York, 1979), pp. 38–39; *The Immigrant Jew in America*, Edmund J. James, ed. (New York, 1907), pp. 298, 316. See also, Cary Goodman, "(Re) Creating Americans at the Educational Alliance," *Journal of Ethnic Studies*, vol. 6, no. 4 (Winter, 1979), p. 19.

13. Goodman, *Choosing* p. 112; Williams, p. 166; "Adjusting to the New World," *Readings in Modern Jewish History*, Eliezer L. Ehrmann,ed. (New York, 1977), p. 371.

14. Irving Howe, *The World of Our Fathers :The Journey of the East European Jews to America and the Life They Found and Made* (New York, 1976), p. 182.

15. Stephan F. Brumberg, *Going to America Going to School: The Jewish Immigrant Public School Encounter in Turn-of-the- Century New York City* (New York, 1986),

pp. 73–5; see also, J. Thomas Jable, "The Public Schools Athletic League of New York City: Organized Athletics for City Schoolchildren, 1903–1914," reprinted in Steven Riess, *The American Sporting Experience: A Historical Anthology of Sport in America* (New York, 1984), p. 234.

16. Roy Lubove, *The Progressives and the Slums: Tenement House Reform in New York City, 1890–1917* (Pittsburgh, 1962), p.189; Robert A. Woods and Albert J. Kennedy, *The Settlement Horizon: A National Estimate* (New York, 1922); *Philanthropy and Social Progress* (Boston, 1892), p. 83; Irene Kaufmann Settlement *Neighbors* 1 (October 25, 1923), p. 4, "Good , Clean Sport,' Motto of C.H.I.," Philip L. Seman Collection, Scrapbook, I (1910–1916),Chicago Hebrew Institute, "News Letter # 11" all quoted from Linda J. Borish, "The Place of Physical Culture and Sport for Women in Jewish Americanization Organizations," (unpublished conference paper, 2001); George Eisen, "Sport, Recreation and Gender: Jewish Immigrant Women in Turn-of-the-Century America (1880–1920)," *Journal of Sport History* vol. 18, no. 1 (Spring, 1991), p. 112; Steven Riess, *City Games: The Evolution of American Urban Society and the Rise of Sports* (Urbana, 1989), p. 165.

17. For more comments on Jewish youngsters in informal play—or swimming, see Bernard MacFadden quoted in Goodman, p. 20 and Eisen, 108.

18. *A.H.*, vol. 96 (January 1, 1915).

19. *A.H.*, vol. 99 (June, 23, 1916), p. 206.

20. *A.H.*, vol. 104 (June 6, 1919), p. 96.

21. Howe, p. 182; "Adjusting to the New World," p. 371; Riess, "Tough Jews," *Sports . . .*, Riess, ed., pp. 67–8. 77.

22. Abraham Cahan, "The New Writers of the Ghetto," *The Bookman* vol. 39 (August, 1914), p. 633. This source is an account by Cahan of an untitled Yiddish story written by Aaron Weitzman.

23. Peter Levine, *From Ellis Island to Ebbetts Field: Sport and the American Jewish Experience* (New York, 1992), p. 36.

24. For references to problems fathers had with sons, see the observations of Arthur H. Gleason in "Religion for the Jew" that appeared in *Harper's Weekly*, reprinted in *A.H.*, vol. 96 (January 29,1915), p. 340. For comments on so-called "half-baked" youngsters and their parents, see Isaac B. Berkson, *Theories of Americanization : A Critical Study with Special Reference to the Jewish Group* (New York, 1920), pp. 185–86. See also on youthful disinterest in synagogue life, "The Weakness of the Synagogue," *A.H.*, vol. 96 (January 8, 1915), p. 276.

25. On Abraham Cahan's statements and explanations about baseball, see Gunther Bart, *City People:The Rise of Modern City Culture in Nineteenth-Century America* (New York, 1980), p.150f and Howe, p.182. The Polo Grounds diagram appeared in the August 29, 1909 edition of the *Forward*.

26. See "A Trumpet for All Israel," *Time Magazine* (October 15, 1951), p. 54 for an account of Schechter's legendary sports statement. See e-mail communication between Ezra Finkelstein and Jeffrey S. Gurock, June 17, 2002 for an alternate version of the statement.

5

America's Most Memorable Zionist Leaders

Jonathan D. Sarna

Jewish Literacy, a widely distributed volume by Joseph Telushkin that promises "the most important things to know about the Jewish religion, its people, and its history," highlights two American Zionists as worthy of being remembered by every literate Jew: Louis Brandeis and Henrietta Szold.[1] Brandeis and Szold are likewise the only two American Zionists to make Michael Shapiro's somewhat idiosyncratic list of "The Jewish 100," a ranking of the most influential Jews of all time.[2] In addition, they are the highest-ranking Zionist man and woman in the journal *American Jewish History*'s small scholarly survey of "the two greatest American Jewish leaders."[3] They have been the subject of more published biographies than any other American Zionists, and they dominate children's textbook presentations of American Zionism as well. They are, in short, the best known American Zionists by far.

Scholars may lament that other critical figures—people like Harry Friedenwald, Israel Friedlaender, Richard Gottheil, Chaim Greenberg, Louis Lipsky, Julian Mack, Emanuel Neumann, Alice Seligsberg, Marie Syrkin, and so many others—have not achieved immortality this way. Stephen S. Wise, Abba Hillel Silver, and Mordecai Kaplan may have come close, but they are neither as well known as Brandeis and Szold nor as universally respected. Kaplan, moreover, is far better known as the founder of Reconstructionism. Whether others deserve greater recognition, however, is not the question to be considered here.[4] That would demand an extensive inquiry into what "greatness" in Zionism entails and how it should be measured. Instead, our question is *why* Brandeis and Szold achieved special "canonical status" among American Zionist leaders, while so many others did not.

Existing studies of American Zionist leadership fail to consider this question. Taking their cue from social scientific studies of leadership, they focus instead on the sources from which Zionist leaders drew their authority, the strategies that they pursued, and the extent to which they preserved tradition or promoted change. Yonathan Shapiro's well-known volume entitled *Leadership of the American Zionist Organization, 1897–1930* (1971), for example, follows Kurt Lewin in distinguishing between leaders from the center (like Louis Lipsky) and leaders from the periphery (like Louis Brandeis), and analyzes differences between the backgrounds, styles and leadership methods of different American Zionist leaders. But questions of long-term reputation and popular memory—why, in our case, Brandeis and Szold won historical immortality while so many others were forgotten—go unanswered.

Here, I shall argue that the historical reputation of Brandeis and Szold rests upon factors that reach beyond the usual concerns of leadership studies. How they became leaders and what they accomplished during their lifetimes is certainly important, but even more is the fact that both Brandeis and Szold became role models for American Jews: they embodied values that American Jews admired and sought to project, even if they did not always uphold them themselves. Brandeis and Szold thus came to symbolize the twentieth-century American Jewish community's ideal of what a man and woman should be. Their enduring reputation reveals, in the final analysis, as much about American Jews as about them.

What Louis Brandeis and Henrietta Szold accomplished in their lives is, in broad outline, widely known. Brandeis (1856–1941), born in Louisville, Kentucky, attended Harvard Law School and went on to become a successful and innovative Boston lawyer, achieving fame as the "people's attorney." During these years he maintained no formal Jewish affiliations, but in midlife, for reasons historians continue to debate, he became attracted to Zionism and in 1914 assumed leadership of the American Zionist movement, transforming its image and identity. He resigned in 1921, following a dispute with Chaim Weizmann, but remained a significant behind-the-scenes player. In 1916, President Woodrow Wilson nominated Brandeis to the United States Supreme Court, the first Jew tio be so honored. He survived a bruising confirmation fight, tainted by anti-Semitism, and served on the Court for twenty-three years, earning a reputation for "prophetic vision, moral intensity, and [a] grasp of practical affairs."[5]

Henrietta Szold (1860–1945), born in Baltimore, Maryland, was the eldest child of Rabbi Benjamin Szold, and served as his amanuensis and aide. Graduating first in her class (and as the only Jew) at Western Female High School, she became a private school teacher, founded a night school for Russian Jewish immigrants, wrote essays for the Jewish press, and then worked for twenty-three years as editor (though without that title) of the

Jewish Publication Society in Philadelphia. She was one of the founders
of Hadassah in 1912, as well as its first national president; she traveled to
Palestine in 1920 to supervise the organization's Zionist Medical Unit; and
she lived for most of her remaining years in Jerusalem, organizing social
services and assuming (in her seventies) responsibility for Youth Aliyah,
the immigration of Jewish refugee children to Palestine. Lauded as "Mother
of Israel" for her tireless efforts on behalf of Jews in need, she believed in
practical Zionism and invested every task that she undertook with a sense
of spiritual purpose.[6]

All of these accomplishments surely earned Brandeis and Szold the ac-
colades showered upon them, but they still leave open the question of why
others, who also achieved a great deal, have in the course of time been
totally forgotten. Why, in other words, has popular memory operated so
selectively in the case of American Zionist leadership, to the advantage of
Brandeis and Szold and the disadvantage of everybody else? No definitive
answer to this question is possible, but five factors stressed by biographers
of Brandeis and Szold seem particularly revealing. At the very least, they
help to explain why the lives of these two Zionist leaders took on special
relevance to subsequent generations of Jews.

First, Louis Brandeis and Henrietta Szold were both native-born, second-
generation Americans, children of Central European Jewish immigrants.
As leaders, they stood in marked contrast to the vast majority of American
Jewish adults (and even greater majority of American Zionists), who were
immigrants, born in Eastern Europe. This disjunction between leaders and
led was common in the early decades of the American Zionist movement.
Every National President of Hadassah until 1939 was American-born, and
not one of the early presidents of the Federation of American Zionists or the
Zionist Organization of America was born in Eastern Europe.[7] The reason is
that native-born leaders like Brandeis and Szold helped to legitimate the Zionist movement. They understood American norms and mores, spoke English without a foreign accent, attracted other native-born Jews to join them,
and made it more difficult for opponents to label Zionism "un-American."
No less important, they served as living proof that those born and bred in
America could, through Zionism, preserve their Jewish loyalties. The life
stories of Brandeis and Szold thus served to reassure immigrants who feared
that their American-born children would assimilate and be lost to Judaism.
Simultaneously, they reinforced one of Zionism's central claims—that it
held the key to Jewish survival.

A second element stressed by biographers of Brandeis and Szold concerns
the quality of their minds: their well-deserved reputation for broad learning
and superior intelligence. Alfred Mason, Brandeis's first major biographer
quotes a Harvard Law School classmate who recalled that "Mr. Brandeis,
although one of the youngest men" in his class, "had the keenest and

most subtle mind of all." Brandeis finished first among his peers, received a special dispensation from the university allowing him to graduate at a younger age than the rules allowed, and was described as late as 1941 as "the most brilliant student ever to have attended the Harvard Law School."[8] Near the end of his life, his "outstanding qualities of great learning" were described by the *Universal Jewish Encyclopedia* in terms usually reserved for the greatest rabbis and scholars, including "keen perception, rare analytical powers, [an] orderly and constructive mind...and profound knowledge of the historical roots of our institutions."[9]

Henrietta Szold's reputation for brilliance was similarly stellar. She graduated top of her class at Western Female High School, commanded German, French, and Hebrew, studied Judaica and the classics with her father (who considered her his "disciple"), audited classes in rabbinics at the Jewish Theological Seminary, and was an omnivorous reader. One biographer described her as "the most learned Jewess in the United States."[10] Another recalled how Szold's "probing mind" revealed facets of problems "that had occurred to no one else and plumbed depths unfathomed by the others." Even Jerusalem's doctors, we are told, "listened agape" while Szold, who had no formal medical training, "expounded before them the interrelationships among the various fields of medicine with the clarity of one long conversant with problems of hospitalization."[11]

Even if exaggerated for effect, the reputation shared by Brandeis and Szold for wide-ranging learning and intellectual brilliance reinforced both a basic Jewish value and a longstanding tradition that rewards wisdom with status. Just as so many of the great heroes of Israel's past were renowned for their genius, so too, according to Zionism's followers, its contemporary heroes. For American Jews, the fact that Brandeis and Szold were smarter than their peers both explained their success and justified the adulation that their followers showered upon them.

One might have expected that Szold, as a woman, would have been held to a different standard. Her formal academic achievements, after all, fell well below those of Brandeis. He held a graduate degree from America's finest university; her highest earned degree was a high school diploma. Moreover, Jews traditionally considered higher education more important for men than for women. Szold herself, however, often condemned this double standard and from an early age championed women's higher education.[12] Through her writings and career, she demonstrated that women were as intellectually able as their male counterparts. Her editorial work at the Jewish Publication Society, in fact, made clear that she was actually *more* able than many of those whose books she tacitly improved.[13] The image of the brainy Miss Szold underscored this feminist lesson by showing that learning and wisdom were no less important for Jewish women than for Jewish men.

Third on the list of revealing characteristics stressed in popular presentation of the lives of Brandeis and Szold is meticulous efficiency. Both leaders, according to their biographers, hated to waste time and championed order and precision—values central to America's ethos, but not to Zionism's. Szold sought to bring efficiency to Zionism as early as 1910. Charged with the task of clearing up what she described as the "almost hopeless condition" into which the Federation of American Zionism's affairs had fallen, she labored "night and day" as "honorary secretary" and within four months was able to report that "the muddle had been cleared."[14] Brandeis, when he took over as leader of American Zionism in 1914, made a similar thrust for efficiency. He installed a timeclock in the Zionist offices, introduced a filecard system for names, and even proposed fines "for absence or tardiness."[15]

Both leaders also personally embodied the values that they preached. Szold, according to those who knew her, led a "systematic, well-ordered life." "One hesitates," one biographer writes (with obvious didactic intent), "even to hint to our somewhat careless younger generation just how meticulous Henrietta Szold really was in all things, whether great or small."[16] Brandeis according to his biographers, was no less punctilious. Philippa Strum, speaks of his "organization," "efficiency," "energy" and "concern for detail." Alfred Leif, writing half a century earlier, reported simply that "He made efficiency a household word."[17]

The meticulous efficiency that these leaders personified and preached reflected modern business values, alluring yet still somewhat foreign to immigrant Jews from Eastern Europe. Traditional rabbis may have taught the virtue of wasting as little times as possible on pursuits other than Torah, but the secular idea that time should be husbanded for productive labor was new. Benjamin Franklin popularized this idea in America, and Frederick W. Taylor transformed it into a "scientific" management technique with his time-study experiments of the 1880's and 90's, aimed at eliminating waste and inefficiency.[18] Something of a "cult of efficiency" developed in early twentieth century America, and American Zionism's main followers, success-oriented East European Jews and their children, stood among its most ardent disciples. To them, Brandeis and Szold appeared as "priest and priestesses" of this new faith, the very antithesis of "old world" habits. In this, as in so many other ways, Brandeis and Szold served as role models, projecting a vision of Zionism fully consonant with modernity and suffused with values that followers sought to incorporate into their own lives.

Closely akin to meticulous efficiency was a fourth characteristic stressed by biographers of Brandeis and Szold: the commitment to hard work. Szold rose early—often at five and rarely after seven—and labored long into the night. In her forties, she sometimes complained about the "crazy orgy of work" to which she subjected herself.[19] Later, at Hadassah, friends recalled that "she worked harder and longer than anyone else on her staff."[20] Even when she was eighty-three she wore out her companions. Norman Bentwich, who was twenty-three years her junior, recalled a day with her at that time as "an experience of physical and intellectual vitality." It involved meetings in different parts of Israel and lasted for seventeen hours, interrupted only by catnaps.[21] Long hours and hard work were for Szold a permissible way for her to compete successfully with her peers—male and female alike. Into old age, she delighted in her victories: her ability to outlast men and women much younger than herself.[22]

Brandeis too was known for working hard, but his secret was efficiency. He once claimed that he "could do twelve months' work in eleven months."[23] He then spent the twelfth month, usually August, on vacation. His days began early, just as Szold's did, but they generally ended at five. "He knew his health limited his work hours," Philippa Strum explains, "so he organized his time to accomplish all that he wished to do."[24] In the time allotted, he completed an astonishing amount of correspondence and legal writing and kept up with a wide array of interests. His secret, as his colleagues noted when he retired, was "vigor," "devotion," and "intensity". One biographer reports that he was happiest "working for leisure and using leisure for work."[25]

This passionate embrace of work as a calling, rather than simply as a means of earning a living, calls to mind the Protestant work ethic, as described by Max Weber, and serves as yet another reminder that this ethic was scarcely confined to Protestants alone.[26] Through their success, Brandeis and Szold demonstrated that for Jews too hard work pays off. Again, they served as role models that others sought to emulate.

In the narratives of Brandeis and Szold, hard work was not only rewarded, it also yielded financial independence and freedom—goals that many an American Jew fervently desired. Brandeis, we are told, had nothing but pity for the man without capital who had "to slave and toil for others to the end of his days."[27] Reputedly, he sought to avoid that sad fate for himself by always living carefully and by accumulating from a young age a fortune substantial enough for him to be his own master, free to select the clients and the causes in which he believed. Henrietta Szold gained financial independence in a different way at age 55 when a group of wealthy admirers rewarded her with an annuity. Like Brandeis, she too was now able to devote herself fully to the causes in which she believed. Shrewdly, if all-too-modestly, she once credited her monthly checks with being "the whole secret" of her success in Palestine. Had she worked equally hard and not been financially independent, she recognized, her devotion would "at best" have gone "unnoted."[28] Freedom and financial independence were magic terms to hardworking, upwardly mobile American Jews of that time; they represented, for them, the essence of the American Dream. This explains, in part, the allure for Jews of occupational choices like law, medicine and accounting, which promised to make this dream come true faster, and was reflected too in the allure of Zion, which at least in its American version offered brawny pioneers something of this same dream on the soil of Palestine. Brandeis and Szold served, in a sense, as poster children for this dream. The freedom and financial independence that hard work brought them amply validated America's promise, and made the Zionist promise seem that much more credible.

The value of hard work went along with the fifth characteristic pointed to by all biographers of Brandeis and Szold: their penchant for Spartan living and their commitment to social justice. In an age characterized by materialism and hedonism, both leaders represented "traditional values"; they firmly opposed the conspicuous consumption so frequently witnessed in their day. Brandeis, for example, was said from a young age to have "limit[ed] his wants to the barest minimum." A biography written in his lifetime spoke of the "Stoic simplicity of his needs." He was known to abhor ostentation and personal debt and to shun the kinds of luxuries that most men of his class indulged in; his ideal instead was to be "economical."[29] His friend, the Catholic social reformer Monsignor John A. Ryan, went so far as to describe his tastes and manner of living as approaching "the standards of an ascetic." Philippa Strum reminds us that this was something of an exaggeration, for Brandeis indulged in horses, canoes, summer homes, servants, and private schooling for his daughters. The image he cultivated, however, did border on the ascetic: he never owned a car, his dinners were "spare in provision," and his office "was furnished with austerity. There was no rug or easy chair." Where others spent more than they earned, he did the opposite and donated the excess to causes like Zionism in which he passionately believed. This was a deeply held value lived out in life and at the same time a silent polemic, an attack on the materialism of American society in general and particularly, one suspects, on the "crude, materialistic Boston Jews" of whom he was so very contemptuous.[30]

Henrietta Szold displayed similar values and ideals. "For decades she had been frugal," her biographer reports.[31] She preached simple household virtues—"economy, order and system."[32] Philanthropy was central to her life, and like Brandeis she preferred to give than to receive. Her own home in Jerusalem was described as "simple [and] tastefully furnished,"[33] while she herself, according to her longtime secretary Elma Ehrlich (Levinger) was "unbelievably straitlaced in all matters great or small."[34] "Scrupulous about the use of public funds," her friend Rose Zeitlin recalled, "Miss Szold rarely indulged in any but second class travel (third when second was not available) . . . On the Palestine roads her travel was by bus and third-class rail, unless a taxi was indispensable. 'I am no more than one of the people of Israel,' she said, when found waiting for a bus on a windy corner. . . . At the hotel where she lived for years a tablemate could not help noticing that invariably she chose the least expensive foods."[35] To Szold, as to Louis Brandeis, crude materialism and conspicuous consumption were anathema. At twenty-seven, she lamented the "rampant materialism" that afflicted "our co-religionists in Europe."[36] Late in life, she deprecated, in a letter to her family, "America's business greed."[37]

Jewish ideals of social justice and American Progressivism underlay many of these attitudes and life patterns. Brandeis and Szold, like other Jewish and Christian social reformers of their day, believed in a better world and conducted their lives according to *its* values, rather than those of their surroundings. Zionism for them served as an extension of this vision. Both strongly supported the 1918 Pittsburgh Program of the Zionist Organization of America which set forth a social justice agenda for Palestine, and both were fired by the ideals of "Social Zionism," which in its American garb advocated the creation of "a model state in the Holy Land—freed from the economic wrongs, the social injustices and the greed of modern-day industrialism."[38] Zionism for them took on the aura of a sacred agenda, at once lofty and prophetic. Indeed, it was their image as latter-day prophets that led so many to revere them—in their own lifetimes and thereafter.

As these shared images illustrate, those who portrayed Brandeis and Szold transformed them into larger-than-life symbols embodying the values, aspirations and ideals that American Jews cherished and hoped to pass along to their children. They held them up as living proof that those who were smart, efficient, hardworking, and righteous could rise to positions of prominence in America and still find time to improve the world—without hiding their faith or abandoning commitments to Jews in need. They validated, through them, some of American Jews' fondest hopes concerning the land that they now called home. Szold and Brandeis thus came to function in American Jewish life as did famous rabbis, scholars, and philanthropists. No wonder Jews carefully tended the memories of their two native "saints" even as they allowed the memories of so many other American Zionist leaders to fall into neglect.

Beyond serving as role models, however, Brandeis and Szold also came to symbolize future directions for American Jews in an era of changing religious identities and new communal challenges. For one thing, they validated alternative modes of Jewish identification. Brandeis was an avowedly secular Jew who displayed no interest in Jewish religious rituals and never belonged to a synagogue.[39] Szold was something of a Jewish seeker: kosher, Sabbath-observant and deeply spiritual, yet fiercely unorthodox in many of her beliefs and practices.[40] Neither fit comfortably into the community's standard religious categories. As a result, both conveyed to American Jews the reassuringly latitudinarian message that they could find their own way in Judaism, for there were many ways to be a good Jew. In marked contrast to those who resisted change fearing assimilation, they extended Zionism's embrace to all who sought to join them. In so doing, they paved the way for the movement's emergence as part of the common-faith "civil religion" of American Jews,[41] and gave added legitimation to the optimistically pluralistic and broadly inclusivistic model of American Jewish communal life that took shape during the interwar years.

Brandeis and Szold reinforced this sense of inclusivism by showing how, in America, Jews of Central European descent could work harmoniously with their counterparts from Eastern Europe for the betterment of Jewish life. While scarcely a new message—the leadership of the Federation of American Zionists had included "uptown" and "downtown" as well as Orthodox and Reform representatives even before 1900[42]—tensions between the two communities continued to divide American Jews well into the twentieth century. Through their Zionist efforts, Brandeis and Szold helped to bridge these divisive tensions by serving as exemplars of intracommunal cooperation. Szold felt particularly strongly about this point. Her friend Alice Seligsberg recalled that she would not permit Hadassah to have more than one chapter in a city, "and that chapter had to include rich and poor, Americanized socially elite and foreign born."[43] In this way, she worked to redirect the agenda of American Jews away from differences rooted in the old-world past and toward the common (if ultimately no less divisive) goal of shaping the Zionist future.

Finally, and perhaps most importantly, Brandeis and Szold symbolized and projected a message of cultural inclusiveness, personally embodying the grand synthesis—Judaism and Americanism, Hebraism plus Hellenism—that so many aspired to but so few actually achieved. Brandeis, compared in his own lifetime to both Isaiah and Lincoln was known to be a devotee both of fifth-century Athens and of Puritan New England.[44] Szold too embraced both Jewish and secular culture. In addition to her much-celebrated Judaic learning, she taught, as a young schoolteacher in Baltimore, subjects as diverse as French, Latin, mathematics, history, botany, and physiology, and throughout her life she maintained an absorbing interest in plants and nature.[45]

In an era when many doubted the ability of American Jews to negotiate both sides of their "hyphenated" identity, Szold and Brandeis served as prominent counter-examples. They provided reassuring evidence that the ideal of inclusiveness could be realized, and that Judaism, Zionism, and Americanism could all be happily synthesized.[46] For this, as much as for their more tangible organizational contributions, American Jews revered them and remembered them. Perhaps at some level they also understood that through them they saw reflected their own aspirations and ideals.

NOTES

1. Joseph Telushkin, *Jewish Literacy* (New York, 1991), pp. 410–413.
2. Michael Shapiro, ed., "The Jewish 100: A Ranking of the Most Influentual Jews of All Time" (New York, 1994); the list is reprinted in Sander L. Gilman, *SmartJews: The Construction of the Image of Superior Jewish Intelligence* (Lincoln, 1996), p. 234.
3. *American Jewish History* vol. 78 (December 1988), pp. 169–200.
4. Evyatar Friesel, "Ha-manhigut Be-tenuah Ha-tsiyonut Be-arstsot Ha-berit, 1900–1930," *Manhig Ve-hanhaga: Kovetz Ma'amarim* (Jerusalem, 1992), pp. 187–202, deals in part with this question.
5. Paul A. Freund, "Louis D. Brandeis," *Dictionary of American Biography*, Supplement 3 (New York, 1973), p. 100; standard biographies include Alpheus T. Mason, *Brandeis: A Free Man's Life* (New York, 1946), and Phillippa Strum, *Louis D. Brandeis: Justice for the People* (New York, 1984).
6. Eric L. Goldstein, "The Practical as Spiritual: Henrietta Szold's American Zionist Ideology, 1878–1920," *Daughter of Zion: Henrietta Szold and American Jewish Womanhood*, ed., Barry Kessler (Baltimore, 1995), pp. 17–33; standard biographies include Irving Fineman, *Woman of Valor: The Story of Henrietta Szold* (New york, 1961), and Joan Dash, *Summoned to Jerusalem: The Life of Henrietta Szold* (New York, 1979).
7. The National Presidents of Hadassah are conveniently listed in Marlin Levin, *Balm in Gilead: The Story of Hadassah* (New York, 1973), p. 270; the presidents of the FAZ and ZOA are listed in the annual volume of the *American Jewish Year Book*. For capsule biographies, see Jacob R. Marcus and Judith M. Daniels, eds., *The Concise Dictionary of American Jewish Biography* (New York, 1994).
8. Mason, *Brandeis*, p. 47; Strum, *Louis D. Brandeis*, p. 33.
9. Seymour S. Guthman, "Brandeis, Louis, Dembitz," *Universal Jewish Encyclopedia* (1948), vol. 2, p. 495.
10. Elma Ehrlich Levinger, *Fighting Angel: Story of Henrietta Szold* (New York, 1946), p. 45.
11. Rose Zeitlin, *Henrietta Szold: Record of a Life* (NewYork, 1952), pp. 47, 64.
12. Alexander Lee Levin, *The Szolds of Lombard Street* (Philadelphia, 1960), pp. 153–155, 257.
13. Jonathan D. Sarna, *JPS: The Americanization of Jewish Culture, 1888–1988* (Philadelphia, 1989), 47–135.
14. Marvin Lowenthal, *Henrietta Szold: Life and Letters* (New York, 1942), pp. 70–74.
15. Strum, *Louis D. Brandeis*, p. 255.
16. Levinger, *Fighting Angel*, pp. 103, 60.
17. Strum, *Louis D. Brandeis*, pp. 46, 249; Alfred Lief, *Brandeis: The Personal History of an American Ideal* (New York, 1936), p. 200.
18. Richard D. Brown, *Modernization: The Transformation of American Life* (New York, 1976); Alan Trachtenberg, *The Incorporation of America: Culture and Society in the Gilded Age* (New York, 1982), p. 69.
19. Sarna, *JPS*, p. 72.
20. Zeitlin, *Henrietta Szold*, p. 117.

21. Norman Bentwich, *My Seventy-Seven Years* (Philadelphia, 1961), p. 200.

22. See, e.g., Levinger, *Fallen Angel*, p. 107; Zeitlin, *Henrietta Szold*, pp. 210–211.

23. Strum, *Louis D. Brandeis*, p. 42.

24. Ibid, p. 38; Lief, *Brandeis*, p. 423; Mason, *Brandeis*, p. 77.

25. Strum, *Louis D. Brandeis*, p. 42; Mason, *Brandeis*, p 634; Lief, *Brandeis*, p. 47.

26 See on this theme, Ewa Morawska, *Insecure Prosperity: Small-Town Jews in Industrial America, 1890–1940* (Princeton, 1996), p. 226, which cites all the relevant literature (n.21).

27. Mason, *Brandeis*, p. 77.

28. Lowenthal, *Henrietta Szold Life and Letters*, pp. 197–198.

29. Lief, *Brandeis*, pp. 22, 47.

30. Strum, *Louis D. Brandeis*, pp. 47–48, 62; for other sources, see Jonathan D. Sarna, " 'The Greatest Jew in the World Since Jesus Christ': The Jewish Legacy of Louis D. Brandeis," *American Jewish History*, vol. 81 (Spring-Summer 1994), p. 350 from where portions of this paragraph are drawn.

31. Dash, *Summoned to Jerusalem*, p. 148.

32. Fineman, *Woman of Valor*, p. 359.

33. Zeitlin, *Henrietta Szold*, p. 70.

34. Levinger, *Fallen Angel*, p. 163.

35. Zeitlin, *Henrietta Szold*, pp. 236–237.

36. Lowenthal, *Henrietta Szold Life and Letters*, p. 28.

37. Michael Brown, "Henrietta Szold's Progressive American Vision of the Yishuv," in Allon Gal, ed., *Envisioning Israel: The Changing Ideals and Images of North American Jews* (Detroit, 1996), p. 65.

38. Bernard A Rosenblatt, *Social Zionism* (New York, 1919), pp. 10–11; Lowenthal, *Henrietta Szold Life and Letters*, pp. 107–108, 203; Jonathan D. Sarna, "A Projection of America As it Ought to Be: Zion in the Mind's Eye of American Jews," in Gal, ed., *Envisioning Israel*, p. 55.

39. Sarna, "The Greatest Jew in the World," pp. 347–349.

40. For an unusual private expression of her religious perplexities ("what do I want?"), see Henrietta Szold to Alexander Marx, (July 3, 1912), Alexander Marx Papers, Jewish Theological Seminary of America, New York.

41. Jonathan S. Woocher, *Sacred Survival: The Civil Religion of American Jews* (Bloomington, 1986), pp. 76–80.

42. Marnin Feinstein, *American Zionism 1884–1904* (New York, 1965), esp. 134.

43. Cited in Goldstein, "The Practical as Spiritual," p. 30.

44. Sarna, "Greatest Jew in the World," pp. 346, 362–363.

45. Zeitlin, *Henrietta Szold*, p. 15.

46. Sylvia Barack Fishman, *Negotiating Both Sides of the Hyphen: Coalescence, Compartmentalization and American-Jewish Values*: The Jacob and Jennie L. Lichter Lecture, University of Cincinnati (Cincinnati, 1996).

6

Encountering Jewish Feminism

Pamela S. Nadell

> In an age when the alienation of young Jews from Judaism is a major concern for the Jewish community, we can hardly afford to ignore fully one-half of young Jews. Thus, the challenge of feminism, if answered, can only strengthen Judaism.[1] 1972

Since the feminist activist-scholar Paula E. Hyman wrote these words more than three decades ago, feminism has challenged Judaism. By the close of the twentieth century, those challenges had revisioned large swathes of American Jewish life. Whether or not that revisioning strengthened Judaism may be debated, but what cannot be questioned is feminism's impact upon American Judaism. Elsewhere in the Jewish world in the State of Israel, feminism has had a different effect; and where it has affected Israeli Judaism, it has done so in other ways, for Judaism as lived out in America is indeed different. This essay uses the single lens of the transformations wrought by feminism in two different Jewish communities to grapple with the question of why America is different.

In the U.S. the term feminism is, of course, associated with the "years of hope" and "days of rage" of the 1960s.[2] In America in those years, a constellation of events—President Kennedy's 1961 Commission on the Status of Women, the 1963 publication of Betty Friedan's *The Feminine Mystique*, and the 1966 founding of the National Organization of Women—propelled women's demands for political, social, and economic change forward in American life. That the constellation of aims and ambitions associated with feminism would also affect religion was evident early on, best exemplified by the National Organization of Women's creation of its Ecumenical Task

Force on Women and Religion. Historians aptly named this era the second wave of American feminism for the first had appeared a half century
before.

As feminism evolved in the 1910s and 1920s, it sought simultaneously
"to achieve sexual equality while making room for sexual difference." The
constellation of ideas, voices, and groups then linked by feminism revealed,
as it would later during the second wave, paradox and heterogeneity, gener-
ating then, as it would later, enthusiasm and hostility.[3]

As participants in the second wave of American feminism, Jewish women
were swept up by the movement. In it they discovered new opportunities
to live lives dramatically altered by its great transformations, especially by
its revolution in women's labor force participation.[4] As Jewish women,
they brought their feminist consciousnesses home to the American Jewish
community.

Propelled by feminism's calls for an egalitarian transformation of American life, the feminist challenge to Jewish life began "as a series of isolated
questionings in the shadow of the women's movement."[5] Eventually,
Jewish feminists voiced a widespread challenge to American Jewish life.
They demanded equal access to the Jewish community, its organizations,
structures, and leadership; equal status within Jewish life, especially within
the synagogue and the body of Jewish law known as *halacha*; and equal
valuing of women's voices, perspectives, and uniqueness. A constellation of
events in the 1970s—Sally Priesand ordained the first woman rabbi, young
women organized as Ezrat Nashim demanding "an end to the second-class
status of women in Jewish life,"[6] the convening of a national Jewish Feminist Conference,[7] the publication of seminal articles,[8] and the founding of
the feminist magazine *Lilith* —shone light on American Jews' encounters
with feminism.

During the last quarter of the twentieth century, these encounters resulted
in remarkable transformations that have touched virtually every aspect of
the American Jewish community. Feminists demanded the restructuring of
American Jewish organizational life, declaring: "Women are stating, in clear
and resounding cadences, that they will no longer be second-class citizens";
and steps were taken to correct the gross gender imbalance that traditionally characterized Jewish communal leadership outside the all female enclaves of its women's organizations..[9]

Judaism's encounters with feminism led to new behaviors in the synagogue as those affiliated, especially, with the liberal denominations of
American Judaism, with the Reform, Conservative, and Reconstructionist
movements, sought to reconfigure the synagogue as an egalitarian institution. In time this came to mean, for some, women wearing the prayer
shawls and head coverings traditionally worn only by men;[10] women
counting in the quorum of ten necessary for a complete prayer service;[11]

women learning Hebrew and the liturgical skills they had never acquired as girls; women taking on new roles in their synagogues, like reading regularly from the Torah; and women elected synagogue presidents.[12]

Moreover, these liberal branches of American Judaism were not the only ones encountering feminism. Feminism also impacted American Orthodoxy. Its observant Jews embraced the twentieth-century innovation of bat mitzvah;[13] participated in a "learning revolution" which transformed what Jewish girls learn in Orthodox educational settings;[14] embraced women's prayer groups, where, because of the single-sex setting, women may perform ritual roles not open to them when men are present;[15] and have, since 1997, held international conferences on Feminism and Orthodoxy under the auspices of the Jewish Orthodox Feminist Alliance (JOFA).[16]

But feminism's impact extends beyond the synagogue walls. Jewish feminism sparked the invention of an array of private prayers, readings, and ceremonies that ritually mark the "invisible life passages" at the heart of the female biological life cycle which traditional Judaism by and large ignored.[17] Feminism inspired new public rituals: the *simchat bat* celebrating the birth of a daughter, adult bat mitzvah for those women who never had the opportunity to have one as teens, and the women's *seder* which places a cup of water on the table for Miriam and tells of remarkable women from the Jewish past.[18] Feminists re-claimed Rosh Chodesh, the new moon, as the women's holiday,[19] and reappropriated *mikvah*, the ritual bath, as a place to celebrate Rosh Chodesh, to mark a milestone, or to bring closure to a crisis.[20]

Feminist transformations within American Jewish life have challenged the androcentric teachings of the Bible, the liturgy of the prayer book, and the giant corpus of rabbinic literature. Religious feminists decry the exclusion of women's voices and visions in these texts. Where they do find women appearing in the Jewish past, they hungrily gravitate to them, reinterpreting their lives to cast them as role models and to teach lessons for today.[21] Feminist challenges to Judaism's androcentric liturgy compelled each of the liberal denominations of American Judaism to revise its prayer books.[22] Seeking to incorporate female voices and perspectives led to the writing of feminist *midrashim*, like the wildly successful *The Red Tent*.[23] Feminists also seek a new theology, one which will "engender a world that Jewish women build together with Jewish men";[24] and they want to rectify inequities in Jewish law that discriminate against women.[25]

But, of all the transformations wrought by Judaism encountering feminism, the most visible and most dramatic was women becoming rabbis. The history of women's quest for rabbinic ordination dates back to the late nineteenth century when the debate over a woman's right to be a rabbi emerged as part of a larger debate about American women's access to all the learned professions. If women wanted to become doctors, lawyers, and ministers, professions which then largely excluded them, why should they also not want to be rabbis? Yet, despite a series of challengers and engagement of the question for nearly a century, it took the collision of second-wave feminism with American Judaism to propel women into the rabbinate. In 1972 in Reform Judaism, in 1974 in Reconstructionist Judaism, and in 1985 in Conservative Judaism, the first women were ordained rabbis.[26] Eventually, the presence of hundreds of female rabbis would further the feminist agenda in American Jewish life.

In fact, the women who became rabbis hold the key to understanding how so many of the innovations wrought by these encounters with feminism became mainstream so quickly. These rabbis' visibility in the pulpit and the impact of their writing has given them enormous influence upon American Judaism even though they rarely invented the contours of feminism's encounter with Judaism. The women who became rabbis stood "on the front line"[27] of Jewish feminism and were often among the first to adopt its revolutionary changes.

More importantly, because of who they are and where they stand, they have had the opportunity to bring feminism home to America's Jews. Touched by feminist rabbis in the classroom, on the *bimah*, over Shabbat dinner, and often at the most vulnerable moments of their lives—as they wed, celebrated their newborns, rejoiced at *b'nai mitzvah*, and mourned the dead—American Jewish boys and girls, men and women encountered a Judaism transformed by feminism. The women who became rabbis laid the bridges over which crossed the feminist critique of Judaism to the homes, synagogues, and communities of modern America's Jews. With more than five hundred female rabbis in America today,[28] they have played a significant role in communicating its agenda to America's Jewish women and men.[29]

My personal snapshots of American Judaism today demonstrate the depth of the transformations wrought by Jewish feminism. At the *kallah* opening the academic year for Reform Judaism's rabbinical seminary, Hebrew Union College, men and women were evenly represented among the faculty and students, a striking contrast to a 1925 photo of College faculty, staff, and students which shows but four women, only one of whom was student, in a sea of a hundred men.[30] The women reading from the Torah on Rosh Hashanah and dancing with it on Simchat Torah in a suburban, Washington, D.C. Conservative synagogue reveal how far American Judaism has come from the 1950s when a rebbetzin's *aliyah* in a Conservative congregation propelled shocked congregants to flee the service.[31] During Sukkot 5765, the *bat mitzvah* girl chanted all twelve chapters of Ecclesiastes from the *bimah* after services, and those sitting on both sides of the *mechitzah* stayed. These prove that, as I write this in 2005, encountering feminism has transformed the public face of American Judaism.

But this book asks us to think comparatively, to see if we can elucidate how and why the American Jewish experience is different. One way to approach this is to contrast Israeli encounters with feminism.

As feminism emerged in the early twentieth century in many parts of the world, it often appeared "in the context of nationalist movements emphasizing self-determination, secularism, democracy, and socialism." One marker of states' modernization became how much their policies "alleviated gender-based inequities and promoted [women's] empowerment." This was no less true of the Jewish society emerging in the *Yishuv* and the new State of Israel. There "the egalitarian socialist orientation of its initial wave of settlers assured an early recognition of gender equality."[32]

Signs of women's equality in Israel's early history seemed everywhere. One had only to point to the female pioneers and their work in the kibutzim, women's compulsory army service, Israel's 1951 Equal Rights for Women Act, and the presumed unparalleled access to political life exemplified by the iconic Golda Meir. But journalists and scholars exposed the reality belying the myths of women's equality, "Calling the Equality Bluff" on the status of women in Israel.[33] They decried David Ben-Gurion's status quo agreement with the National Religious Party, which gave the religious courts full jurisdiction in personal matters, as "a compromise between socialist men and Orthodox men, at the expense of women."[34] The omission of provisions for civil marriage and divorce made the 1951 Equal Rights for Women Act a lie. The *halutzot*'s reality meant working "sixteen-hour days cleaning shirts and peeling vegetables."[35] In the army women were diverted into sex-segregated, gendered roles; and, while men serve the state by defending it, women serve it by bearing the next generation of defenders.[36]

These exposes grew out of and helped fuel an encounter with second-wave feminism in Israeli society and culture. Former Knesset member Marcia Freedman believes that the Yom Kippur War constituted the "defining national moment" when a resurgent feminism surfaced in Israel. By 1973, a nascent feminist movement had emerged among small groups of women meeting in Haifa, Tel Aviv, and Jerusalem, who, influenced by American Jewish feminists, had developed a feminist critique of Israeli society. Then the war left Israel stunned and not only because of the initial military disasters. The war exposed the fact that, with all the men gone, "the country all but shut down"; that there was not a single female bus driver in the entire nation; and that, when women sought to take part in the defense of their very homes, the government told them to knit caps and bake cakes for the soldiers. The war laid the groundwork for the "first of the second-wave of Israeli feminists," and they borrowed their early organization, ideology, and tactics from the American Women's Liberation movement.[37]

Since then feminists, seeking to integrate women into the political, social, and economic life of the nation, have evolved an array of strategies to raise consciousness about women's issues.[38] Through the Israel Women's Network and other forums, they have found venues for pressing the chief institutions of the nation—the government, army, and workplace—to tear down barriers to and to promote women's advancement. That, in 2005, Israeli feminists remained highly critical of how little their society had accommodated their demands,[39] does not negate the weight of their advocacy for women's rights, as they fought for workers' compensation for sexual harassment and championed legislation promoting women's equality in sports.[40] These encounters with feminism keep issues of women's status before the nation, even though Israeli feminists are so frustrated by the pace of change that they quote Lewis Carroll's *Through the Looking Glass*:

> "A slow sort of country!" said the Queen. "Now, HERE, you see, it takes all the running you can do, to keep in the same place. If you want to get somewhere else, you must run at least twice as fast as that!"[41]

But what about the Israeli encounter with Jewish feminism? In a recent survey of the status of Jewish feminism in Israel, scholar and feminist activist Naomi Graetz, concedes:

> The critique of patriarchy that has become widely accepted among religious Jewish feminists in the United States has taken its time penetrating the religious milieu of Israeli society. This is partially because feminist concerns have mostly focused on political and social change rather than on religious change, and partially because of the traditional nature of Israeli society as a whole.[42]

Graetz reports that, where changes have occurred—in granting women *aliyot*, permitting them to read from the Torah, having women serve as synagogue presidents and as members of ritual committees, inserting the matriarchs into the *amidah*, counting some twenty women rabbis—these transformations have largely taken place in Reform and Masorti (Conservative) Israeli congregations.[43] In these synagogues American immigrants to Israel are significant presences, and it is those immigrants who have interjected into Israeli religious life the Jewish feminism which first emerged in the United States.

Writing of the American "inspiration to the Israeli feminist movement," journalist Rochelle Furstenberg observed the high percentage of Americans in Reform and Conservative congregations promoting egalitarian worship for Israelis; that the first Israeli female rabbi, Na'ama Kelman, came out of America; that the spiritual leader of Jerusalem's *Kehillat Yedidya* is the American-born Deborah Weissman; and that of the women studying for Orthodox ordination, Haviva Ner-David learned how to lay *tefillin* when she was living in Washington, D.C. as Haviva Krasner.[44] Where Jewish feminism has found a foothold in Israel, it did so first through the influence of those whose feminism was inspired by their intimate experience of America's difference.

Nevertheless, these feminists helped spawn a "quiet revolution" among some within Israel's Orthodox world. However, its focus is not on the transformation of the synagogue, for most synagogues in Israel are traditional or Orthodox, not Reform or Masorti. Nor is it on the ritual invention characteristic of American Judaism's encounter with feminism. Rather its focus is on higher Jewish learning, on women's advanced study of sacred Jewish texts, and on what acquisition of such knowledge portends. Before the twentieth century, when most women in the world had limited access to education, the question of women's formal Jewish education was largely moot. However, the encounter with modernity's challenges of assimilation and secularization led rabbinical authorities to approve girls' Jewish educations, chiefly to make them better mothers equipped with the learning needed to safeguard the piety of the next generation.[45] This change, however, paved the way, likely unintentionally, for Orthodox women's eventual desire for higher Jewish learning.

Like other aspects of Israel's encounter with feminism, this too was set into motion by those who came from America. Many of the first Israeli settings for women's higher Jewish learning, like Michlalah,[46] Midreshet Lindenbaum, Matan, and Nishmat, were all founded by American-born immigrants to Israel.[47] Although Graetz refers to "the cross-fertilization of ideas and practices between Israeli and American Jewish women,"[48] that initial fertilization began as a one-way bridge crossing feminism from America to Israel.

But, in Israel, this encounter with religious feminism has deepened: "Women's study is becoming an authentic Israeli orthodox form." From it have flowed transformations of Israeli Judaism improbable within the American context. Women's institutions of higher learning have pioneered programs for training "halakic advisors" and legal advocates to represent women and men in divorce and custody cases before the rabbinical courts which hold jurisdiction over these matters in Israel. Once again the American influence is evident. Shlomo Riskin, a charismatic teacher who had been rabbi of one of New York's leading Orthodox synagogues, created the first Israeli program for training female rabbinical court advocates. A graduate of New York's Stern College, Nishmat founder Rabbanit Chana Henkin set up a program to train women advisors in the laws of family purity, authorizing them to answer *halachic* questions on menstruation, sexuality, and the new reproductive technologies.[49]

Thus, encountering religious feminism led to different responses within Israeli Judaism. Why?

In *Two Worlds of Judaism: The Israeli and American Experiences*, Steven Cohen and the late Charles Liebman concluded that American Jews and

Israeli Jews are "Jewish in a different way." They discovered that aspects of Jewish identity important to one community are often "Judaically irrelevant to the other"; whereas "symbols, stories, concepts, and allusions" that hold meaning for one community are "often understood differently, if at all, by the other." They hypothesized numerous reasons for the difference—America's Jews are a tiny minority; Israeli Jews constitute a majority; America's Jews are more Westernized; Israeli Jews have a higher percentage of the Orthodox. While they refrained from proclaiming two Judaisms because Judaism still rests in both communities upon "a common past," they understood that encountering modernity had produced "marked differences in how American and Israeli Jews have refashioned aspects of their religious life."[50]

Liebman and Cohen discovered that "personalism, voluntarism, moralism, and universalism" define American Jews' interaction with their tradition.[51] These attributes explain why Judaism as lived out in America is unique, and why its response to feminism—a topic they utterly ignored—is different. These characteristics explain the particularity of American Judaism and illuminate American Jews' embrace of feminism's agenda in the last quarter of the twentieth century. The emphases on personalism and voluntarism mean that, in America, Jews decide for themselves which religious traditions to observe. They volunteer to uphold rituals from the Jewish past, like lighting Chanukah candles,[52] even as they feel free to incorporate new vibrant concepts, especially those which they believe are ethically right, which constitute a universal good. Feminism, especially the liberal, egalitarian model trumpeted in the U.S. by second-wave feminists,[53] stands among these ethical charges and universal rights. Thus, American Jews have showed themselves willing to transform their synagogues to welcome women to the *bimah* and to embrace the baby naming ceremonies and the women's seder that have become hallmarks of American Judaism's encounters with feminism.

But Judaism, as lived out, in Israel is different. Liebman and Cohen observe:

> The idea of personal religious innovation, so common among American Jews, is underdeveloped and far less legitimate in Israel. Even though the majority of Israelis are non-Orthodox, they tend to regard Orthodox spokesmen as the most authoritative interpreters of Judaism....Even secular Israeli Jews believe that there is a proper, authoritative (that is, Jewishly legal) way to observe Jewish law and custom.[54]

The keys to the proper, authoritative, correct observance of Jewish law and custom lie within Judaism's sacred texts. Not surprisingly then, granting women access to those texts, especially to the Talmud, represents the most significant response of the Israeli encounter with the religious feminism first imported from America. In America, where Judaism is publicly expressed in the synagogue, the synagogue became the chief target of Jewish feminists. In Israel, where Judaism is publicly expressed in many venues, higher Jewish learning which would ultimately afford access to the Jewish legal system became the first target of religious feminists.

Those promoting women's higher Jewish learning in Israel have been extraordinarily careful not to couch this transformation as a revolution. In the United States from the beginning Jewish feminists proudly asserted their feminism, asking, as Orthodox feminist Blu Greenberg did, not only "What Judaism can learn from feminism?", but also "What can feminism learn from Judaism?"[55] But in Israel, even though a

> revolution is taking place . . . most of the orthodox community denies that it is a revolution. . . . Revolution is identified with the breakdown of tradition, and these women cherish and want to promote the tradition.[56]

Hence they do not speak of a feminist revolution. Rather they explain that their learning "enhances Jewish traditional values." It reveals women to be "deeply and sincerely religious." These women learn for its own sake (*Torah l'shmah*), and their learning is carefully integrated, as is that of their husbands, within the framework of their lives, within the context of their traditional families.[57]

Similarly, the new opportunities for women's halachic authority propelled forward by women's higher learning are never trumpeted as a great transformation. In America, those who championed women rabbis stated proudly that Sally Priesand's ordination heralded "women finally entering into, and helping to shape, the conversation of the Jewish people."[58] Those leading the way for female halachic advisors carefully explain that they neither "replac[e] rabbis nor do they aspire to be rabbis." They assert: "Women halachic consultants are an evolution, not a revolution," to be praised for enabling the proper functioning of Jewish law. Because modesty and self-consciousness prevent too many women from consulting with a rabbi on intimate questions of menstruation and conception, women decide such matters on their own; and that is "terribly wrong," a violation of *halacha*.[59] Thus training female halachic advisors upholds Jewish tradition, maintains *halacha*. The traditional form is kept, even as, from the perspective of the outside observer, a striking social and educational change has occurred.[60]

The result is that, in both the United States and Israel, feminism has unquestionably affected Judaism. But it has done so in ways unique to each setting. The divergent outcomes engendered by Judaism's encounters with feminism do not result from dissimilar conceptions of feminism. In both settings feminists embrace liberal feminism which asks for equal access to the tradition for women. Rather the feminist innovations accepted—in the United States the push for the egalitarian synagogue and ritual equality, in Israel the promotion of Orthodox women's higher learning—ripple out from "two worlds of Judaism," each uniquely marked by its encounter with modernity.[61] Just as American Jews and Israeli Jews understand modern Judaism differently, so too have they embraced different aspects of the feminist challenge to Judaism. Viewing contemporary Jewish life through the prism of its encounters with feminism thus affirms that America is indeed different.

NOTES

My thanks to Hebrew Union College Professor Wendy Zierler and Professor Rela Geffen for their comments on an earlier draft of this paper.

1. Paula E. Hyman, "The Other Half: Women in the Jewish Tradition," 1972; rpt. in *The Jewish Woman: New Perspectives*, ed. Elizabeth Koltun (New York, 1976), pp.105–113, 112.

2. Todd Gitlin, *The Sixties: Years of Hope, Days of Rage* (New York, 1987).

3. Nancy F. Cott, *The Grounding of Modern Feminism* (New Haven, 1987), quotations, pp.10, 282.

4. By 1990, three-quarters of Jewish women aged 25–44 and two-thirds of those aged 45–64 showed up in the labor force; Sidney Goldstein, "Profile of American Jewry: Insights from the 1990 National Jewish Population Survey," *American Jewish Year Book* vol. 92 (1992), pp.77–173, 115–16.

5. Anne Lapidus Lerner, "'Who Hast Not Made Me a Man': The Movement for Equal Rights for Women in American Jewry," *American Jewish Year Book 1977* vol. 77 (1976), pp.3–38.

6. "Jewish Women Call for Change, 1972," in *The American Jewish Woman: A Documentary History*, ed. Jacob Rader Marcus (New York, 1981), pp. 894–896, 896.

7. Shirley Frank, "Women--Writing the History of the Future," *Attah* (1973), pp. 4–5.

8. See, for example, Rachel Adler, "The Jew Who Wasn't There: Halakhah and the Jewish Woman," 1973; rpt. in *On Being a Jewish Feminist: A Reader*, ed. Susannah Heschel (New York, 1983), pp.12–18.

9. Jacqueline Levine, "The Changing Role of Women in the Jewish Community, 1972," in *The American Jewish Woman: A Documentary History*, ed. Jacob Rader Marcus (New York, 1981), pp. 902–07; Tamara Cohen, Jill Hammer, and Rona Shapiro, "Listen to Her Voice: The Ma'yan Report; Assessing the Experiences of Women in the Jewish Community and Their Relationship to Feminism," (New York, 2005).

10. At the 1973 National Jewish Women's Conference, Rachel Adler excited many, not only by wearing tallit (prayer shawl) and tefillin (phylacteries), but also by showing other women how to put them on; Rachel Adler, e-mail communication, 6 May 2005.

11. Irving Spiegel, "Conservative Jews Vote for Women in Minyan," *New York Times*, 1 September 1973, p. 1.

12. A few women became synagogue presidents before the second wave of feminism burst forth; Pamela S. Nadell, *Women Who Would Be Rabbis: A History of Women's Ordination, 1889–1985* (Boston, 1998), p. 129. As a result of Jewish feminism, by 2005, women becoming synagogues presidents were commonplace everywhere except among the Orthodox. On the first woman to head an Orthodox congregation in Washington, D.C., see Paula Amman, "Beth Sholom Breaks Ground: First Local Orthodox Shul to Elect Woman President," *Washington Jewish Week*, April 7 2005, p. 9.

13. Norma Baumel Joseph, "Ritual Law and Praxis: Bat Mitsva Celebrations," *Modern Judaism* vol. 22, no. 3 (2002), pp. 234–60.

14. Rochelle Furstenberg, "The Flourishing of Higher Jewish Learning for Women," in *Jerusalem Letter* (Jerusalem: Jerusalem Center for Public Affairs, 2000).

15. This is discussed in greater detail in Deborah E. Lipstadt, "Feminism and American Judaism: Looking Back at the Turn of the Century," in *Women and American Judaism: Historical Perspectives*, eds. Pamela S. Nadell and Jonathan D. Sarna (Hanover, NH: 2001), pp. 291–308.

16. *JOFA: Jewish Orthodox Feminist Alliance* [web page, accessed May 6, 2005]; www.jofa.org.

17. Debra Orenstein, *Lifecycles: Jewish Women on Life Passages and Personal Milestones*, vol. 1 (Woodstock, VT, 1998), p. 117. Orenstein lists an array of moments which Jewish men and women should honor in their lives. They include first love, first sexual experience, weaning, finding out the biopsy is negative, becoming a grandparent, cooking a grandmother's recipe, and "discovering Jewish feminism"; pp. 119–20.

18. Nadine Brozan, "Waiting List Grows as Seders for Women Increase in Popularity," *New York Times*, March 16, 1999, p. B5. There is no standard text for these *seders*. Reflecting the grassroots nature of this transformation, women in the synagogue and Jewish communal groups sponsoring the *seders* tend to write their own, borrowing and adapting from various texts that circulate privately.

19. Lenore Bohm, "The Feminist Theological Enterprise," *CCAR Journal* (Summer 1997), pp. 70–79.

20. Elyse Goldstein, "Rabbi Elyse Goldstein," in *Half the Kingdom: Seven Jewish Feminists*, ed. Francine Zuckerman (Montreal, 1992), pp. 71–88, 82–83.

21. For example, see Deborah R. Prinz, "Lilith: Lust and Lore," *CCAR Journal: "Wisdom You Are My Sister: Twenty-five Years of Women in the Rabbinate* (Summer 1997) pp. 62–69; Lynn Gottlieb, *She Who Dwells Within: A Feminist Vision of a Renewed Judaism* (New York, 1995), pp. 7–8; Elyse Goldstein, ed., *The Women's Torah Commentary: New Insights from Women Rabbis on the 54 Weekly Torah Portions* (Woodstock, VT., 2000).

22. For the new liturgies, see Chaim Stern, ed., *Gates of Prayer for Shabbat and Weekdays: A Gender Sensitive Prayerbook* (New York, 1994); *Kol Heneshamah*, (Wyncote, PA., 1994); Leonard S. Cahan, ed., *Siddur Sim Shalom for Shabbat and Festivals* (New York, 1998).

23. First published in 1997, Anita Diament's *The Red Tent* (New York) has gone through multiple reprintings and is available in more than twenty countries; http://www.jwa.org/this_week/week40.html.

24. Rachel Adler, *Engendering Judaism: An Inclusive Theology and Ethics* (Boston, 1998), 212. Her introduction surveys developments in feminist Jewish theology. The first, now classic work on this subject, is Judith Plaskow's *Standing Again at Sinai: Judaism from a Feminist Perspective* (San Francisco, 1990).

25. They are especially concerned with solving the plight of women chained by religious law to marriages that are no longer tenable; *JOFA: Jewish Orthodox Feminist Alliance*.

26. This history is detailed in Nadell, *Women Who Would Be Rabbis*. See also the film *And the Gates Opened: Women in the Rabbinate* (New York: Jewish Theological Seminary of America, 2005).

27. Reform rabbi Laura Geller acknowledges that "most of the systematic work in the area of Jewish feminist theology has been done by women scholars who are not themselves rabbis and that the same holds true for much of the most creative work in prayer and liturgy"; Laura Geller, "From Equality to Transformation: The Challenge of Women's Rabbinic Leadership," in *Gender and Judaism: The Transformation of Tradition*, ed. T.M. Rudavsky (New York, 1995), pp. 243–53, 245–46.

28. For statistics, see Lipstadt, "Women and American Judaism," p. 305, n. 2.

29. This is discussed more fully in my "Bridges to a Judaism Transformed by Women's Wisdom," ed., Prell, Riv-Ellen, *Women Remaking American Judaism* (Detroit, 2007).

30. This *Kallah* was held at the URJ Kutz Camp at Warwick, New York, for the New York campus of HUC-JIR in August 2004. The 1925 photo appears in Nadell, *Women Who Would Be Rabbis*.

31. Deborah Dash Moore, *To the Golden Cities: Pursuing the American Jewish Dream in Miami and L.A.* (New York, 1994), pp. 120–21.

32. Kalpana Misra, "Introduction," in *Jewish Feminism in Israel: Some Contemporary Perspectives*, ed. Kalpana Misra and Melanie S. Rich (Hanover, NH., 2003), pp. xiii–xix, xiii, xv.

33. See, for example, Natalie Rein, *Daughters of Rachel: Women in Israel* (New York, 1979); Lesley Hazelton, *Israeli Women: The Reality Behind the Myths* (New York, 1977); Barbara Swirski and Marilyn P. Safir, eds., *Calling the Equality Bluff: Women in Israel* (New York, 1991).

34. Barbara Swirski and Marilyn P. Safir, "Living in a Jewish State: National, Ethnic and Religious Implications," in *Calling the Equality Bluff: Women in Israel*, ed. Barbara Swirski and Marilyn P. Safir (New York, 1991), pp. 7–17, 12.

35. Lesley Hazelton, "Israeli Women: Three Myths," in *On Being a Jewish Feminist*, ed. Susannah Heschel (New York, 1983), p. 66.

36. Hazelton, *Israeli Women*.

37. Marcia Freedman, "Theorizing Israeli Feminism, 1970–2000," in *Jewish Feminism in Israel: Some Contemporary Perspectives*, ed. Kalpana Misra and Melanie S. Rich (Hanover, NH., 2003), pp. 1–16, 1–5.

38. Misra, "Introduction," pp. xvi.

39. Ruth Sinai, "Advocacy Groups Tell Us All Is Not Well with Women's Rights Here," *Haaretz* February 3, 2005. The full report appears at *Israel Women's Network* [web page, accessed May 26, 2005]; http://www.iwn.org.il/iwn.asp.

40. *Israel Women's Network.*

41. Ibid. Israel Women's Network, Report Submitted to the United Nations Commission on Women, (February 2005), p. 2.

42. Naomi Graetz, "Women and Religion in Israel," in *Jewish Feminism in Israel: Some Contemporary Perspectives*, ed. Kalpana Misra and Melanie S. Rich (Hanover, NH., 2003), pp. 17–56, 17–18.

43. Ibid., pp. 21, 25.

44. Furstenberg, "The Flourishing of Higher Jewish Learning for Women"; Haviva Ner-David, *Life on the Fringes: A Feminist Journey toward Traditional Rabbinic Ordination* (Needham, MA., 2000).

45. Norma Baumel Joseph, "Jewish Education for Women: Rabbi Moshe Feinstein's Map of America," *American Jewish History* vol. 83, no. 2 (1995), pp. 205–222.

46. The Jerusalem College for Women (Michlalah) was founded by an Irish-born immigrant and his Chicago-born wife.

47. Furstenberg, "The Flourishing of Higher Jewish Learning for Women."

48. Graetz, "Women and Religion in Israel," p.19.

49. Furstenberg, "The Flourishing of Higher Jewish Learning for Women," quotation, p. 5. Other indications of the American influence in Israeli feminism are the many American women who were the founders, in 1988, of the group which evolved into Women at the Wall, whose quest to pray with a Torah at the Western Wall incited violence and sparked an on-going legal battle; Phyllis Chesler and Rivka Haut, eds., *Women of the Wall: Claiming Sacred Ground of Judaism's Holy Site* (Woodstock, VT., 2003). Also, the first M.A. program in Jewish women's and gender studies in Israel opened at the Schechter Institute of Jewish Studies in 1994, which, of course, is affiliated with the American Conservative movement, and its director, Renee Levine-Melammed, also comes from the United States.

50. Charles S. Liebman and Steven. M Cohen, *Two Worlds of Judaism: The Israeli and American Experiences* (New Haven, 1990), pp. 2, 158–59.

51. Ibid., pp. 158–59.

52. In 2000, 75 percent of American Jews reported that they light Chanukah candles "all the time," and only 8 percent said they never lit them; American Jewish Committee, "2000 Annual Survey of American Jewish Opinion," (New York, 2000).

53. For a summary of the difference between liberal feminism and cultural feminism, see Paula Hyman, "Jewish Feminism Faces the American Women's Movement: Convergence and Divergence," in *American Jewish Women's History: A Reader*, ed. Pamela S. Nadell (New York, 2003), pp. 297–312, 305–06.

54. Liebman and Cohen, *Two Worlds of Judaism*, pp. 158–59.

55. Blu Greenberg, "Judaism and Feminism," in *The Jewish Woman: New Perspectives*, ed. Elizabeth Koltun (New York, 1976), pp. 179–92.

56. Furstenberg, "The Flourishing of Higher Jewish Learning for Women," p. 1.

57. Ibid.

58. Donna Berman, "Introduction," *CCAR Journal: "Wisdom You Are My Sister: Twenty-five Years of Women in the Rabbinate* (Summer 1997), pp. I–IV, I.

59. Chana Henkin, "Yoatzot Halachah: Fortifying Tradition through Innovation," *Jewish Action* 1999.

60. This echoes Sally Priesand's determination to uphold—not overturn—Jewish tradition by becoming a rabbi; Nadell, *Women Who Would Be Rabbis*, p. 155.

61. Michael Meyer locates Reform Judaism as one response to the encounter with modernity; Michael A. Meyer, *Response to Modernity: A History of the Reform Movement in Judaism* (New York, 1988).

7

Judaism and the Pluralist Dynamic

Peter L. Berger

It is rather rare that one is asked to take up a topic that one addressed twenty-five years ago. This is such an occasion. In December 1978 Rabbi Alexander Schindler, in a presidential address to the board of the Union of American Hebrew Congregations, proposed that Judaism should actively seek converts among religiously unaffiliated people of whatever ethnic background. There was quite a bit of debate about this at the time. I was invited to address the issue from a sociological point of view, which I did in an article published in *Commentary* in May 1979. Basically, I said that, while I could not speak to the normative issues raised by Schindler, I thought his proposal made sense sociologically in the context of American religious pluralism. I still think so, and for a moment I was tempted to save myself some work by resubmitting the old article with just a brief new preface. I rejected the temptation, because my understanding of pluralism has developed since (I hope, in a useful way). What follows here, then, is a new formulation, even if the conclusion remains pretty much the same.

Twenty-five years younger, I had more *chutzpah* in 1979 than I have now (after all, old age is supposed to lead to greater mellowness). But even then I found it necessary to make a reservation that I must repeat now: I can only address this topic as a sociologist—that is, as an attempt at analysis. I cannot offer prescriptions. If my analysis has merit, any ensuing prescriptions would have to come from within the Jewish community, not from an outsider such as myself.

Just what is the "pluralist dynamic?" The term "pluralism," as far as I know, was popularized (if not coined) in the 1920's by Horace Kallen. As the suffix indicates, it was intended to refer to a moral position—one that

105

celebrates the racial, ethnic, and religious plurality of America. But the term has increasingly been used in a simply descriptive sense—that is, as referring to the empirical fact of such plurality, in America or anywhere else, regardless of whether one celebrates it or not. It is in this sense that I am using the term here: Pluralism means the co-existence of diverse human groups in one society in a state of civic peace. *Religious* pluralism is a particular instance of this phenomenon, and it is this that concerns us here.

Religious pluralism has an institutional dimension, in the relation of religious groups to each other and to the state. It also has a cognitive dimension, within the consciousness of individuals. This we will look at in a moment. But, clearly, the institutional dimension by itself has far-reaching implications. It means, first of all, that every religious group must give up the claim to have a societal monopoly guaranteed by the state. In other words, there must be at least a degree of religious freedom. Such a state of affairs is commonly associated with democracy, which is almost certainly a mistake. To be sure, religious freedom is usually one of the rights established in a democratic regime—as, for example, in the bill of rights that Thomas Jefferson was instrumental in passing through the legislature of colonial Virginia. However, in many countries religious freedom (usually within certain limits) was inaugurated by the autocratic rulers of the *ancien regime*—as, for example, by Joseph II of Austria, or Frederick the Great of Prussia—or, for that matter, by the Moghul Emperor Akbar. There was a high degree of religious freedom in the late Roman Empire—where, as Edward Gibbon observed, the people believed that all religions were equally true, the philosophers that all religions were equally false, and the magistrates that all religions were equally useful.

Put simply: Religious freedom means that religious institutions can no longer rely on the state to usher people into their sanctuaries. This changes the relation of these institutions to their constituencies. Increasingly, persuasion must take the place of coercion. Also, increasingly, religious institutions find themselves in competition with each other, as individuals are free to abandon or even change their affiliation. The result is the emergence of a market of religious options, and religious institutions have to accommodate themselves to this situation, even if their normative self-understanding resists such accommodation. The modern history of the Roman Catholic Church is a paradigmatic case of this.

The relation of religious institutions to each other also changes as a result. In order to preserve the civic peace, they must develop rules of amicable engagement (whether explicitly or implicitly). This may involve public assurances of mutual respect, the establishment of joint agencies for this or that common good, or agreements to refrain from poaching on one another's demographic bases. A nice example of the last of these amicable gestures is what, in an earlier period of American Protestantism, used to be called "comity." This referred to formal agreements between mainline churches to refrain from actively trying to recruit each other's members. Implicitly, this then came to include Catholics. And in the 1940's Reinhold Niebuhr created a stir by arguing that Christian churches should not try to convert Jews. In America today, with the notable exception of a large segment of Evangelical Protestantism, "comity" has now come to include just about any religious group that does not engage in blatantly illegal conduct.

Some of this is perhaps obvious. Less obvious is the cognitive effect of pluralism, within the consciousness of individuals. This can be summed up in a simple proposition: Religion increasingly loses its taken-for-granted status in consciousness. Put differently: Religious certainty becomes harder to obtain. The reason for this is deeply rooted in human psychology. Human beings are intrinsically social and their definitions of reality are significantly influenced by their social milieu. There is ample evidence from social psychology that individuals feel certain in their beliefs (religious or other) to the degree that there is consensus about these in their milieu. *Pluralism disrupts such a consensus.* As people with different beliefs intrude into the milieu in which other beliefs were previously taken for granted, this taken-for-granted quality is weakened. Within consciousness, beliefs "percolate" up from the "deep" level of supposedly self-evident certainty to more "superficial" levels of choice, which may range from easily changed opinions to desperate acts of faith (Kierkegaard's famous "leap") to fanatical reaffirmation of what had previously been a relaxed worldview (about as good a description of fundamentalism as one can give).

Before developing this further, one additional observation: This cognitive aspect of pluralism is obviously enhanced under the conditions of religious freedom. But the pluralist dynamic begins to have the afore-mentioned cognitive effects even in the absence of religious freedom. The social presence of "others," with whom one is forced to interact within one's milieu, acts to undermine the old certainties even if the state seeks to uphold the old religious monopoly. Of course the state, conspiring with the traditional monopolistic institution, can use force to prevent the 'others" from doing their subversive job. Under modern conditions, with mass communications and mass movements of people, this is quite difficult. The disintegration of the Catholic monopoly in Spain in the waning years of the Franco regime is a good example of this.

I understood the cognitive dimension of pluralism early on in my work in the sociology of religion. At the time, though, I made an important mistake: I thought that, because of this cognitive dynamic, pluralism fostered secularization—that is, the decline of religion. And since pluralism, for very understandable reasons, is enormously enhanced by modern conditions, I further thought that modernization necessarily leads to secularization. Under the pressure of empirical data, I gradually changed my mind about this linkage (just about the time that I responded to Schindler's proposal): It turns out that the modern world, with some notable exceptions that need not concern us here, is far from being secularized, indeed is full of very powerful religious explosions. Pluralism indeed undermines taken-for-grantedness and confronts the individual with many choices. *But among these choices are religious ones.*

I would now describe the impact of pluralism on religion as follows: It affects *how* one believes, but not necessarily *what* one believes. For example, a modern Catholic may affirm in perfectly good faith all the creedal positions of his tradition, but he will have *chosen* to do so; by contrast, the same propositions were assumed to be self-evidently true in his ancestral village, requiring no acts of choice by an individual (though, of course, there always were more fervent and less fervent Catholics—but that is another matter). Put differently, the pluralist situation *internalizes the market* that has been established in the sphere of religious institutions. The American phrase "religious preference" beautifully describes this situation.

The Catholic Church insists on assent to specific doctrinal formulations. Adherents of traditions that emphasize practice rather than doctrine, such as Hinduism and indeed Judaism, might be seen as relatively immune to the cognitive development just described. I think that is not so: Practice also requires a cognitive frame of reference within which it makes sense. If only because every cohort of children will ask *why* one should observe caste purity or a dietary code, the explanation will have to operate with specific cognitive propositions. These propositions may or may not be taken for granted, and socialization into a religious tradition will differ significantly in the two cases.

Religious pluralism has occurred in different periods of history, in different places—as already mentioned, in the Hellenistic world and in Moghul India, but also in Confucian China, along the Silk Road, in Sicily under the Hohenstaufens. But modernity has brought about an enormous increase in both the scope and the acceleration of pluralism in most of the contemporary world. America, for easily understood historical reasons, has been in the vanguard of this development. To use a phrase of Talcott Parsons, America has been the "lead society" of religious pluralism. The old Protestant "comity" has been steadily expanding. In 1955 Will Herberg published his very insightful book *Protestant—Catholic—Jew.* About the same time the phrase "Judeao-Christian civilization" came into common usage. Since then there has been further expansion of this "comity," to the point where Diana Eck, with only a little exaggeration, could say that America is the most religiously diverse society in the world.

Max Weber made the classical distinction between two forms of religious institutions—the church, into which one is born, and the sect, which one joins. Richard Niebuhr, in his 1929 book *The Social Sources of Denomination-*

alism, added a third form, a distinctly American innovation—the denomination, which he defined as a church that accepts the legitimacy, *de facto* if not necessarily *de jure*, of other churches. These typologies can be criticized (for one thing, they are hard to apply outside Christianity), but they point to an important empirical fact: Religious institutions become denominations insofar as they are constituted of the voluntary association of their adherents. I think it was American Catholics who coined the term "Protestantization" to describe recent developments in their church. The term is apt, but it primarily refers not to this or that theological influence, but rather to the social form taken by the church as a result of pluralism—precisely as, *de facto*, a voluntary association competing with others in a religious marketplace. I don't want to insult the English language by proposing, instead, the term "denominationalization." Still, in America, every religious institution, sooner or later, and willy-nilly, becomes a denomination.

Let me sum up these general considerations: Modernization does indeed foster pluralism, which has accordingly become a global phenomenon. This need not go together with secularization. What it does bring about is a huge shift in human experience—*from fate to choice*. This affects all areas of life, behavior as well as consciousness. The consumer must choose between a vast array of competing goods and services, the citizen between competing political scenarios. And modernity in general confronts every individual with a multitude of choices between career patterns, biographical trajectories, life-styles, belief systems and even identities. Freud could say that biology is destiny. He did not see sex transformed into gender—a biological term mutating into a grammatical term—the former grounded in ontology, the latter obviously artificial. Perhaps it denotes a certain climax in this movement from fate to choice that we can now speak of "sexual preferences." It should not be surprising that this transformation of the life-world of human individuals affects religion as well.

After all this, it is high time for me to get to Judaism. And there is a distinctive Jewish aspect to the pluralist dynamic that I have tried to describe (all too briefly, alas). It comes from the combination of religion and ethnicity: Judaism understands itself as the religion *of a people*. More or less by definition, peoplehood is a matter of fact, not choice. In terms of Halachah, a Jew is a child of a Jewish mother: One does not choose one's mother! And while the concept of the Covenant as an engagement of God with his particular people goes back to the earliest traditions of the Hebrew Bible, Jewish identity was indeed a matter of fate rather than choice through most of history. A notable exception was the Hellenistic period, when Judaism attracted converts from a significant number of people who were *not* born of a Jewish mother. But even the converts were perceived as being, so to speak, "naturalized" into the Jewish people (I suppose the Book of Ruth provided the paradigm for this perception). In any case, the episode of proselyting Judaism came to an end as Jews had to exist—whether tolerated or oppressed—in societies defined in terms of Christianity and, later, of Islam. Once again, in empirical fact, Jewish identity was a matter of fate.

The eastern European *shtetl* is frequently perceived in antithesis to the Jewish situation in contemporary America, and with good reason. In, say, the Russian Pale of Settlement there was nothing chosen about being a Jew. To be sure, most of the time this was not a particularly pleasant identity—"hard to be a Jew" as the Yiddish saying had it. All the same, both the ethnic and religious identity of Jews was taken for granted. It was fated. Conversion to the dominant religion was one possible avenue of escape from this fate. There were powerful pressures against such apostasy within the Jewish community, and few individuals chose to go that way. But for them even escape from their Jewish fate was far from complete: Russian anti-Semitism was ethnic as well as religious, and the convert to Christianity was viewed with suspicion and hardly welcomed with open arms. *Mutatis mutandis*, a similar situation prevailed in western Christendom. The melancholy story of the *conversos* in Spain and Portugal may be cited as an example.

The coming of assimilation in western and central Europe changed this situation to a considerable degree—a development, with its horrendous *denouement* in the Holocaust, which we cannot pursue here. But the history of Jewish immigration from Eastern Europe to America took a happily different course. For a while, in areas of dense Jewish settlement, as on the Lower East Side of New York, the *shtetl* was, as it were, transported. I would think that first-generation immigrants in such localities, enveloped in a massively Jewish milieu, also experienced their Jewish identity as fated, though that fate was certainly less oppressive than it had been in the old country. But this type of transported *shtetl* did not last. And as Jews moved into the mainstream of American life they found themselves increasingly in a very different situation.

What happened now, of course, is that Jews found themselves immersed in an exuberant pluralism, experienced empirically as a fact of existence, but also legitimated by the American political ideology of freedom and rights. This situation has put the traditional taken-for-granted identity under considerable pressure. Disturbingly, Jewish identity has indeed become a matter of choice. Needless to say, this choice is not absolute. It is constrained by strong ties of family and friendship, by deeply ingrained feelings of loyalty, and reinforced by the synagogue and other Jewish institutions. Individual conversions to other religions have continued to be relatively sparse, except for those motivated by marriage to non-Jewish spouses. But there has been the much less dramatic choice of simply de-emphasizing Jewish identity in the individual's behavior and consciousness, revealingly expressed in the typical American phrase "I happen to be Jewish." Coupled with a low Jewish birthrate (a function of class rather than ethnicity), all of this has led to a demographic hemorrhage that has understandably alarmed Jewish sociologists.

Theoretically, there are two major possibilities of restoring a challenged taken-for-grantedness—one society-wide, the other sub-cultural (that is, by constructing enclaves within society). In the case of Jewish identity, the former is only possible in Israel. While that society has identity problems of its own, being Jewish still has a self-evident quality which it lacks anywhere else. American Jews, of course, have the option of making *aliyah*, and those who how have done so frequently express their satisfaction with a situation in which their Jewish identity is unproblematic in a way it was not in America. For the great majority of American Jews who stay put there is the possibility of an intense identification with Israel, which naturally has become a focus of Jewish identity. The fact remains that they are *here*, not *there*. The identification with Israel is itself a choice, not to be taken for granted. It must be reinforced by Zionist institutions of one kind or another, and it is not irreversible. Dissatisfaction with various aspects of Israeli reality has weakened the identification with Israel for some American Jews. In any case, identification with Israel is a vulnerable project for restoring taken-for-granted Jewish identity in America.

Obviously, the sub-cultural possibility is more plausible in America. The project here is to create a milieu in *America* that will be so strong as to make Jewish identity taken for granted again. This is clearly the aim of many Jewish institutions, some religious, some not. I have no doubt that for many individuals the aim is realized, as it has with other sub-cultural constructions in America. The largely successful project, before the Second Vatican Council, to create a Catholic sub-culture in America is a prime example; its rapid collapse in recent decades may also serve as a *caveat*. Erecting sub-cultural barriers against the pluralistic turbulence of American society is a difficult undertaking.

There still exist more or less intact "transported *shtetls*," famously in the Williamsburg and Boro Park sections of Brooklyn. I can imagine that someone growing up in one of these enclaves can still inhabit an intact, taken-for-granted world of Jewishness. By now there is copious literature on this world, popularized in the novels of the late Chaim Potok. The same literature, however, also indicates the fragility of this world. Pluralistic America beats against its barriers all the time, and it provides an ongoing temptation. I further imagine that even the most fully socialized individual in these communities knows that, at any time, there is a simple choice of escape: All that he, or she, has to do is take a subway and move to Manhattan!

Throughout history the strongest factor making Jewish identity as fate has been anti-Semitism. It is thus not surprising that anti-Semitism as a perennial threat is frequently cited as a reason for holding on to Jewish identity. The memorialization of the Holocaust has been important in this context.

In no way do I want to be critical of this memorialization: The Holocaust is the most horrific crime in the history of western civilization and its memory must never be allowed to be pushed aside. Nevertheless, as a focus of Jewish identity *in America* it is problematic. There is, for one, a problem in asking young people born decades after it to anchor their identity in an event of unspeakable horror. More importantly, though, there is the empirical fact that anti-Semitism in America has been steadily waning over the last fifty years. Could this happy development be reversed? Of course it could. But so could every good thing in our experience. It is difficult to base an identity on a future threat that is at present un-experienced (I am speaking, of course, about America. One may be less sanguine about the situation in Europe, not to mention the Muslim world).

I cannot refrain from telling an anecdote here. Some years ago I was on a panel with a prominent American rabbi. I have forgotten the topic of discussion, but I do remember one exchange. At one point the rabbi said he is telling his children that the Holocaust could return, even in America. He then turned to me and asked, "Do you think I am paranoid?" I replied that, on the contrary, he was not paranoid enough: He could only imagine that violent hatred would be turned on him because he was Jewish. But, given the right circumstances, he could be violently hated for being white, bourgeois, American, or for that matter a heterosexual male. I don't remember what he replied.

If the preceding observations have merit, the most plausible grounding of Jewish identity in contemporary America would be religious—that is, with Judaism as a living religious tradition being the focus. But such an identity could be based in two different institutional forms. It could be maintained within an essentially sectarian institution—that is, a sub-culture that is turned inward, that avoids interaction with the wider society, and that imposes a rigorous discipline on its members. Alternatively, religious identity can be maintained in the typically American institutional form of the denomination—open to outside society, in dialogue with the latter, and tolerant of considerable variety within it. Both possibilities have inherent problems. The sectarian institution is under constant pressure from the outside, its defensive barriers must be kept in good repair, and the social life of its members must be kept under control. This requires a great deal of effort, and the slightest breach in this social and cognitive Maginot Line risks a floodtide of outside cultural influences rushing in, at which point the sectarian project threatens to collapse. Again, the post-Vatican-II history of the Catholic sub-culture may serve as a good example. The denomination, on the other hand, risks a steady erosion, a relativization, of its tradition as it engages in dialogue with everybody and everything around it. The relativization is nicely caught in a joke that somewhat violates the etiquette of ecumenical discourse: How does the Unitarian version of the

Lord's Prayer begin?—"To Whom it May Concern."—When the tradition has been thus eroded a point is reached where it loses, as it were, its market niche—in other words, whatever appeal it may have originally had. The prime example of such a development is mainline Protestantism. It remains to be seen to what extent Evangelical Protestantism will follow the same trajectory; at present, different elements within it straddle the sectarian/denominational divide.

Back to Schindler's proposal of a missionary Judaism: What he had in mind, of course, was a denominational model. He did not envisage a Jewish equivalent of aggressive Christian evangelism; he observed the rules of "comity" by designating only religiously unaffiliated Gentiles as fair game for the Jewish outreach. In any case, Judaism here would fully enter the competitive religious market created by American pluralism. Schindler expressed confidence that such a self-confident Judaism would prove attractive to many people looking for spiritual meaning and sustenance in their lives. It is not for me to say whether the stance proposed by Schindler is acceptable in terms of normative Judaism. But I can say that, *sociologically*, his proposal makes sense.

There is an interesting social-psychological dimension to this issue. Any community facing the exodus of substantial numbers of its members must ask the question, "How can I keep my children inside?" The pluralist dynamic, however, leads to a situation in which the line between insiders and outsiders is blurred. This means that one must use similar language in addressing either group. The child, who no longer takes adherence to the community for granted, must be targeted by the same missionary enterprise. Some years ago I met a Sufi poet. He showed me a poem he had written about the boundary that, in traditional Muslim thought, divides the Realm of Islam from the Realm of Unbelief. The last line of the poem read, "Today this boundary runs through the soul of every Muslim." *Mutatis mutandis*, the same can be said of every other religion in the modern pluralist situation.

8

From Treifene Medina to Goldene Medina: Changing Perspectives on the United States among American Haredim

Chaim I. Waxman

Contrary to the impression conveyed by many, including Moshe Davis and Marshall Sklare, American Orthodox rabbis were not monolithic. As Jeffrey Gurock has demonstrated, there were among them what he appropriately labels "resisters and accommodators."[1] As he portrays it, the Orthodox rabbis who were immigrants from Eastern European were more resistant to American society and culture, while their colleagues who were American or immigrants from Central Europe were more accommodating to American society and culture.

The popular perception of the Orthodox as resisters, if not rejectionists, probably derives from statements by or attributed to not more than a handful of American Orthodox rabbis at the end of the nineteenth and beginning of the twentieth centuries. The best known among these were Rabbis Moses Weinberger and David Wilowsky but, even with them, the pictures are not as clear as they are often portrayed. Weinberger (1854–1940) immigrated from Hungary in 1880, sought to be a rabbi in New York City but was unsuccessful. Although he became a businessman to make a livelihood, he remained close to the rabbinic field and frequently practiced it unofficially. In 1887, he wrote a pamphlet, *Jews and Judaism in New York* which, fortunately, has been meticulously translated and edited by Jonathan Sarna, under the title *People Walk on Their Heads*.[2] This work is a broad, stinging critique of the condition of traditional Judaism in New York. However, although Weinberger did discourage some of his fellow scholars in Eastern Europe from migrating to the United States, he did not say that it was forbidden to migrate, nor did he issue any broad opinions about the wisdom of migrating. He did warn those who would have anticipated becoming rabbis in the United States that the chances of successfully fulfilling their rabbinic aspirations were poor to nil and they might be better off remaining in Europe. Although he was not optimistic about the prospects of any significant improvement in the Jewish condition, he was not despondent. He remained convinced that the path to improvement lay in the establishment of yeshivas and the development a strong rabbinate.

Rabbi Jacob David Wilowsky (1845–1913) was an outstanding Talmudic scholar who was community rabbi and the founder of a prominent yeshiva in Slutsk, Belarus. He was the author of several commentaries on the Jerusalem Talmud and was known as "The Ridvaz," an acronym for his Hebrew name. He first arrived in the United States to raise money to complete his works on the Jerusalem Talmud. During his less than a half-year visit, he addressed a meeting of the Union of Orthodox Congregations, in New York City, and was quoted as having condemned anyone who came to America, "for here, Judaism . . . is trodden under foot. It was not only home that the Jews left behind them in Europe; it was their Torah, their Talmud, their Yeshebahs (sic), their Chocomim (sic)."[3]

Be that as it may, shortly thereafter, Wilowsky himself immigrated to the United States and, at a rabbinical convention in Philadelphia, was recognized as the *"Zekan Harabanim,"* the Elder Rabbi in the United States. He served as rabbi for one year, in Chicago, but then became disillusioned and, in 1905, left for Safed, in the Holy Land, where he remained for the rest of his life.[4] Despite his own brief stay and emigration, Wilowsky was not fatalistic about the future of Judaism in the United States. As Weinberger, he was highly critical of the condition of Judaism in the United States. However, as he indicated in the Introduction to his commentary on the Torah, he saw the Jewish sojourn and experience in the United States as having ultimate religious significance, as per the Midrash he quotes at his opening. He concludes his Introduction by exhorting his readers to establish yeshivas for the children of this and future generations. This is hardly the advice of an individual who believes that Judaism is doomed in the United States.

In fact, there were hardly any rabbis in the United States who actually believed that it was a *"treifene medina"* and that there was no future for Judaism here. To the extent that there were such views, they were those of rabbis and the traditional masses in Eastern Europe. Interestingly, however, even in Eastern Europe, it was more often the perspective of the secular Zionist than of the Orthodox rabbi. While many East European Orthodox were wary of emigration to he United States and some may have actually banned it outright, there were prominent individuals among them who were less wary, if not actually proponents of such emigration. Perhaps the most outstanding such individual was Rabbi Chaim Soloveitchik (1853–1918) who said,

> I know that the conditions [in America] are defective, but there is a greater possibility there, complete freedom, which is absent in Russia, and if diligent people arrive there, they can correct a great deal; and I am perplexed, how is it possible for our rabbis and leaders to remain in their places and to see how holiness is destroyed among millions of Jews . . . If we wish to fulfill our obligations, the obligation of the hour, we should go to America to improve Judaism there and to build a secure haven there for our people and out Torah, until we return to Zion.[5]

Returning to *American* Orthodox rabbis, there clearly was hostility among many of them to American culture, especially its individualism and secularism. Some, such as Weinberger, even went so far as to criticize the Constitutional notion of separation of religion and state. But criticisms such as these were not unique to Orthodox rabbis. As Kimmy Caplan points out,[6] some Reform rabbis were likewise critical. Nor did one have to be Jewish to be so critical. Both Protestantism and Catholicism had their versions of "Resisters" and "Adaptationists." In Protestantism, there were and are the "Fundamentalists" and "Modernists," and in Catholicism there were the conservatives and the "Americanists." These were the religious reactions to what Peter Berger saw as the consequences of modernity, especially religious demonopolization and pluralization. As he put it, "The pluralistic situation presents the religious institutions with two ideal-typical options. They can either accommodate themselves to the situation, play the pluralistic game of religious free enterprise, and come to terms as best they can with the plausibility problem by modifying their product in accordance with consumer demands. Or they can refuse to accommodate themselves, entrench themselves behind whatever socio-religious structures they can maintain or construct, and continue to profess the old objectivities as much as possible as if nothing had happened. Obviously there are various intermediate possibilities between these two ideal-typical options, with varying degrees of accommodation and intransigence."[7]

During the second half of the twentieth century American Orthodox Judaism was increasingly divided into two major categories, the "Modern Orthodox" and the "Ultra-Orthodox," or "Haredim." Again, these are the current versions of those two ideal-typical options, though today they have developed more elaborate and sophisticated ideologies legitimating their respective stances. Essentially, they represent two different perspectives on the larger society and culture. In brief, one sees everything as clear, black and white, we and they, good and evil; the other sees complexity, dilemmas, tensions, and inner struggles. One hears a call to engage the larger society and world; the other views a need to seal oneself off from contamination by the larger society and world. One adheres to a staunch conservative socio-political ideology which views the nature of humans as inherently evil, while the other holds out hope for the ability of humans to improve themselves and the world. The foremost philosopher of Modern Orthodoxy in the twentieth century was the late Rabbi Dr. Joseph B. Soloveitchik, who lived in and identified with Boston from the early 1930s until his death in 1993.[8]

Though there has been little change in the stance of the "Resisters" toward modern non-material culture, there was a distinct shift in their stance toward separation of religion and state during the twentieth century. As mentioned previously, early on, Moses Weinberger and others viewed many of the problems in American society and culture as rooted in the freedoms established in the Constitution, especially the separation of religion and state. A number of developments during the first half of the twentieth century contributed to a change in that stance. Perhaps the most glaring manifestation of the change in stance is in a *derasha*, sermon, delivered by Rabbi Moshe Feinstein, in February 1939, in commemoration of the 150th anniversary of the United States Constitution. Rabbi Feinstein (1895–1986) was born in Starobin, Belarus, where his father was Rabbi. In 1921, he became Rabbi of Luban, where he served until his emigration to the United States, in 1937, where he headed a yeshiva in New York and became a leading authority of Jewish religious law, Halakha, within Orthodox circles. In the conclusion to his 1939 sermon he said:

> And so, the government of the United States, which already 150 years ago established its law that it will not uphold or favor any faith but will allow everyone to do as they see fit, and the government will serve only to assure that no one harms another, they are thus following the will of Almighty God, and they therefore succeeded and grew during this time. And we are obligated to pray for them that Almighty God shall have them succeed in wherever they undertake . . .[9]

Rabbi Feinstein's public lauding of the practice and principle of separation of religion and state did not indicate his support of the adaptationist perspective and certainly was not an endorsement of secularism. Rather, it was an expression of support for the notion of religious freedom, that is, religious demonopolization. This is clear in much of his public activity as well as in his responsa. For example, in his major collection of responsa, there is a discussion of the permissibility of the Jewish and non-Jewish public school children participating in a common non-denominational prayer service in school, and Rabbi Feinstein supported it. This is not the place to discuss the details of that responsum but in it, he emphasizes the non-denominational character of the prayer and says that "the governors of our land are generous people and do not wish to impose their belief on other citizens and they therefore wrote this prayer which is obvious that it was instituted so that each person can have his own religion in mind."[10]

Rabbi Feinstein's approval of non-denominational prayer in public schools essentially gave support to the efforts of the Lubavitch hasidim who had long spearheaded the released time program which allowed for prayer in public schools.[11] The Lubavitch Rebbe staunchly supported prayer not only for Jewish children but for Christians as well, in the firm belief that traditional Judaism wants Christians to be religious, so long as Jews are free to offer their own prayers and are not proselytized. Rabbi Feinstein averred in his responsum that non-Jews obviously perform a *mitzvah*, a religious act, when they pray, "otherwise, what praise is it that it will be called a house of prayer for all nations, if non Jews don't have a mitzvah when they pray."[12]

The sources behind the change in the stance of the "Resisters" toward separation of religion and stance were both internal American and external. Externally, the deterioration of the conditions for Jews in Europe and, especially, the rise of Hitler and Nazism and the hope that the United States would be a haven for refugees probably toned down, if not stifled any public criticism of the American government. Moreover, with the shifting of the larger American culture from anglo-conformity to increased tolerance, if not actual cultural pluralism, the Orthodox began to take a more favorable stance to American society. They came to perceive possibilities of recreating their subculture on American soil and they began by doing precisely what Weinberger and Wilowsky had called for at the turn of the century. Among the refugee arrivals were a number of Orthodox leaders who had been heads of advanced rabbinical seminaries, *yeshivot gedolot*, in Eastern Europe and almost immediately upon their arrival in the United States, they set about to reconstruct those yeshivas on American soil. Such leaders as Rabbi Aaron Kotler, Rabbi Abraham Kalmanowitz, and Rabbis Eliyahu Meir Bloch and Mordechai Katz reestablished their advanced yeshivas and their conceptions of Orthodoxy in Lakewood, Brooklyn, Cleveland, and elsewhere, in the Eastern European mold. These institutions then spawned a generation of knowledgeable and ideologically committed Orthodox Jews, many of whom were to subsequently establish other advanced yeshivas in dozens of American cities.

As a first step, the National Society for Hebrew Day Schools, Torah Umesorah, was founded in 1944 by Rabbi Shraga Feivel Mendelowitz, with the objective of encouraging and assisting in the founding of Jewish day schools-elementary and high schools that would provide intensive Jewish education along with a quality secular curriculum-in cities and neighborhoods across the country. The number of day schools grew tenfold and enrollments grew almost as much between the years 1940 and 1965, and the rate of growth accelerated between then and 1975. These day schools and yeshiva high schools were located not only in the New York metropolitan area, but in 33 states across the country. By 1975, every city in the United States with a Jewish population of 7,500 had at least one day school, as did four out of five of the cities with a Jewish population of between 5,000 and 7,500. Among cities with smaller Jewish populations, one out of four with population of 1,000 Jews had a Jewish day school.[13]

It should be emphasized that instituting this type of day school was in itself an adaptation to modernity, although this case may not quite be a support for Alan Wolfe's thesis of the impact of American culture on American religion.[14] Be that as it may, many of the very same rabbinic leaders who spirited the day school movement, had previously been adamantly opposed to this type of school, which combined both sacred and secular education. With the efforts of the leadership of the new immigration, there was a virtual boom in the growth of the day school movement from World War II to the mid-1970s. Since then, day schools have become recognized as valued institutions within Conservative and Reform Judaism as well, and by the 1990s, non-Orthodox day schools were the fastest growing phenomenon in the American Jewish community.[15]

Among the WWII refugees were also many members and some leaders of Hasidic sects, such as Belz, Bobov, Chernobyl, Lisk, Munkatch, Novominsk, Satmar, Skver, Stolin, Talin, Trisk, and Zanz, to name some of the more prominent ones. The Hasidim, perhaps even more than others, were determined to retain their traditional way of life even within the modern metropolis and they were largely successful in achieving that goal.[16]

By the 1970s, there emerged a "Haredization of American Orthodox Jewry," that is, American Orthodox Jewry became more punctilious in its ritual observance and it turned inward, in the sense of decreasing cooperation with the Conservative and Reform branches, as was documented and analyzed by Samuel Freedman.[17] Two important societal developments emerged during the late-1970s and 1980s to significantly affect the character of American Orthodoxy. The first was a socio-cultural development in the United States as a whole and, as almost everywhere else, the patterns of Jews are, in part, reflections of what happens in the larger society and culture This was pointed out by the German apostate and poet, Heinrich Heine (1797–1856), when he said, *"Wie es sich christelt, so judelt es sich"* ("As Christianity goes, so goes Judaism"), which is actually a variation of a similar statement asserted centuries earlier Rabbi Yehuda Hehasid (c. 1150–1217), in his well-known work, *Sefer Hahasidim*: "It is known that as is the Gentile custom in most places so is the Jewish custom."[18] With respect to the "turn to the right" in American Orthodoxy, it was, in large measure, a reflection of the broader turn to the right and rise of fundamentalism in a variety of different countries and continents. If, in mid-century United States, secularization appeared to be the wave of the future, an inevitable consequence of modernity—so much so that sociologist Peter

Berger predicted that by the year 2000, "religious believers are likely to be found only in small sects, huddled together to resist a worldwide secular culture"[19]—by the 1980s, Berger recanted and by the closing decades of the century he averred that the world today "is as furiously religious as it ever was."[20] Much of the tone and character of both the baseball pennant race and, especially, the presidential election campaigns, in 2004, were highly infused with religious terminology as well as religion itself. Moreover, "On the international religious scene, it is conservative or orthodox or traditionalist movements that are on the rise almost everywhere."[21] The forces of moderation have widely been replaced by fundamentalism and it has become fashionable to reject the culture—although not the technology—of modernity in favor of "strong religion."[22] It should, therefore, be no surprise that American Orthodoxy moved to the right; it was reflecting a pattern in the larger society and culture and, as it did so, it felt increasingly closer to those on the right of Protestantism and Catholicism than it did the modernist within in own fold. This was a product of the emergence of what James Davison Hunter calls "culture wars" in the United States, and the shifting of the significant boundaries from the vertical, separating religions, to the horizontal, separating the conservatives from the modernists.[23]

By the turn of the twentieth century, however, while turning inward institutionally, haredi Orthodoxy in America began to manifest newer, more open patterns interpersonally. For example, whereas in mid-century religious outreach was the province of the Modern Orthodox, with the haredim being somewhat suspicious of *ba'alei teshuva*, the newly-religious,[24] by the end of the century the haredim were heavily engaged in religious outreach, in the National Jewish Outreach Program (NJOP), the Association for Jewish Outreach Programs (AJOP), with which hundreds of Orthodox outreach organizations are affiliated, and in the Orthodox Union's National Conference of Synagogue Youth (NCSY), among others.[25] Ironically, the Modern Orthodox who pioneered religious outreach turned inward and, institutionally, are hardly engaged in such activity. For the most part, the Modern Orthodox have become defensive and are much more likely to engage in intellectual discussions among themselves rather than actively reaching out beyond their borders. Likewise, as Adam Ferziger has demonstrated, the Modern Orthodox rabbinical seminaries have turned more inward and emphasize Halakhic expertise, while the more right-wing institutions have programs which train rabbis in religious outreach.[26]

To some extent, this also reflects the modernity of the Modern Orthodox. Their very modernity means that they are less likely to be affiliated and actively involved with communal organizations. This is a phenomenon characteristic of the larger American society and culture, and not unique to the Modern Orthodox. The political scientist Robert Putnam amassed considerable data indicating that Americans were, at least until 9/11, increasingly detached from social groups such as community, were increasingly less likely to join parent-teachers associations, unions, political parties, as well as host of other social groups.[27] Although there is recent evidence of Modern Orthodox strength and institution-building,[28] it still appears that the focus is on intellectual discussion among peers rather than active engagement and involvement with the broader population of America's Jews as well as the larger American public.

The haredim, on the other hand, moved precisely in the direction of outward involvement. Thus, Agudath Israel, for example, became very active in the public sphere during the second half of the twentieth century. It has a full-time office in Washington, D.C., as well as others across the United States, and actively lobbies all branches of federal, state and local government on issues that it views as having Jewish interest. Its public relations specialist frequently writes columns in Jewish newspapers across the country and internationally, expressing the Aguda perspective on broad issues of Jewish interest. Indications are that the haredim are increasingly attached to the larger society and view living their Orthodox lifestyle as a right within the larger society rather than as set apart from it. One possible indication of their emotional attachments to the larger society may be reflected in the widespread display of American flags on homes and businesses in heavily Orthodox neighborhoods following the World Trade Center disaster of September 11, 2001. Though inconclusive in and of itself, the additional fact that the national office of Agudath Israel sent out strongly-worded letters imploring its members to contribute to the fund for families of firefighters and police victims of the disaster appears to indicate a deep sense of identification with the tragedy as Americans and to reflect a sense of being an integral part of the society rather than isolated from it.

It should be noted that this may also be a consequence of a basic difference between Christian and Jewish conservatives and how they carry out their lives as cognitive minorities. For Christians, the symbol is the "mighty fortress" which, according to Luther is God who acts as a trusty shield and weapon and the fundamentalists interpret this as entailing removing oneself from involvement in the larger society. For conservative Jews, the objective is to build a fence (*seyag*) around the Torah, to shield it from distortion but not for the refraining from societal involvements. Socio-historical circumstances in Eastern Europe did encourage isolation from society and that carried over to the initial perceptions of American society. However, once they felt physically secure and legitimately autonomous religiously, the Orthodox began to feel themselves as part of the society and to praise the political system which made that possible. They also began to feel comfortable in partaking in some arenas within the popular culture which had previously been alien to traditional Judaism, such as sports and music.

As Jeffrey Gurock indicated, the notions of "recreation" and "leisure time" were alien to Jewish immigrants[29] and, I would add, traditional Judaism. With respect to sports, it is commonplace to find American haredi yeshiva students intimately involved as ardent fans of professional sports and even participating in betting pools as well as engaging in athletics, albeit non-professionally.[30] Exercise is now a "kosher"activity,[31] as are sports. That the very notion of "leisure time" was alien in haredi circles in Eastern Europe may be further support for Alan Wolfe's thesis of the transformation of American Religion.[32]

With respect to music, there is today what might be called parallel structure to the American pop culture music industry, with a broad new genre of American haredi music being created, much of which resembles very much the larger popular music but with a Jewish twist.[33] Haredim have also developed a genre of literature which had been alien to conservative traditional Orthodoxy, namely, fiction.[34] All of this is possible in an American society which tolerates, if not encourages, both religion and religious diversity.

Haredim have now adopted modern methods of inspirational self-help. Aguda conventions and Haredi publications are replete with "cutting edge" psychological and educational, as well as medical topics. Both the producers and the consumers of these materials are not isolated and do not retreat from the larger society and culture. They are very much engaged in it. They have learned to be in it and to use it for their ends.[35]

On several occasions during the 1980s, Rabbi Menachem Mendel Schneerson, the Lubavitcher-Habad Rebbe, expressed very positive attitudes toward the United States and proclaimed its government to be a "*malkhut shel chesed*," a benevolent polity. For example, in 1982, he said,

> "By the grace of G-d, we are in a country which is a which is a benevolent polity in which the President announces and encourages the observances of the seven Noahide commandments, and with the strong emphasis that this is not merely human law but the commandment of G-d, the Creator of the world and its ruler."[36]

In the 1990s, a haredi rabbi published a volume of responsa in which he explicitly praised America and exhorted observant Jews not only to uphold its laws but to conform to its cultural norms as well. In a responsum concerning the growing tendency of haredi Americans to wear their prayer shawls in the street on the Sabbath, he wrote,

> We, the surviving Jews of Poland and other lands of Eastern Europe, who have borne witness to the cruelty and brutality exhibited towards us by a majority of the gentile governments and populations in those countries, must bear in mind that the non Jews of the United States could also have chosen to act with cruelty and hatred towards Jews, as did those in Eastern Europe. Who would

have stood in their way? Instead, they chose the path of justice and fairness, granting equal rights to all men, regardless of nationality. They have also assisted - and continue to assist - millions of Jews all over the world in a variety of ways. Therefore, we must show them our gratitude for all this. We must be second to none in our steadfast observance of this country's laws, we must pray for her welfare, and we must display the American flag outside our homes on every national holiday with no religious connection. In this manner, we will demonstrate that we rejoice in the successes and achievements of this country, and are profoundly grateful for all it has done for us.[37]

For many Haredim, America enabled them to develop their version of "authentic Judaism," perhaps even more fully and certainly without most of the tensions and struggles that, from their perspective, Haredim in Israel experience. They feel, in some ways, more "at home in America" than in Israel. This is probably even more so for the hasidic haredim than for the Lithuanian-type Haredim because the hasidim have a long tradition of involvement in business. Be that as it may, some Haredim feel that it is less *"shver tzu zein a Yid"* ("difficult to be a Jew") in the United States than it is in Israel.

Israel does, of course, have religious significance for them as *Eretz Israel*, the Holy Land, as well as the home of the largest or second largest Jewish community and certainly the home of the largest number of Orthodox Jews. Contrary to popular mythology, they are overwhelmingly not anti-Zionist and certainly not anti-Israel. On the contrary, as the 2001 National Jewish Population Survey (NJPS) reconfirms, Orthodox Jews in the United States have much stronger ties with Israel than do other American Jews. For example, when asked about their level of attachment to Israel, 66 percent of the Orthodox indicated that they are *very* attached emotionally, as compared to 42 perecnt for Conservative and 17 percent for Reform Jews.

Likewise, 81 percent of the Orthodox respondents said they visited Israel, as compared to 58 percent of the Conservative and 26 percent of the Reform. In addition, of those who have visited, 72 percent of the Orthodox have visited more than once, as compared to 62 percent of the Conservative and 30 percent of the Reform respondents.

Nevertheless, the Haredim, like the vast majority of America's Jews, are in no rush to make aliya, to immigrate to Israel. Though the Orthodox—Haredi as well as Modern—probably comprise at least 80 percent of contemporary American *olim*, the total annual number of American olim is around 2,000 or less individuals.[38] The Haredim have deep ties with Israel. It is a significant place to visit—and they do so much more than other American Jews—but America is now their home. America has enabled them to create "a life apart"[39] which, ironically, has enabled them to feel that are a part of America. They can now live in almost any neighborhood while retaining their separate communities. In New York, for example, they have become a significant part of the Orthodox Jewish population in Manhattan's West Side,[40] as well as in the affluent suburban "Five Towns," in Nassau County. They identify as haredi while simultaneously living an affluent, consumptive life style. In other words, to borrow and adapt the title of one of the late Frank Sinatra's best known songs, they do it their way.

NOTES

I appreciate the very constructive comments of Steven Katz, Kimmy Caplan, and Adam Ferziger, who read various drafts of the paper.

1. Gurock, Jeffrey, S., *American Jewish Orthodoxy in Historical Perspective* (Hoboken, N.J., 1996), pp. 1–62.

2. Sarna, Jonathan, D., (ed.), *People Walk on Their Heads: Moses Weinberger's Jews and Judaism in New York* (New York, 1982).

3. "Union of Orthodox Congregations," *American Hebrew*, vol. LXVIII, no. 7 (January 4, 1901), p. 236. Interestingly, the newspaper report states that Wilowsky labeled anyone who comes to America as a "Poshe Yisrael," a Jewish sinner. Arthur Hertzberg, cites Abraham J. Karp, "The Ridwas, Rabbi Jacob David Wilowsky, 1845–1913," in Arthur A. Chiel, ed., *Perspectives on Jews and Judaism: Essays in Honor of Wolfe Kelman* (New York, 1978), p. 223 (not 233). Moreover, Hertzberg has Wilowsky saying "that whoever comes to America is a heretic because Judaism is trodden here underfoot." (Arthur Hertzberg, "'Treifene Medina': Learned Opposition to Emigration to the United States," *Proceedings of the Eighth World Congress of Jewish Studies* (Jerusalem, 1984), p. 25.

4. "Brief Biography of the Author," in *Sefer nimukei haridvaz 'al hatora*, (Chicago, 1904, New Edition, 1992).

5. Quoted in Kimmy Caplan, *Orthodoxy in the New World: Immigrant Rabbis and Preaching in America (1881–1924)* (Jerusalem, 2002), p. 85 [Hebrew]; my translation.

6. Ibid.

7. Berger, Peter, L., *The Sacred Canopy: Elements of a Sociological Theory of Religion* (Garden City, 1967), p. 153.

8. His major works in English are "The Lonely Man of Faith," first published as an article in *Tradition*, vol. 7, no. 2, Summer 1965, pp. 5–67., and then as a book (Garden City, N.Y., 1992), and *Halakhic Man*, translated from the Hebrew by Lawrence Kaplan (Philadelphia, 1983). Some of his perspectives and involvements can be gleaned from his published letters, *Community, Covenant and Commitment: Selected Letters and Communications*, edited by Nathaniel Helfgott (Jersey City, N.J., 2005).

9. Feinstein, Moshe, Rabbi, *Darash Moshe* (New York, 1988), *Derush* 10, p. 416.

10. Feinstein, Moshe, Rabbi, *Igrot Moshe, Orach Chaim* 2 (New York, 1963), p. 197.

11. On the involvements of the late Lubavitcher Rebbe, Rabbi Menachem Mendel Schneersohn, in the Released Time program, see Sue Fishkoff, *The Rebbe's Army: Inside the World of Chabad-Lubavitch*, (New York, 2003).

12. Feinstein, *Igrot Moshe*, op. cit.

13. For a history of Torah Umesorah and Jewish day schools in the United States, see Alvin I. Schiff, *The Jewish Day School in America* (New York, 1966); Doniel Zvi Kramer, *The Day Schools and Torah Umesorah: The Seeding of Traditional Judaism in America* (New York, 1984).

14. Wolfe, Alan, *The Transformation of American Religion: How We Actually Live Our Faith* (New York, 2003).

15. Avi Chai, *Jewish Day Schools in the United States* (New York, 1994); Hanan Alexander, "Literacy, Education and the Good Life," paper delivered at the Workshop on Language, Culture, and Jewish Identity, Tel-Aviv University, School of Education, Dec. 28, 1998.

16. This theme is captured in the 1997 award-winning documentary film by Menachem Daum and Oren Rudavsky, "A Life Apart: Hasidim in America." See also Jerome Mintz, *Hasidic People: A Place in the New World* (Cambridge, M.A., 1998); George Kranzler, *Hasidic Williamsburg: A Contemporary American Hasidic Community*, (Northvale, N.J., 1995), esp. Ch. 8, pp. 207–231; Israel Rubin, *Satmar: Two Generations of an Urban Island*, 2nd ed., (New York, 1997); William Shaffir, "Montreal's Hassidim Revisited: A Focus on Change," in Simcha Fishbane and Jack N. Lightstone, (eds.), *Essays in the Social Scientific Study of Judaism and Jewish Society*, (Montreal, 1990), pp. 305–322.

17. Freedman, Samuel, G., *Jew vs. Jew: The Struggle for the Soul of American Jewry*, (New York, 2000). The "move to the right" in American Orthodoxy was already apparent in the 1960s. See Charles S. Liebman, *Aspects of the Religious Behavior of American Jews*, (New York, 1974), p. 150. See also Haym Soloveitchik, "Rupture and Reconstruction: The Transformation of Contemporary Orthodoxy," *Tradition*, vol. 28, no. 4 (Summer 1994), pp. 64–130; reprinted in Roberta Rosenberg Farber and Chaim I. Waxman, (eds.), *Jews in America: A Contemporary Reader*, (Hanover, 1999), pp. 320–376.

18. #1101. Rabbi Yehuda Hehasid was a major figure among Pietists of Germany in the 12ᵗʰ and 13ᵗʰ centuries. His work, *Sefer Hahasidim*, was the most important work in ethical literature which the Pietists produced.

19. "A Bleak Outlook is Seen for Religion," *New York Times*, February 25, 1968.

20. Peter L. Berger, (ed.), *The Desecularization of the World: Resurgent Religion and World Politics* (Washington, D.C., 1999), p. 2.

21. Ibid., p. 6.

22. Almond, Gabriel, A., R. Scott Appleby, and Emmanuel Sivan, *Strong Religion: The Rise of Fundamentalisms Around the World*, (Chicago, 2003).

23. Hunter, James, Davison, *Culture Wars: The Struggle to Define America*, (New York, 1991).

24. Pelcovitz, Ralph, "The Teshuva Phenomenon: The Other Side of the Coin," *Jewish Life*, vol. 4, no. 3, (1980), pp. 16ff.

25. Shafran, Avi, Rabbi, "I Have a Dream," http://www.jlaw.com/Commentary/ ihaveadream.html. Habad-Lubavitch, the most prominent hasidic movement in the United States, was a most notable exception to this pattern. Its major focus has

consistently been on religious outreach to all Jews and it utilizes cutting-edge technology in its outreach and public relations activities. Since the death of the Rebbe, in 1994, the movement has experienced struggles internally as well as with some other Orthodox groups, because of its increasing proclamations of him as the Messiah, a notion which others view as antithetical to Judaism. In addition to the work by Fishkoff cited above, see Janet S. Belcove-Shalin, (ed.), *New World Hasidim: Ethnographic Studies of Hasidic Jews in America* (Albany, 1995); Lis Harris, *Holy Days: The World of a Hasidic Family*, (New York, 1985); Shaul Shimon Deutsch, *Larger Than Life: The Life and Times of the Lubavitcher Rebbe, Rabbi Menachem Mendel Schneerson*, 2 vols. (New York, 1995); David Berger, *The Rebbe, The Messiah, and the Scandal of Orthodox* Indifference, (London, 2001). One other exception to the pattern was the Rabbinical Seminary of America, Yeshiva Chofetz Chaim of Queens, NY, which had a specific outreach component and, in the past several decades, has opened branches in cities across the United States, as well as in Israel.

26. Ferziger, Adam, S., "Training American Orthodox Rabbis to Play a Role in Confronting Assimilation: Programs, Methodologies and Directions," Bar-Ilan University, Faculty of Jewish Studies, Rappaport Center for Assimilation Research and Strengthening Jewish Vitality, Research & Position Papers, 2003.

27. Putnam, Robert, D., *Bowling Alone: The Collapse and Revival of American Community*, (New York, 2000).

28. Chaim I. Waxman, "American Modern Orthodoxy: Confronting Cultural Challenges," *Edah Journal*, vol. 4, no.1, (Spring 2004/Iyar 5764).

29. Gurock, Jeffrey, "Immigrant Jews and the Challenge of American Athleticism," paper presented at the Conference, "Why Is America Different," Boston University, Elie Wiesel Center for Judaic Studies, October 25, 2004. For a detailed analysis, see Jerffer S. Gurock, *Judaism's Encounter With American Sports* (Bloomington, 2005).

30. Caplan, Kimmy, "Haredim and Western Culture: A View from Both Sides of the Ocean," in Meir Litvak, (ed.), *Middle Eastern Cultures and the West: Accommodation or Clash of Civilizations?* (Tel Aviv, 2006), pp. 269–288.

31. Max Gross, "Exercising to a Rabbinic Beat," *Forward*, May 7, 2004.

32. Wolfe, *The Transformation of American Religion*.

33. www.shlockrock.com, www.veroba.net, Mattisyahu, Blue Fringe, Soul Farm, The Chevrah, and even Mordechai Ben-David and Avraham Fried, to name a few.

34. Finkelman, Yoel, "Medium and Message in Contemporary Haredi Adventure Fiction," *Torah Umadda Journal*, vol. 13, 2005, pp. 50–87.

35. See, for example, the highly popular books by psychiatrist, Abraham J. Twerski, especially *Getting Up When You're Down: A Discussion of Adult Malady—Depression and Related Conditions*, (Brooklyn, 1995); idem., *The Shame of Silence: Spouse Abuse in the Jewish* Community (Pittsburgh, 1996); and idem., *Successful Relationships: At Home, At Work, and With Friends: Bringing Control Issues Under Control* (Brooklyn, 2003). Also see the works of Akiva Tatz, *Anatomy of a Search: Personal Drama in the Teshuva Revolution* (Brooklyn, 1987).

36. Schneersohn, Menahem, Mendel, "Likutei sihot 'al parshiyot hashavu'a hagim umo'adim", vol. 25, *Bereishit*, 2nd ed., (Brooklyn, 1997), p. 419. I thank Yitzchak Kraus for pointing me to this source.

37. Schwarz, Yom Tov, Rabbi, (ed.), and (trans.), Schwarz, Avraham, Leib, *Eyes to See: Recovering Ethical Torah Principles Lost in the Holocaust,* (New York, 2004, p. 289 (Hebrew ed., Brooklyn, 1997).

38. Nefesh B'nefesh, the major organization promoting American aliya, claimed that, in 2004, there were almost 3,000 American olim. However, according to Israel's Central Bureau of Statistics, the figure was actually 1,890 American olim; in 2005, it was 2,045, and in 2006, it was 2,157.

39. This was the theme of the 1997 award-winning documentary film by Menachem Daum and Oren Rudavsky, "A Life Apart: Hasidim in America."

40. Leibovitz, Liel, "Orthodox Boom Reshaping West Side," *Jewish Week,* July 2, 2004.

9

From Many, One? Reflections on the Notion of American Jews

Arnold Eisen, Chancellor,
The Jewish Theological Seminary

My concerns in this essay will come clearly into view if we listen for a moment to the closing peroration of Israel Friedlander's otherwise sober rumination from nearly a century ago on "the problem of Judaism in America." That problem, in a word, was assimilation, an alarming result of the "apparent incompatibility of Judaism with modern life and culture." Emancipation and Enlightenment had resulted in indifference, apostasy, decomposition. "The dawn of the Jews is the dusk of Judaism," lamented Friedlander, a professor of Bible at the Jewish Theological Seminary and—as we see in this address—a faithful disciple of the cultural Zionist theorist Ahad Ha'am. Jews confronted truly bleak alternatives in the modern diaspora: either return to the ghetto (which should not be considered) or complete absorption into Gentile society (which well might occur). "But is there really no escape?" Friedlander wonders aloud? Was there no future for Jews in America? At this point the tone of the essay alters markedly, as Friedlander turns to the precedent of "the great Jewish-Arabic period," especially during the Golden Age in Spain. That precedent, he argues, establishes "irrefutably" that Judaism is compatible with freedom. Friedlander then proceeds to paint a picture of what American Jews might look like if his hopes—and the community's possibilities—were realized.[1]

That vision of the American Jewish self—a person neither ghettoized nor assimilated, neither solely American nor less than fully American, neither hopelessly fragmented nor in any simple sense whole—has proven remarkably enduring, even dominant, since Friedlander first gave it expression a century ago. The key components of this identity are easily recognizable. First, the modern American Jew would combine "American energy and success with that manliness and self-assertion which is imbibed with American freedom."[2] (The elements comprising this portion of the self, we note, are attributed exclusively to America.) Second, compromises between the demands of Judaism and the reality of America would be required—but that was true of any happy marriage, Friedlander observes; he then portrays the partnership without any hint of compromise, speaking only of fulfillment. Indeed, third, his vision positively soars as he depicts that happy outcome of the Jewish marriage with America—and pointedly avoids explicit division of the self into American and Jew.

> We perceive a community great in number, mighty in power, enjoying life, liberty and the pursuit of happiness: true life, not mere breathing space; full liberty, not mere elbow room . . . men with straight backs and raised heads, with big hearts and strong minds, with no conviction crippled, with no emotion stifled, with souls harmonious developed, self-centered and self-reliant . . . blending the best they possess with the best they encounter . . . Everyone that will see them will point to them as a community blessed by the Lord.[3]

Virtually no twentieth century American Jewish religious thinker, from modern Orthodoxy on the "right" to Reform and Reconstructionism on the "left," has significantly dissented from the main points of Friedlander's formulation. The optimism which he voiced without hesitation has been tempered over time, particularly on the matter of wholeness: successful integration of the self's two major parts. But America ("the best they encounter") is still believed to provide the Jew (in Friedlander's words) with energy, success, self-assertion, straight back, raised head, liberty. Judaism's contribution ("the best they possess") is often defined only vaguely in contemporary essays as it was in Friedlander's, but it remains a matter, as ever, of spirit, ethics, meaning, depth, culture, God. America remains by and large the self's outside, while Judaism lies within. America is form, Judaism content. America is body, Judaism is soul. American is adjective, Jew or Judaism is noun. America is opportunity. Judaism is the age-old substance which turns present opportunity into unprecedented fulfillment.

I shall first briefly review the variations on this theme offered by major American Jewish religious thinkers over the course of the twentieth century (a debate which I have examined in detail elsewhere).[4] I shall then juxtapose the notion of self set forth by these thinkers, including implicit assumptions concerning whether selves can or should be whole or hyphenated, with two other sets of very recent writings, one by philosophers and the other by social scientists, on the vexed and ever-confusing definition of self.[5] My aim is not to survey, let alone analyze, the vast and ever-growing body of work in many disciplines on this matter, just as I shall not attempt to offer an exhaustive summary of rabbinic views of the American Jew. I want only to show just how difficult and controversial the notion of

American Jew remains. If those who hold that identity are "ambivalent," as sociologist Charles Liebman famously claimed thirty years ago,[6] there are ample reasons for them to be so—not least widespread confusion over what it means to be a self in America today, and what sort of self a Jew and American can and should aspire to become.

THE AMERICAN JEWISH SELF

Let us begin with Mordecai Kaplan, whose often-elaborated call for American Jews to live in two civilizations seems to resolve the problem of identity in one brilliant stroke, but in fact only points up difficulties which are not easily resolved. Jews could only survive as such in modern America, Kaplan argued in his masterpiece, *Judaism as a Civilization* (1934), if they came to regard themselves as essentially different from non-Jewish Americans. They would only do that if their difference took the form of real "otherness" (in who they were) rather than mere "unlikeness" (in a single feature such as religion). Kaplan wanted Judaism to be intuitive, taken for granted, a core element of every American Jewish self. He proposed to accomplish that end by persuading American Jews to see Judaism henceforth not as religion but as "civilization: that nexus of a history, literature, language, social organization, folk sanctions, standards of conduct, social and spiritual ideals, esthetic values, which in their totality form a civilization."[7]

"Totality" was the key. A civilization, he wrote, "demands that the foundations of personality in the child be laid with the materials which the civilizations itself supplies."[8] Kaplan laid out a comprehensive vision of Jewish culture involving attachment to a homeland in Palestine, revival of Hebrew, knowledge of Jewish history, the practice of Jewish "mores, laws and folkways," and a communal social structure far more encompassing than the synagogue—all this above and beyond Jews' participation in American life.[9] In one extraordinary passage in a later work, *The Future of the American Jew* (1948), Kaplan even urged Jews to reconstitute their people as a "security-affording, authority-exerting, soul-stirring corporate entity," suggesting that world Jewry unite, elect a parliament, enact a constitution, and apply for representation at the United Nations.[10]

In other passages, however, Kaplan recognized that Jews in America could never "live Judaism" as their "primary civilization" as they could in Palestine, and could not even "live Judaism" as a "co-ordinate civilization" as they might in a situation of substantial cultural autonomy. Judaism in America could survive only as a "subordinate civilization. Since the civilization that can satisfy the primary interests of the Jew must necessarily be the civilization of the country he lives in, the Jew in America will be first and foremost an American, and only secondarily a Jew."[11] Jews could only be as Jewish as circumstances allowed.

This is a damning concession indeed. The two parts of the self are woefully out of balance. The American side is destined to triumph over the Jewish. Kaplan addresses the problem later in the book by noting that Jews need Jewish civilization because America was simply not constituted to offer its citizens, Christian or Jewish, the "salvation," i.e. self-fulfillment, which every true culture provides to its members. Americans could turn to their nation for "literary and esthetic values," and of course owed the state civic allegiance. But Gentile Americans, possessed no less than Jews of a hyphenated identity, had to turn to Christian civilization for "moral and spiritual sanctions" i.e. for values. They had no choice, seeking fulfillment, but to be American Catholics or American Protestants.[12] American Jews did not have that option. As a result, Kaplan wrote in another telling passage, Jews would depend upon America primarily for social and economic security but for all the rest, for all that really mattered where self-fulfillment was concerned, there would be Judaism and it alone.[13] Yet immediately after observing that the "elementary needs of human existence" and key events in every Jewish life should constitute an occasion for the practice of Jewish folkways, Kaplan adds that this could only occur "whenever they do not involve an unreasonable amount of time, effort, and expense . . . what is reasonable will depend on how intensely Jewish one is."[14] Here as elsewhere, as Liebman pointed out long ago, Kaplan probably spoke the mind of a great many American Jews.[15]

He also spoke for their theologians, I believe, though most would have been less willing to make peace explicitly with the societal and cultural realities to which Kaplan deferred. It would not stretch the point too much, I think, were we to say that for Abraham Joshua Heschel, a leading thinker associated with the Conservative movement, as for Eugene Borowitz, a leading Reform thinker and author of that movement's 1976 statement of principles, and for Joseph Soloveitchik, the intellectual authority of modern Orthodoxy in America for half a century—America is pre-eminently means, Judaism end. America is, while Judaism is forever. America is often obstacle, sometime ally, but Judaism is the protagonist in the American Jew's life drama, the source of his or her blessing, the path to his or her fulfillment. American values are sometimes good and often not so good. America rescues, but only Judaism saves.

This is not to say their views on this matter (or anything else!) are uniform or of a piece. They are not. Soloveitchik's notion of the "covenantal community" and its obligations are not those of Borowitz or Kaplan. Soloveitchik's notion of the human being split from God's creation onwards— legitimately split, inevitably so, eternally so—into "Adam I" seeking majesty and control over nature by use of God-given reason, and "Adam II" seeking

covenant with God and human fellows—makes explicit a positive valuation of the culture outside the covenant. That valuation is sometimes present but never quite so explicit in the Heschel or even in Kaplan.[16] Heschel's
notion of mitzvah as "pattern for living," or prophetic "sympathy" with the
divine "pathos," did not win assent from any of the others. Nonetheless,
this telling paragraph from a 1957 address by Heschel captures something
essential in all four rabbinic views:

> We are all committed to the ideal of the modern Jew. By modern Jew I mean
> a person who lives within the language and culture of a twentieth-century
> nation, is exposed to its challenges, its doubts and its allurements, and at the
> same time insists upon the preservation of Jewish authenticity in religion and
> even cultural terms. But let us not forget that the modern Jew is but an experi-
> ment, and who can be sure that the experiment will succeed.[17]

The modern Jew, we note, lives inside a particular language and culture,
is exposed to challenges, doubts and allurements (which we gather should
be overcome, and (unlike premodern, non-hyphenated Jews) is deemed an
experiment. His or her identity is in doubt. Even Soloveitchik's bifurcated
Jewish self must sooner or later withdraw from modern culture (especially,
we gather, its American variety) and stand apart. Adam II commitments simply cannot be made understandable to that culture. At a certain point, "the
dialogue between man of faith and the man of culture comes to an end."[18]
Soloveitchik accords America far more than political allegiance, respect
for its culture's aesthetic achievements or gratitude for social and economic
security. This difference from the "outside/inside" schema is not trivial.
It brings Soloveitchik more into line with what I take to be the way most
American Jews actually think about their identities. I shall return to this
matter in the conclusion. At this point we need note only that the Kantian
division of self into something resembling "phenomenal" (Adam I) and
"noumenal" (Adam II), with its roots as old as the body/soul distinction
and the separation of Jew from Gentile, sacred from profane, Sabbath
from weekdays, remains central to Soloveitchik's picture of the American
Jew, as it does in the accounts offered by the other Jewish thinkers I have
mentioned. Rabbis all; charged with articulating faith commitments which
of course trump other loyalties; acting as spokesmen for a minority culture
threatened by wholesale absorption into the majority—the four Jewish
thinkers not surprisingly give the bulk of their attention and devotion to
the Jewish side of the hyphen. That imbalance is to be expected, and poses a
serious obstacle to full adoption by Jewish selves in America of the models
their rabbis propose. But I believe that all four thinkers posed to the reader,
sometimes explicitly, a more serious problem as well: whether the view
of self they proposed is; whether hyphenated identity of any sort, on any
terms, makes sense.

A brief foray into recent philosophical and social-psychological literature on identity should help us answer this question. Even a cursory reading of this literature shows that the rabbis have not been alone in their concern to depict and make the case for hyphenated selves; the coherence, stability and legitimacy of identity have long been at issue in this country, for a host of reasons. It is not at all clear, we find, that an American Jewish self harnessed firmly to its hyphen, or any other such identity, can long endure.

IN SEARCH OF IDENTITY

Against the charged background of recent debate over multiculturalism, several recent philosophers have vigorously disputed whether it still makes sense to speak of identity of any sort whatever.[19] The word connotes one-ness, after all, and implies unity.[20] Charles Taylor, in his acclaimed work *Sources of the Self*, 1989), made a strong case for the possibility of a self who is reasonably whole even if that self is not homogeneous and derives from modern sources as diverse as the movements of Enlightenment and Romanticism.[21] Others have disagreed, however, arguing that substantive diversity is a fact among individuals as among societies. What is more, that heterogeneity is a good, and should be nurtured at the very core of the self. The self, too, is multicultural, divided, "cosmopolitan," or at minimum should retain the freedom to become so, i.e. not to be defined as any one thing for very long. If that is the case, identity becomes nominal, selfhood a fiction or mere label. In part, as historian Philip Gleason points out, this recent debate over "one" versus "many" in identity goes back to the very beginning of the modern period. Hume and Locke called into question on empirical grounds the notion of a united self which had rested for centuries on Christian belief in an eternal soul.[22]

The current literature asks a related set of questions as well, these too related to the matters of concern to the rabbis: whether selves can be formed at all, or are legitimately formed, or are perhaps formed, when the developing individuals and their families are active participants in strong communities (religious or ethnic) and shaped by the distinctive cultures of those groups. Communitarian thinkers, like the rabbis we surveyed, answer these questions unqualifiedly in the affirmative. Liberal thinkers for whom individual autonomy, or cosmopolitan openness, or a combination of both, is the highest good argue the opposite case. They claim that strong communities inevitably stifle individual development by precluding options and thereby limiting autonomy. Liberal communitarians, like many Jews, are caught in the middle: seeking to balance commitment to a tradition they prize with loyalty to notions of self imbibed with the air of America, and unflagging effort to keep all their own options open.

Take, for example, the political philosopher Michael Sandel, who defends the legitimacy of "allegiances [that] go beyond the obligations I voluntarily incur and the 'natural duties' I owe to human beings as such . . . To some I owe more than justice requires or even permits . . . in virtue of those more or less enduring attachments and commitments which taken together partly define the person I am."[23] The last phrase is the most relevant here. Sandel's claim is that the various components of our identity—whether cultural or religious—do not arise as a result of associations we join, but stem from connections which are partly constitutive of the persons we are. We thus owe more to the individuals who share that core, given aspect of our selfhood than we do to others. Indeed we may be duty bound to develop this element in our own persons, at the expense of other things we might do or become.

Charles Taylor comes to much the same conclusion by pointing to the self's need for and right to recognition, which in many cases flows from participation in a particular community or culture. The group, its ideas and its commitments enable me to become the person I am; its members are the people who best know me in depth and so can provide me with the recognition I require.[24] The presumption here is that we do not simply select ideas for selfhood from the supermarket shelves of American culture and other sources, constructing as we go. Rather, certain possibilities for the self are enlivened for and in us by the exemplary lives of people we know and love. We therefore require strong sub-cultures, in order to grow, and that in turn means that we require strong communities.

Jurgen Habermas—a strong proponent of individual autonomy—makes his surprising case for both sub-cultures and sub-communities this way.

> The integrity of the individual legal person cannot be guaranteed without protecting the intersubjectively shared experiences and life contexts in which the person has been socialized and has formed his or her identity. The identity of the individual is interwoven with collective identities and can be stabilized only in a cultural network that cannot be appropriated as private property any more than the mother tongue itself can be.[25]

Self, for Habermas as for Taylor, requires community; autonomy depends upon group loyalties. All three thinkers thus provide philosophical support for the legitimacy of a self who is very much defined by attachment to a collective. Unlike the rabbis, they skirt the "ontological" issue of whether the self is "primordial," i.e. given with birth, fixed for life, or "optionally cultivated," that is, "achieved" in the course of social interaction, and as such fluid, one attribute among others.[26] The issue is rather ethical and social-psychological. Who should we be—and what enables us to be so? Their answers are very much in accord with the substantive Jewish commitments for which Kaplan, et al. argued so vigorously.

Thinkers who dispute the significance of the sort of attachments praised by Sandel, Taylor and Habermas claim that these ties, far from being fundamental to identity, can be severed rather easily—and indeed be severed, either because strong ethnic or religious identities, however formed, impede autonomy, the ability of selves to choose which identity they will become, or because single identity breeds narrowness and intolerance, or both. Amartya Sen, for example, reminds us eloquently that inside even the strongest communities, there is and must be room for serious difference. "Many of the 'cultures' that are frequently interpreted in rigidly narrow terms by contemporary religious leaders contain enormous internal variations of attitudes and beliefs." The same holds true inside the self. "The neglect of our plural identities in favor of one 'principal' identity can greatly impoverish our lives and our practical reason." He refuses to allow the borders of his own self to be identical with those of any religion or tribe. Autonomy demands that such clear demarcation be eschewed.[27] This is of course a concern advocates of a Jewish self have been addressing throughout the modern period, especially in America. Leon Wieseltier joins the debate at a somewhat different but related juncture. He attacks the sort of "identity politics" which would measure the worth of a person or idea in accordance with ethnic or religious provenance, affiliation or interest. Hence his polemic "against identity, an idea whose time has gone." "The thinner the identity, the louder," he remarks. Or again: "Authenticity is a paltry standard by which to appraise an idea or a work of art or politics . . . a reactionary ideal. And speaking strictly, it is an anti-ideal. It says: what has been is what must be. It is the idolatry of origins." More pointed still: "'I love it because it is mine.' This is the language of identity. Properly translated, this means: I do not love it, I love me."[28] None of the rabbis argued in this manner, of course. Even Kaplan, who has sometimes been accused of ethnic chauvinism—Jewish is good, simply by virtue of being Jewish—time and again called for "ethical nationhood" and set values as the main work of civilization. Wieseltier does however show the weakness of any appeal to ethnic "survival" for its own sake. The rabbis, of course, stood opposed to such models of the Jewish self. The hyphen in that sort of selfhood may not stand for long, they agreed, because it does not stand for much.

Steven M. Cohen and I encountered virtual unanimity among the American Jews we interviewed several years ago concerning the autonomy of the self to make its own decisions, unbound by group notions of what Jewish identity demands. As one informant (a salesman in Queens) put it, "if you want to be involved in something that's very dear to your heart that's fine, but don't sit there and tell me about something that is clearly an option in life, that I have to be doing it, and I should be doing it, because I am this [Jewish]." He was seconded by the Chicago lawyer who said there is nothing whatever about Judaism that he does not like, because "I elect to observe it as I elect to observe it. If something is potentially annoying, I avoid it."[29] Such commitment to personal freedom of choice where religious belief and practice are concerned is widespread among Americans of all denominations. Commitment is legitimate in their eyes, and highly valued, so long as it is freely chosen—and re-chosen again and again. Observances which are not personally meaningful, in their view, should not be practiced. One has a right to abjure them. It is right to do so, and it would be wrong to do the opposite. Practice undertaken in the name of God or tradition precludes autonomy—just as Kant proclaimed over two centuries ago in his classic manifesto, What is Enlightenment?[30]

Jeremy Waldron puts forth the more controversial (and to my mind more interesting) case for the "cosmopolitan" or "mongrel" self who rightly avoids all commitment to singular identity, whether chosen freely or not. A post-modern individual, he writes, though "he may live in San Francisco and be of Irish ancestry, does not take his identity to be compromised when he learns Spanish, eats Chinese, wears clothes made in Korea, listens to arias by Verdi sung by a Maori princess on Japanese equipment, follows Ukrainian politics, and practices Buddhist meditation techniques."[31]

One might be tempted to claim that Waldron only deals with externals in this breezy portrait of contemporary life, that his focus is accessories to the self such as music and food, while the core of the self—the subject of the many verbs he deploys; the "Jew" as the rabbis would have it—remains unified and unique. I am not sure. Jews have negotiated modernity, I have argued elsewhere, not so much by retaining or transforming beliefs about rather abstract matters such as God, revelation and immortality but through practices and their accompanying meanings. These practices have inevitably been altered by the way Jews did a host of other mundane things in response to demands made upon them by the surrounding societies: how and what language they spoke, for example; how they walked and dressed; what and with whom they ate; the sort of music they listened to and sung, inside and outside the synagogue.[32] External and internal matters are not easily kept separate where the self is concerned—a major problem with the rabbis' attempt to divide up the American Jew in this fashion. Waldron is less convincing when he argues in effect that contemporary selves are the sum assemblage of the activities in which they engage. But that we are touched by these daily features or life, that we are shaped by their very diversity and multiplicity, split apart or at least diffused, and forced as a consequence us to wonder who we are, really—of this there seems little doubt.

That is perhaps why the philosopher Michael Walzer takes pains to critique the "postmodern project." He rejects "a life without clear boundaries and without secure or singular identities," one in which "the associations that these self-made and self-making individuals form are likely to be little more than temporary alliances that can be easily broken off when something more promising comes along." Walzer's problem with this sort of self-cum-project is that it "undercuts every sort of common identity and standard behavior."[33] He rather favors what he considers the best of the emerging American reality: namely that we are both this and that; that there are still boundaries, but they are blurred by all the crossings;"[34] or, as he put it elsewhere, the hyphen in identity works as a plus sign rather than a divider, and Americans can live their lives on either side or both. The point is to embrace difference in the United States and yet maintain a common life, a vigorous citizenry and responsible selves.[35] He does not explain how this can be accomplished, or at what cost to the respective sides of the hyphen. That is of course the issue which most concerned the rabbis—and led them to insist that one side of the hyphen must necessarily have normative primacy over the other.

Waldron does not want our selves to be defined by either singular or hyphenated identity. His dismissal of religious loyalties in particular is consistent with his emphasis upon the fact and legitimacy of sweeping diversity (and is all too typical of many secular liberal philosophers). He himself contrasts "lifestyles" with "background assumptions." The former have to do with the music we listen to and the clothes we wear. The latter, in his words, "govern our views of life, agency and responsibility." However, he then equates the difference between Catholics and Methodists with the taste for campfires as opposed to opera, and writes caustically that if cosmopolitan selves leave churches in droves and the churches die out, "it is like the death of a fashion or a hobby, not the demise of anything that people really need."[36] Here one sees perhaps the deepest problem that Jewish religious thinkers are likely to have with the postmodern view of the self. All choices are okay, because none matters very much. The notion of ultimacy indicates nothing more than subjective or communal preference. Oneness and belief in The Good are mutually dependent, as monotheists have claimed for centuries.

Arguments about the place of religion are integral to discussions of identity. Philip Gleason's "semantic history" of the term "identity" makes it clear that recent usage, from whatever point of view, coincided with the resurgence of interest in ethnicity in the 1960s, that in turn followed upon and countered Will Herberg's famous prediction a decade earlier "that the ethnic identities of an immigrant-derived population had transformed themselves into religious identification with organized Protestantism, Catholicism, or Judaism."[37] The famous psychologist Gordon Allport too linked "identity" to "ethnicity" in his classic 1954 study of prejudice.[38] Contemporary evidence seems to support Herberg's analysis; the cultural differences which remain and thrive in America today, whether among recent immigrant groups or among ethnic groups of Asian or European origin several generations removed from immigration, are often perceived as belonging to ethnicity but are almost without exception strongly connected to beliefs, practices and communities. Think of Haitians or Koreans, Italians or Jews, Mexican-Americans or African-Americans (the last of course involuntary immigrants brought here on slave ships). Even the sort of "symbolic ethnicity" which Richard Alba and other sociologists, following Herbert Gans, believe is all that remains of the more vigorous ethnic differences that were once strengthened by "structural" factors such as where one lived, whom one married, what one worked at, how much money one made, etc.—even these "symbolic ethnicities" cannot entirely be separated from religious observances, especially festivals centered on food.[39]

Indeed, it seems harder and harder to separate the two. Recent research, for example, has pointed to the role of nostalgia in maintaining religious ties, and vice versa. Loyalty to ancestors is no longer just a tried and true means of securing loyalty to God. It often serves as an end in its own right, thriving where faith in the strict sense no longer exists, but supported by traces or echoes of that faith. *The Jew Within* amply supports this suggestion. Waldron's preference for the "mongrel self" therefore requires the denigration of religion in particular that he provides. Faith is involved integrally with even the most symbolic of ethnicities and retains its hold on many Americans (though on far fewer Europeans). Religion is strengthened through links to the very features of daily life which Waldron values and seeks to diversify, and so sets limits to those features. The hyphen in contemporary American identities may join far more than two parts of a given self. But it remains in place nonetheless, supported in many cases by religion. Jewish Americans are in this case not unusual.

This persistence of religion explains, finally, why liberal writers on multiculturalism almost invariably slip or jump from talk of ethnicity to talk of religion whenever they want an example of group loyalty more robust than most white ethnicity in contemporary America. The case in point, in fact, no matter what the point at issue, seems regularly to be the Amish or the Jews. Both groups combine religious with ethnic difference, and manifest that difference (in the behavior of some adherents) in distinctive dress and mores. Waldron wants to reduce religion to the level of ethnicity: encouraging difference by trivializing it, as it were; removing its substantive sting. The historian David Hollinger, by contrast, wants to build a "postethnic America" in which ethnicity attains the more substantial status of religion—precisely by becoming a purely voluntary association. "Ethno-racial cultures ought to look after themselves much the way religious cultures have been expected to do," i.e. be sustained by voluntary affiliations rather than public subsidies, and stay out of the public sphere.[40] Hollinger likes the fact that religions, however much they matter to people, can be chosen and abandoned—which may ironically not be the case with ethnicities.

Jews have of course sought and invoked both self-descriptions over much of the past century: that of a constitutionally protected religion expanded with the penumbra of ethnicity and "peoplehood;" and an ethnic group ennobled and lent weight by ethics and traditions associated with religion. They have tried to preserve this degree and sort of difference from the great majority by means of the social pressure and persuasion which only a tight community can bring to bear—the strategy articulated eloquently and programmatically by Kaplan 70 years ago. The hyphenation in the American Jewish self has been supported by a further hyphenation on the Jewish side, as it were, separating and linking ethnicity and religion. If America is "outside," and Judaism "inside," the latter too has an external (ethnic) and internal (religious) portion. Both hyphens have arguably served American Jews fairly well, allowing for and supporting identities which could not have been sustained on other terms. But the philosophical literature we have just surveyed carries a twofold caution for this ambition. First: ethnicity detached from strong community and normative claims about the good life may not seem worth protecting, and likely cannot be sustained, except at the price (gladly paid by Waldron) of any notion of unified selfhood. Second: liberal philosophy is by nature suspicious of hereditary attachment, religious or ethnic, as an infringement on autonomy. That is all the more true when such attachment smacks—as both "religion" and "tradition" do—of irrationality. Hyphenated American Jewish identity may or may not be legitimate, depending on the philosopher and sort of identity concerned. It can never be anything other than precarious.

Yet such identity may in fact be the way American selves these days, according to several recent articles by social psychologists. Daphna Oyserman and Hazel Rose Markus, while stressing again and again how little we know of the ways identity is actually developed and/or constructed in America and other cultures today, insist as well that identity is not developed or constructed in only one way. Culture makes a difference in this respect as in others. Nor is the "sociocultural self" developed in America or elsewhere likely to comprise one element exclusively. We are "social selves," and we are complex.[41]

"What has become increasingly clear," Oyserman and Markus write, "is that although terms such as identity and self-concept suggest a single, monolithic entity, phenomena like identity and self should be viewed as plural and diverse even within the individual. . . . it is no longer feasible to refer to *the* self-concept."[42] Sociologist Sheldon Stryker concurs. "Self is often written about in the singular in the literature on the topic. . . . Nevertheless, a multiplicity of selves conceptualization currently reigns."[43] Stryker, while arguing against return to the view of unified self, points up two dangers with the "multiplicity of selves conception." It can lead to a "situationalism" that "renders the concept of self superfluous in accounts of social behavior."[44] It also discounts the fact of consistency and stability of behavior across time and across situations, and ignores the "phenomenological validity to the sense of continuity of self, to the perception of self as the 'same' over time and situations." We see ourselves as "whole" and in some sense are. We are not just ephemeral beings, nor aggregations of thoughts and action. We are selves.[45]

Note the stance midway between singular and "mongrel" identity in this approach; the support for possible hyphenation grows when we consider that "within an individual's collection of the self, some are tentative, fleeting, even peripheral, others are highly elaborated and function as enduring, meaning-making, or interpretive structures that help individuals lend coherence to their own life-experience."[46] We choose who we will be, but choose not indiscriminately or randomly but creatively, from among available possibilities real or ideal. "Individuals develop or construct their selves and identities within a field of overlapping groups and collectivities."[47] If that is the case—as the rabbis all believed it was—the race is on to influence and shape this choice. "Recent studies on ethnic identity in various parts of the world reveal that those groups that are in the minority with respect to language, skin color, and religion are those most likely to define themselves in these terms."[48]

Two other features of this approach are relevant to our concerns. First, the research finds ground for and tension inside the sociocultural self, without loss of that self's unity. Each of us receives, and responds to, internalized, contradictory and sometimes negative messages. The latter may handicap performance. Energy may be required to sustain identity in the face of it. But the self endures.[49] Second, formal as well as substantive features of identity vary across cultures. It is not just a matter of a self believing this or that positively, or valuing A as opposed to B. The very concept of being an individual distinct from others, a self who stands essentially apart from one's group (the authors call it "ontology or theory of being") is a variable. If modern America demands that we be individuals, that we are to be judged by personal success in competition with others, as opposed to a collectivist view of self which judges according to group membership and prizes friendly interaction, Soloveitchik's Adams I and II might have captured a cultural conflict that is both empirically verifiable and, as he argued, threatening to American Jewish identity. For it is not just a matter of being the same self but choosing varying commitments but of being a different sort of self entirely. The viability of his proposed hyphen, as of the others proposed by the rabbis, is called into question.

CONCLUSION

It seems reasonable to say, on the basis of studies such as *The Jew Within*, that the millions of choices made by individual American Jews week by week and year by year with regard to the weight assigned each part of their multiple, complex identities will play a far greater role than almost anything else—birth, upbringing, or environment, for example—in determining the next stage in the 350–year experience of the American Jewish hyphen. Jews have been major players for a century now in American debates concerning pluralism, multiculturalism and the legitimacy of difference, for very good reason. Both theology and "sociology," the demands of covenant and the quest for normalcy, have left them little choice.[50] Like other minorities, Jews continue to define and negotiate the parameters of their identities at the same time as they work to convince America that the models of self which they adopt are legitimately and properly American. All this seems unlikely to change any time soon.

What has apparently changed of late, and will continue to change, is the repertoire of self-conceptions among which Jews choose, and the diverse thoughts and behaviors which comprise and enact these identities. Waldron can be usefully taken as a well-founded warning against over-simple dichotomies when it comes to identity: we as opposed to them, as if either side is undifferentiated; essence versus accessory, as if food and clothing and music do not matter in fixing the sense of self; I as part of one and only one We, as if each self is blocked off from all that surrounds it. This to my mind is the major failing of the Jewish thinkers surveyed and many others who espouse similar views. One cannot neatly define "the Jew" as opposed to "the American" inside the hyphenated American Jew, ignoring diversity, difference, complexity and sheer idiosyncrasy. One cannot picture the Jew as a unity standing opposite the American who is multiple (a clear and direct echo of the ancient opposition between "Israel"—"one people"—and "the nations," the "seventy nations," the world in all its diversity. To the degree that Jews really are hyphenated selves, at home in America and not merely residents of America, it is impossible to separate neatly "the Jew" from all he or she does in daily life as "American" or to delineate the purely "Jewish" from the "non-Jewish" sources for beliefs, practices, assumptions, ethics, ethos, temperament, character, neurosis, etc, at the very deepest levels of who American Jews are. That is all the more true when one seeks to make the division in simplistic terms such as outside/ inside or form/substance or opportunity/ends.

It is true, of course, that many American Jews retain a self of themselves that is larger than the time and place they inhabit. They feel attached to Israel, for example, a place far away, and to the Jews who live there. They themselves or their parents or their grandparents were in most cases immigrants: individuals who did not always live in America, and so can fairly easily see themselves as not living here. Such Jews cannot identify entirely with the American side of the hyphen. They can imagine being Jews joined by the hyphen to different nations and culture. Put another way: Jew necessarily remains the noun in their notion of self, American the adjective. One does seem essential, the other a blessed accident, but an accident nonetheless.

I would argue, however, that even the various aspects of these selves cannot be thoroughly compartmentalized into Jew and American, and could not function well in this culture if they were. That will be all the more true in coming decades, for a larger and larger portion of the American Jewish population will have the hyphen in its genes, as it were, and not just their identities. Children of intermarriage, if the Reform experience with patrilineal descent is a reliable indication, are far more willing to call themselves Jews and even affiliate with Jewish institutions than they are to convert to Judaism in order to earn the right in the eyes of some other Jews to call themselves such. Sociologist Bruce Philips, discussing the "multi-racial paradigm" of identity, highlights its emphasis upon the feature of between (or among) various models for relating the identities built into the self. Some mixed-race individuals do define themselves as exclusively black or white only. Others insist on being both, or "biracial." Still a third group opts for "protean identity;" they "will sometimes identify as black, at other times as white, and still other times as biracial."[51] Jews, who are not marked as such in most cases by appearance, and so are able to "pass" for non-Jews, presumably have much greater opportunity for such serial choosing than groups who are presumed by others to be X or Y because of external features. Pressure on the hyphen in identity is therefore enormous, and will likely only increased in years to come.

This degree of choice is particularly evident in how intermarried couples elect to raise their children, and in whom those children eventually elect to marry. The results for Jews indicate a great preponderance of choice away from the Jewish side of the hyphen. Phillips finds that two thirds of children born to intermarried couples are currently not being raised as Jews—whether because hyphenated identity is perceived as too difficult for a self to bear, or a competing noun such as "Christian" is regarded as more desirable, or the attraction to the majority identity of American cannot be resisted. The great bulk of these children do not marry Jews.

American Jewish thinkers committed to the hyphen thus have a complex task. They must of course convince other Jews that the Jewish side of the hyphen in the self is worth sustaining, even at great cost. But they also have to find ways of making sense of hyphenated identity, or—if they choose to sacrifice the hyphen for a singular self—of that identity; either choice will require defense of the very notion of identity itself. Such is the cultural moment in which we live. Friedlander's confidence in the happy marriage of Jew and American inside one self seems dated a century after its appearance; it is at best hope and not prospect. I expect we will hear more of Soloveitchik's insistence on a self divided, committed to both sides of its hyphen but resigned to loneliness, in faith and covenant that no amount of at-homeness in American culture can overcome or assuage.

NOTES

1. Israel Friedlander, "The Problem of Judaism in America," in *Past and Present: Selected Essays* (New York, 1961), pp. 159-184. See also the reprint of Friedlander's essay, with accompanying contemporary responses, including one by the present author, in *Conservative Judaism*, vol. 56 (2004).

2. Ibid., p. 181.

3. Ibid., pp. 183-84.

4. Arnold Eisen, "Jews, Judaism and the Problem of Hyphenated Identity in America," in *Ambivalent Jew: Charles Liebman in Memoriam*, ed. Stuart Cohen and Bernard Susser (New York, 2007). That piece too is based on the conference at Boston University in Fall 2004. Earlier versions of both articles were delivered in draft at Fairfield University and Stanford University. I am grateful to audience members at Fairfield and to conference participants at Stanford and Boston for helpful suggestions and ideas.

5. Philip Gleason, "Identifying Identity: A Semantic History," in *Speaking of Diversity: Language and Ethnicity in Twentieth-Century America* (Baltimore, 1992), pp.123-149.

6. Charles Liebman, *The Ambivalent American Jew: Politics, Religion and Family in American Jewish Life* (Philadelphia, 1973).

7. Mordecai M. Kaplan, *Judaism as a Civilization: Toward a Reconstruction of American-Jewish Life* (Philadelphia, 1994), pp. 177-78,

8. Ibid., p. 196.

9. Ibid., pp. 186-208.

10. Mordecai M. Kaplan, *The Future of the American Jew* (New York, 1948), p. 80.

11. Kaplan, *Judaism as a Civilization*, pp. 215-216.

12. Ibid., p. 516.

13. Kaplan, *Future of American Jew*, p. 437.

14. Ibid., p. 439.

15. Charles Liebman, "Reconstructionism in American Jewish Life," in *Aspects of the Religious Behavior of American Jews* (New York, 1974), pp. 254ff.

16. This section of the paper draws upon the article cited in note 4 above. For the relevant passages in Soloveitchik, see especially Joseph B. Soloveitchik, *The Lonely Man of Faith*, trans. Lawrence Kaplan (New York, 1992), pp. 1-46. For further insight into the Jew-Gentile distinction see Joseph B. Soloveitchik, *Halakhic Man*, trans. Lawrence Kaplan (Philadelphia, 1982), especially pp. 3-48. For relevant passages in Borowitz, see for example Eugene B. Borowitz, "The Autonomous Jewish Self" (1984), in *Studies in the Meaning of Judaism* (Philadelphia, 2002), pp. 215-233; Eugene Borowitz, *The Mask Jews Wear* (New York, 1973), pp. 10-11, 72-78, 96, 125; Eugene B. Borowitz, *Exploring Jewish Ethics: Papers on Covenantal Responsibility* (Detroit, 1990), pp. 57, 132, 398, 407-12; and Eugene B. Borowitz, *Renewing the*

Covenant (Philadelphia, 1991), pp. 288-94. For a fine set of essays about this last book, see Peter Ochs, ed., *Reviewing the Covenant* (Albany, 2000).

17. Abraham Joshua Heschel, "The Individual Jew and his Obligations" in *The Insecurity of Freedom*, (Philadelphia, 1966), p. 197. For other passages in Heschel's writings relevant to our subject see for example, Abraham Joshua Heschel, *Man is Not Alone: A Philosophy of Religion* (New York, 1991), pp, 8, 77; Abraham Joshua Heschel, *The Sabbath* (New York, 1952), p. 12; Abraham Joshua Heschel, "Religion in a Free Society" in *The Insecurity of Freedom: Essays on Human Existence*, pp. 3-5, 21; and Abraham Joshua Heschel, "No Religion is an Island" in Susannah Heschel, ed., *Moral Grandeur and Spiritual Audacity* (New York, 1996), pp. 236-38.

18. Soloveitchik, *Lonely Man of Faith*, p. 106.

19. Derek Parfit, *Reasons and Persons* (Oxford, 1984). See especially chapters 14-15.

20. Gleason, *Identifying Identity*, p. 124. Gleason usefully explains the usages—sometimes synonymous, sometimes not—of "identity" and "self." Ibid., pp.129-36.

21. Charles Taylor, *Sources of the Self: The Making of the Modern Identity* (Cambridge, MA., 1989).

22. Gleason, "Identifying Identity," p. 125.

23. Michael Sandel, *Liberalism and the Limits of Justice*, (Cambridge, 1982), p. 179.

24. Charles Taylor et al, *Multiculturalism: Examining the Politics of Recognition* (Princeton, 1994), pp. 33, 39, 57-71.

25. Jurgen Habermas, "Struggles for Recognition in the Democratic Constitutional State," trans. Sherry Weber Nicholsen, in Taylor, *Multiculturalism*, pp. 128-30.

26. Cf. Gleason, "Identifying Identity," p. 132, who notes the reappearance in these debates of the ancient idea of the soul.

27. Amartya Sen, "Other People: Beyond Identity, in *The New Republic* (Dec. 18, 2000), pp. 23-30. Quotations from pp. 28 and 25 respectively.

28. Leon Wieseltier, "Against Identity: An Idea Whose Time Has Gone," in *The New Republic* (Nov. 28, 1994), pp. 30-32.

29. Steven M. Cohen and Arnold M. Eisen, *The Jew Within: Self, Family and Community in America* (Bloomington, 2000), pp. 36-37.

30. "Enlightenment," Kant begins, "is man's release from his self-incurred tutelage...man's inability to make use of his understanding without direction from another....'Have courage to use your own reason' - that is the motto of enlightenment." Immanuel Kant, "What is Enlightenment," in *Foundations of the Metaphysics of Morals and "What is Enlightenment*," trans. Lewis White Beck (Indianapolis, 1976), p. 85.

31. Jeremy Waldron, "Minority Cultures and the Cosmopolitan Alternative," in Will Kymlicka, ed., *The Rights of Minority Cultures* (Oxford, 1995), pp. 93-95.

32. Arnold M. Eisen, *Rethinking Modern Judaism: Ritual, Commandment, Community* (Chicago, 1998). See in particular pp. 1-12, 107-134.

33. Michael Walzer, *On Toleration* (New Haven, 1997), p. 88.

34. Ibid., p. 90.

35. Michael Walzer, *What it Means to be an American* (New York, 1992), pp. 45, 17.

36. Waldron, "Minority Cultures," pp. 98, 100.

37. Gleason, "Identifying Identity," p. 126.

38. Ibid., p. 129.

39. See Richard D. Alba, *Ethnic Identity: The Transformation of White America* (New Haven, 1990); and Herbert Gans, "Symbolic Ethnicity" The Future of Ethnic Groups and Cultures in America," *Ethnic and Racial Studies*, vol. 2 (1979), pp. 1-20.

40. David A. Hollinger, *Postethnic Ameica: Beyond Multiculturalism* (New York, 1995), pp. 14, 24.

41. Daphna Oyserman and Hazel Rose Markus, "The Sociocultural Self," in J. Suls. ed, *Psychological Perspectives on the Self. Volume 4: The Self in Social Perspective* (Hillsdale, 1993), pp. 187-90. I am indebted to my student Joel Astman for bringing this and related pieces of work to my attention and for furthering my thought on the matter of the "bi-cultural self." See also Hazel Rose Markus and Shinobu Kitayama, "Culture and the Self: Implications for Cognition, Emotion, and Motivation," in *Psychological Review* 1991 (98:2), pp. 224-53.

42. Ibid., pp. 190-91.

43. Sheldon Stryker, "Further Developments in Identity Theory: Singularity Versus Multiplicity of Self," eds., Berger, J., and M. Zelditch, *Sociological Theories in Progress: New Formulations* (Newbury Park, 1989), pp. 40-41.

44. Ibid., p. 42.

45. Ibid., pp. 42-43. See also Sheldon Stryker, " Identity Theory: Developments and extensions" in K. Yardley and T. Honess, eds., *Self and Identity* (New York, 1987), pp. 89-103.

46. Oyserman and Markus, "Sociocultural Self," p. 191.

47. Ibid., p. 193.

48. Ibid., p. 199.

49. Ibid., pp. 202-205.

50. See on this issue Arnold Eisen, *The Chosen People in America* (Bloomington, 1983).

51. Bruce Phillips, "'Half-Jewish: The Jewish Identity of Mixed Parentage Jewish Adults," forthcoming in *Contemporary Society*. Phillips quotes from Kerry Ann Rockquemore and David L. Brunsma, *Beyond Black: Racial Identity in America*, (Thousand Oaks, CA, 2002).

10

Superbowl Parties, Women Rabbis and Freedom Seders: Twenty-first Century Jewish American Synergy

Rela Mintz Geffen

INTRODUCTION

There is no doubt that Jewish Americans and American Judaism live in a symbiotic relationship. Major interpretations of the future of the American Jewish community have been based on a series of Jewish community sponsored demographic analyses of the extent of the interaction between American civil religion and popular culture, and the identity and identifications of American Jews. Whether termed assimilation, acculturation or accommodation, the glass half empty/glass half full debate simmered following the first *National Jewish Population Survey* (NJPS) in 1971, burned brightly during the decade following the 1990 NJPS and came to a head during the controversy over estimated American Jewish population figures surrounding the United Jewish Community's NJPS 2001. Most public debate about the future of the American Jewish community has centered around the definition of a Jew, the size of the population and factors affecting shrinkage such as interfaith marriage and below replacement level birthrates.

In stark contrast to the debate about population size, this essay is focused on the vitality and quality of American Jewish institutional and spiritual life. In it we aim to elucidate a number of late twentieth century trends in American life and forces from within the Jewish community which have interacted to foster a vibrant and particularly American Judaism in the first decade of the twenty-first century. To cite a platitude, these interactions create a whole that is greater than the sum of its parts. This view is in line with one economics based definition of synergy from the corporate world that a combined enterprise will perform better than the previously separate companies because it is more efficient. But, does synergy always lead to a "better" result? Not necessarily. For the purposes of this essay we will employ a definition of synergy that states that synergism takes place "when agents . . . work harmoniously together, or where the total effect is more affective than the individual part. (There is) mutual reinforcement making the sum greater than the parts."

The idea here is that the combined parts have properties that are more or less than their sum (positive-sum or negative-sum rather than zero-sum). The negative-sum version is sometimes called dysergy, leaving synergy to mean only beneficial effects, or what we might call a "value-added" effect. One more characteristic of synergy is germane to this analysis. Synergy characterizes the behavior of whole systems unpredicted by the behavior of their parts taken separately. Though synergy is sometimes the result of planning, at other times it is serendipitous and has the power to surprise us. To give one example of this potential for surprise, who would have predicted that dancing separated by gender at simchas (religious festivities) in the Orthodox Jewish community would lead to regular dance classes for women at many synagogues during the last two decades of the twentieth century?

So, we have two parallel forces, Judaism and Americanism. Sometimes they work together so that the joint effect, positive or negative is greater than the sum of each individual process. It is the thesis of this essay that America is different because its cultural, political and religious context shapes a unique version of Judaism, a novella or what is called a *Hiddush* in traditional Jewish discourse. The examples that follow to support this thesis come from the spheres of everyday life such as food, the search for meaning in life, the Jewish and American calendars, gender roles, the academy and life cycle rituals. In each case we shall see the fusion of American and Jewish norms and values played out in popular culture.

KOSHER SUPERBOWL PARTIES AND SPINOZA BAGELS

One impact of secularization on religion has been to narrow its sphere of influence in everyday life. Traditional Judaism is counter-cultural in this respect as the mitzvah (commandment) system central to it is pervasive. One of the most pervading sets of commandments relates to food. Traditional Jews may not consume any cooked food unless it meets biblical and rabbinic guidelines as to type and its preparation has been supervised by acceptable religious authorities.. In other places and other times the dietary laws and the civil or official religion of the country in which Jews lived moved on parallel tracks, never to interact. In America, however, even some who scrupulously adhere to the dietary laws choose to participate in

American rites. An example of this synergy can be found in a superbowl menu for the kosher restaurant on Manhattan's Upper Westside called "Dougie's Bar-B-Que & Grill." Only the kashrut symbol of the Orthodox Union stamped on the "pigskin" pictured on the side of the full page newspaper advertisement alerts the discerning reader to the fact that this menu of Fire Poppers, Buffalo Wings, B-B-Q Ribs and Three-foot Heros is aimed at Jews who observe the dietary laws. This approach eschews employing the psychological device of compartmentalization, that is, the separation of Jewish and American celebrations, a modus operandi typified by the enlightenment maxim that one should "be a Jew at home and a human being in the street." On the contrary, these Jewish Americans wish to enjoy the Superbowl (which is always on Sunday, and thus, like Thanksgiving, the quintessential American festival that is always on Thursday doesn't pose a conflict with Sabbath observance) with family and friends as they munch on "traditional" tailgating foods tailored to the occasion.

Just as committed Jews have included American civil religion in their lives, so too has American commerce incorporated Jewish symbols even when not catering to a targeted Jewish market. Trader Joe's store brand of bagels features a picture of the great (though excommunicated) 17th century Jewish philosopher Benedict (Baruch) Spinoza along side the tag line "It Bagels The Mind." To be sure, there is also a kashrut supervision symbol (KVH) and the designation Parve (can be eaten with meat or dairy) in the upper right hand corner. However, this chain of over 200 stores across the United States including Nevada, New Mexico and Oregon is marketing the bagel by appealing to those who shop for food prepared without artificial additives. (Incidentally, Trader Joe's line of English muffins is named for Disraeli and Gladstone – clearly someone in management has a sense of humor). On its website, the chain provides a nine page list of the foods it carries which have kosher certification with the following introduction:

> This kosher product list has been produced in an effort to make shopping a bit easier for our favorite label reading customers…We sail the culinary seas in search of new and exciting products. How does this affect our kosher shoppers? Because our products span the globe, you may spot kosher symbols that you do not recognize. Our list was compiled to help you become more familiar with kosher governing agencies that may not be from your neighborhood.

THE INFLUENCE OF MULTICULTURALISM

American business seeks to market its wares to an ever more diverse population. They try to do this while being politically correct and utilizing the cultural idiom of their new target audiences. The next example is one of a failed but noble attempt by a Boston area food chain to reach out to

Muslim shoppers. This ordinary looking advertisement by a large chain would draw a gasp or perhaps a sign, by someone with even a superficial knowledge of Islam. Alas, in contrast to the spirit of the month of fasting, the cheerful ad wishes potential Moslem customers a "Happy Ramadan." Insult is added to injury by the offer of whole boneless pork loin as the featured main dish with which to "celebrate" the occasion, and further illustrates the ignorance of the misguided but well intentioned marketing department that tried to cash in on multiculturalism. Some years ago, in a similar well-meaning attempt that went awry, a large supermarket chain in the Philadelphia area featured *hallah* bread in the center of its full page Passover advertisement.

A more felicitous example in praise of diversity is the "Mixed Blessing" greeting card (Figures 10.1 and 10.2). The manufacturer notes on the card's verso that "Our multicultural celebration combines Hanukkah, Christmas and Kwanzaa." As in the case with most cards of this type the fact that it is printed on recycled paper is mentioned as well. The assumption here, as with the Spinoza bagels and natural foods, is that those who appreciate religious and ethnic harmony while valuing diversity will also favor environmentally sound practice. Less tasteful but in the same vein is the Hanukkah card shown (Figure 10.3) parodying Christmas carols which includes a boxed section on the reverse explaining the virtues of its recycling program.

Figure 10.1.   Mixed Blessing greeting card (front).

MixedBlessing®

Our multicultural celebration combines Hanukkah, Christmas and Kwanzaa

printed on recycled paper

illustration by Alice io Oglesby

1.75 MC4

©1996 MixedBlessing, Inc. P.O. Box 97212, Raleigh, NC 27624 1-800-947-4004
Printed in USA

Figure 10.2.   Mixed Blessing greeting card (back).

Figure 10.3.   Hanukkah card.

SPIRITUALITY AND KABBALAH

The end of the twentieth and the first decade of the twenty-first century have witnessed an explosion of spiritual exploration in the United States. Perhaps this is a millennial occurrence. Some of the searching has been within mainline and evangelical Protestant denominations and movements and some has been of a more exploratory, new age variety.

It is fashionable to be on an individualistic spiritual quest, or journey. Within the Jewish community there is a parallel phenomenon with individual "returnees", born again Jews (known as *baalei* or *hozrei b'teshuva*) becoming observant and joining a variety of existing traditional communities. There are also some who seek their own, sometimes syncretistic paths either because they were brought up in dual faith households or because they meld Judaism with Buddism or Hinduism. These are now common enough that they have nicknames such as "Jewbu" or "Hinjew." Representatives of the establishment Jewish community visited the Dalai Lama so that he might learn about survival in diaspora from the world's experts. Roger Kamanetz, one member of the groups, returned and wrote a book entitled *The Jew and the Lotus* and lectured around the country speaking about "What I learned about Judaism from the Dalai Lama."

One of the most interesting synergies has taken place between non-Jewish celebrities and the medieval Jewish mystical system known as Kabbalah. Promoted widely by the late Rabbi Philip Berg, a multicultural version of Kabbalah has taken hold in Hollywood and New York. Promotional material set out in a coffee house in Center City, Philadelphia refers to Kabbalah as the "key that unlocks all the mysteries of life, the secret code that governs the universe." At the open house where Kabbalah is being promoted, philosophy will be explained but many goods will also be sold. The reader notes that classes and most goods are free or discounted but Kabbalah Mountain Spring Water and The Zohar (the classic foundational text of Kabbalah) are excluded! What a mix of the two trends noted above, traditional religion and the individualistic new age search for meaning. While not as minimalist as naming bagels for Spinoza, this incorporation of Jewish tradition for the non-Jewish masses is a remarkable phenomenon.

The most well known example of the Kabbalah influence is the championing of it by pop star Madonna, who has now changed her name to Ha-Malka Esther (Queen Esther) and who makes pilgrimages to Israel to encircle the graves of Jewish saints to seek their blessing for her life. According to one article "Madonna strikes a new pose for Shabbat" carried in *The Jewish Advocate* in September 2004, she spent five days in Israel with 2,000 other devotees of Kabbalah from around the world including Marla Maples, ex-wife of Donald Trump. Clearly Madonna has not left Catholicism, however she has taken on observance of certain Jewish laws and folk customs such as refraining from cooking on the Sabbath and lighting candles at the graves of famous Kabbalists. The Kabbalah-celebrity phenomenon has led to a renewed popularity of the study of the Jewish mystical system in liberal and even secular Jewish circles.

THE GENDER REVOLUTION

Whatever the relative valences of the American feminist movement from without or the internally sparked Jewish women's movement, it is clear that they interacted and that the synergy yielded major changes across the spectrum of American Judaism between 1975 and 2000. Other papers in this volume deal with this revolution in greater detail. Here, several examples are worth noting. Major arenas within which Jewish women's roles and opportunities expanded included classical and modern Jewish scholarship, synagogue professional and lay leadership roles, life cycle rituals and community leadership. The rhetoric accompanying these changes was also important as it helped to shift the imagery of the phrase Jewish woman. Thus, in November of 1999 Yeshiva university, the bastion of modern Orthodoxy advertised itself to the world through a full page in the in the *New York Times* with the title "My daughter the Doctor", boasting that the medical school acceptance rate for YU's Stern College for women had been 100% in the previous year. That same year, they began to recruit for a graduate program in Talmudic studies for women, touted as a "full-time two-year post-graduate program for women in Gemara and *Torah she'al Peh*." The fact that the program was only open to students with at least two years formal Talmud study on the college level indicated that there was a population of Orthodox women who had been studying Talmud (a subject previously forbidden to women) for some time.

It was clearly utilizing the skills learned in the civil rights struggle and under the influence of their awareness of the general American feminist movement of the mid to late 1960's that, according to Paula Hyman

A small Jewish feminist group, which we called *Ezrat Nashim*, presented the "Call for Change" to the Rabbinical Assembly of the Conservative movement on March 14, 1972 and disseminated it to the press. The rabbis received it in their convention packets, but we managed to arrange a face-to-face session with the rabbis' wives. *Ezrat Nashim* grew out of a study group on the status of women in Judaism that formed in the fall of 1971 in the New York Havurah, a countercultural community of young Jews who studied, observed Judaism, and engaged in politics together . . . We were all well-educated , in both Jewish and secular terms, and had been deeply affected by the nascent American feminist movement in which we participated. Within several months we determined that if any Jewish issue required political action, it was this one, the status of women. At the time we were ten women, the oldest of whom was 27. We chose to target the Conservative movement because most of us had grown up in its ranks, and because the Reform movement was already moving on the issue while Orthodoxy presented too many obstacles. (statement written for the Jewish Women's Archive website)

Many of the projects which *Ezrat Nashim* and similar groups undertook were parallel to those initiated in the general feminist movement. These included writing non-sexist stories for Jewish children; writing Jewish women back into history; creating life-cycle rituals to welcome baby girls into the world; lobbying for identical curriculum in Jewish studies for girls and boys and fighting for access to to top lay and professional leadership positions in Jewish communal life.

The celebration of a girls's Jewish coming of age became close to universal thanks to the Jewish feminist movement. Not only did public festivities become normative by 1980, but in the Reform, Reconstructionist and Conservative movements, girls took part in the synagogue rituals previously open only to boys while among the modern Orthodox, they gave learned discourses at luncheons, and sometimes, even in the synagogue at the close of the services.

A final example of Jewish-American interaction is a sign accompanying centerpieces at a Bat Mitzvah luncheon in a large Conservative synagogue around the year 2000. Replacing costly floral centerpieces with scrolls indicating contributions to various charities in honor of guest;, books to be donated to Jewish libraries; canned foods for shelters; or sporting goods to be donated to schools in impoverished areas was an innovation of the last quarter of the twentieth century. Perhaps this could have taken place in Jerusalem or Paris as well. However, the centerpieces at Talia's Bat Mitzvah were made up of animal food designated for the Society for the Prevention of Cruelty to Animals. This particularly American mix would not have been acceptable outside of the United States.

CONCLUSION—WHY IS AMERICA DIFFERENT?

This essay has focused on the interplay of Jewish and American forces as they fostered the vitality and quality of American Jewish institutional and spiritual life particularly in the last quarter of the twentieth century. This synergy created a whole that is greater than the sum of its parts, as was the case with the gender revolution and the ability to combine America civil religion with traditional Judaism on occasions such as Thanksgiving and Superbowl Sunday. On the other hand, some of the parts may be superficial and/or negative, as has been the case with much of the popularity of Kabbalah. "Why is America Different?" The short answer proposed here is that America is different because of the fusion of its multi-cultural ethic and popular cultural forms with Judaism in a synergistic relationship.

11

American Anti-Semitism: The Myth and Reality of American Exceptionalism

Michael N. Dobkowski

Philip Roth in his important new political novel, *The Plot Against America*, imagines an alternative American history in which America has gone fascist, and ordinary life is subverted by ideologically driven national politics and mass hatreds. Hitler's allies control the White House, anti-Semitic mobs roam the streets brutalizing and killing, reminiscent of the Brown shirts in Nazi Germany, and the lower-middle-class Jews of Weequahic in Newark, N.J., cower behind locked doors waiting for the inevitable.[1]

In Roth's version of history, the Republicans nominate Charles A. Lindbergh for president in 1940 and he defeats F.D.R. in a landslide on an isolationist plank. "Keep America Out of the Jewish War" reads a button worn by Lindbergh supporters rallying at Madison Square Garden. And so he does: he signs nonaggression pacts with Germany and Japan that will keep America at peace while Europe burns and six million European Jews are exterminated. Lindbergh, in real life as in the novel, was an admirer of Adolf Hitler, a recipient of the Nazi Service Cross of the German Eagle and was hostile to Jews and what he believed was their excessive influence.[2] We know that fascism took over most of Europe in those years and Roth posits an ingenious "what if" and skillfully closes the gap between far-fetched hypothetical and possible reality. He shows how quickly the rights and democratic values of American life are lost under the authoritarian guidance of President Lindbergh and his "Just Folks" program which sets out to break up Jewish families by scattering Jewish children into the Christian heartland where they can be absorbed and assimilated. He has columnist and radio personality, Walter Winchell, (Jewish), running for president in 1944 until he is killed by as assassin. Roth describes Jewish school children "heatedly debating whether Walter Winchell's crisscrossing the country with his soapbox to flush into the open the German-American Bundists and the Coughlinites and the Ku Klux Klanners and the Silver Shirts and the American Firsters and the Black Legion and the American Nazi Party and their thousands of unseen sympathizers to reveal themselves for what they were—was good for the Jews or bad for the Jews."[3] As the society darkens with the isolationist clamor that it is only the Jews who want war, their plot against America, Walter Winchell counters that the plotters are Nazi sympathizers who would destroy the constitution, while some Jews say other Jews just don't appreciate how real the threat is.

In *The Plot Against America*, Roth's incredible imagination opens up reflections on deep aspects of the American Jewish experience. Who are America's Jews? How and why do they see themselves assimilating (or not) into the heartland of America? How do gentiles really see Jews? What is the true nature of Jewish identity? One is reminded of Sartre's troubling and flawed observation that the world decides what it means to be Jewish. It is not up to Jews.[4]

The novel is, on many levels, dark, fable-like, disturbing, preposterous and, as Paul Berman writes in his New York Times book review "creepily plausible."[5] Roth seems to be playing with the emotions of the reader. "You think swastikas are only for other countries?" And then you turn the pages and find yourself astonished and afraid, like the young narrator of the novel, Philip, who begins the novel with the lament that "fear presides over these memories, a perpetual fear . . . I wonder if I would have been a less frightened boy if Lindbergh hadn't been president or if I hadn't been the offspring of Jews."[6]

What I would like to do in this essay, using Roth's novel as a backdrop, is to reflect on the plausibility of his scenario and on the nature of American anti-Semitism, particularly as we try to put it in the context of the history of anti-Semitism generally, as well as to understand its place in American history specifically. Let me begin with a few general reflections. There apparently has been a ready market for anti-Semitism, religious and racial, medieval, modern, and now postmodern. George Steiner attributes this perpetual hatred of the Jews to their "invention of conscience." That is how Steiner characterizes Moses' demand for obedience to law, Jesus' demand for love and sacrifice, and Marx's demand for perfect Justice. These demands of perfection by Jews that are unfullfillable are the source of deep and bitter resentment of the people who devised them. Others say it is because Jews have chosen to be "a people who dwells apart," as the Biblical Pagan prophet Balaam proclaimed, unwilling to assimilate or submerge their identity. "The longest hatred," as Robert Wistrich, one of the foremost interpreters of the history of anti-Semitism called it, has continued in response to a simple observation: that Jews are perceived to be different from the people among whom they live. From ancient times through the centuries of Christian hegemony in Europe, and Muslim hegemony in the Middle East, dislike, even hatred of the Jews, grew out of their commitment to their own religion and their rejection of those of others. Jews are, of course, not responsible for the negative reactions of the dominant cultures to them—merely the recipients of that prejudice. Victims are never responsible for their victimization. During the 1500 years of Christian hegemony in Europe, the roots of that hatred were religious and theological, as many have pointed out. In the modern era, the hatred sprang from religious roots secularized, with the Jewish difference being more and more attributed to race and ideology. Common to both religious and secular forms of anti-Semitism, however, were deeply hostile reactions to Jews as a people singularly apart—for centuries the most visible of European minorities in a continent defined as Christian to the core: and in Muslim countries becoming increasingly hegemonic, the most visible non-Muslim minority. The key, it seems to me, is that in a world in which difference is increasingly a source of conflict, the otherness of the Jew appeared salient and pernicious.[7]

Now when this tendency is brought to the new world with the Europeans who settled here, there were new conditions and circumstances that clearly contributed to lessening the potency and centrality of anti-Semitism. Yes, fear and prejudice against Jews persisted in the folk memories and popular traditions that the immigrants brought with them here. But they were filtered through the prism of a democratic society in the making, of a frontier sensibility that paid less attention to religious ideas than the practical challenges of making a go of it in a land with limitless opportunities but formidable challenges, and a society where there were other outsiders, other potential victims. Hatred of the other increasingly found on this soil more convenient targets—other immigrants, racial, religious and national minorities to focus on.

The important thing to say at this point, however, is that the unique tenacity of anti-Semitism with an enduring spatial and historical reach is reinforced by the fact that it reared its head, with varying degrees of intensity, even in democracies like the United States. Obviously, America has been different than Europe and the rest of the world on this issue; clearly, overt political, structural and violent anti-Semitism has been much less of a factor here, but that does not mean that America has been free of its influence. To be sure, if we look at the American Jewish experience in the broad stroke and with comparative lenses we must come away impressed by the tremendous accomplishments of this community—the unprecedented access to political office, college admissions, virtually every sector of the economy, employment, housing, culture. Jews have achieved significant economic, social and political successes in America. An Orthodox Jew was nominated for the vice presidency in 2000 with almost negligible backlash. But, we have to look at why and how this was achieved, at what cost, and examine the struggles that were necessary to secure these opportunities and we have to also evaluate American anti-Semitism in terms of American values and expectations and ask the question, in the final analysis, should America be held to a higher standard? And if it is, perhaps our overall assessment of the extent and impact of American anti-Semitism needs to be modified, or at the very least, qualified.

Elsewhere I have argued that anti-Semitism has been far more important and pervasive in our national history than most scholars were willing to admit and that its persistence over time in different social and economic contexts throws some doubt on the socioeconomic or structural explanations of its existence.[8] Instead, taking a cue from Jean Paul Sartre's classic essay *Anti-Semite and Jew*, it is the "idea" of the Jew that animates the anti-Semite. I draw attention to the ideological origins of this tendency that focuses on the various images of Jews as enemies of Christianity, as materialists, as international conspirators, as quintessential outsiders. It is certainly true that pride in America as a haven for the oppressed and the liberal traditions of tolerance, individuality, and equal opportunity helped create, as Jonathan Sarna has pointed out, the ambivalent attitude Americans have had concerning Jews, often combining feelings of hostility with feelings of friendship and acceptance.[9] But it is also true that, during certain key periods in our history this ambivalence slides into outright hostility. I want to focus briefly on the two decades from 1920–1940 as the period that, I believe, witnessed the most significant eruption of anti-Semitism in our history and ask whether it should force a re-evaluation of the significance of this social pathology in the context of the overall American Jewish experience.

The fact remains that anti-Semitism erupted even in reformist and freedom-loving sectors of American society. The democratic impulse was not and may not always be resolute enough to overcome the psychological and social momentum of anti-Semitic stereotyping.[10] True, America never visited mass physical oppression upon its Jews. But there are more subtle forms of oppression—economic, social, and cultural—that are also damaging and painful. In addition to the ideological factors, Jews faced the serious problem of social discrimination. Saratoga, Nahant, Newport, Long Branch, Lakewood, even New York City became battlegrounds. Signs like "No Jews or Dogs Admitted Here" were common in many of America's finest resorts. Advertisements in the *New York Times* and the *New York Tribune* often used euphemisms like "restricted clientele," "discriminating families only," and "Christian patronage." Rather than accept this discrimination, some prominent Jews, including Nathan Straus, retaliated by buying several of the leading hotels that excluded Jews.[11]

Discrimination at summer resorts, private schools, and clubs increased during the years before World War I. The Century Club in New York rejected the distinguished scientist Jacques Loeb because he was a Jew. Most Masonic lodges excluded Jews. Some of the most prestigious preparatory schools, such as Exeter, Hotchkiss, and Andover, had small Jewish quotas. After 1900, few Jews were elected to the Princeton clubs or to the fraternities at Yale, Columbia, and Harvard. The literary and gymnastic societies at Columbia excluded Jews. As a result, Jewish students gradually formed their own fraternities, the first appearing at Columbia in 1898. The anti-Semitic feelings also infected college faculties. It was common knowledge that few Jews could gain entry to or advancement in American academic circles.[12]

Social discrimination reached a climax in the quota systems adopted by colleges and medical schools in the years after World War I. Many colleges set limits on Jewish enrollment. Some established alumni committees to screen applicants. Others, under the pretext of seeking regional balance, gave preference to students outside the East, thereby limiting the number of Jews, who were heavily concentrated there. The most common method of exclusion came with the introduction of character and psychological examinations.

Before the 1920's scholastic performance was the most important criterion in admissions policies. Now admissions committees devised tests to rank students on such characteristics as "public spirit," "fair play," "interest in fellows," and "leadership," traits not usually associated in the popular mind with Jews. Here we see that negative imagery can have social consequences. According to the prevailing opinion, "public spirit" and "interest in fellows" were Christian virtues; Jews were excessively clannish and cared only for their group. "Leadership" also was seen as a Protestant virtue; Jews exhibiting it would be regarded as aggressive and pushy.[13] By 1919 New York University instituted stringent restrictions and introduced psychological testing. Chancellor Elmor Brown justified this policy, citing the "separateness" of the Jewish student body.[14] Columbia University cut the number of Jews in the incoming classes from 40 to 20 percent. At Harvard, where elite Protestant students and faculty feared the university's becoming a "new Jerusalem," President A. Lawrence Lowell in 1922 recommended a quota system, openly adopting what other institutions were doing covertly. "There is a rapidly growing anti-Semitic feeling in this country," he wrote in June of that year, "caused by . . . a strong race feeling on the part of the Jews."[15] Smaller colleges, perhaps more rigid than some large, urban ones, used more subjective criteria such as requiring a photograph of the candidate and enforcing a geographic distribution. The problem was even greater in medical schools, which erected formidable barriers throughout the country, severely limiting Jewish enrollments and causing undue hardship.[16] The adoption of a Jewish quota that began explicitly at Columbia, New York University and Harvard reflected the behind-the-scenes policy between 1920 and the mid 1940's at most eastern private liberal arts colleges and elite universities, in the major state universities in the South and Midwest, and nationally in many medical, dental, and law schools. As Marcia Graham Synnott has argued, the reason for these limitations was "to perpetuate the economic and social position of middle and upper-middle-class, white native-born Protestants." This policy also had social and economic implications because "few manufacturing companies, corporate law firms, private hospitals, or such government bureaucracies as the State Department welcomed Jews."[17]

The 1920s also saw the proliferation of "restrictive covenants" in housing through which owners pledged not to sell their homes and property to Jews and other undesirable groups. Economic discrimination also grew. Jews could not find positions in banking, insurance, and public utilities firms. Employment agencies found that Jews were unacceptable to most employers. The Alliance Employment Bureau in New York City, for example, wrote to Cyrus Sulzberger, president of the United Hebrew Charities, in 1908: "We are finding great difficulty in placing our Jewish boys and girls, an increasing number of employers absolutely refusing to take them." The Katharine Gibbs School for secretarial training informed a Jewish applicant in 1928 that its policy was "not to accept students of Jewish nationality." Insurance companies such as Connecticut Mutual Life Insurance Company, the Shawnee Fire Insurance Company, and the New Jersey Fire Insurance Company, urged their agents not to insure Jewish clients because they were "an extraordinary hazardous class."[18]

The most significant ideological attack against Jews occurred during the 1920s and 1930s. It focused not on religious issues or Jewish social climbing but on race and political subversion. A resurgent Ku Klux Klan activated the myths about Jews as Christ killers and race polluters. More significantly, the country witnessed the resurrection of the international stereotype of the Jew as half banker and half Bolshevik, conspiring to seize control of the nation. This belief, having been foreshadowed during the Civil War, emerged in the 1890s during the Populist ferment and crystallized in the early 1920s around auto magnate Henry Ford. In May 1922, Ford's newspaper, the *Dearborn Independent*, launched an anti-Semitic propaganda campaign without precedent in American history. It lasted for about seven years. In time, the newspaper "exposed" Jewish control of everything from the League of Nations to American politics, from baseball and jazz to agriculture and movies. If any pattern of ideas activated discrimination, it was the conspiratorial ferment to which, Henry Ford, and the Ku Klux Klan contributed.[19]

This intensification of ideological anti-Semitism and discrimination in the United States was happening at the worst possible time for European Jews who would soon need havens of refuge from Nazi Germany. If their destination was the United States, a logical and attractive choice because of its humanitarian traditions and because much of the rest of the world was closed off to them, the immigration laws of the United States marked the first hurdle for the Jewish immigrants and later refugees. In 1924, Congress, responding to a wide range of restrictionist pressure, passed the Johnson-Reed Bill or National Origins Act as it was subsequently named. It provided for an annual immigration of 164,667, 2 percent of each European nationality represented in the United States population in 1890. The new quota, effective July 1, 1929, would be 153,714 based on the proportional representation of the respective nationalities in the United States population in 1890.[20]

The quota allotments as finally determined in 1929, reveal as much about the racist thinking of the period as they do about the national origins of the American people of 1890 upon which they were based. Of the quota, 81.9 percent was assigned to the nations of Northern and Western Europe; 54 percent to Great Britain and Ireland alone. Under this formula, the German quota was 25,557 and the Austrian 1,413 annually, and even these were unfilled during the 1930's because of the overly scrupulous interpretation of the law. In the 1920s no one needed to apologize for racist opinions, for racism was a popular doctrine accepted in many intellectual and scientific circles. In an America swept by Red Scares and xenophobia to new degrees of prejudice and in a nation turning its back on world affairs, the question of inner unity and homogeneity took on increased import. The isolationist reaction of the 1920s not only pressed home the danger of world entanglements in a more conscious and articulate manner than ever before, but also underscored for those sensitive to increased immigration the threat that national enclaves within would impede the fortress America concept.

Nativism echoed through the halls of the universities. It swayed the policies of the American Legion and rumbled in the "Konklaves" of the Ku Klux Klan; it unleashed a new torrent of interest in restrictive immigration legislation.[21]

The majority of the American people, including many liberal and labor leaders, were opposed to the reform of existing immigration laws and regulations. Joseph Chamberlain, prominent law professor, friend and advocate of refugees, wrote in 1934 to James G. McDonald, League of Nations High Commissioner for Refugees Coming from Germany, that although economic factors opposing increased immigration were most important, "there were nevertheless some outcries based on racial grounds. The Bureau of Immigration was really alarmed over the demonstration, and is nervous over the possibilities of difficulty being made by the A. F. of L., so that they are treading very cautiously in respect to allowing immigrants to enter." On November 20, 1939, Walter White, Secretary of the NAACP wrote: "There appears to be a growing opinion that huge hordes of immigrants are pouring into the United States and are displacing native-born or naturalized Americans in jobs. I believe that a good deal of this is being stirred up by anti-Semitic and other groups."[22]

There were anti-refugee and anti-immigration campaigns in nation-wide publications throughout this period. Refugees were accused of being wealthy, parvenu, conspicuous consumers. The group, it was charged, had not only "taken over" exclusive hotels, "overrun" fashionable resorts, and "paraded" in expensive restaurants and night clubs, but was attempting to shape American cultural and intellectual life and had often behaved in an arrogant, self-assertive, ostentatious and rude manner.[23] In 1934–37, *The Saturday Evening Post* published numerous editorials and articles demanding immigration restriction. This was significant, for George Horace Lorimer's magazine had a circulation of a record 3 million copies a week in 1937, higher than any other magazine up to that time. The writers argued that the number of foreigners in the United States must be cut down because of unemployment, but they placed even more emphasis on the undesirability of most refugees. They called the émigrés a *moral menace* and warned that "thousands of foreigners . . . foment strikes, work to overthrow our political system, and aim at the disaffection of the men in the Army and Navy." In referring to the refugees, one editorial asked whether we should "allow our indignation to deprive us of our common sense?" Congressman Martin Dies of Texas answered in a later issue: "What our unhappy country needs today is more so-called selfish patriotism and less fatuous internationalism . . . We must cease being made the dupes and willing victims of European duplicity, deceit and cunning."[24] The Hearst newspapers likewise flooded the country with anti-refugee publicity directed chiefly against the alleged Communist activities of the foreign-born.[25]

Other influential commentators followed suit. Sociologist Henry Pratt Fairchild was opposed to loosening the quota restrictions because he did not want to exacerbate American anti-Semitism. "Any increase in numbers of the outsiders to the point where they become definitely conspicuous is a sure sign for the rise of antipathy and perhaps active opposition."[26] Journalist Jane Ellsworth referred to the émigrés as a "cultural plague . . . Out of step with America's development, the European émigré is equipped with intellectual tools, psychologies, philosophies—all outmoded products of the decadent, have-been nations . . . The European is stymied by his Old World sophistry, the tiredness and failure of his nation."[27] Another observer queried whether "Americans want their children taught by refugees from Europe and American civilization affected by alien scholarship? . . . Must or should America shoulder problems, burdens and anxieties thrust upon her because of the violent policies of European dictators? Must we help the alien at the expense of our own citizen?"[28] Still another referred to "the choking atmosphere of defeatism . . . in refugee-dominated New York."[29]

Negative portrayals abounded. "No doubt, we all know the type of German Jew," one critic remarked, "who has been flung out of Germany. Yet for many years he continues to find fault with his new environment, saying tauntingly "in our country'—i.e., in Germany—'these or other things are better and more beautiful.' The German-Jewish immigrant, who behaves so ungraciously, certainly makes a nuisance of himself."[30] A Black commentator found the German Jew to be a "loud-spoken insensitive braggart . . . He must be seen at any price. He talks loudly, displays his money, jewelry and clothing, annoying everybody with fabulous stories of his wealth and importance."[31] Senator Robert Reynolds of North Carolina, a leading restrictionist, had printed in the *Congressional Record* an attack on refugees for "systematically building a Jewish empire in this country."[32] These images and opinions did little to contribute to a forthright and sensitive reception of the refugees.

Two public opinion surveys, one conducted before the Anschluss in March 1938 and the other after Kristallnacht in November, demonstrated how little even these two shocking events affected people's attitudes toward the refugees. Roughly the same percentage thought that refugees should not be admitted. In reply to a question in the first poll: "What is your attitude toward allowing German, Austrian, and other political refugees to come into the United States?" 4.9 percent thought that we should encourage them to come even if we must raise the immigration quotas; 18.2 percent thought that we should allow them to come in but not raise the immigration quotas (making 23.1 percent); 67.4 percent said that with conditions as they are we should try to keep them out. On November 22, 1938, the question asked was: "Should we allow a large number of Jewish exiles from Germany to come to the United States to live?" Twenty-three percent answered in the affirmative and 77 percent in the negative.[33] In a 1939 *Fortune* poll, the question asked was, "If you were a member of Congress would you vote yes or no on a bill to open the doors of the United States to a larger number of refugees than are now admitted under our immigration quotas?" 8.7 percent replied "yes," 83 percent, "no."[34] The message was clear; refugees were not welcome.

The reasons for wanting to keep the doors of America shut were basically consistent throughout the 1930s: an ostrich-like isolationist sentiment; a Depression decade fear that refugees would take jobs away from Americans; the difficulty of raising money to assist them; concern lest émigrés add to the relief rolls; desire to guard against the importation of alien and radical philosophies and attitudes; belief that it was impossible to make pioneering types out of city dwellers, especially Jews; fear that refugees were aliens and aliens bred crime; the anti-immigrant and anti-Semitic attitudes which prevailed; and the feeling that the whole Hitler mess was a European, not an American problem.[35]

With the approach of World War II, these issues were further clouded by events in Europe. As Hitler proved to be virulently anti-Semitic, American Jews, and many others, began to argue for intervention in the affairs of Europe, a stand resented by isolationists committed to keeping America out of the impending conflagration. On September 11, 1941, another fateful 9/11 date, American aviation hero Charles Lindbergh warned that the Jews and President Roosevelt were conspiring to bring the nation into a war against Germany and that it would be catastrophic for America. He said that." . . . no person of honesty and vision can look at their pro-war policy here today without seeing the dangers involved in such a policy, both for us and for them. Instead of agitating for war, the Jewish groups in this country should be opposing it in every possible way . . . Their greatest danger to this country lies in their large ownership and influence in our motion pictures, our press, our radio and our government."[36]

This sentiment fed into a form of Catholic anti-Semitism best represented by Father Charles Coughlin, who spoke for the beliefs of small-town America. Beginning in 1936 in his journal, *Social Justice*, and on his widely aired radio broadcasts (with 20 to 30 million listeners); he began to argue that European fascism was a legitimate response to the more pernicious threat of communism that was largely inspired by Jews. His diatribes continued until 1942, when he was finally taken off the air. But Fritz Kuhn's German-American Bund, Gerald L.K. Smith, Dudley Pelley, and other pro-Nazi and anti-Semitic groups and individuals kept the issue alive. More than one hundred ant-Semitic organizations were formed in the United States in the 1930s, including the Silver Shirts, the Friends of Democracy, and the National Union for Social Justice.[37]

The situation became more acute when European Jews began to seek refuge in this country. The growing isolationism and xenophobia of the 1930s, as well as public opinion polls of the period, have shown how stereotyping, how the idea of the Jew, reinforced insensitivity and misunderstanding and contributed to the government's inertia in the face of an unprecedented human tragedy. The critical decade of the 1930s was clearly characterized by a high degree of acceptance and approval of anti-Semitism in America. Although claiming some sympathy for the plight of the refugees, from a distance, most Americans remained unalterably opposed to admitting them.

Consequently, only approximately 127,000 refugees, or an average of a little over 18,000 a year, came to the United States between 1933 and 1940. Without congressional action, 183,112 could have entered the United States from Germany and Austria, for example, the principal countries from which emigration was still possible before 1940. Obstruction, red tape, restrictionism, and anti-Semitism, kept out at least 55,000 others.[38]

Yes, overt political, structural and violent anti-Semitism has been much less of a factor here than in Europe. The sum of the individual cases of American anti-Semitism before WW II may seem relatively insignificant. But when viewed from the point of view of the callous lack of concern for Nazi refugees and the refusal to admit them that led to certain death for countless thousands—we can use the 55,000 figure as a very low-end estimate—then the reality becomes painfully disturbing. This is violent anti-Semitism American style—indirect, couched in bureaucratic inertia and legality and polite obfuscations and rationalizations, but deadly none-theless. And it was largely motivated by ideological factors, the "idea of the Jew," the images that animated the Charles Lindbergh's of America and may have inspired Philip Roth to write his novel which, in retrospect, may not appear as fantastic and unrealistic as some may suppose.

If America is held to a higher standard because of its professed values, and I believe it must in any evaluation of this problem or any major social ill here, it is these values that have been stained by our behavior in the 1920's and 30's. Sure, we have to celebrate the unprecedented accomplish-ments of American Jews in the most tolerant diasporic experience in Jewish history—that is clear. But we also have to ask whether the experiences then should give us some pause about our sense, maybe inflated sense, that these benefits are permanent and that they may, in fact, be more fragile than we would like to believe. This brings me back to the Roth novel.

The anti-Semitism Roth describes comes mostly from an isolationist resentment—from the belief that the Jews have a separate agenda, are not loyal citizens and that they, and not the Nazis, bear responsibility for the war and are trying to advance their own selfish interests at everyone else's expense. As the novel rushes to its wild end, with America beset by *coup d'etats* and mob vio-lence and a president who has disappeared, Roth has German radio denounc-ing a conspiracy by "the warmonger Roosevelt—in collusion with his Jewish Treasury Secretary, Morgenthau, his Jewish Supreme Court Justice, Frankfurter and the Jewish investment banker, Baruch" with help from half-Jew La Guar-dia, and Governor Lehman." . . . to return Roosevelt to the White House and launch an all-out Jewish war against the non-Jewish world."[39] Roth also has Mayor La Guardia say: "There's a plot afoot all right, and I'll gladly name the forces propelling it—hysteria, ignorance, malice, stupidity, hatred, and fear. What a repugnant spectacle our country has become. Falsehood, cruelty, and madness everywhere, and brute forces in the wings waiting to finish us off . . . How it must please the Fuhrer to be poisoning our country with this sin-ister nonsense. Jewish interests. Jewish elements. Jewish usurers. Jewish retali-ation. Jewish conspiracies. A Jewish war against the world. To have enslaved America with this hocus-pocus! To have captured the mind of the world's greatest nation without uttering a single word of truth! Oh, the pleasure we must be affording the most malevolent man on earth!"[40]

In this conspiratorial rant, it is possible to detect a few echoes from our own time. During the last decade, in what many see as the emergence of a new anti-Semitism, large numbers of people in Europe and the U.S. have taken up the view that if extremist political movements and terrorism have swept across the Muslim world and if radical Islamists and their supporters and fellow-travelers target the U.S., Israel and its crimes against the Palestinians must ultimately be to blame. And if the U.S. has been drawn into a war with Iraq, it is because of the disproportionate influence of the neoconservatives, many of whom are Jewish. And if there has been a disturbing escalation of violence directed against Jews in Europe and an escalation of heinous language, cartoons, placards accusing Israel of the most unspeakable crimes, approaching blood libel charges, it is because of Sharon and his "Nazi"-like policies. And if there is violence and intimidation on American and Canadian University campuses directed at Jewish students it is because they support Israel, a racist state. And if there are modern day Baathists and radical Islamists who likewise speak about an all-out Jewish war for control and for cosmic evil, sometimes with phrases and concepts and books that have been lifted directly from the European and American ultra right and fascists of the 1930's, then maybe there are some tentative connections between these two periods, connections that go beyond a novelist's imagination.[41] Now, like then, there are mad, conspiratorial ideas floating around that seem to be finding a home not only among the die-hard committed anti-Semites, but among the fellow-travelers who would be surprised to be lumped together with Nazi-era sympathizers. As journalist and novelist Jonathan Rosen wrote several years ago in a *New York Times Magazine* piece, "I have awakened to anti-Semitism. I am not being chased down alleyways and called a Christ killer . . . I do not feel that prejudicial hiring practices will keep me out of a job, and I am not afraid that the police will come and take away my family . . . But in recent weeks I have been reminded, in ways too plentiful to ignore, about the role Jews play in the fantasy life of the world. Jews were not the cause of WW II . . . Jews are not the cause of WW III, if that's what we are facing, but they have been placed at the center of it in mysterious and disturbing ways."[42]

That is why it is important to take a new look at that earlier period in U.S. history to see how close we came to the unthinkable and to re-evaluate the scope of American anti-Semitism with those decades as the fulcrum. We may come away with a renewed sense of the dangers of ideologically driven hatred, then and now, of the realization that ideas can kill, both directly and indirectly, by preventing a nation from saving potentially tens of thousands of the desperate and helpless Jews who could have come here within quotas but did not thus begging for a re-evaluation of the claim that America never visited mass violence against Jews—it did not directly kill Jews, certainly, but indirectly its policies and attitudes contributed to the significant loss of Jewish life. America is different, but maybe not different enough.

NOTES

1. Philip Roth, *The Plot Against America* (Boston, 2004).

2. A. Scott Berg, *Lindbergh* (New York, 1998).

3. Roth, *The Plot Against America*, p. 267.

4. Jean-Paul Sartre, *Anti-Semite and Jew* (New York, 1965).

5. Paul Berman, "What if it Happened Here?" *The New York Times Book Review* (Oct. 3, 2004), pp. 1, 14–16, 28.

6. Roth, *The Plot Against America*, p. 1.

7. See George Steiner, *Language and Silence* (New Haven, 1998), Dennis Prager and Joseph Telushkin, *Why the Jews?* (New York, 1983), Joshua Trachtenberg, *The Devil and the Jews* (Philadelphia, 1983), Norman Cohn, *Warrant for Genocide* (New York, 1967), and Robert Wistrich, *Antisemitism: The Longest Hatred* (New York, 1991).

8. Michael N. Dobkowski, *The Tarnished Dream: The Basis of American Anti-Semitism* (Westport, CT., 1979).

9. Jonathan Sarna, "Anti-Semitism and American History," *Commentary*, Vol.17 (March 1981), pp. 42–47.

10. John Higham, *Send These To Me: Jews and Other Immigrants in Urban America* (New York, 1975), pp. 131–35.

11. *Ibid.*, pp. 48–49.

12. *Ibid.*, pp. 150–52.

13. See Stephen Steinberg, "How Jewish Quotas Began, *Commentary*, vol. 52 (September, 1971), pp. 71–72.

14. *New York University Daily News* (May 11, 1923), p. 4.

15. A. Lawrence Lowell to A. C. Ratshevsky, June 7, 1922, American Jewish Committee Archives, General Correspondence, 1906–32 (New York City), folder D-E, s.v. "discrimination."

16. Higham, *Send These To Me*, pp. 159–62.

17. See Marcia Graham Synnott, "Anti-Semitism and American Universities: Did Quotas Follow the Jews?," in David A. Gerber, ed., *Anti-Semitism in American History* (Urbana, 1986), p. 234. See also Lawrence Bloomgarden, "Our Changing Elite Colleges," *Commentary*, vol. 29 (February, 1960), pp. 152–6; Synnott, *The Half-Opened Door: Discrimination and Admissions at Harvard, Yale and Princeton, 1900–1970* (Westport, CT: Greenwood Press, 1979); and Dan A. Oren, *Joining the Club: A History of Jews and Yale* (New Haven, CT., 1985).

18. American Jewish Committee Archives, G-C 1906–32, Cyrus Sulzberger Folder.

19. See Neil Baldwin, *Henry Ford and the Jews* (New York, 2001), Joseph Bendersky, *The "Jewish Threat," Anti-Semitic Politics of the U.S. Army* (New York, 2000), and Higham, *Send These To Me*, pp. 169–72, 187–88.

20. John Higham, *Strangers in the Land: Patterns of American Nativism 1860–1925* (New York, 1971); Robert A. Divine, *American Immigration Policy, 1924–1952* (New Haven: 1957).

21. *Ibid.*

22. Quoted in Zosa Szajkowski, "The Attitude of American Jews to Refugees from Germany in the 1930's," *American Jewish Historical Quarterly*, vol. 61 (December, 1971), pp. 101–2.

23. Emily Post, "The Refugees," *New York Herald Tribune*, May 28, 1944; S.F. Porter, "Refugee Gold Rush," *American Magazine*, October 1942; "Rules for Refugees, Royal or Otherwise, while in America," *Life*, December 16, 1940; "May We Offer Apologies for 'Life's Boorishness?'", *PM* (December 24, 1940).

24. Isaac F. Marcosson, "The Alien in America," *Saturday Evening Post*, April 6, 1935, pp. 22, 110 ff; May 19, 1934, p. 22; Martin Dies, "The Immigration Crises," April 20, 1935, pp. 27, 105; Stewart, p. 237.

25. *Interpreter Release*, April 15, 1935, p. 142; May 7, 1935, p. 192.

26. Henry Pratt Fairchild, "Are Refugees a Liability? A Debate: New Burdens for America," *Forum* (June 1939), pp. 317.

27. Jane Ellsworth, "Backwash from the Wave of the Future," *Scribner's Commentator*, vol. 10 (June 1941), pp. 7–9.

28. Abbott Hamilton, "Refugee Scholars and American Education," *Scribner's Commentator*, vol. 10 (December 1941), pp. 90–92.

29. *Scribner's Commentator*, vol.10 (July 1941), pp. 3.

30. Willi Schlamm, "Cultural Dilemma of the Refugee," *Jewish Frontier*, vol. 6 (February 1939), p. 8.

31. Lewis K. McMillan, "An American Negro Looks at the German Jew," *The Christian Century*, vol. 55 (August 31, 1938), p. 1034.

32. U.S. *Congressional Record*, 76th Cong. 1st sess., p. 4546.

33. "The Fortune Quarterly Survey," *Fortune*, vol. 18 (July 1938), p. 80; Hadley Cantril, Milder Strank, eds., *Public Opinion: 1935–1946* (Princeton, 1951), p. 385; Stewart, pp. 360–61.

34. "The Fortune Quarterly Survey," *Fortune*, vol. 19 (April 1939): 102–104.

35. See Feingold, Friedlander, Morse, Wyman, and Stewart, p. 362.

36. The text of the speech appears in full at www.pbs.org/wgbh/amex/lindbergh/filmmore/reference/primary/desmoinspeech.html.

37.See Baldwin, *Henry Ford and the Jews*; Michael Barkun, *Religion and the Racist Right: The Origins of the Christian Identity Movement* (Chapel Hill, 1994); Berg, Lindbergh, Alan Brinkley, *Voices of Protest: Huey Long, Father Coughlin and the Great Depression* (New York, 1983); Leonard Dinnerstein, *Uneasy at home: Antisemitism and the American Jewish Experience* (New York, 1987); Dinnerstein, *Antisemitism in America* (New York, 1994); Glen Jeansonne, *Gerald L.K. Smith, Minister of Hate* (Baton Rouge, 1997); Donald Strong, *Organized Anti-Semitism in America* (Washington, D.C., 1941); and Donald Warren, *Radio Priest: Charles Coughlin, The Father of Hate Radio* (New York, 1990).

38. See Saul Friedman, *No Haven for the Oppressed* (Detroit, 1973); Henry Feingold, *The Politics of Rescue* (New Brunswick, NJ, 1970); Arthur D. Morse, *While Six Million Died* (New York, 1967); David Wyman, *Paper Walls* (Amherst, 1968); Wyman, *The Abandonment of the Jews* (New York, 1984); Walter Laqueur, *The Terrible Secret* (Boston, 1980); and Michael Dobkowski, *The Politics of Indifference* (Washington, DC, 1982).

39. Roth, *The Plot Against America*, pp. 309–10.

40. *Ibid.*, pp. 315–16.

41. See Ron Rosenbaum, ed., *Those Who Forget The Past* (New York, 2004); Gabriel Schoenfeld, *The Return of Anti-Semitism* (San Francisco, 2004); Abraham Foxman, *Never Again?* (San Francisco, 2003), and Paul Berman, *Terror and Liberation* (New York, 2003).

42. Jonathan Rosen, "The Uncomfortable Question of Anti-Semitism," *The New York Times Magazine*, November 4, 2001.

12

To Make "a Jew": Projecting Anti-Semitism in Post-War America

Donald Weber

To see your own face look to what you say of the Jews.

—Cynthia Ozick[1]

In this moment her eyes had made a Jew of him.

—Focus[2]

For the anti-Semite, the Jew is a living Rorschach inkblot . . . the anti-Semite sees whatever he needs to see in the Jew.

—Anti-Semitism and Emotional Disorder[3]

In the wake of Word War II and the horrors revealed by the Holocaust, Americans were confronted by the dark legacy of European anti-Semitism. For young writers like Saul Bellow and Afred Kazin, the palpable shock of Nazi genocide was revealed in the darkness of the movie theaters, in footage of the liberation of concentration camps, and in the sickening images of bodies piled in mass graves. Commenting later on the impact of watching these terrifying newsreels, Bellow recalled the "deeply troubling sense of disgrace and human demotion" in witnessing these images; he was appalled and sickened that "the Jews had lost the respect of the rest of humankind."[4] Working in the shipfitting department of the Brooklyn Navy Yard during the war (deferred from the draft because of an injury), a young Arthur Miller pondered the fate of anti-Semitism in America after the war. "It is no longer possible to decide," Miller wrote in the Afterward to a later edition of his 1945 novel, *Focus*, "whether it was my own Hitler-begotten sensitivity or the anti-Semitism itself that so often made me wonder whether, when peace came, we were to be launched into a raw politics of race and religion, and not in the South, but in New York."[5]

To judge from the evidence of post-war American literary and popular culture, the matter of anti-Semitism in America, with its complex social and psychological manifestations, and the larger question of the fate—resilience—of American ideals in light of the sordid revelations of the Holocaust, consumed writers, filmmakers, and dramatists alike. In works as various as Hollywood's two film portraits in 1947 of anti-Semitism, *Crossfire* and *Gentleman's Agreement*, Arthur Laurents's stage play *Home of the Brave* (1945), Saul Bellow's *The Victim* and Miller's *Focus*, his first and only published novel, the meaning of Jewish identity in relation to various forms of anti-Semitism—genteel in *Gentleman's Agreement*, brazen in *Home of the Brave*, murderous in *Crossfire*, psychologically complex and ambiguous in *The Victim* and *Focus*—became perhaps *the* overarching subject of post-war cultural expression.

In America of the 1940's, the "scientific" study of anti-Semitism preoccupied psychologists and sociologists, as evidenced in the collection of *Jews in a Gentile World* (1942), subtitled "The Problem of Anti-Semitism," and *Anti-Semitism and Emotional Disorder* (1950), based on a series of essays published in the late 1940s by its authors, Nathan W. Ackerman and Marie Jahoda (sponsored by the American Jewish Committee under the "Studies in Prejudice" series, which produced the famous post-war study, *The Authoritarian Personality* [1950]). Its deepest readings, however, are to be found in *Focus* and *The Victim*, post-war novels that explore in profound ways the social-psychological dynamics of anti-Semitism as an obscene system of belief afflicting American society in general (*Focus*) and subverting the possibilities of intimacy across the ethnic divide (*The Victim*). Setting these texts in dialogue reveals how the "great hatred," to recall the title of Maurice Samuel's 1940 study of anti-Semitism, enabled authors as different as Miller and Bellow to dramatize the modern condition of "alienation"—the label often ascribed to the moment of post-war America writing marking the emergence of the so-called Jewish American novel. In retrospect, Miller's *Focus* may be said to have inaugurated the thematic strain of American literature concerned with the figure of the Jew as the *face* of modernity itself.[6] Anticipating Sartre's famous *Reflexions sur la question juive* (1946), published in the United States as *Anti-Semite and Jew* in 1948, *Focus* explores the intrinsic and extrinsic figurations of the Jew projected by the Gentile imagination. With Sartre, Miller's novel images "the Jew" as a terrifying reflection in the eyes of the gentiles—the uncanny sign of alienation, the specter mirroring the condition of modernity itself.

Looking back, Miller recalled "the sense of emergency that surrounded the writing of" *Focus*.[7] Sixty years later, readers may wonder at the situation of crisis that stirred the young playwright, who was not yet thirty, to compose it. The straightforward plot of the fable-like *Focus* concerns the psychic journey of Lawrence Newman (does Miller echo Henry James?), a self-consciously mannered, middle-level office worker whose job is to screen applicants for a restricted company. He prides himself on being able to tell—to "make," or identify, as in street language—a "Jew" when he sees (or smells, or suspects) one. When he fails to flag an applicant who, after she is hired, turns out to be a Jew, thus unsettling the placid gentile tones of the office ("'Miss Kapp is obviously not our kind of person, Newman,'" remarks Newman's supervisor; "'I mean, she's obvious. Her name must be Kapinsky or something.'"), Newman is ordered to get fitted for a pair of glasses.[8] Yet it turns out that wearing glasses *makes* Newman look "Jewish" in the eyes of the world ("a little Hebey," according to his anti-Semitic next-door neighbor), even in the eyes of his invalid mother. *Focus* is thus a moral-political fable enabling Miller to explore the transformations in consciousness of an anti-Semite who begins, acutely, to feel persecuted by a world that now "makes" a "Jew" of him, despite himself.[9]

At a crucial point in his journey, from generalized resentment to emergent empathy, Newman begins to identify with the preyed-upon neighborhood newspaper vendor Mr. Finkelstein, who challenges Newman's own slowly destabilized, abstracting anti-Semitism by forcing Newman to look at him (Finkelstein) and thus at himself (Newman) face to face. In the end, Newman joins Finkelstein in defending his life and property against local "Christian Front" hooligans (Miller's version of the quasi-Nazi collective who follow the anti-Semitic rantings of an unnamed Father Coughlin-like figure, a "priest from Boston"). Questioned in a police station after fighting off the neighborhood anti-Semites with a baseball bat, battered and psychically altered by the "cleansing fury" of his actions, Newman has the following exchange with the policeman, to whom he has reported the assault:

> "How many of you live there? . . ."
> "There are just the Finkelsteins on the corner . . .
> "Just them and yourself?" the policeman interrupted.
> "Yes. Just them and myself," Mr. Newman said.[10]

This is *Focus*'s concluding dramatic dialogue: Newman's "confession" that he, too, lives among "you people," a testament to Newman's striking personal growth, from his previous garden variety, genteel anti-Semitic stereotyping to an awakened psychic space of self-identification as a "Jew."

As it turns out, Saul Bellow did not admire *Focus* when it was published in late 1945. Writing in the *New Republic*, the thirty-year-old novelist, in the midst of composing his own meditation on anti-Semitism, which he published less than two years later as *The Victim*, felt that in Newman Miller had created a character not fully adequate to the situation. "He is not conscious enough," Bellow observed of Newman. "If only he had more substance to begin with." Bellow continued: "He finds himself in Mr. Finkelstein's predicament. He tries to escape it, but fails; the gift of glasses is not to be refused; and eventually he accepts his identification as a Jew as a course of wisdom and justice and attains to the dignity of a brother's keeper . . . [I]t would be splendid to believe it. But the whole thing is thrust on him. He is too docile."[11]

For Bellow, Newman's psychological passage from antisemite to honorary "Jew" (think of the conclusion to Bernard Malamud'a novel *The Assistant* (1957) in this respect, where Frank Alpine undergoes a ritual circumcision, the physical and symbolic expression of his awakened "Jewish" empathy), remains too pat, uncomplicated. Whatever form of "dignity" he may "attain"—and "dignity" is, perhaps, the key word in *The Victim's* vision of what it takes to be human—feels unearned. Why doesn't Newman (in Bellow's cynical speculation) simply "carry his baptismal certificate around to the neighbors as proof that he was not a Jew?"[12] Bellow's question, designed to expose the thinness of Miller's characterization, radically misses the point about Newman's reversal (so to speak) of gentile fortune. What Miller understood sixty years ago—in an insight that carried, as Matthew Jacobson has argued,[13] a substantial charge of social criticism—is that there can be no *material* defense against the perverse "logic" of antisemitism, no *rational* proof of Newman's hereditary "gentile" identity, since the act of being "taken" as a "Jew" exposes the "raving" unconscious of the antisemite himself.[14]

Listen to Lawrence Newman, in one of his early reflections, bordering on epiphany, on the meaning of his "new," glasses-transforming "Jewish face":

> For he knew that in the old days in the glass cubicle [where, in an uncanny New World version of *judenrein*, Newman labors, separating Jew from gentile] no proof, no documents, no words could have changed the shape of a face he himself suspected.
>
> A face . . . The monstrous mockery of the thing started tears to his eyes. He got up and started walking again as though to find ahead of him in the dark the clue to his confusion. Was it possible, he wondered, that Mr. Stevens looked at me and thought me untrustworthy, or grasping, or loud because of my face? . . . Because I am not untrustworthy and I am a quiet person . . . There must be something he could do that would henceforth indicate to an employer that he was what he was, a man of great fidelity and good manners. . . .
>
> His face. Besides a lamppost on a corner he came to a halt. *He* was not this face. Nobody had a right to dismiss him like that because of his face. Nobody! He was *him*, a human being with a certain definite history and he was not this face which looked like it had grown out of another alien and dirty history.[15]

In this complex interior monologue, we overhear Newman's psychic confusion and despair as he begins his bewildering rite of passage. Entering the territory of "alienation," Newman tries to fathom, to rationalize how he could be seen ("taken") for what he believes he "knows" he is not. Tellingly, his only recourse is denial of the imagined (hallucinated?) accusations of "bad manners," or of being "loud" and "grasping." He has no identity, we might say, except through negation of stereotypes. Unconscious (for now) of the operation of antisemitism as ideology, Newman nevertheless begins to feel the existential-political process that would empty him of individual history and replace it with one the defines him, both in his own eyes and in the eyes of the world, as "alien and dirty." (In this respect his tears betray the dislodging of emotion—another gesture towards empathy, self empathy.) Newman thus begins his eventual transforming encounter with the haunting face of the "Jew": the uncanny image he sees in the mirror is that of the "Jew" and the "antisemite." Both, ironically, are his.

At the beginning of *Focus*, Miller emphasizes Newman's strict personal habits. Newman strives to be neat, to appear unruffled in public. Indeed, "When he awakened [in the morning] there would hardly be a crease in the bedding and his reddish hair, trained flat from the part on the left side, would really not need combing." Taking the train downtown from Brooklyn, "He wore a starched collar and a meticulously-tied cravat. . . . His fingernails were roundly pared and shone baby pink. There was hardly a crease in his soul." Newman's obsessions at the level of the body, however, bespeak a soul struggling for *self*-mastery; his neat, "creaseless" habits betray a latent fascist mentality: "Walking *neatly* now, watching along the already baking sidewalk, he tried to think of his block and the houses all identical standing there like pickets on a fence. The memory of their sameness soothed his yearning for order."[16]

The political-psychic drama of *Focus* follows Newman, the crypto-fascist antisemite, in his overturning passage from order to chaos, figured in his ultimate identification with the "dirty history" of the Jews. In the process, he relinquishes (in Miller's understanding of historical stereotypes) an ingrained "gentile" fear of intimacy and "Jewish odors" ("He did not want to touch the odor" emanating from "the old cooking" in Mrs. Finkelstein's kitchen) to enact a form of "Jewish" empathy with it (in Jacobson's reading), political solidarity across an imagined racial divide.[17] Lawrence Newman thus undergoes, we might say, an apocalyptic "creasing" that leaves its deepest mark at the level of his buried "Jewish" soul.

The internal drama of *Focus* turns on Newman's complicated—and charged—face-to-face encounters, first with Miss Hart, a young woman to whom he refuses a job at his firm because he "takes" her for a Jew, and Mr. Finkelstein, the local newspaperman down the block, who enlists his help in the fight against neighborhood harassment.

When he first gazes at Miss Hart, Newman registers only her loud, flashy "theatrical" style, and in a reflexive anti-Semitic reaction conjures obstacles to her being hired (her lack of experience with an electric typewriter proves fatal). "She had the vitriol of the Hebrews, he thought, and their lack of taste. He watched her calves go. She was overdressed, overpainted." Miss Hart (who at the end of the job interview aggressively confronts Newman in stating that she is, in fact, an Episcopalian!), in turn, quickly reads the hidden meaning of the situation, and, to Newman's horror, takes *him* to be a "Jew": "In this moment her eyes had made a Jew of him."[18]

Caught in her own fixing gaze, Newman finds himself sexually attracted to Miss Hart (whom, remarkably, he eventually marries). In reaction, he discovers an unaccustomed lust that makes him *feel* like a "Jew"; and since all "Jews" harbor a "sensuous lust for women," evidenced "in the dark folds of their eyes and their swarthy skin," the emotion produces an unwelcome, abject disgust. By rendering the mind of an antisemite tangled up in stereotyping, in transcribing how an antisemite might rationalize his unsought attraction to an imagined libidinous "Jewess" who has taken *him* for a "Jew," Miller's Newman undergoes a series of powerful psychological affects, an internal ordeal of shame, rage, denial, and self hatred that exposes how the racist imagination talks to itself:

> She was taking him for a Jew.
> His lips parted. He wanted to run out of the office [shame], and then he wanted to hit her [rage]. She must not do that with her eyes!
> He sat there unable to speak to her through his hate. And yet the perspiration on the palms of his hands was to him the sign of embarrassment also, for he was polite to an extreme and he could not say that he was not Jewish without coloring the word with his repugnance for it, and thus for her [denial]. . . . In disgust with himself [because of his guilty desire] he got up. His jaw clenched against the pain of his own corruption, and she saw it and seemed to take it for an expression of anger.[19]

Newman's vexed, dumb (speechless) reaction to being fixed as "Jew" dislodges his own buried terror over the incivilities attendant with Jewish identity itself ("imposters," "no tradition of nobility," "Their houses smelled," "Their sensuous lust for women")—a vile litany abstracted, of course, from a long history of racist stereotyping that he accepts as truths to experience.

What is Miller's aim in exploring Newman's psychic ordeal during this liminal phase of the character's passage? The answer, in part, lies in Miller's demystifying attempt to expose the conundrums of racist mentality itself: how the anti-Semitic (totalitarian?) mind rationalizes its view of the world; how it projects its own guilty longings onto taboo objects of desire; how, above all, its particular way of seeing and feeling resists the possibilities—really, the potential—of intimacy in a world riven by tribal barriers. *Focus*, that is, tries to imagine the conditions under which, unmediated by histories of oppression and stereotype, potentially emancipating, *face-to-face* encounters can take place.

The agent of such self-liberating potential is Mr. Finkelstein, Miller's symbol of the Jew who turns his indignation over the history of personal and collective oppression into a mode of dignity. From his perch on the corner, Finkelstein watches each morning as Newman discovers his—Newman's—garbage pails turned over, with his private refuse spilled into the street, and his obsession with neatness and order overturned. These harassing acts are committed by the local anti-Semitic "Christian Front," which means, as Mr. Finkelstein explains to Newman, "'Somebody's got you marked for a Jew.'"[20]

Their shared experience as victims of prejudice slowly brings Newman closer to his neighbor. "What," Miller has Newman ask himself, "was Finkelstein to him?" This is a key question, voiced in a (now familiar) Bellovian register, concerning the matter of individual responsibility and our relation to other people (core matters interrogated in *The Victim* as well). Inexorably, Newman feels more and more drawn to Mr. Finkelstein. He listens attentively to the Jew's "deep voice"; beneath its "quavering" tones, the confused antisemite *senses* "some intense emotion."[21] Listen, as Lawrence Newman's gentile/genteel front of resistance begins to soften; no longer repelled by the dangers of intimacy, he seeks an answer to the question of his own hollow existence:

> And yet as they walked along the dark street Mr. Newman felt a sharp curiosity. What had Mr. Finkelstein to say to him now? Despite himself he felt drawn to this man. It was not that he thought of himself as being in the same situation as the Jew [note the Sartrean echo] walking leisurely beside him, for consciously he did not think of himself that way. It was only that he saw the man in possession of a secret that left him controlled and fortified, while he himself was circling in confusion in search of a formula through which he could again find his dignity.[22]

In Sartrean terms (that is, Sartre's particular way of understanding Jewish identity in *Anti-Semite and Jew*), we might say that at this moment Mr. Finkelstein represents the "authentic" Jew, linked by bonds of history and memory to his people. In this respect, the Old World parable of the shtetl-bound Itzik, which Finkelstein recalls at his father's grave, seems important as a cautionary tale on how to become the duped middleman for the gentiles. The parable fills Finkelstein with indignation; he vows never to be an "Itzik," playing the fool for the master. (Realizing how his accommodating, self-interested behavior leads to the death of his family and community, Itzik goes mad.) In a subsequent impassioned face to face encounter,

Finkelstein challenges Newman ("'You look at me and you don't see me. You see something else.'") to feel his (i.e., Finkelstein's) passion, to acknowledge his existence. The result is transforming: "Where once [Newman] had seen a rather comical, ugly, and obsequious face, now he found a man, a man throbbing with anger. And somehow his anger made him comprehensible to Newman. His clear anger, his relentless and controlled fury opened a wide channel into Newman's being . . . he had no complaint against Finkelstein in particular and he could not face the man like this. . . ."[23]

The voicing of Finkelstein's righteous anger, we might say, *creases* Newman's very being. Anger clarifies; it confers humanity. To recall another Bellovian theme, this emotional exchange with Finkelstein (now no longer "the Jew") begins to open a channel to Newman's soul, replacing antisemitc abstractions with the flesh and blood and pain and despair of Jewish history (memory?) itself. That is why Newman can't "face" Finkelstein; for an antisemite, such a face-to-face encounter is apocalyptic, a threat to his very being. As a result, Newman himself undergoes an astonishing consciousness-*razing* transformation, an ordeal by identification that literally overwhelms his previous self, displacing the "Northern man that he *was*"[24] with the soul of a "new-man," an agent able to act in the world with a measure of dignity.

To achieve such a condition, however, Newman must first begin to "make" himself a "Jew"—or, at least, sense how the "gentile" imagines Jews feel under the palpable weight of his judging gaze. In his present liminal condition, caught between his once secure non-Jewish self and a new-man waiting to be born, Newman becomes displaced in the city, which "kept carving a new shape against his soul . . . it scoured silently against the sides of this mind."[25] (In this striking image, Miller suggests that the crust of Newman's closed world is being softened, penetrated by figures arriving, implicitly, from the East. It also recalls Henry James' anxious sense of witnessing, just forty years earlier, the Old World's unsavory invasion at Ellis Island.) His certainties gone, his confidence assaulted, Newman feels "off balance":

> He could no longer simply enter a restaurant and innocently sit down to a meal. Certain tall and broad types of fair-haired men, with whom he fancied his appearance most in contrast, threw him off balance. When they happened to be seated nearby he found himself speaking quite softly, always wary of any loudness in his tone. . . . When he spoke he kept his hands under the table, although he had always needed gestures. In the glances of people, in the fleet warpings of their eyes, he sought to learn where he stood. . . . The things he had done all his life as a gentile, had been turned into the tokens of an alien and evil personality.[26]

In this astonishing reflection, we witness the newly self-conscious Newman experience—perhaps at the level of paranoia—what might be called the David Levinsky syndrome: the ghetto Jew's restaurant anxiety, the self-monitoring—really, repressing—of voice and gesture signifying the shame and self-hatred that comes with the territory of alienation. And like his American namesake, James's Christopher Newman, at sea in the Old World, Lawrence Newman also finds himself "off balance," seeking "to learn where he stood" in the eyes of a world he takes as authorizing, legitimizing his own, no longer stable, identity.

On one level, Miller places Newman in such destabilizing situations in order to explode the foundations of anti-Semitic thinking itself: If a gentile like Newman can be compelled to act (an feel) like a ghetto Jew, then the attendant stereotypes can, perhaps, be drained of local, self-arraigning power; thus demystified, this debilitating habit of mind can be exposed as a debased psychological-political structure of feeling, overcome by seeing through its external and internal impositions. By contrast, David Levinsky cannot, alas, see through his own shame and self-hatred. Yezierska's daughters of loneliness continuously struggle to overcome the syndrome. Henry Roth's Ira Stigman flees an imagined parvenu world by heading downtown.

At the same time, Newman's self-hatred seems like a necessary stage in a process leading to its ultimate shedding. He must "make" a "Jew" of himself; he must "take" himself for a "Jew" on the road to dignity. In this respect, Newman's antisemitic wife Gertrude's exasperated critique of her husband, after the newly married couple is, ironically, turned away by a restricted resort hotel, "'[W]hy do you always let them make a Jew out of you?'" resonates with terrific irony.[27] She will never understand that Lawrence needs to undergo such soul-altering shame situations, for they provide the kind of deep creasings of the self that, for Miller, are the (pre) conditions for achieving humanity. In the final pages of *Focus*, we witness Lawrence Newman's baptism into an alternate congregation, the tribe of empathy. Significantly, it is a baptism by violence, leading to feeling and, ultimately, identification.

As Mr. Finkelstein suspects, the neighborhood Christian Front seeks to terrorize him into flight. During the attack, anticipated and defended against with baseball bats, Newman and Mr. Finkelstein are each wounded but survive. "'All right, you Hebrew bastards,'" one of the attackers screams, while leaving the scene, "'This is a warm-up.'" Verbally marked as a "Hebrew," Newman begins to see Mr. Finkelstein in new ways. After Finkelstein is bloodied, Newman "took out his handkerchief and put it to Mr. Finkelstein's nose." His empathic gestures continue, first at the level of face-to-face mirroring: "Newman looked at [Mr. Finkelstein's] upturned eyes, his strained and helpless eyes. . . . [Mr. Finkelstein has just received a bloody nose and other physical injuries.] He could not break his gaze away and kept staring into Finkelstein's eyes." Newman also begins to sob, in disbelief "at

the way his tears were flowing." Then, in almost motherly fashion, Newman helps put Mr. Finkelstein to bed and, to his amazement, finds himself
"assured and empty of fear."[28] In the wake of the violence and the shared
resistance, Newman gains, it appears for the first time in his life, a feeling of
inner security, of spiritual grounding:

> In all his life he had never known such calm, despite the torrent of blood rush-
> ing through him. Within his raging body a stillness had grown very wide and
> very deep and he stared at his image feeling the texture of this peace. It was
> almost a tone he seemed to be hearing, level and low and far away. He stood
> there listening to it.[29]

What is the ultimate source of Newman's "stillness?" At one level, his
newly found "peace" literally overcomes the antisemitic "rage" of the attackers; the calm arises in the wake of scattering such raving hatred. But for
Miller, Newman's transformation appears even more profound. When the
police officer taking down his story assumes that Newman is a Jew ("How
many of you people live over there?"), Newman chooses not to correct the
assumption, for such a "denial was to repudiate and soil his own cleansing
fury of a few moments ago."[30] Purified of his great hatred, Newman sees
Finkelstein with new eyes; at the same time, he sees himself reflected in
that mirror. The image confers a kind of peace. Above all, he has found the
answer to the cosmic questions—"what is dignified?" "'Have you a good
heart?'"—that Newman asks Mr. Finkelstein, anxious about his neighbor's
physical condition.[31] *Focus* implicitly poses the same questions of Newman,
and, perhaps, to the novel's readers in 1945 as well.

Miller wrote *Focus*, he tells us, just as world War II was ending, at the
threshold of a hoped for universal peace; he wasn't sure, looking back,
"whether after peace came, we were to be launched into a raw politics of
race and religion."[32] At the end of *Focus*, Miller allows Newman a kind of
revelation, a vision of society no longer consumed by difference. Newman,
we're told, "longed deeply for a swift charge of lightning that would with a
fiery stroke break away the categories of people and change them so that it
would not be important to them what tribe they sprang from. It must not
be important anymore."[33]

Such utopian yearning enables *Focus*, according to Matthew Jacobson,
to envision "a truly progressive politics based upon the deconstruction of
race," "a solidarity uniquely attuned to race, not as a biological bond, but
as a historical process."[34] To be sure, Newman's personal apocalypse registers Miller's own larger, hopeful vision concerning race relations, at least
in post-war New York City. In this respect, he voices a Sartre-like argument
for the eventual elimination of difference in the next era of social relations.
In 1946, *Réflexions sur la question juive* imagined a post-Jewish, indeed a
post-multicultural France—a society in which antisemitic "projections"

and enmity toward "the other" would ultimately vanish under the sign of a authentic socialist (i.e., classless, rather than ethnically particularized) state. As Michael Walzer explains, social deformations like antisemitism are "for Sartre inevitable consequences of pluralism. . . . the fight [against antisemitism and all degrading forms of human relationships] will never be won until pluralism, indeed groupness itself, is definitively transcended."[35]

Despite Sartre's hope, the war revealed the tenacious power of groupness; in our own time, the claims of ethnic identity and the emergence of "identity politics" in general have tended to resist the appeal of transcendence. In this respect, *The Victim* ("Bellow's most specifically Jewish book," according to Leslie Fiedler)[36] also explores the question of affiliation and belonging, of "tribal" mentality and the limits of "groupness." It examines the complex psychological dynamic between a Jew who imagines himself the victim of gentile persecution and an antisemite who feels himself victimized by the Jew's intentional behavior *as a Jew*. Their vexed and mutually accusatory relationship allows Bellow to pose the larger questions concerning human responsibility, guilt, revenge, the meaning of dignity, and the possibility of empathy in a jittery post-war world of recrimination and pain. *The Victim* thus participates in and is deeply shaped by the key themes that occupied both Jewish American expression and Post-war American culture in the late 1940s.

The Victim was Bellow's second novel. When it appeared in late 1947, it was heralded by important critics like Diana Trilling, Leslie Fiedler, and Elizabeth Hardwick as a brilliant work of fiction. Its reception elevated the thirty-two year-old Bellow into the ranks of major American novelists. He has the "chance," observed Hardwick, "to become the redeeming novelist of his period."[37]

Reading *The Victim* over sixty years later, the interpretive challenge remains gauging the levels of complexity in Bellow's portrait of Asa Levethal, the city Jew, alone in New York during a few sultry weeks in August (the novel famously opens, "On some summer nights New York is as hot as Bangkok")[38] and Kirby Allbee, a down-on-his luck, antisemitic WASP, who suddenly surfaces with a long-harbored grievance against Leventhal, whom he associates with the beginning of his fall into destitution. At first Leventhal is baffled by Allbee's accusation ("'You ruined me.'");[39] he feels innocent of the charge, and resists any claim of responsibility for Allbe's personal situation. The core drama of *The Victim* involves Allbee's literal stalking—haunting—of Leventhal, his obsession with the Jew as the symbol of all his woe. As Hardwick recognized long ago, "More than anything else [Allbee] seems to want Leventhal to recognize the possibility of his guilt."[40]

What is the source of Allbee's grievance? The short answer concerns a fairly convoluted story (Fiedler speaks of *The Victim's* "slow, gray, low-keyed exposition")[41] involving Leventhal's search, after the war, for a new job in publishing. Although Leventhal knew Allbee socially (and then only indirectly), Allbee agrees to recommend Leventhal for a position to his employer, Rudiger, the editor of *Dill's*, where Albee himself works. During the subsequent interview, Leventhal engages in a heated argument with Rudiger; as a direct result—at least in Allbee's reading of the episode—Allbee is fired by Rudiger. In his own mind, Allbee links Leventhal's outburst at Rudiger with his own loss of a job, thus marking the onset of his financial and personal ruin. Allbee has now materialized, after years of decline and personal tragedy (his wife died a few years before in a car accident) to remind Leventhal of his forgotten but still outstanding moral and monetary debts. But more than anything else, Allbee seeks retribution and confession from Leventhal *as a Jew*.

The deeper meanings contained in the Leventhal-Allbee "story," however, are located in the rich if (at times) abstract narrative that shapes *The Victim's* dense plot: the psychologically charged exchanges between Allbee and Leventhal played out as a version of Bellow's own Sartre-like drama of "antisemite and Jew." As the novel unfolds, Allbee surfaces from nowhere, a return of the repressed figure from Leventhal's unconscious. As a native New Yorker, Allbee is obsessed with the "swarming" (to recall Henry James's own unsettling encounter with the Lower East Side) presence of upstart Jews in *his* city. The object of his passion (desire?) is Leventhal, the second-generation son of an immigrant father sensitive, we soon discover, about the subject of Jews—specifically, their manners and civility—in a gentile world.

The origins of the complicated Allbee-Leventhal "relationship," the source of their eventual debate, begins with a troubling episode: a social gathering during which a Jew named Harkavy behaves in ways that shamed Leventhal and "delighted" Allbee.[42] *The Victim*'s deep analysis—in effect, its genealogy of antisemite and Jew—requires a close reading of this moment of ethnic-social drama, for the scene contains the foundations of the novel's profound evocation of Jews ill at ease—haunted—in the New World, struggling to locate a zone of stability under the condition of psychic exile, alienated even in the familiar territory of post-war New York City.

The incident in question takes place at a party, where a group of mixed company (Jews and gentiles), including Leventhal's boss (at the time) Williston, Allbee and his wife, and Leventha's roommate Dan Harkavy gather together and witness Harkavy's comic "performances." Harkavy, we're told, loves an audience. In Bellow's description: "he liked to talk and at these parties he was easily kindled, for some reason. Any trifle made him enthusiastic, and when he spoke his hands flew up and his brows slanted up, sharpening the line of his nose." His subject—really his shtick—amounts to a comic routine "giving imitations of auctioneers, in reality [in Leventhal's assumption] burlesquing his father." Crucially, during these antic performances Leventhal watches *Allbee* watching Harkavy, for Leventhal is obsessed with Allbee's reactions. During these routines, "Allbee studied him, grinning and curious; Harkavy appeared to delight him."[43]

For his part, Leventhal is "annoyed" at Harkavy's spectacle, above all at his friend's utter lack of self-consciousness at playing the type of the comic Jew before Allbee's "grinning and curious" gaze. For some reason, Leventhal is shamed by Harkavy's unconscious gesticulations; during these routines, "for all his traits," Leventhal muses, "the Jewish especially, became accentuated"—a brilliant description, pointing toward Harkavy's "Jewish" gestures and suggesting his theatrical inflections [is Harkavy imitating Milton Berle? Eddie Cantor? Or perhaps Bellow's own dear friend and legendary mimic, Isaac Rosenfeld?], including the unwelcome accents (in Leventhal's ears at least) that sound from his "Jewish voice." (Harkavy's routine also *accentuates* his "Jewish" nose.) Leventhal "watched" this spectacle, we're told, "unsmiling and even forbidding," thus offering another great touch by Bellow: chagrined by Harkavy, Leventhal privately seeks to banish these "Jewish" gestures so relished by Allbee. If the aim of shame is invisibility, then Leventhal wishes Harkavy would disappear.[44]

Leventhal's private ordeal of witnessing *a shanda for the goyim* ("shame before the gentiles") isn't over, however. At one of these parties, while in a drunken state, Allbee asks Harkavy to stop his singing (in this instance) of "spirituals and old ballads," protesting that "'It isn't right for you to sing them. You have to be born to them. It's no use trying to sing them.'" He further presses Harkavy, charging that he is not "bred" to sing this music; instead, he requests, "'Then sing any Jewish song. Something you really got feeling for. Sing us the one about the mother.'"[45] Enjoying the collective wince in the wake of his wicked antisemitic "advice" (at least that's how the aghast audience appears to take Allbee's impertinence), he surveys the shocked assembly of friends; then, "deeply pleased; he smiled at Harkavy . . . and he even had a glance for Leventhal, too."[46]

Bellow focuses so intensely on this early, determining episode in *The Victim* because it highlights the main characters' respective habits of imagination. Years later, ruined and degenerate, Allbee continues to be literally consumed by the matter of "breeding." He announces his once-proud lineage as a descendant of Governor Winthrop, now usurped by the children of immigrants. The irony continues to astonish him: "His voice vibrated fiercely; there was a repressed laugh in it." A dethroned New York aristocrat (think of Tom Buchanan knocked off his polo pony by Mr. Finkelstein), Allbee feels utterly *displaced* in his city where the cafeterias now serve only "Jewish" food; where people with names like "Lipshitz" publish books on Emerson and Thoreau (is Bellow gently satirizing his friend Alfred Kazin, author of *On Native Grounds* [1942]?); where "the children of Caliban were running everything." Above all, Allbee is obsessed with the (bodily) figure of Leventhal as "Jew." He is fascinated, for example, by Leventhal's "Jewish" hair ("It's like an animal's hair," he exclaims in wonder): "'Your hair amazes me. Whenever I see you, I have to study it. . . . Is it hard to comb?'" and assumes, on the evidence of a photograph, that Leventhal's absent wife must have descended from ancestors in eastern Europe.[47]

Thus Allbee constructs Leventhal as a textbook "Jew" who has usurped Allbee's position in the city. He can't "see" Leventhal, face to face, for a history of stereotyping and a personal rage at feeling unhoused, adrift on the streets of his old home, mediate the encounter. A paranoid consumed by "descent" identity, a social scientist manqué driven by a morbid fascination with a new Jewish New York, Allbee seeks to examine Leventhal (as he had earlier studied Harkavy) as "Jewish" specimen; he desires to know, up close, the source of his personal pain, embodied in the figure of Leventhal.

The unwelcome encounter with Allbee forces Leventhal to re-examine his own life. Allbee's sudden appearance disrupts Leventhal's usually "impassive" composure—the habitual demeanor of his public, "indifferent" face[48]—adding yet another complication to his summer of crisis (in a subplot, Leventhal's brother's son is very sick on Staten Island, compelling the uncle to assume the role of surrogate father while the brother is in Texas, searching for work and a new home). Indeed, Allbee's invasion (at least that's how it feels to Leventhal, even if out of a growing concern he invites Allbee into his apartment) challenges Leventhal's deepest assumptions; his sudden return dislodges long-buried anxieties about Leventhal's identity as son, as brother, as husband and (above all) as "Jew." "Eventually he had to have a reckoning with himself,"[49] Leventhal admits. It's a crucial moment of honest (if rare) introspection, among the earliest articulations of the now familiar Bellovian invitation to self-analysis. During the course of *The Victim*, Leventhal begins to recognize Allbee's claim upon him, which means that Leventhal begins to learn (to recall Newman's dilemma in *Focus*) the meaning of "dignity," what *in-deed* is truly "dignified."

In this respect, a key sequence in *The Victim* involves Leventhal's re-interpretation of the "primal scene" that haunts Allbee: the fateful encounter with Rudiger at *Dill's* which, Allbee feels, cost him his job. As it turns out, for all his confidence about the meaning of his behavior with Rudiger, upon deeper reflection, prodded by his ex-boss Williston, Leventhal begins to feel unsure of his true motivations. Could Allbee be right? Did he intend for Allbee to lose his job, in revenge (unconscious or not) for the antisemitic behavior (however benign) toward Harkavy? For Leventhal, the condition of his very soul seems at stake.

These questions literally haunt Leventhal as he revisits the argument with Rudiger. To distill this key episode, on Allbee's recommendation, Leventhal, in search of a better position, is granted an interview with Rudiger, but their exchange immediately turns sour, descending into a shouting match. Rudiger insults Leventhal's sense of his abilities as a writer; in reply, Leventhal insults Rudiger by stating how much he feels *he* could improve *Dill's* magazine, but since the business of newspapers amounts to a "guild," "'Any outsider hasn't got a chance.'"[50] Let me quote at length from Bellow's narration of this incident, related (of course) from Leventhal's perspective:

> The air between them must have shaken, it was so charged with insult and rage. Under no circumstances could he [Leventhal] imagine doing now what he had done then. But he had determined not to let his nose be pulled. That was what he told himself. "He thinks everybody who comes to him will let his nose be pulled." Too many people looking for work were ready to allow anything. . . .
> "Get out!" Rudiger cried. His face was aflame. He rose with a thrust of his stocky arm while Leventhal, evincing neither anger nor satisfaction, although he felt both, smoothed the groove of his green velours hat, and said, "I guess you can't take it when people stand up to you, Mr. Rudiger."
> "Out, out, out!" Rudiger repeated, pushing over his desk with both arms. "Out, you case, you nut, you belong in the asylum! Out! You ought to be committed!"
> And Leventhal, sauntering toward the door, turned and retorted, made a remark about two-bit big shots and empty wagons. . . . He did remember, and very clearly, too, that he was elated. He congratulated himself. Rudiger had not pulled his nose.[51]

Looking back, struggling to remember what in fact he had said to set off Rudiger (Allbee accuses him of swearing), Leventhal feels mortified. During this heated exchange, Leventhal remains utterly in character, always projecting an "impassive" mask of composure, an air of "indifference" before the eyes of the world. "Angry and tense" during the interview, Leventhal "managed to present a surface of dry, uncaring calm."[52] Beneath Leventhal's façade of indifference, however, raw emotion rages, uncontained affect reigns (rains?), linked, at some level, with his self-consciousness as "outsider"—to the closed newspaper guild, perhaps to the world in general. Without directly acknowledging his situation, Leventhal nonetheless *feels* his outsider status as a Jew.

"He had determined not to let his nose be pulled." Significantly, Leventhal voices this private injunction three times in recalling the Rudiger incident. Clearly, the shame of having one's nose pulled is associated with his threatened, self-conscious Jewish identity shaped, ultimately, by a history of stereotyping. Indeed, Leventhal's sense of Jewish identity seems formed in visceral reaction to the limited models of selfhood available in his horizon of experience (i.e., Harkavy, his absent brother, his immigrant father). In his row with Rudiger, Leventhal refuses to play the part of the passive, insinuating Jew of the gentile stereotype, a figure hovering near the surface of his imagination. (Are long Jewish noses naturally more accessible to gentile pulling? Do Jews push their big noses forward so that they may be pulled?) "Too many people looking for work were ready to allow anything,"[53] he tells himself; the act of letting one's nose be pulled issues in degradation, in the loss of self-worth, indeed, of self image.

Leventhal's psychic defense against playing—*being taken for*—the Jew of his own worried self-reflection finds curious expression in his studied act of composure (Bellow speaks of Leventhal's "appearance of composure"), which masks his growing rage during the interview, as well as the "elation" he experiences after his feigned display of control incites (excites?) *Rudiger* into making a scene. Rudiger, that is, *acts out* the rage that Leventhal tries to keep under wraps. In a complex scene of "projection," it may be that Rudiger's loss of composure is the source—and aim—of Leventhal's private Jewish "delight," he performs what is clearly an exaggerated exit, "sauntering toward the door," "smooth[ing] the groove of his green velours hat"—a show (shtick?) emphasizing his own false "indifference."[54] His behavior can thus be read as a way of getting even with Rudiger, the arrogant reminder (and symbol) of Leventhal's own outsider status.[55]

At the same time, perhaps unconsciously, Leventhal's actions appear as an act of revenge against Allbee. Although he can't *as yet* admit the possibility, Leventhal's behavior, nevertheless, might be construed as a belated response to being uncomfortably fixed (during the Harkavy incident), if only for a second, by Allbee's antisemitic gaze. Watching Allbee watching Harkavy's "Jewish" performance, we recall, made Leventhal cringe, for Harkavy's gesticulations bring to light the repressed Jewish self that Leventhal seeks to keep buried: the *accent*uated Jew of his deeply embedded shame and self-hatred. Thus the antisemitic Allbee doesn't *make* Harkavy a "Jew" (although he takes him for one); Allbee remains a passive, if "delighted," witness to Harkavy's Jewish shtick. And Harkavy doesn't in theory make a "Jew" of himself, since he appears at ease in his performing (Jewish) self. In the end, it is Leventhal who makes a "Jew" of Harkavy. To recall the core rhetoric of *Focus, Leventhal* takes Harkavy for a "Jew"; in the process, he projects his own shame-ridden anxiety as a Jew onto Harkavy. Thus the figure of Harkavy, under repression, haunts Leventhal as much as it does Allbee.

Throughout *The Victim*, then, Leventhal's stance toward Jewishness and Jewish identity remains problematic, ambivalent. Joining, for example, in the intimate cafeteria banter about the figure of Disraeli with fellow Jews (including Haravy, along with an older man named Schlossberg, who voices perhaps the most important speech in the novel on "dignity"), Leventhal surprises the group by his critique of Disraeli's "nerve" in taking on British society: "'People laughed at his nose, so he took up boxing; they laughed at his poetic silk clothes, so he put on black; and they laughed at his books, so he showed them. He got into politics and became the prime minister. He did it all on nerve. . . . But I don't admire it.'"[56] In light of his own "nervy" behavior with Rudiger, Leventhal's *spiel* sounds a bit disingenuous. After all, refusing to have his nose pulled is Leventhal's personal mark of honor.

Why is Leventhal so sensitive on the matter of "Jewish" nerve (and "Jewish" noses?), in the same way that he is "annoyed" by Harkavy's "Jewish" antics at the party? (Significantly, Harkavy's "upbraids" Leventhal after the Disraeli speech, charging, "'Why, you're succumbing yourself to all the things that are said against us.'"[57] He's essentially accusing Leventhal—correctly—of Jewish self-hatred. Later, still fuming over Leventhal's statement, he accuses him of embracing "ghetto psychology.") *That* question requires an understanding of Leventhal's vexed relation to (in his eyes) the narrow, grasping world of his immigrant father, a "turbulent man, harsh and selfish toward his sons."[58]

Without warning, while riding in a cab uptown, Leventhal is reminded, powerfully (he "suddenly felt his face burning"), of his merchant father's often-repeated Yiddish rhyme:

> Ruf mir Yoshke, ruf mir Moshke,
> Aber gib mir die groshke.

(Leventhal translates the aphorism as "Call me Ikey, call me Moe, but give me the dough." The more precise translation would be, "Call me Joe, call me Moe, but give me the dough.") recalling his father's crass business philosophy makes Leventhal feel ashamed and disgusted. "What's it to me if you despise me?" his father spat at the *goyim*. "What do you think equality with you means to me? What do you have that I care about except the *groschen*?" "That was his father's view," Leventhal told himself; "but not his. He rejected it and recoiled from it. . . . It gave Leventhal pain to think about his father's sense of these things."[59] At the deepest level of his identity as Jewish son, Leventhal "recoils" from the father's ghetto mentality. A key word, *recoils* conjures a taut winding of the self, a soul (really, heart) constricted ("impassive," "indifferent"), wrapped tight, closed in upon itself. But *recoiling* also implies an inevitable counter-gesture of *uncoiling*, a contrapuntal release, a *loosening* of the heartstrings of empathy. In this respect, the ultimate drama of *The Victim* charts Leventhal's progress in matters of what might be called heart expansion. To achieve the dignity of "exactly human" (to recall the exemplary vision of Schlossberg, the novel's other Old World Jewish voice), Leventhal must also reject a mode of selfhood born of denial, constructed out of a need to bank on stereotypes.

Despite his rejection of the immigrant father's cosmic paranoia "to be freed by money from the power of his ["imaginary"] enemies," Leventhal's mask of "indifference," his "unaccountably impassive' demeanor, and above all his anxiety about "composure" betray an uneasy relation to Jewish patrimony. As strategies of defense, they mask reservoirs of affect, which include Leventhal's buried feelings of anger and betrayal (linked with his wife's confessed affair at the threshold of their marriage), the need to be well-liked (as in his impulse to force a moral contrast between his absent brother and his own acts of responsibility as surrogate father to his nephew Phil), to have his way (as with Rudiger and Williston), and shame over "Jewish" behavior in general. His physical reaction to the Yiddish rhyme, reflecting the shame he feels in recalling his father's ghetto mentality, exposes his tangled relation to an immigrant Jewish world under repression, an ambivalent realm of belonging that continues, at an unconscious level, to control his own complex behavior. Following John Clayton's key insight, Leventhal's consuming self-hatred generates his habit of defensive pride.[60]

The latent power of *"Yoshke"* and *"Moshke"* also begins to explain the generalized anxiety that hovers around Leventhal in the wake of Allbee's accusations. Leventhal's immediate response to Allbee's charge is denial. Allbee is an antisemite, Leventhal keeps reminding himself; he has chosen, gentile that he is, to "dissolve" his self in alcoholism and self-pity; he's merely looking for a handout. At least this is how Leventhal initially tries to explain away Allbee and his indictment, He abstracts Allbee in precisely the same way that the antisemite empties humanity out of the Jew (at one point Leventhal even notes his "breathing in [Allbee's] odor.')[61]

But Allbee's ultimate office in *The Victim* is to help to uncoil, to release *Leventhal*, to enable *him* to break through his shell of indifference, to help Leventhal begin to feel. In this respect, Allbee plays Finkelstein to Leventhal's Newman; each set of doubles has powerful face-to-face encounters. Significantly, during this tropical New York summer of personal reckoning, Leventhal already senses a change in the psychic atmosphere:

He wondered why it was that lately he was more susceptible than he had ever been before to certain kinds of feeling. With everyone except Mary [his absent wife] he was inclined to be short and neutral, outwardly a little like his father [this recognition seems important], and this shortness of his was, when you came right down to it, merely neglectfulness. When you didn't want to take trouble with people, you found the means to turn them aside. . . . You couldn't find a place in you feelings for everything.[62]

It takes a disorienting conversation with his gentile ex-boss Williston for Leventhal to begin to gain an altered perspective on the past. After Allbee surfaces in his life, Leventhal rushes to Williston, seeking confirmation of his own reading of the Rudiger incident. Despite Leventhal's "pushy" demand to meet, his face-to-face encounter with the always-composed Williston proves unnerving; "he began to feel unsure of his ground. . . . He suddenly felt weak and confused; his face wet. He changed the position of his feet uneasily on the soft circle of carpet."[63] Here is a portion of their exchange:

Williston: "You were wrong."

Leventhal: "Maybe . . . My nerves were shot. And I never was any good at rubbing people the right way. I don't know how to please them."

Williston: "You're not long on tact, that's perfectly true."

Leventhal: "I never intended to hurt Allbee. That's my word of honor."

Williston: "I believe you." . . .

Leventhal: "I don't see what he's after. I can't find out what he wants."

Williston: "You ought to . . . You certainly ought."[64]

In the wake of this demystifying moment, Leventhal's strategies of indifference and impassivity begin to lose their defensive power; softened under the pressure of self-analysis, he begins to feel the palpable truth of Allbee's claims. In the process, Leventhal emerges as a recognizable Bellovian hero, a self overwhelmed, consumed by a need to understand what primal forces drive the human heart. After the unnerving conversation with Williston, Leventhal "felt that he had not said everything had had come to say. The really important things, the deepest issues, had not been touched."[65] Lying in bed, Leventhal revisits in his mind the scene with Rudiger and winces in recollection: "He stifled his emotion altogether and all expression, merely moving his lids downward. He did not try to spare himself; he recalled them all, from his attack on Williston tonight to the original scene in Rudiger's office. When he came to this, he turned on his back and crossed his bare arms over his eyes."[66] Leventhal's telling gesture—he covers his eyes in defense against shame—opens him to the truth of his intentions, which include, he now admits, the possibility of revenge. He has begun to "see," indeed perhaps begun to recognize what Allbee is "after."

Thus the source of Leventhal's convicting shame—his revelation—is the memory of the "scene" at Rudiger's. For all his appearance of composure, to his discomfort Leventhal now sees that he had, literally, lost it, while "losing his head at *Dill's*." As he recounts, Rudiger "made me believe what I was afraid of"; under his judging gaze, Rudiger made him feel unworthy and rejected. His deepest self thus insulted, Leventhal became "his own worst enemy."[67]

Having reached this insight—that his defensive pride (an instinctual backlash that surfaces in the wake of self-hatred) determined his behavior at *Dill's*—Leventhal no longer can claim antisemitism in defense of his actions or summon the history of Jewish stereotyping in anticipation of an imagined (gentile) reading of his intentions: "'If you believe I did it on purpose, to get even," Leventhal heatedly says to Williston, strenuously defending himself against the (presumed) "gentile" charge of "plotting" to have Allbee fired, "'then it's not only because I'm terrible personally but because

I'm a Jew.'" But a clear-eyed rational Williston refuses to accept Leventhal's "logic": "'You were fighting everybody, those days,'" he reminds Leventhal; "'You were worst with Rudiger, but I heard of others.'" "'The Jewish part of it,'" he points out to Leventhal, in the role of sober analyst, "'is your own invention.'"[68]

Stripped of all his defenses, Leventhal is left alone with Allbee; the result is a gradual but steady recognition of the legitimacy of Allbee's claims, not simply with respect to the incident at Dill's but, more importantly, in relation to Allbee's struggle to recover his own dignity after a long ordeal of degradation. At the same time, Allbee undergoes his own personal reckoning, a rite of passage that involves moving beyond his own dehumanizing abstractions born of antisemitism to see Leventhal face to face. If in the beginning each figure becomes the other's stereotype,[69] as in an ancient script, in the end Leventhal and Allbee each achieves a kind of dignity, perhaps even a mutual empathy. They achieve the dignity of the "exactly human"—not more or less—in the famous words of old Schlossberg. The signs of dignity, we might say, are inscribed in gestures of recognition and forgiveness: Leventhal and Allbee each begins to soften his respective grievances with the world, adjusting expectations, refusing to displace or project personal disappointments onto the "other."

Signigicantly, Leventhal moves from impassivity to empathy as he begins to *feel* Allbee's presence in his life. It represents a momentous transition. Exchanging instinctual feelings of "harassment" for a kind of hospitality, we witness his habitual "indifference" undergo a sea-change, as Leventhal begins to "read" Allbee's self-pity not as mere "performance" (Leventhal is often struck by Allbee's display of "gentlemanly" "manners," noting, for example how, "In crossing his legs, Allbee gave a twitch to his stained, loose-hanging trousers")[70] but as a legitimate plea for recognition and, if possible, mercy ('*hab rachmones*," "have mercy," is, ultimately, Allbee's request, though he can't voice this ardent plea—as do characters everywhere in Malamud—in the *mamaloshen*). "'You ought to realize,'" Allbee confesses, "'that I'm not entirely' . . . he stumbled, 'that I'm not entirely under control.'"[71] This seems like a key confession; after all, Harkavy's "Jewish" antics showed him to be out of control as well. Slowly, Leventhal begins to read in deeper, indeed more empathic, ways. Moved to look closer, Leventhal scans Allbee's face: "The slant of the shadows on his pale, fleshy face made it look infirm. The marks beneath his eyes brought to Leventhal's mind the bruises under the skin of an apple. . . . [S]uddenly he had a strange, close consciousness of Allbee, of his face and body, a feeling of intimate nearness such as he had experienced in the zoo when he had imagined himself at Allbee's back, seeing with microscopic fineness the lines of his skin, and the smallest of his hairs, and breathing his odor."[72] This moment of intimacy recalls the close encounter that Newman has with Finkelstein: his heightened attention to the Jew's voice followed by the dislodging of emotion and empathy toward his "Neighbor," and so on. So moved (if still nervous and skeptical), Leventhal invites Allbee inside his home.

Leventhal's progress toward intimacy continues, as Allbee literally takes over Leventhal's apartment, and eventually, in a key scene, his bed. These adjustments in physical space have an impact on Leventhal's psyche as well: "Allbee bent forward and laid his hand on the arm of Leventhal's chair, and for a short space the two men looked at each other and Leventhal felt himself singularly drawn with a kind of affection. It oppressed him, it was repellent. He did not know what to make of it. Still, he welcomed it, too. He was remotely disturbed to see himself so changeable."[73] Allbee's presence, we might say, begins to overturn Leventhal's strictly coiled world. This striking moment of "Jewish-gentile" mirroring highlights Leventhal's core ambivalence: the desire for human contact and identification in counterpoint to a (congenital?) hardness of heart and fear of change, of losing control. Looking back, we can now read his own strategy with Rudiger as a conscious labor of control, a *performance* designed to contain his out-of-control emotions, to display a show of "poise." Drawn to Allbee's situation, at some level Leventhal recognizes himself in Allbee. Reversing Ozick's profound dictum, among the epigraphs above, to know oneself in *The Victim*, the Jew must gaze into the mirror of the antisemite. In Allbee's mirror, Leventhal sees his own struggle to understand what constitutes "manners" as well as what is "dignified."

As *The Victim* moves toward "closure," which includes a brilliant comic epilogue that takes place a few years later, Bellow continues to complicate the Leventhal-Allbee relationship. In another scene of role reversals, we watch *Leventhal* watch Allbee in an embarrassing moment of exposure, a farcical situation (as Leventhal renarrates it in his head) of Allbee being caught—literally—naked by Leventhal in bed (Leventhal's bed) with a woman. Reimagining the pathos and comedy—and, to be honest, the pleasure—of witnessing the spectacle of mannered Allbee out of control, Leventhal feels both supremely empathic for the woman ("It must have been frightening, sickening for her to hear the crash of the door and then run out of bed. . . . He found himself regretting the whole incident")[74] and wildly amused at poor Allbee's helpless fumblings at the moment of exposure:

[Thinking about the women's expression] It now struck him that there was more amusement in it than fear, and he could see, too, how with a grain of detachment it was possible for her to find the incident amusing. He began to remember how Allbee had stumbled in pulling up his pants and how comically he had held out the woman's stockings to her. It was low, it was painful, but it was funny. He grinned, *his eyes dilated and shone*; he gave way explosively to laughter. . . . When he had done laughing and coughing, his face remained unusually expressive. Yes, and *he ought not to leave himself out of the picture,* glaring at them both. Meanwhile, Allbee was burning, yet *trying to keep his head*. The woman must have grasped that *he did not dare say what he felt*. Perhaps he had been boasting to her, telling lies about himself, and that was why his predicament amused her [emphases added].[75]

All kinds of ironies and reversals abound in this, Bellow's intimate transcription of Leventhal's richly empathic reflections. In nice contrast to the Harkavy episode—which, we recall, gnawed at Leventhal—the tables are turned on the pathetic Allbee who, shorn of his "gentile" composure, performs the burlesque clown for Leventhal's own "delight" (to recall the key word that so troubled Leventhal). Yet Leventhal's reaction, in its generosity of feeling, also appears out of character. (Can Allbee's "delight" in Harkavy's pathetic performance be called "generous?" Perhaps not.) Leventhal's eyes dilate and shine (is he about to shed tears that accompany unbuttoned, enthusiastic laughter?); they're enlarged, like his expansive heart, in direct response to Allbee.[76] At the same time, Leventhal does not separate himself from the scene of farce; he, too, is implicated in the comedy, as witness and participant—another sign of Leventhal's emergent empathy. Finally, to complete the stunning set of reversals, Leventhal watches Allbee's losing effort in shame management, unconscious that the comic situation recalls his own not so funny scene with Rudiger, where he, too, lost his head, and could dare not say what he truly felt.

Thus by the end of *The Vicitm*—I refer now to the epilogue—the initially fixed positions of the "antisemite" and the "Jew" have become blurred; the unhealthy zones of stereotyping and mutual enmity have been breached, giving way to empathy and perhaps, at some level, identification. Each has helped engineer the other's transformation. Leventhal enables Allbee to move beyond despair and recrimination by slowly making room for Allbee, first in his home and (at some level) in his heart. Based on the evidence, Allbee, it appears, has worked through his suicidal impulses, arriving at a healthier, better "adjusted" relation to the larger world. This is in radical contrast to our last image of Allbee (before the Epilogue), crouching at Leventhal's open door, inhaling gas fumes, seeking only his own death, not intending, he claims, Leventhal's. ("'Me, myself!' Allbee whispered despairingly." Not surprisingly, after this ordeal Leventhal's self reverts to *its* familiar territory of defense: "He looked impassive, under the cloud of his hair."[77]

In the remarkable final pages of The Victim, at Leventhal's and Allbee's chance encounter a few years later in the lobby of a Broadway theater, we observe each character's "progress." Leventhal, Bellow remarks, has stopped lashing out against the world. "Something recalcitrant seemed to have left him"; "he was not exactly affable, but his obstinately unrevealing expression had softened." Looking "years younger," his wife pregnant, Leventhal is about to fulfill a generative office we caught only a glimpse of during his fatherly gestures with his nephew Philly. (A subplot in *The Victim* concerns Asa's tender parental relationship with his sick nephew, who sadly passes away at the end of the novel.) What has softened (of course, only to a degree) in Leventhal is his heart; he is now more inclined to empathy, rather than bristling against the insults of the world.[78]

Tellingly, however, Bellow expresses *The Victim*'s deepest wisdom through the example of Allbee who, unlike the still baffled Leventhal, has apparently acquired a self-preserving, ironic sense of humor. Indeed, Allbee seems to have taken to heart the key insight that, earlier, Leventhal had noted of Allbee, without really recognizing the import of his observation (even in the Epilogue Leventhal continues to be either deaf or unresponsive to comic nuance): "By clowning," Leventhal says of Allbee, reflecting on the incident in the bedroom, "he could pass off his own feelings."[79] Burlesque as emotional release; clowning as way to salve the pain of incurred or imagined insult; accentuated routines as a mode of defense; comedy as revenge. Of course these are among the familiar strategies of Jewish humor. Indeed, by the end of *The Victim*, Allbee has become something of a (Jewish?) comedian.

Meeting Leventhal and his expectant wife, Allbee cracks ("smil[ing] broadly, displaying his teeth"), "'Congratulations. I see you're following orders. "Increase and multiply."'" Still (alas) in character, Leventhal can only respond "with a dull, short nod"; he misses, that is, Allbee's genial tone, above all the levels of irony embedded in Allbee's line.[80] In light of their shared history, Allbee's joking (to my Jewish ears at least) sounds like the self-mocking humor of an ex-antisemite who, nevertheless, acts the role of the wise-ass antisemite for someone who shares, or can remember, their previous intimacy. The joke banks on intimacy; only Leventhal knows—or ought to remember—how unironic Allbee used to be, when he was obsessed with Leventhal's "animal"-like, "Jewish" hair, or protested Harkavy's singing. "'Increase and multiply'" amounts to Allbee's shtick, his way of "signaling" (a key word in sociological-anthropological studies of ethnic humor) that he is a changed man. "'You haven't changed much,'" Allbee remarks, again, with an ironic tone. "'I wasn't the one who was going to change much,'" Leventhal dryly admits, in reply. At last Leventhal voices a truth about himself.[81]

In yet another striking example of self-transformation through humor, voiced perhaps in this instance, from within a less self-conscious comedic space, Allbee utters a startlingly ironic line. We overhear Allbee, arriving late to the theater, arguing with a cabbie about overcharging ("'He took us the long way around'"), exclaiming, "'Does he think I don't know the city? I'm no greenhorn here.'"[82] In light of his earlier obsessive exchange with Leventhal on the matter of "breeding," recalling the unsettling scene of immigrant Jews overtaking his New York, Allbee's statement registers, on many levels, with even more stunning irony. As voicecd by someone like Allbee, "'I'm no greenhorn'" could mean any one (or more) of the following:

"I'm not a 'Jew,'" either an innocent immigrant (recall that *greenhorn* is a key word in Cahan and Yezierska) or a "Jew" in general.
"I'm not a 'greenhorn' Jew, but rather a Jew who knows the city."
"I've lived in New York all my life, so I know when I've been taken for a ride."
"Don't make a [greenhorn] Jew of me."

Whichever meanings one might choose, the point is that, finally, Allbee appears at ease in "Jewish" New York; he can now appropriate—crucially, without rancor or despair—the latent resonances of "greenhorn" for his own purposes, ironically or not. In this respect, Allbee's gesture seems related to Newman's at the end of *Focus*, though obviously from a very different perspective. For Allbee now seems to identify as a "Jew"—not, of course, as a Jew fresh off the boat or a Jew as a matter of "descent," but rather as a symbolic "Jew" in—and of—the city: argumentative, wise-ass, ironic, refusing to be "taken."

And, finally, Allbee appears to be reconciled with a universe that tends to ignore him. "'I've made my peace with things as they are,'" he confesses to Leventhal; "'I'm not the type that runs things. I could never be. I realized that long ago. I'm the type that comes to terms with whoever runs things. What do I care? The world wasn't made exactly for me. What am I going to do about it?'"[83] Arriving at this hard-won reality principle (recall the Freudian vogue among New York intellectuals in the forties and fifties), a worldview at odds with the paranoid isolationist maxims of Leventhal's immigrant father, living on "the old system," Bellow's phrase (and title of a great 1967 story) connoting Old World styles of belief and behavior, Allbee's personal insight sounds with the authority of a lifetime of pain, loss, and humiliation. "'When you turn against yourself,'" he continues, voicing perhaps the deepest insight any character is allowed in *The Victim*, "'nobody else means anything to you either.'" Significantly, Allbee utters these heartfelt words in a "bitterly shame-faced and self-mocking" mood; "he took Leventhal's hand and pressed it."[84]

Thus in *The Victim*, the self may be healed through a psychic journey from self-hatred to empathy, a condition of selfhood that, in the end, Allbee appears to have achieved more than his "victim." Allbee, that is, seems to have worked through his grievances, to have adjusted his expectations: Adjustment through self-mockery. Chafing under the system, Leventhal, by contrast, continues to worry about "who runs things." In light of Talcott Parsons's famous observations in "The Sociology of Modern Anti-Semitism," does Leventhal remain an "emotional victim?" True, his previous "impassive," "recalcitrant" self has been softened, but it remains unclear whether his heart now inhabits a zone of enlarged feeling. After all, "Leventhal pulls his hand away" from Allbee at the very end.[85] Reversing (unconsciously?) the office of the "Jew" in *Focus*, Bellow's Allbee serves as the agent of Leventhal's choosing, or effort to choose, "dignity."

In *Focus*, the antisemite gazes into the Jew's face in order to be spiritually cleansed; in *The Victim* the Jew must learn how to read the antisemite in order to read himself. In each drama, a heart is stirred to empathy, piercing layers of stereotype, breaking through the crust of animosity. Despite his critical dismissal, Bellow, like Miller, participated in the post-war examination of Jewish-gentile relations. Would the possibilities of such mutual recognition lead to personal and social renovation, if not redemption? The answer to these ultimate questions remains open, unresolved. But for both Miller and Bellow, the "situation" of the Jew was crucial for resolving the political and psychological dilemmas of post-war America. Whatever the future might bring, the "Jew" would figure in the outcome.

NOTES

1. Cynthia Ozick, participant in "Is There a Cure for Anti-Semitism?" *Partisian Review*, vol. 61 (1994), p. 388.

2. Arthur Miller, *Focus*, (New York, 1945), p. 33.

3. Nathan W. Ackerman, and Marie Jahoda, *Anti-Semitism and Emotional Disoder: A Psychoanalytic Interpretation* (New York, 1950), p. 58.

4. James Atlas, *Bellow: A Biography* (New York, 2000), p. 126.

5. Arthur Miller, "The Face in the Mirror: Anti-Semitism Then and Now," "Afterward" to *Focus* [1945] (London, 2000), p. 213. Looking back in 2003 about his encounter with anti-Semitism and the origins of *Focus*, Miller reflected: "The anti-Semitism I ran into all over the place was fierce. And yet there was no sign of any recognition of it or acknowledgement of it in the public domain, not in novels, not in plays . . . and I felt it had to be unearthed. It had to be brought to light." Quoted in Hilary Leila Krieger, "Withstanding the Crucible," *The Jerusalem Post*, June 19, 2003 [Internet edition].

6. Malcolm Bradbury asserts that *Focus* "has some claim to being the first post-war Jewish-American novel, appearing at a time when that distinctive genre underwent a powerful, internationally influential revival." "Arthur Miller's Fiction," in *The Cambridge Companion to Arthur Miller* ed., Christopher Bigsby (Cambridge, 1997), p. 215. Michael Walzer speaks of "The Jew in Europe" as "the exposed face of modern life" in the Preface to Jean-Paul Sartre's *Anti-Semitism and the Jew* (New York, 1997 [orig. 1948]), p. xviii. "The post-war writers," observes Morris Dickstein, "moved away from social problems toward metaphysical concerns about identity, morality, and man's place in the larger scheme of the universe." Both *Focus* and *The Victim* amply illustrate this point. Morris Dickstein, *Leopards in the Temple: The Transformation of American Fiction, 1945–1970* (Cambridge, M.A., 2002), p. 63.

7. Miller, "The Face in the Mirror," p. 214.

8. Arthur Miller, *Focus*, p. 17 ("a little Hebey," p. 175).

9. In this respect *Focus* uncannily anticipates the core rhetorical/philosophical discourse of Sartre's *Anti-Semite and Jew.*

10. *Focus*, p. 155; p. 217.

11. Saul Bellow, "Brothers' Keepers" [review of Arthur Miller, *Focus*], *The New Republic*, vol. 114 (Jan. 7, 1946), p. 30.

12. Bellow, "Brother' Keepers." p. 30.

13. For a strong reading of *Focus*, which connects the novel to Laura Z. Hobson's *Gentleman's Agreement*, see Matthew Jacobson, *Whiteness of a Different Color: European Immigrants and the Alchemy of Race* (Cambridge, Ma., 1998), pp. 187–99.

14. "It is not a natural and clean anger," Maurice Samuel observes of anti-Semitism in *The Great Hatred*; "it is rage, plus disgust at the sight of something both dangerous and repulsive. It is the difference between being fighting mad and raving mad." *The Great Hatred* (New York, 1940), p. 143.

15. *Focus*, pp. 66–7. Newman's agony over the loss of social identity at the level of his "face" looks forward to Miller's later cautionary 1952 fable *The Crucible*, where John Proctor, falsely accused of witchcraft, agonizes over losing his "name"—and thus his "history"—if he accepts the judges' *devil's* bargain to save his life. Mr.Finkelstein also voices a Proctor-like accusation against the anti-Semites of the Christian Front. "'I will not move,'" he tells Newman, who has asked him to consider leaving the neighborhood. "'I like it here. I like the air. . . . I don't know how to fight them but I will fight them . . . They are a gang of devils and they want this country.'" *Focus*, p. 182–3. Thus anti-Semitism in the 1940s looks forward to blacklisting in the 50s. Each ideology of negation *possesses* a totalitarian face. Miller, it should be remembered, refused to answer the summons to appear before HUAC.

16. *Focus*, p. 3; p. 58; p. 13 (emphasis added).

17. *Focus*, p. 6. On the utopian aspect to the ending of Focus see Jacobson, *Whiteness of a Different Color*, p. 198.

18. *Focus*, p. 32; p. 35; p.34.

19. *Focus*, p. 34; p. 32–34. In Jacobson's view, in *Focus* Miller provides "a stunning treatment of the complex process of projection. . . ." In the figure of Lawrence Newman (p. 192). In the late 1940s "projection" was taken to be the core psychological affect of anti-Semites.

20. *Focus*, p. 134. Anticipating one of key issues of *The Victim*, Miller has Newman ask himself, "What was dignified, what is God's name was Dignified!" p. 137.

21. *Focus*, p. 135; p. 166.

22. *Focus*, p. 165.

23. *Focus*, p. 168; p. 169. In this respect, Finkelstein offers Newman a (psychoanalytic) mirror reflecting the gentile's deepest anxieties. "What do you see that makes you so angry?" (p. 166) Finkelstein asks? The query exposes the complex dynamic of anti-Semitic projection limned in *Focus*.

24. *Focus*, p. 186 (emphasis added).

25. *Focus*, p. 184.

26. *Focus*, pp. 185–6.

27. *Focus*, p. 117. Further ironies abound, especially in relation to the film version of *Gentleman's Agreement*. Passing as a Jew, Gregory Peck as "Phil Green"

confronts the manager at the restricted Flume Inn on the matter of admitting Jews. In the tense exchange, Peck—who has made a "Jew" of himself—seeks to expose the hotel's genteel anti-Semitism, but his moral outrage remains helpless before the steely gaze of the Inn's manager who, made uneasy by Peck's increasingly belligerent tone, quickly banishes the "loud" "Jew" from the lobby. During this scene the palpable shame Peck begins to "feel" his self-declared "Jewish" identity in new ways. For a fuller reading of *Gentleman's Agreement* along with *Crossfire*, the other famous 1947 film on anti-Semitism, see Donald Weber, "The Limits of Empathy: Hollywood's Imaging of Jews ca. 1947," in Jack Kugelmass, ed., *Key Texts in American Jewish Culture* (New Brunswick, 2003), pp. 91–104.

28. *Focus*, p. 209; p. 210.

29. *Focus*, p. 212.

30. *Focus*, p. 217.

31. *Focus*, p. 211.

32. Miller, "The Face in the Mirror," p. 213.

33. *Focus*, p. 217.

34. Jacobson, *Whiteness of a Different Color*, p. 198.

35. Walzer, "Preface" to Sartre, *Anti-Semite and Jew*, p. xx-xxi.

36. Leslie A. Fiedler, "Saul Bellow," in *Saul Bellow and the Critics* ed. Irving Malin (New York, 1967), p. 6. Fiedler also reviewed The Victim in the *Kenyon Review*, vol. 10 (1948), 526–7.

37. Elizabeth Hardwick, rev. of *The Victim*, *Partisan Review*, vol. 15 (1948), p. 114. Other significant reviews include Diana Trilling in *The Nation* 166 (Jan. 3, 1948), pp. 24–5, and Martin Greenberg, "Modern Man as Jew," *Commentary*, vol. 5 (1948), 86–7.

38. Saul Bellow, *The Victim* (New York, 1947), p. 3.

39. *The Victim*, p.77.

40. Hardwick, review of *The Victim*, p. 116. Morris Dickstein helpfully situates Bellow's second novel in terms of "forties concerns" (racism and anti-Semitism); yet it is "almost a parody of the literature of social protest." *Leopards in the Temple*, p. 61.

41. Fiedler, "Saul bellow," p. 6.

42. *The Victim*, p. 39.

43. *The Victim*, p. 39.

44. *The Victim*, p. 39. For the complicated genealogy of Harkavy's "Jewish" antics see Sander Gilman's chapters on "the Jewish voice" and "the Jewish nose" in the *The Jew's Body* (New York, 1991), pp. 10–37 and 169–93.

45. Is Allbee thinking of the classic "My Yiddishe Mama"? Written by Jack Yellen, it was a huge hit for Sophie Tucker in the mid-thirties, and for the Barry Sisters in the forties. Thanks to Mount Holyoke master librarian Bryan Goodwin for this factoid.

46. *The Victim*, p. 40; p.41.

47. *The Victim*, p. 144; pp. 144–5; p. 244. In an early exchange Allbee notes with interest the picture of Leventhal's wife and seeks to divine her "descent" intentity:

Albee: She's positively Asiatic.
Leventhal: She comes from Baltimore.
A: First generation?

Her mother is native-born, too. Further back than that I don't know. [Here Leventhal sounds like Sara confessing her lack of genealogical memory to Hugo in *Bread Givers*.]
A: I'm willing to bet they came from Eastern Europe, originally . . . .It's apparently enough; it doesn't need any investigating. Russian, Poland . . . .I can see at a glance. (p. 72).

Recent scholarship on *The Victim* highlights the racialized dimension of the Allbee-Leventhal relationship. See, for example, Philip McGowan, "The Writing of Blackness in Saul Bellow's *The Victim*," *Saul Bellow Journal*, vols. 16–17 (2000 and 2001), pp. 74–103.

48. *The Victim*, p. 7; p. 13. Elsewhere Bellow notes Leventhal's "unimpassioned face." (p. 98).

49. *The Victim*, p. 241. In this respect Leventhal's looming personal crisis looks forward to Bellow's Tommy Wilhelm in *Seize the Day* (1956).

50. *The Victim*, p. 44.

51. *The Victim*, pp. 44–45.

52. *The Victim*, p. 44.

53. *The Victim*, p. 45.

54. *The Victim*, p. 45.

55. "Composure, if it is a quality," observes Adam Phillips, "is the least innocent of virtues." "Provoked by an excess of excitement, composure becomes a way of accommodating such experience, a belated refusal; it becomes, in fact, a superstition of confidence in the integrity of the self." Asa's mask of composure inscribes, in effect, Phillips's stunning observation about the raging underbelly of composure, acted out at the end of this remarkable scene: "And there is always the mind as the theater of revenge." Adam Phillips, "On Composure," in Phillips, *On Kissing, Tickling, and Being Bored: Psychoanalytical Essays on the Unexamined Life* (Cambridge, Ma., 1993), pp. 42; 45.

56. *The Victim*, p. 130.

57. *The Victim*, p. 130.

58. *The Victim*, p. 216.

59. *The Victim*, p. 111. Leventhal's "recoil" may also explain his reading of Harkavy's comic routine as generational burlesque. It may be Leventhal's unconscious (taboo) desire to parody his own father that accounts for his complex response.

60. Leventhal's "self-hatred leads to ugly defensive pride," observes John Clayton, in the strongest reading of *The Victim*. See John Clayton, *Saul Bellow: In Defense of Man* (Bloomington, 1968), p. 148.

61. *The Victim*, p. 160. Is this Bellow's stunning reversal of the long history of the anti-Semite's olfactory revulsion against and imagined "Jewish odor"? "The smell of the Jews," writes Sander Gilman, "the *foeter judaicus*, is the medieval mephitic odor always associated with the Other." Sander Gilman, *Jewish Self Hatred: Anti-Semitism and the Hidden Language of the Jews* (Baltimore, 1986), p. 174.

62. *The Victim*, p.98.

63. *The Victim*, p.113; pp. 118–9.

64. *The Victim*, p. 119.

65. *The Victim*, p. 119. Morris Dickstein nicely observes, "Asa Leventhal foreshadows the blocked feelings, the sense of entrapment and asphyxiation of the Hapless

Tommy Wilhem in *Seize the Day*, whose whole life comes unstuck in just twenty-four hours." See Dickstein, *Leopards in the Temple*, p. 63.

66. *The Victim*, p. 120.
67. *The Victim*, p. 120.
68. *The Victim*, p. 166.
69. Cf. Clayton, *Saul Bellow*, p. 148: "Asa is in danger of becoming Allbee's kike."
70. *The Victim*, p. 160; p. 162.
71. *The Victim*, p. 160.
72. *The Victim*, p. 160.
73. *The Victim*, p. 224.
74. *The Victim*, p. 276.
75. *The Victim*, p. 276.
76. On the matter of Leventhal's "expansiveness" see Clayton, *Saul Bellow*, pp.159–60.
77. *The Victim*, p. 283.
78. *The Victim*, p. 285.
79. *The Victim*, p. 277.
80. *The Victim*, p. 292.
81. *The Victim*, p. 292. Leventhal, however, continues to stereotype Allbee, remarking, "You still drink." Leventhal, that is, implicitly thinks of Allbee as a *"shicker,"* the pejorative Yiddish slur for gentiles who drink.
82. *The Victim*, p. 289.
83. *The Victim*, p. 294.
84. *The Victim*, p. 294; 293.
85. *The Victim*, p. 294. Cf. Talcutt Parsons, "The Sociology of Modern Antisemitism," p. 8:

> It is not surprising, therefore, that Jews have often displayed rather extreme sensitiveness in matters touching self-respect and status. So long as their emotional attachments were limited exclusively to the Jewish community and all that mattered to them was the honor in which they had been held in their own community, they remained comparatively free from conflicts. As soon, however, as they are permitted, through emancipation to participate as a member of the larger community, the balance was largely lost and they found themselves torn between two worlds and victims of serious emotional difficulties.

At the end of *The Victim* Bellow's Asa Leventhal remains torn by such historic conflicts.

13

Jews in the United States: How Good It Has Been

Leonard Dinnerstein

In perhaps no other country in the world have Jews fared as well, and over as long a period, as they have in the United States and the British colonies before that time. Although some Jews may recall their "golden age," during most of the fifteenth century in Spain, and have been, from time to time welcomed and respected in different parts of Europe at one time or another, never have there been such opportunities for peaceful coexistence with gentiles, and economic opportunities, as they have consistently had in the United States. Social equality came, went, and not only returned, but grew to the point in American society where others would like to be like them and not the other way around. That does not mean, of course, that there have not been difficult periods which frightened Jews in this country, and which seemed to be quite threatening to their welfare, but in no other country in the world—not even Israel—have they had the freedom to follow their own pursuits as they have had, and still have, as American citizens. In the United States they have been able to lead normal and productive lives without always having to look over their shoulders.

For a number of reasons, all of which in combination have worked well for most white males in the United States, Jews have been able to exploit their talents and take advantage of economic and educational opportunities. Some of the factors that have made this situation unique are, in no particular order, a Constitution, a separation of church and state, a rhetoric of tolerance of, and opportunities for, all white males, no official class barriers, an amalgamation of people with a shared Protestant faith, an expanding economy, a tradition of political parties never forming official ties with religious groups, and the idea, generally prevalent in our rhetoric and internalized in our culture, that hard work leads to productive accomplishment. Moreover, and this has been true for Jews as well as for other white males, there has been largesse on the part of the federal, state, and local governments to spur economic development. What comes to mind immediately are (1) the Homestead Act of 1862 which the federal government granted to anyone willing to cultivate the land for five years and (2) the G. I. Bill of 1944 which helped returning veterans further their career goals with governmental assistance. Finally, although some people might think of other factors that I have not mentioned, there was, as historian Frederick Jackson Turner wrote more than a century ago, an ever expanding frontier for those individuals who wanted to start new lives away from developed regions. Continual immigration brought people from Europe and Asia and while a huge majority originally settled on the East or West Coasts, millions also moved inland until the whole continent was connected. Discontented white people have always had the opportunity to move elsewhere in the United States to start life afresh.[1]

The United States, despite its firm roots in England and the Protestant faith, has always been a polyglot nation that welcomed all white people to share its beneficence. A rhetoric glorifying cultural pluralism is certainly part of the American ethos despite the fact that immigrants were expected to shed their native values and quickly conform to the existing folkways and mores of the dominant culture. Even when they did not, however, Caucasian newcomers were looked down upon, not legally discriminated against.[2]

Unlike most other countries in world history, people who have risen from the bottom of the social ladder to the top have never been accorded the kind of respect that Americans have shown to those who have pulled themselves up by their own bootstraps. Perhaps the best example is Abraham Lincoln, one of our most revered Presidents, who rose from a modest beginning to the pinnacle of American power. Similarly, Andrew Carnegie, one of the richest men in America in the late nineteenth century, has been glorified in textbooks because he arrived in the United States as a poor seven year old from Scotland and who by stealth, determination, and hard work, accumulated one of the greatest fortunes ever known.

Just as the opportunities for accomplishment remained broad, so too did the liberalism of American rhetoric. A belief existed, and still exists in this country that anyone could come and join with the establishment once he accomplished what the elite had won for themselves or their children. Foreigners were always encouraged to emulate the paths taken by previous generations of newcomers. Thus Jews in the 18th and 19th centuries in the United States ranked amongst the elite in business and social measurements. They were amongst the founders of some prestigious men's groups, like the Philadelphia Club, and in 1830, Jews constituted 5% of the white population in the state of South Carolina. They held a number of high level positions in state government at that time which certainly was not common in any other Christian nation.[3]

In colonial America both British policies and settlers' needs combined to provide a relatively good situation for Jews. The British, anxious to enhance their riches provided land to white males willing to take it; the colonies did the same thing. Unlike the Spanish and French governments, the British allowed self rule to their colonists in almost all matters except for trade. Therefore people of different nationalities and religions were both welcomed and encouraged to help with economic development. The colonists, who considered Indians "savage" and African Americans inferior beings because of their skin color, both needed and welcomed white people regardless of their cultural backgrounds. To be sure, problems were greater for Catholics than for other white people because the Protestants were particularly hostile to their faith, but there were too few Jews to constitute a threat. The Jews who were in the colonies numbered perhaps 1,000 at the time of the American Revolution; lived mostly in New York City, Philadelphia, Charleston. Savannah and Newport, Rhode Island. Where trade was important they stood at the same level as Christians in their freedom to pursue their economic interests.[4]

Two things observed amongst Jews in colonial America, are that unlike Europe, (1) there were never any ghettos, although Jewish families tended to live in close proximity to one another, and (2) those who wished to do so, found marriage with Christians an easy road to assimilation. Both of these factors have always been true in the United States, for Jews and other Caucasians. At the end of the nineteenth and beginning of the twentieth centuries scions of wealthy Jews often married Christians and their offspring moved into the mainstream. For the most part, Jews who wanted to marry Christians have rarely been denied the opportunity to do so, and in some sections of the nation, especially the South, they have been encouraged in that pursuit. For example, there were no Jewish heirs of Jews who settled in Virginia before 1840 while in the nineteenth century successive generations of Sheftalls in Georgia counted fewer and fewer Jews.[5]

Another significant difference from Jewish experiences in Europe was the establishment of a Constitution and a Bill of Rights. The Constitution prohibited official affiliation of the federal government with religious bodies and forbade religious tests for those who wished to hold public office. The Bill of Rights added safeguards for individual white males like freedom of speech, freedom from religious restrictions by the federal government, freedom from "unreasonable" search and seizures, fair and speedy trials, and the right not to incriminate oneself. These safeguards, for the most part honored almost to the letter, are still part of the Constitution. Although the provisions of the Constitution did not prevent private bigotry and unwarranted physical attacks, unlike in Europe at various times, such activities against Jews were never sponsored or supported by governmental officials.

Moreover, the fact that the structure of government has remained secure and continuous, even in the face of a Civil War in the mid-nineteenth century, has provided stability and confidence among American people. No matter how charged the rhetoric of political campaigns may have been, Americans have united behind the victorious candidates and parties without raising significant questions about their right to govern. And new administrations, no matter how broad their proposals may have been during political campaigns, have always functioned within the guidelines originally set by the Constitution and its subsequent modifications. One especially important amendment, the 14th, guaranteed citizenship to all persons born or naturalized in the United States. That meant that anyone born or naturalized within its boundaries had the legal rights and privileges of every other person in the United States. This provision has been observed more often in the breach rather than in its execution since local circumstances often dictated which "rights and privileges" individuals of different ethnic and religious backgrounds might enjoy. Nonetheless, this has been particularly reassuring for members of white minority groups who, in other countries in the world, often found the tenets of government altered when new groups have come to power, especially if those governments had achieved their goals by revolutions or *coup d'etats*.[6]

Americans, although practicing what one might call an English speaking culture derived from the British and New England heritage, almost always fostered economic development and there were always opportunities for enterprising white males to exploit their own individual talents. Moreover, they were free to travel anywhere in the United States to do so. For those who sought opportunities outside of developed areas there were always fledgling communities in which to embark on new endeavors. For those who wanted to start new businesses or create heretofore unheard of or unusual enterprises, the opportunity existed not only to do so but to patent their ideas or discoveries. Never have there been federal restrictions on which occupations white males might pursue although several state governments, until well into the nineteenth century, required both voters and office holders to take oaths declaring their belief in Jesus Christ and the Christian faith.[7] There existed also, at different points in time, decisions made by other private citizens that in effect limited social and economic opportunities for minority groups. For the Jews, these occurred in having difficulty obtaining credit from lending institutions in the nineteenth and twentieth centuries, and restrictions in job, housing, and recreational pursuits before the passage of the Civil Rights Act in 1964.

Similarly, with the development of public education, in the North before the Civil War and in the South afterwards, Jewish males had the same legal options as other white males. Although education *per se* was not a significant factor in Jewish economic accomplishments before the twentieth century, it was nonetheless a stepping stone for socio-economic advancement, especially in the second half of the twentieth century. In the frontier West of the late nineteenth century, for example, Jewish peddlers and storekeepers not only found a niche but often became bankers because they were among the few people in their small communities who knew how to read, write, and do arithmetic. These skills made them the natural leaders to whom others turned for guidance and assistance. For example, in frontier Arizona, Idaho, and Colorado, several Jewish names have been associated with banks, major stores, and political development. Of all the frontier territories, however, Jews made their biggest impact in New Mexico.[8]

Family values and strong networks among Jews stressed the importance of learning and hard work, and when these factors were present, individuals thrived. Where prejudice and bigotry existed, Jews often sponsored or employed coreligionists who could not find work elsewhere. In the nineteenth century especially, Jewish businessmen or aspiring businessmen, found it difficult to get credit from American bankers but used the Jewish networking associations to get it from other Jews.[9] Jews who were creative about their economic choices never had to worry about governmental or religious interference in the United States. Nonetheless, most Jews found it prudent not to challenge local folkways and mores; they hoped to be good citizens and they accepted as many of the cultural norms as a practicing Jew could without converting to the Protestant faith. Not until after the Second World War in the United States did Jews, or at least their major defense organizations (which frequently preferred to be called "community relations agencies"), successfully induce state and federal governments to legally prohibit discrimination in several areas of private life such as education, travel, housing, public amusement, and resorts.[10]

Moreover, since the end of World War II, American Jews have become influential lobbyists and have communicated their sentiments to elected officials in local, state and federal governments. The nature of the American political system is such that any group which combines money, brains, and organization, usually has a good chance to have legislators—and executives—work for their goals by transferring suggestions into legislation. By the 1970s, and, in fact even earlier, legislators and executives in the different levels of American governments not only passed legislation that Jews favored, or appointed individuals to high office that Jews recommended, but also paid careful attention in foreign policy to issues that Jews favored. Foreign governments, in fact, have been amazed by the influence that American Jews have had in the development of United States foreign policy.[11]

Perhaps the best example of that is American policy toward Israel. Ever since the United States became the first nation to recognize the establishment of Israel in 1948, this government has consistently supported that state's right to exist. Moreover, American politicians, at every level, have almost always sympathized—and even praised—Israeli politicians for the stances that they have taken even when other nations in the world have been less supportive or more critical. Only twice has an American President intervened to actually counter a position Israel has taken in foreign policy. The first time it occurred was in 1956 when President Dwight D. Eisenhower condemned Great Britain, France, and Israel for trying to take over the Suez Canal. Eisenhower's strong condemnation of that action led all three nations to retreat and forced the British Prime Minister, Anthony Eden, to resign from office. On the other hand, when in 1967, Israeli planes bombed "The Liberty," an American ship in the Mediterranean Sea, both sides were quick to say that it had been an accident even though documents available in archives opened later suggested that the bombing might have been deliberate.[12] The other President who did not follow the advice of Jews and officials of the Israeli government, Jimmy Carter, lost Jewish support when he sought reelection in 1980. Carter tried to deal "even-handedly" in the Middle East which most Jews and Israelis viewed as a negative stance.[13]

Another important observation that affected Jews in the United States is that despite the sometimes questionable practices of both ordinary people as well as officials of the federal, state, and local governments, Americans have always engaged in self praise about this country being the land of the free and the home of the brave. With few exceptions, almost all white immigrants were welcomed to join our nation until the 1920s, when Congress erected barriers to bar Asians and limit the number of southern and eastern Europeans (e.g. primarily Italians and Jews) from entering the United States. Politicians, July 4th speakers, government officials, and the people at large have nevertheless generally subscribed to the idea that Americans are an amalgam of different European backgrounds and therefore welcomed other white people who they believed would choose to acculturate and then eventually assimilate with members of the majority. Almost all foreigners have been, and are, encouraged to, drop their "foreign" characteristics, dress, and faith, and behave like other Americans while adopting some Protestant denomination as their own. White people who did that generally found acceptance as "real Americans" as did their children and grandchildren. Marriage to persons of "foreign" backgrounds generally remained class oriented and rarely did old line Americans marry beneath their station. Marriage to people of high status, however, regardless of place of birth, was usually acceptable.

During the last half century our rhetoric of welcome and economic opportunity are still the same but now we proclaim, without most Americans really meaning it, that we are a classless, multi-cultural, and gender neutral, society. In truth, however, although women and minorities are encouraged to exploit their talents in any way they chose, there are still many people who harbor old beliefs about the "place" of women and members of different ethnic groups.

For Jews, there have always been less intense feelings against them in the United States than existed in Europe. The history of the Jews in Europe, despite the periodic good times, has been one of slander, stoning, expulsions, hanging, and drowning. Jews have been charged with causing riots, poisoning wells, kidnapping and mutilating Christian children for religious purposes, and fomenting wars and revolutions. In their economic dealings they have been suspected of shady and ruthless practices which they foisted on Christians. While several of these charges have also been attributed to Jews in the United States they have not been as many, as severe, or as quickly supported by church and governmental institutions. In fact, even when churches and members of the government have quietly supported and/or encouraged blatant anti-Semitism, the official rhetoric has always been circumspect and more often critical of public bigotry. In Europe, however, it would be difficult to find centuries where Christian voices were officially accepting of Jews as simply people of a different faith.[14]

Finally, in the United States and in no other country in the world since the passage of the Constitution in 1787, has the head of state, regardless of the man who occupied the highest electoral office in the nation, so frequently rallied to the cause of American Jewry. When specifically confronted with direct examples of anti-Semitism many an American President took a firm stand specifically opposing that type of bigotry. Practically every history of American Jews includes the comment of President George Washington to a delegation of Newport, Rhode Island, Jews visiting with him in 1790, that this nation gives "to bigotry no sanction, to persecution no assistance."[15] In 1840, after thirteen Jews had been arrested in Syria for allegedly having killed a Christian to use his blood for religious purposes, President Martin Van Buren's Secretary of State, John Forsyth sent a letter of protest to the Syrian government.[16] During the American Civil War, when General Ulysses S. Grant barred Jews from his military area in Tennessee, President Abraham Lincoln overruled him and rescinded the order.[17] In the mid-1880s, President Grover Cleveland appointed an Ambassador to Austria who had a Jewish wife. The Austrians refused to accept the man for that reason. Cleveland, offended for the United States, therefore refused to send another in his stead and left the *charge d'affairs* to head the embassy. Theodore Roosevelt appointed the first Jewish member of the Cabinet, Oscar Strauss, in 1905 and then in January, 1921, President Woodrow Wilson, along with former President William Howard Taft, headed a list of protesters against the anti-Semitism spewed forth in Henry Ford's newspaper, *The Dearborn Independent*. Without mentioning either Ford or his newspaper, Wilson and

Taft joined others denouncing "an organized campaign of anti-semitism" that encouraged "prejudice and hatred . . . because we are convinced that it is wholly incompatible with loyal and intelligent American citizenship."[18]

Without a doubt, the President most revered by American Jews, and who did the most for them while he served in the White House from 1933–1945, was Franklin Delano Roosevelt. At a time when anti-Semitic rhetoric and behavior reached their pinnacle in the United States, when Jews could not find employment with non-Jewish businesses, and when churches allowed ministers and priests almost unrestricted freedom in their attacks upon Jews, Roosevelt not only came to their aid but demonstrated, to a greater extent than anyone else in the nation, or any previous occupant of the White House, how much he valued Jewish contributions to the United States and to his own administration. Roosevelt liked surrounding himself with people of sparkling wit and intellect. He had been Governor of New York, where he had had many Jewish advisors, and as President he brought more Jews into the federal government than had all of his predecessors combined.

His formidable tasks as President required, as he put it in his first inaugural address on March 4, 1933, "action and action now," and he was not about to allow any factors like race or religion thwart his goals of relief, reform, and recovery for the nation. Within the Agricultural and Interior departments Jews served at various levels. Roosevelt consulted frequently with Harvard Law School Professor Felix Frankfurter about policy, and through Frankfurter, sought the advice as well of Supreme Court Justice Louis D. Brandeis. Roosevelt's Secretary of Labor, Frances Perkins (the first American woman to hold a cabinet position) claimed that she also liked to have about her quick, bright, alert people from an "urban Jewish background."[19]

Within the White House Roosevelt did not start out with many Jewish advisors but during his terms in office he brought in Judge Samuel Rosenman, who had been his chief counsel when he served as Governor of New York, technically as a "speech writer," but, in effect, especially from 1937–1945, as his closest personal advisor. David Niles of Boston served as his aid for minority affairs, and Benjamin ("Ben") V. Cohen sat in the White House and wrote proposals for some of the administration's major domestic legislative accomplishments, such as the social security act, the regulation of public utilities, and the wages and hours acts.[20]

During World War II both Rosenman and Niles kept telling Roosevelt to keep away from the refugee issue. Neither the State Department nor the War Department wanted to do anything to help European Jews escape the clutches of the Nazis. Within the United States pollsters registered their highest scores of gentile anti-Semitism. Nonetheless, in the fall of 1942, despite the words of his closest advisors and the evidence of the nation's hostile feelings towards Jews, the President tried to increase American immigration quotas. Vice President Henry Wallace, Speaker of the House of Representatives Sam Rayburn (d-Texas), and Majority Leader Alben Barkley (D-Kentucky) told him that if he made any effort to change quotas Congress would be more likely to cut, rather than to add, them for Jews.[21]

The results of the November, 1942, Congressional elections forced Roosevelt to work with his smallest Democratic majority in Congress and the largest number of outspoken anti-Semites (10) that he had had to deal with in his twelve years as President. Many "New Deal" agencies were scrapped by this Congress.[22] Nonetheless, Roosevelt again attempted to assist European Jews in peril by requesting Congressional permission for emergency powers to control the flow of persons and information into and out of the country.[23] An incensed House of Representatives turned down the request. Historian David Wyman not only captured the mood of the country, but expressed the views of a majority of legislators, when he wrote that

> many Americans were prejudiced against Jews and were unlikely to support measures to help them. Anti-Semitism had been a significant determinant of America's ungenerous response to the refugee plight beforePearl Harbor. During the war years, it became an important factor in the nation's reaction to the Holocaust.[24]

After World War II, Jews in government, particulary in Democratic administrations, were par for the course. Until Roosevelt's era they had not been. Contemporary critics who disliked "that man" in the White House condemned many of Roosevelt's programs as the "Jew Deal." This designation rankled the President no end. Nonetheless, he did not hesitate to appoint Jews to most administrative positions where he thought that they had the requisite skills and judgment. Prominent legislation regarding American Indians was prepared by Jews in the Department of the Interior. Ben Cohen, who had served the President in the White House from 1935–1941, worked for the State Department during World War II.

Bigotry, of course, existed along with tolerance throughout all of American history but one would find it difficult to find as popular, and as outspoken, an anti-Semite as Father Charles Coughlin of the Roman Catholic Church whose vitriolic broadcasts from 1938 to 1942 stirred Catholics and others into violent physical and verbal attacks upon Jews, especially in New York and Boston. No member of the church hierarchy criticized Coughlin publicly and not until President Franklin D. Roosevelt threatened to bring charges of sedition against Father Coughlin in 1942 for remarks undermining the war effort, did Catholic Church officials give him the choice of continuing in politics and resigning from the priesthood, or ending his political pronouncements and resuming the activities of a parish priest.

Coughlin chose the latter and refrained from public political activity for the rest of his life.[25]

To be sure, silencing of Coughlin did not bring about an era of tolerance. In fact the anti-Semitism prevalent in the United States during World War II has been measured by pollsters as having been the strongest in this nation's history. Not until after World War II ended did the bigoted public and private rhetoric of non-Jewish Americans begin to subside. Much of the credit for the new direction must be given to the more tolerant attitudes that were gradually developing in the United States after World War II, as well as the tremendous economic expansion that occurred. Prosperity, wartime experiences as well as the business of daily life, weakened anti-Semitism. However, one must not ignore the important work of the Jewish agencies that actively campaigned for legislation to end divisive policies. They carried their messages to state, local, and ultimately the federal legislators, and their efforts proved worthwhile. State and local legislation eliminating discrimination in housing, employment, travel, education, and public recreational facilities appeared in the second half of the 1940s.[26] To be sure, legislation did not lead to instant alteration of actions but the bills that passed and the edicts that were issued signaled that discriminatory behavior no longer had moral and legal sanction. Not until passage of the 1964 Civil Rights Act, however, did Congress make any significant attempt to bar public discrimination. Bigotry could not be erased from people's minds and hearts but people's legal ability to act out their prejudices was severely limited.

Even an era of heightened anti-Semitism in the United State, however, especially during World War II, can only be described as "intense" in American terms. Aside from episodes of children being bullied and beaten in some major American cities, like Boston and New York, hostility toward Jews in the United States can in no way be compared to the savagery of the prejudice that existed at that time in Poland, Rumania, and Germany. The United States, I again reemphasize, passed no restrictive legislation designed to harm or curtail the activities of Jews in the country. To be sure, social anti-Semitism was rife, and many churches allowed lower level officials to utter anti-Semitic remarks, but, for the most part, Jews lived their daily lives without strife or fear. In many parts of the United States hundreds of thousands of Jews believed that they always had to be on their best behavior to prevent arousing public manifestations of anti-Semitism, which, they believed, their Christian neighbors might engage in. For the most part, life for Jews in America continued with all the assorted joys, pleasures, and problems that people must deal with on a daily basis.

Changes did come, not only in the United States but in other countries as well. And while in the United States people have a greater degree of freedom of speech than elsewhere, other nations, to promote the end of bigotry, have passed legislation that has made the expression of vicious and irrational remarks about members of minority groups punishable by law. Despite this factor, in no other country in the world have the opportunities been as extensive, or as restrictive about official religious ties, as they have been in the United States over a period of centuries. Although some countries which are democratic in practice do have established state religions, like Great Britain, Denmark, and Israel, or allow churches to provide public education with financial support from taxpayers, like Germany and Canada, these conditions, with some minor exceptions, have never existed in the United States.

On the other hand no other nation in the world has been as friendly toward, and as tolerant of, the government in Israel as has the United States. While in many places attitudes towards Israel, its people, and its government, change according to evaluations of contemporary events, in the United States the powerful influence of American Jewry has made such variations in policy untenable. The nature of the American political system has given disproportionate influence to well organized and well-financed groups. No other country in the world is responsive to so many lobbying organizations as is the United States. Using whatever resources they have at their command, hundreds, if not thousands, of different American economic, social, and religious groups can win the ear, and the policies that they seek, from members of the legislative body and the executive branch of local, state and federal governments. Fortunately for American Jews, they are one of the most potent of the lobbying groups in areas where they unite and take a strong stance on an issue, such as support for the people and the government of Israel.

Yes, America is a Christian country with a majority of citizens who are Christians, but because of the wisdom of the founding fathers, and the evolution of the American political system as it exists today, various minorities have the opportunity to exert influence upon the government. Furthermore, no legal barriers have ever been established by the federal government to prevent Jews, or other white minorities, from obtaining equal economic opportunities and equality of treatment before the law. For these myriad reasons, America has always been different for Jews. Opportunities to live fruitful and decent lives have always been legally present.

NOTES

1. Richard D. Heffner, *A Documentary History of the United States* (New York, 2002), pp.213ff.

2. Leonard Dinnerstein and David M. Reimers, *Ethnic Americans* (4th edition: New York, 1999), p. 7.

3. Hasia R. Diner, *The Jews of the United States* (Berkeley, 2004), pp. 24ff.; Leonard Dinnerstein, *Antisemitism in America* (New York, 1994), pp. 90–91; Howard M. Sachar, *A History of the Jews in America* (New York, 1992), p. 30; Frederic Cople Jaher, *The Urban Establishment* (Urbana, 1982), pp. 596, 650.

4. Naomi W. Cohen, *Jews in Christian America* (New York, 1992), p. 19; Sachar, *History of the Jews*, pp. 16–17.

5. Myron Berman, *Richmond's Jewry: 1769-1976* (Charlottesville, VA, 1967), chapter 4; Stephen Birmingham, *"Our Crowd": The Great Jewish Families of New York* (New York, 1967), passim.

6. Cohen, *Jews in Christian America*, pp. 30ff.

7. New Hampshire was the last state to eliminate the requirement that voters had to take the oath of being believing Christians. This occurred in 1877.

8. Leonard Dinnerstein, "Jews in the 'Old Southwest,'" *Journal of the West*, vol. 38(January, 1999), pp. 88–89.

9. *Ibid*, pp. 89–90.

10. Leonard Dinnerstein, *Uneasy at Home* (New York, 1987), pp. 178ff. The best book on the formation and effectiveness of the American Jewish defense (or community relations) agencies is Stuart Svonkin, *Jews Against Prejudice* (New York, 1997).

11. J. J. Goldberg, *Jewish Power* (Reading, MA., 1995), pp. 5, 13, 15 and chapter one *passim*.

12. Robert Dallek, *Flawed Giant* (New York, 1998), pp. 429–430.

13. Goldberg, *Jewish Power*, pp. 57, 58. Arlene Lazarowitz, "President Jimmy Carter and the American Jewish Community," presented at the Western Jewish Studies Association Conference, Tempe, AZ., March 13, 2005.

14. Dinnerstein, *Antisemitism in America*, pp. xxii ff.; Nicholas de Lange, "The Origins of Anti-Semitism: Ancient Evidence and Modern Interpretations." in Sander L. Gilman and Steven T. Katz, eds., *Anti-Semitism in Times of Crisis* (New York, 1991), p. 23.

15. Morris U. Schappes, *A Documentary History of the Jews in the United States* (3rd edition; New York, 1972), p. 80.

16. *Ibid*, pp. 208–209.

17. Steven V. Ash, "Civil War Exodus: The Jews and Grant's General Orders No. 11," *Historian*, vol. 44 (August, 1982), p. 511.

18. Henry L Feingold, *Zion in America* (New York, 1974), pp. 232, 270; Dinnerstein, *Antisemitism in America* (New York, 1994), p. 83.

19. Dinnerstein, *Uneasy at Home*, pp. 62–63.

20. *Ibid*, pp. 62ff.

21. Robert Dallek, *Franklin D. Roosevelt and American Foreign Policy, 1932–1945* (New York, 1979), p. 446.

22. Dinnerstein, *Antisemitism in the United States*, p. 44.

23. H. G. Nicholas, ed., *Wartime Dispatches, 1941–1945* (London, 1981), p. 117.

24. David S. Wyman, *The Abandonment of the Jews* (New York, 1984), p. 9.

25. Dinnerstein, *Antisemitism in the United States*, pp. 132ff.

26. Dinnerstein, *Uneasy at Home*, pp. 181ff. See also, Svonkin, *Jews Against Prejudice*, for a much more detailed analysis.

14

Anti-Semitism Today

Abraham Foxman

Anti-Semitism, apparently the oldest and most resilient form of hatred known to humankind, has recently moved into an alarming new phase, crossing boundaries of every type—geographic, national, political, religious, and cultural.

A frightening coalition of anti-Jewish sentiment is forming on a global scale. We see it in dozens of manifestations.

We see it in the proclamations of Iran's President Mahmoud Ahmadinejad, who called for "Israel to be wiped off the face of the earth," and said "Some European countries insist on saying that Hitler killed millions of innocent Jews in furnaces . . . we don't accept this claim . . ."

We see it in Russia in the brazen daylight attack at a synagogue in Moscow, in which at least eight worshippers were wounded by a knife-wielding assailant who reportedly yelled, "I will kill Jews!"

We see it at the prestigious Ukrainian University, MAUP, which has become a hotbed for anti-Semitic incitement.

We see it in France, where anti-Semitism has exploded, and in the streets of Paris where Ilan Halimi, a 23-year-old French Jew was kidnapped, tortured, and brutally murdered by his captors, because "Jews have money."

We see it in the spread of outlandish conspiracy theories, including the continuing bizarre claim that the Israeli Mossad destroyed the World Trade Center on 9/11, bolstered by the fabricated "evidence" that four thousand Jews did not report for work that day because they were in on it.

We see it in the scores of racist and anti-Semitic websites that pollute the Internet, enabling hatemongers to cross-pollinate globally and spread their venom on a scale never before possible.

We see it in Arab/Muslim mass media, where the proliferation of vicious Nazi-like stereotyping of Jews, conspiracy theories, and Holocaust denial messages are poisoning the minds of a generation of Muslim youth.

We see it in the messages of hate preached in Middle Eastern mosques and broadcast electronically around the world, influencing Muslim immigrants in Europe to commit acts of vandalism and violence against Jewish victims.

We see it in the proliferation of outrageous comparisons between fascism and Zionism—the depiction of Israelis as Nazis, of Jewish leaders as Hitlers, and of Israeli treatment of Palestinians as worse than the Holocaust.

We see it in the resurgence of age-old anti-Semitic stereotypes, frauds, and forgeries, including the reappearance of the long-discredited *Protocols of the Elders of Zion* and the continued spread of the infamous "blood libel" that blames Jews for the murder of innocent non-Jews.

Most alarming, these signs of the new anti-Semitism are visible on every continent and in virtually every country of the world.

The last half-decade has witnessed a horrific resurgence of anti-Semitism in Europe, less than sixty years after the murder of six million Jews in the Holocaust—the crime of crimes that many of us believed would make a rebirth of full-blown anti-Semitism practically impossible. Physical attacks on Jews and their institutions are taking place from France to Russia, Spain to Poland, while governments look the other way or respond too slowly and too ineffectually. Leading European news media are filled with stories slanted against Israel, further heating up a climate in which leadership of the Jewish community is virtually alone in its battle against anti-Semitic attacks. In England, some Christian clerics use anti-Jewish rhetoric suppressed since the Holocaust. Not only are we hearing the cry of "Zionism is racism" and attacks on the legitimacy of the State of Israel, but also the old, destructive "replacement theology"—the notion that Judaism has been superseded as a religion—which we thought Christianity had finally outgrown.

In the nations of Asia and Latin America—even in countries where Jews are few in number—anti-Semites are spreading their hatred, often thinly disguised as anti-Zionism. As a consequence, Jewish communities large and small are becoming increasingly vulnerable. Worshipers on the High Holy Days are attacked; synagogues are targeted by rock-throwers and bomb-planters; children who dare to wear the Star of David are subject to taunts and beatings.

And even in America, the land of freedom and tolerance where Jews have historically enjoyed greater acceptance than anywhere else other than the State of Israel itself, disturbing signs of the spread of anti-Semitism are visible. On college campuses, peace demonstrations all too often degenerate into attacks on Israel, replete with thinly-veiled anti-Semitism language and imagery. Among African-Americans, too many leaders find it advantageous to flirt with anti-Semitism in the guise of communal pride.

Some politicians on both the left and right find it expedient to blame Israel and the American "Jewish lobby" for everything from the war in Iraq to the difficulties of the ongoing battle against terrorism.

Thanks to modern methods of communication, from cable television and cell phones to the Internet, the latest anti-Semitic whispers spread faster, farther, and more quickly than ever. As a result, a worldwide community of hate is developing that links seemingly incompatible forces into a loose network of bigots with many shared enemies, objectives, and policies. Individuals and groups who otherwise agree on little find common cause in their hatred of the Jews. Thus, African-American anti-Semites are swapping ideas with extremist Islamic clerics from Indonesia and Pakistan; xenophobes and reactionaries from the European far right are abetting the efforts of Holocaust deniers at universities in the US and Britain; armed nationalist militants in the Rocky Mountains are studying and learning from the acts of terrorists from Saudi Arabia and Palestine.

People are not born bigots. They must be taught to hate. And today, millions are learning that deadly lesson. In a time of growing political tensions, cultural anxieties, and economic uncertainties, the age-old temptation to lash out at "the other" is too enticing for many to resist—whether that "other" is Jewish or Black, Arab or Hispanic, immigrant or gay. And when people indulge that temptation to scapegoat and to hate, violence and death result, as history and the pages of today's newspapers make all too clear.

It's time to join forces against this spreading evil before it's too late. Now, more than ever, the motto "Never again!" must become a rallying cry for all people of good will—for Jews and Christians, Muslims and Hindus, and lovers of freedom everywhere who profess no creed. Our responsibility is to speak out and to act when tolerance is threatened—and not just in our own backyards, or when our own families or friends are in danger, but in all times and places.

There's no better way for me to close than with the words of Elie Wiesel, the much admired philosopher and teacher, Holocaust survivor, and winner of the Nobel Peace Prize: "Whenever men or women are persecuted because of their race, religion, or political views, that place must—at that moment—become the center of the universe."

All of us who profess to love freedom must learn to live in the spirit of those words—for in a world as deeply and closely linked as ours, only when tolerance is the rule in every land can the freedom of anyone be truly secure.

15

The NYT: The Newspaper American Jews Love to Hate

Ari L. Goldman

We are here to celebrate the 350th anniversary of the arrival of Jews in America. This is also the year that the *New York Times* celebrates its 153rd anniversary.

Which, of course, raises the question: What did Jews complain about for 197 years?

This is a variation on an old joke about Jews and Chinese food, with the punch line being: What did Jews eat for 1,063 years.

The joke works because, like Chinese food, the *New York Times* is a habit among American Jews. Jews are devoted to the *Times*. They read it daily and, even on vacation, are known to go to great lengths to find it. And this is not only a New York phenomenon. A friend of mine who lives in a fancy Chicago high rise once told me, "I know every Jew in my building."

"A mezuzah on the door?" I asked.

"No, they get the *New York Times* delivered."

The odd thing, however, is that they don't like the paper. Jews depend on it, but they also have a distrust and even a contempt for the *Times*, America's newspaper of record.

In this talk I want to explore this issue by looking at four things:

- The role of newspapers in Jewish life
- The Jewish roots of the *Times*
- The *Times'* coverage of the Holocaust and Israel
- The changing role of newspapers in general

While we Jews like to think of ourselves as The People of the Book, sometimes I think we have become The People of the Newspaper. Part of this is the innate Jewish survival instinct. We need to know what is going on because trouble may just be around the corner.

But more than our anxieties and curiosities, I believe that journalism is very much in the tradition of Jewish learning. Think of Torah. Torah is truth, something that newspapers also aspire to capture. Torah also tells the story of the Israelites, warts and all. It doesn't pretty things up or hold back. All the prophets, including Moses, sinned and the Children of Israel did their share of straying as well. The Torah, like a good newspaper, tells it all.

Look at the Talmud. There is never just one opinion, numerous voices are heard. Rav and Shmuel, Hillel and Shammai. They are all engaged in great debates. The Talmud lets everyone have his say. So too with good journalism, we hear Republicans and Democrats, the prosecutor and the defense attorney, the Red Sox and the Yankees.

It is little wonder to me that Jews found a home in journalism, which brings us to Adolph Ochs, the son of German Jewish émigrés, who bought the *New York Times* in 1896. The *Times*, founded in 1851, was an undistinguished newspaper and Ochs transformed it, promising to deliver the news "without fear or favor."

He ran a contest for a slogan. He got many entries but settled on his own slogan: "All the News That's Fit to Print."

Ochs was the son-in-law of Rabbi Isaac Meir Wise, the 19th century leader of Reform Judaism. Both Ochs and his successor as publisher, Arthur Hays Sulzberger, his son-in-law, were self-conscious about their Judaism, insisting that it was a religion and not a community or a nation. Sulzberger was a member of the highly anti-Zionist organization the American Council for Judaism.

The *Times* of that era didn't want the paper to appear "too Jewish" and was cautious about giving bylines to people with Jewish-sounding names. The paper clipped the "Abraham" off of several by-lines, leaving us with writers like A.H. Raskin, the great labor reporter, and A.M. Rosenthal, the legendary foreign correspondent who later became the newspaper's executive editor.

The anti-Semites were watching. In fact, they pointed out that the TIMES spelled backwards is SEMIT(E).

The Times even ran advertisements for jobs, resorts and apartments with code words that essentially meant "no Jews need apply." Among the terms were "restricted" or "selected clientele." Curiously, Sulzberger allowed the *Times* to run these ads. He didn't want to appear too Jewish.

This was reflected most dramatically in the coverage of the Holocaust. The Times' failure to properly cover the Holocaust has been well documented, especially in a new book by Laurel Leff called *Buried by The Times*.

The *New York Times* of the 1940's was also anti-Zionist. Sulzberger favored Jewish settlement in the Dominican Republic or Honduras but not in Israel. To him Judaism was a religion, not a nation or a people.

From those early days and right through to today, there have been efforts among Jews to boycott the *Times*. But all these efforts have been short-lived. We can't live with it . . . and we can't live without it.

Of course the tone has changed. Since 1948, the paper has been in support of a Jewish state. Not always agreeing with the government, but certainly favoring Israel's right to exist within the community of nations.

How else has the *Times* changed?

Well, technically speaking, it's not a Jewish newspaper anymore. The current publisher, Arthur Ochs Sulzberger Jr., the great-grandson of Adolph Ochs, is an Episcopalian.

And after a succession of Jewish executive editors—Abe Rosenthal, Max Frankel, Joseph Lelyveld—the top editor (Bill Keller) is not Jewish.

The *Times* is not what it was in other ways too. It is not the news leader it once was.

I'll cite two reasons, one big and one small. The big one is the Internet and the small one is the Jayson Blair scandal.

In 2002, a scandal rocked the paper. A young reporter was found to have copied an article from a Texas newspaper, stealing quotes and scenes and even making things up. He never went to Texas. He never left Brooklyn. Upon investigation, it was revealed that he fabricated over 50 articles over a two-year period.

What was most astounding about the scandal was that it had gone on for so long. The incident revealed how remote the paper had become from its readers and how remote the editors were from the reporters. It raised questions about the paper's standards with regard to hiring, discipline and promotion, and revealed wide failures by management.

You all know what happened. The top editors, Howell Raines and Gerald Boyd, were forced to resign. The paper revamped its standards and promised to be more transparent. The Times installed a public editor who twice a month second-guesses the decisions and judgments of the newspaper.

Unthinkable just a few years ago.

This is not your grandfather's *New York Times*. It is no longer beyond reproach.

The big reason for change is the Internet.

No newspaper has the influence it once did.

When I ask academic audiences if they are *Times* readers, most hands go up. But when I ask if their children read the paper, the hands come down. Young people are not reading the Times, or other newspapers. They get the news they want from Jay Leno or John Stewart.

And I'd venture to say that even your relationship with the paper has changed. When it lands on your doorstep, you already know the basics. You got it from your favorite Internet sites or from CNN, FOX, MSNBC or from all-news radio. People turn to newspapers for something more: in depth reporting, analysis, a sense of what is going to happen next.

Sure, reading the *Times* can be infuriating. We can grouse about the coverage of Israel and about the paper's failures in the present and the past, but we read it because nothing has quite taken its place. For many of us, the *Times* provides a sense of stability in a fast-changing world. The question I will leave you with is this: What will our children hold on to? And what will they complain about?

16

Confessions of a Jewish Journalist

Gary Rosenblatt[1]

The Letter to the Editor in the Jewish Advocate of Boston complained that "while we Jews have been shouting from the housetops that we believe in democratic ideals and principles . . . the Jewish press, for some reason, will not permit any criticism of some of our so-called leaders." It went on: "No progress will be made if the Jewish press continues their policy of white-washing the lack of action on the part of our leaders."

The letter was dated Aug. 29, 1941.

Some things never change.

We are the People of the Book, and we have produced many famous and talented journalists, in addition to literary writers and historians. But Rabbi Stephen Wise once made reference, dismissively, to "the Jewish weaklies," and the fact is that Jewish newspapers still haven't achieved stature or the respect of the community they serve.

Why is that?

I am not a historian, I'm a journalist. So I would like to share some observations from my 32 years as an editor of Jewish newspapers, in Baltimore and New York, and focus on what role Jewish journalism does, and does not - and should - play in American Jewish life.

When people ask about my role as editor and publisher of the largest Jewish newspaper in the U.S., I tell them it's not unlike being the host of a large family dinner.

I don't know about your family, but in mine, that means being sensitive to a wide variety of relatives, some of whom don't speak to each other. My job as host is to be as inclusive as possible, to keep the conversation going, to try and make it interesting, and if people disagree, that's alright, as long as they're respectful of each other.

That's not unlike editing a weekly newspaper for the world's largest Jewish community, one where people have passionate views and differences—political, religious, ideological, etc.—and enjoy expressing them, and where each group has a large enough critical mass that it feels it need not have much to do with any other group.

So my job is to keep the conversation going, through the pages of the newspaper, allowing people to have their say, but with a degree of tolerance, if not respect.

Easier said than done.

A painful but instructive lesson for me came in 1993, when I had been editor of The Jewish Week for only a few weeks, and wrote a column in which I suggested that Orthodox, Conservative, Reform, Reconstructionist and secular Jews could all learn from each other. A day later, a noted Orthodox rabbi called to berate me for mentioning his denomination in the same sentence as the more liberal streams. It was a disappointing but liberating experience, reminding me I could never please everyone, nor should I try.

The journalist for a Jewish newspaper walks a delicate line, seeking to be true to both his craft and his community. Balancing these two competing mandates—uncovering the news and caring deeply about the community—is always difficult.

About a year ago I received a call from a rabbi pleading that we not write about a Jewish college student who had fallen from a dorm window at New York University the day before, an apparent suicide. The story had been front-page news in the dailies, but the rabbi said the family requested specifically that The Jewish Week not cover the story, since it would only add to their grief.

If we honor the request, we show empathy, but if we make no mention of the incident, do we not lose our credibility?

The deeper question, though, is what could we write about the tragedy that would be different from what had already been published, which raises the central question: how should a Jewish newspaper differ, if at all, from a general newspaper? What is Jewish news?

Historically, the Jewish press in America has been caught between two conflicting mandates. While the First Commandment for journalists is to probe, uncover and shed light on the truth in the shadows, the First Commandment of the Jewish community is to cover up - to present a united front and prevent, at all costs, *a shandeh far de goyim*, a scandal in the eyes of the Gentiles.

On the one hand, then, the duty to expose; on the other hand, the need to protect.

It is a constant tension, and the pressure to publish "good news" about the Jewish community—its synagogues, charities and organizations—is powerful, as is the resistance to exploring problems within that society.

There are so many complex problems we face—the increase in assimilation, the Mideast conflict, the structure and governance of our own voluntary Jewish community—and there is an abiding need to promote Jewish loyalty and unity. Yet pursuit of that need to the exclusion of others would make cheerleaders out of journalists. We would lose our most precious commodity: credibility.

Yes, we journalists sometimes bruise egos and make mistakes. But journalism is not a science. It's a process, an evolving historical snapshot whose focus and perspective change from day to day. Our job is to take the most accurate picture, at that moment, and keep on developing our skills as best we can.

A Jewish newspaper should serve as a corrective within society. And its reporting on the many aspects of Jewish cultural, political and religious life should be proof positive that We Are Not One. We Jews may be united in support of the State of Israel and the continuity of the Jewish People, but we are passionate and outspoken in our differing views about how best to ensure those and other goals. The more views that are reported on and reflected in the Jewish newspaper, the more vibrant the community - and the more reason younger people will want to identify with that community.

Indeed, the greatest threat to American Jewish survival is boredom. "We Are One" may be an effective fund-raising slogan, but if the community stifles discussion and debate, why bother to become involved. Disputation is a sign of life, an indication that people care passionately about issues. Just check the Talmud for proof of that healthy tradition, one we should pass down to our children.

With healthy debate and honest coverage, though, comes controversy, and sometimes communal embarrassment.

Several years ago, when we wrote about a rabbi accused of abusing teenagers in his charge for more than three decades, most of the community was supportive. But there were those, including rabbinic leaders, who accused us of *Lashon Hara*, spreading gossip, a frequent criticism leveled at the Jewish press.

It is true that the Chofetz Chaim, whose writings focused on the scrupulous need to observe the mandate not to gossip about others, would not have been a newspaper editor. But even he noted occasions when communal responsibilities outweighed the embarrassment of an individual.

For me, the Biblical verse of Leviticus 19:16 represents the paradigm for the ethical journalist. "You shall not be a gossipmonger among your people, you shall not stand aside while your fellow's blood is shed, I am the Lord."

On the one hand, we are commanded not to spread gossip because it demeans one's neighbor, insidiously and behind his back, in ways that he cannot counter. Throughout the ages immeasurable harm and bloodshed have come about through gossip, and the journalist knows full well the power he or she has to destroy through character assassination.

But the balance of the verse warns us not to "stand aside," not to shrink from responsibility. Knowing that one's words are powerful and can do damage does not mean we can ignore reporting on wrongdoing, but rather that we must be particularly careful with our facts and mindful that the stakes are high. If the circumstances are important enough, we are obligated to take a stand, speak out and help correct an injustice.

The verse concludes, "I am the Lord," reminding us that if and when we can write with both accuracy and compassion, walking that thin line of advocating for a just cause without unfairly attacking innocent people, our task can take on a measure of holiness.

And if we succeed, surely the Jewish press will come to deserve the respect it strives to achieve.

NOTE

1. Gary Rosenblatt is editor and publisher of The Jewish Week of New York, the largest Jewish newspaper in the U.S. (www.thejewishweek.com).

17

Portraits of America in Jewish Culture

Stephen J. Whitfield

America was more than a place; it was also an idea. It has been more than a country; it has also been charged with myth, made into an object of faith, emblazoned as a repository of hope. Its geography has not been its limit. America has also been injected into the dream-life of millions; and this essay is intended to illustrate the ways in which Jews have enriched that dream-life, through their participation in the nation's culture.

A century ago, even as Jewry happened to be celebrating 250 years of its history on American soil, nativist hostility and racist ideology were rampant. A Harvard-educated Progressive intellectual like President Theodore Roosevelt did not hesitate to pepper his private correspondence with terms like "spicks" and "chinks" and "dagos" and "wops." Though he avoided equivalent terms for Jews, it was far from certain whether hyphenated Americans could become authentic Americans. Take the *Encyclopedia Britannica*, which published its eleventh edition in 1911. Its twenty-four volumes may constitute the most famous compendium of knowledge since Diderot's. The 1911 article on "Migration" pays special attention to the United States, where tension erupted between the descendants of the earlier immigrants from the British Isles as well as Germany and the newcomers from Eastern and Southern Europe. The article noted that emigration was sometimes less the result of the radiance of American ideals than of "the desire to get rid of undesirable members of the community." Push rather than pull especially accounted for "the expulsion of the Jews," an instance of "the effort of a community to get rid of an element which has made itself obnoxious to the local sentiment."[1]

The gates which might admit that element were nevertheless still open. In that same year, 1911, in "Song to America, Land of the Free," lyricist Solomon (Sholem) Shmulewitz managed to string together every cliché that the historian might expect as he urged listeners to "honor this free land/Especially when it comes to the Jew/Who gains rights, happiness and freedom." He recommended swift naturalization, because "You have a voice when you are a citizen," and also endorsed the Protestant ethic: "Work and you will make money." And thus "blessed be this free land."[2] A less programmatic song was composed during the era of the First World War. "A Briv fun Amerike" ("A Letter from America") belonged to a popular, poignant genre that addressed the separation of relatives. The question that is posed in "A Briv fun Amerike" is: who can invoke a transcendent claim—the mother left behind in Russia who needs to be cared for, or the wife who warns against a return to Russia, where military conscription remains a threat?[3] This is the dilemma that was the stuff of song as well as melodrama, the revelation of a tragic situation that cannot be satisfactorily resolved.

But what if a son returns to Eastern Europe after all? What happens to the family when geography and culture have split Old World and New? This is the chasm exposed in Isaac Bashevis Singer's story, "The Son from America." It is a tale that is packed with minimal but precise details and yet manages to convey a grander meaning, as Singer contrasts a *shtetl* whose inhabitants have only the bare necessities with the country overseas, where abundance and even excess are evident. Nothing newsworthy occurs in Lentshin, which is too tiny even to have a cemetery. Samuel has left Lentshin four decades earlier; and when he comes back, his parents, Berl and Pescha, barely recognize him. So mixed is his Yiddish with English that his parents can hardly understand him. So tall has Samuel grown that he must stoop to enter the door of the hut where his parents live—as though his size were a metaphor for a republic that has outstripped in power and prosperity the societies from which the immigrants had stemmed. He wants to contribute to the welfare of the *shtetl* as well as to help his aged parents, with funds brought from America. But in Lentshin desires are so limited and so moderate that all demands are met. The synagogue does not need enlargement (or a building fund); the population is stable. There is nothing that philanthropy can do to alter or improve the lives of Samuel's parents or of their neighbors.

The village seems almost timeless, frozen in history. Pescha learns of "a heretic by the name of Dr. Herzl" who wants Jews to move to Palestine; the crazy ideas that can emerge "in the big cities" amaze her.[4] (That is how the reader knows that the story is set about a century ago.) Otherwise virtually nothing in "The Son from America" reveals a particular decade. Samuel is self-assured. He is a businessman, reputedly a millionaire, who had begun life in America as a baker. (He tells the villagers that Jews in America live so comfortably that they eat *challah* even on weekdays.) How Samuel became rich is unexplained. But one advantage that he undoubtedly enjoys is that, in the dynamic economy of the New World, enterprise itself is not scorned. (In Henry James's *The American*, Christopher Newman loses the prospect of marriage in the Old World partly because he is "a commercial person.") I. B. Singer's American has flourished under conditions that encourage commercial acumen. Because of America, the son of Berl and Pescha is not marked as merely an extension or a continuation of his parents. Indeed he walks too fast for the tempo of Lentshin, so that Berl advises his son to "slow down."[5] He has gone so far beyond this *shtetl* that, when he touches his passport at the end of the Sabbath, the reader knows that departure will be forever. Samuel is never again to traverse the huge distance back.

The emotional claims of Eastern European Jewry are powerfully invoked in "To America," which the Yiddish poet H. Leyvik wrote a little more than half a century ago, when American Jewry was celebrating its Tricentennial. Born in Tsarist Byelorussia as Leyvik Halpern, H. Leyvik (1888–1962) had been imprisoned and subjected to forced labor for Bundist revolutionary activity, but in 1913 escaped from Siberia and reached New York, where he worked as a wallpaper hanger. "To America" is a haunting meditation on his failure, in the forty-one years since he found refuge "in the bounty of your freedom," to express gratitude for U. S. citizenship "with joy, with praise, with pure admiration." Partly because he felt guilt at leaving behind the world of his own father, partly because of his solidarity with the trapped and doomed Yiddish writers of mother Russia, partly because Leyvik had to "carry my Yiddish song/In fear, through your streets and through your squares,/Clenched in my teeth, as a forsaken cat might carry/Her kittens, in search of a cellar, a place of rest," he could not bring himself to confess the depth of his indebtedness. To articulate such appreciation would also require staring into the abyss into which his comrades and contemporaries had fallen. That realization would be too painful. But now, in "old age," the poet could ruefully express what he should have done in 1913; he "should have/Fallen prostrate to your earth and touched it with my lips." By 1954, however, he could find himself "embracing the glare of intimacy and farewell, America."[6]

For that first generation like Leyvik, a sort of proprietary relation was felt for an adopted land that was both alluring and alienating. Take "America and I," a short story (or perhaps better classified as a narrative essay) that Anzia Yezierska published in 1922—exactly between the appearance of a previous collection of short stories, *Hungry Hearts* (1920), and the John-son-Reed Act that in 1924 slammed the gates shut against the very immigrants whose lives she had nominated herself to reveal. Probably born in Pinsk, four decades earlier, Yezierska showed such literary promise that she seemed poised to make the transition from serious fiction to Hollywood scenarios. Her work in the movie industry nevertheless left her deeply dissatisfied, and the high literary reputation that she currently enjoys had to await the revival of feminism. Yezierska is best known for exposing and condemning the subordinate role of women in the Jewish family, which she attributed to the subordinate role of women within Judaism itself. But in "America and I," the narrator reaches beyond the dynamics of the family to the sting of alienation. "I was in America, among the Americans, but not of them," she writes, adding that "I only feel I'm different—different from everybody." From the opposite angle, the influential nativist Madison Grant (flaunting the surnames of two Presidents) had also addressed the challenge of assimilation. "The swarms of Polish Jews," he wrote in 1916, "adopt the language of the Native Americans; they wear his clothes; they steal his name; and they are beginning to marry his women, but they seldom adopt his religion or understand his ideals."[7]

Yezierska's narrator would have welcomed the chance to understand the ideals of the Anglo-Saxon. But she faced the impediment of exploitation, experienced as a terrible ordeal—whether working without wages as a live-in domestic, whether toiling in a sweatshop, whether sewing on buttons in a basement, or whether working in a factory. The anonymous narrator who struggles in an unnamed city realizes that her craving is not merely for a rewarding vocation, for a life without pain, but also for a collective embrace, for inclusion. "As a young girl hungry for love sees always before her eyes the picture of lover's arms around her, so I saw always in my heart the vision of Utopian America." But she realized that such a Utopia would be unattainable. The soul of the immigrant could not bridge the chasm with America as she had imagined it would be. She could not expect the actuality to resemble "the America of my dreams," the "chimera of lunatics and crazy immigrants."[8]

But rather than accept disenchantment, or allow her dreams to sour into repudiation, or consider a return to the Old World, the narrator identifies with the Pilgrims. They too had needed to cultivate fortitude and persistence, to prevail against the adversity of nature and the enmity of the indigenous population. Her "great revelation" was to see America as "a big idea—a deathless hope—a world still in the making. I saw that it was the glory of America that it was not yet finished. And I, the last comer, had her share to give, small or great, to the making of America, like those Pilgrims who came in the *Mayflower*." In inaugurating the process of immigration, the Pilgrims had also exemplified the power of religious differences that had compelled them to seek refuge across the Atlantic. (Yezierska's narrator nevertheless feels a less complete identification than was the invocation of the aesthete Bernard Berenson—who had been born in a Lithuanian *shtetl*—to "our Puritan forebears." That third-person possessive led the art historian Meyer Schapiro to quip that Berenson must have believed that his "ancestors were rabbis on the *Mayflower*.") Yezierska's narrator realizes that immigrants like herself ought to envision her adopted land as an unfinished country, just as the Puritans had, so that even newcomers had something to give, something to contribute. And if only the immigrants would be offered the chance to live beyond the "drudgery they hate," to enrich the spirit of the nation, then the gap "between the American-born and myself" could be bridged. Yezierska's short fiction is a piece of propaganda, a defense of the aspirations of the hyphenates. "America and I" is also a sign of anxiety that the welcome mat was being pulled, and a record of the process from steerage to sweatshops that was tarnishing the ideal that made America so compelling. Yezierska was among the first to understand that to write about her own people meant to write not just *to* her people, but to "the American-born" as well. "In only writing about the Ghetto, I found America."[9]

Only four years before the publication of "America and I," a patriotic revue was produced to promote the First World War, *Yip! Yip! Yaphank* (1918). Among the songs that its composer, Irving Berlin, intended for the show was "God Bless America." But then he realized that the song was "just a little sticky"; he "couldn't visualize soldiers marching to it." Fast-forward to two decades later, when the gathering storm of war was becoming too ominous to be ignored. He made a small number of changes in what he had composed, especially so that "God Bless America" would avoid so reductive a classification as "a war song." Indeed what is striking about what became the unofficial national anthem is that there is nothing martial about it. Berlin injected no strutting chauvinism, no nationalistic glory. He shows no rockets' red glare, and does not even sound "a bugle call/Like you so never heard before,/So natural/That you want to go to war."[10] A song that was composed amid the feverish patriotism of the First World War, a song that became a sensation just as war was about to erupt again in Europe, is remarkably free of jingoistic excess.

To be sure this most versatile of song-writers could achieve topicality and intricacy, as in "Puttin' on the Ritz" (1928), getting "dressed up like a million dollar trouper,/Trying hard to look like Gary Cooper,/Super duper." But the timeless quality of so much of Berlin's work stemmed from the realization that simple songs were the hardest to write, and he modestly noted that a limited formal education compelled him to produce lyrics that were spare in their vocabulary. The wisdom of that approach was revealed in "God Bless America." The Munich crisis had climaxed only two months earlier. With national peril a distinct threat, Irving Berlin had shown other song-writers how to inspire love of country. Yet none of his rivals could match Berlin's flair for tapping into the *Zeitgeist*, for expressing sentiments to stir the public that it had not quite realized it harbored. (During the Second World War, when the Office of War Information called for song-writers to provide the appropriate collective feelings set to music, the ditties that the sheet music publishers and recording studios were forced to sift through bore such unpromising titles as "You're a Sap, Mr. Jap," "Let's Put the Axe to the Axis," and "To Be Specific, It's Our Pacific.")[11]

But when Kate Smith introduced "God Bless America" on CBS radio on November 11, 1938, not even the composer had anticipated how popular his song would quickly become. Fortunately for him, the marketplace was the only standard Berlin had by which to assess what he had written. "The mob is always right," he claimed;[12] and it quickly appreciated that song, which was sung at both political parties' conventions in 1940.[13] Those who, like Berlin, knew Yiddish did not have to wait until Mandy Patinkin recorded a version of "God Bless America" in 1998. They could also enjoy a remarkably maudlin song—with words and music by Harry Schlecker—which came out in 1940: "Ich dank dir Gott far America." There "the Jew can live a free life/Because freedom, equality, democracy rule here. . ."[14] Note the contrast with "God Bless America," which refers to no political ideas or institutions whatsoever, as though the land were still unformed, as though everything but nature itself was unconceived, or at least unfinished—just as Yezierska's narrator had realized.

Another war would put patriotism on the defensive. The military intervention in Vietnam was so disastrous that virtually everything that Berlin had championed seemed to be going out of style. In 1973, only three years after Yezierska herself died, Berlin made his last public appearance, when he sang "God Bless America" at a White House dinner for returning prisoners of war. He realized that public taste had shifted: "It was time for me to close up shop." He was fated to live until 1989, having shaped an idea of America more inescapably than any other Jewish immigrant. Indeed no other seemed more fully to personify an ideal of America than Irving Berlin, who didn't see the point of "American composers [trying to]. . . write imitation European music which doesn't mean anything." Instead, he proclaimed in 1915: "I'm writing American music." His songs were supremely democratic, as George M. Cohan asserted—"music you don't have to dress up to listen to."[15]

Berlin lacked the training to write a symphony, not even the "American Symphony" that David Quixano, the violinist at the center of Israel Zangwill's play, *The Melting-Pot* (1908), had wanted to compose. But the aspirations and the gratitude of the son of a part-time cantor throbbed all the same. Berlin cherished a society in which, as Benjamin Franklin insisted in 1782, the hierarchical rigidities of the Old World had been largely—if not entirely—abandoned. When Americans meet a stranger, Franklin noted in a plea for Europeans to consider settling here, they don't ask who he is but rather: "What can he do?"[16] What was supposed to count is not ancestry but talent. Only a year after the dissemination of this pamphlet, the financier Haym Solomon (an immigrant who had, in effect, taken Franklin's advice) wrote to his relatives back in Poland: "Your *yichus* [pedigree] is worth very little here."[17]

The native-born children of Yezierska's Ghetto dwellers also had their say. None was more articulate than Alfred Kazin, who wrote of his parents: "We were the only conceivable end to all their striving; we were their America."[18] (Later this metaphor could be taken quite literally. In 1971 Abbie Hoffman and his wife Anita Kushner Hoffman named their baby son America, to accelerate the era when "nations will be named after people and people will be nations.")[19] Alfred Kazin's contemporary, Delmore Schwartz, noted that "to be the child of immigrants from East Europe is in itself a special kind of experience." The second generation was often in some sense bilingual—with English as "the one spoken with ease in the streets and at school, but spoken poorly at home." An author with such a background is therefore given "a heightened sensitivity to language, a sense of idiom."[20] Those who were born in the era of the Great War were seared by the Great Depression, while also—in entering the wider society—experiencing the pang of anti-Semitism, which peaked in the 1930's. Schwartz's protagonist (and alter ego) Shenandoah Fish has to confront such bigots, and tells them that his own "ancestors, in whom I take pride, but not personal pride, were scholars, poets, prophets and students of God when most of Europe worshipped sticks and stones; not that I hold that against any of you [,] for it is not your fault if your forebears were barbarians groveling and groping about for peat or something."[21]

The disappointments run deeper, however, since mobility can run downward as well as upward, as revealed in Schwartz's "America! America!" (1948). Shenandoah Fish's mother recounts the saga of their neighbors, the Baumanns, a family in which the drive to succeed in business is badly transmitted to the sons, who are shiftless. The second generation somehow fails to make it, because attractiveness of personality does not compensate for defect of character. The social skills that the Baumann children so easily acquired could not quell the dissipation of energy and ambition and ingenuity that had enabled their father to become a go-getter of an insurance agent. The failure is odder because "the wonders of America" were so central to the conversation of the Baumann household: "When the first plane flew, when elevators became common, when the new subway was built," whichever Baumann was reading a newspaper would exclaim: "You see: America!" And when Oscar Straus is picked to become the first Jew to serve in a President's Cabinet, the reaction in the Baumann household was: "America! America!" So dynamic, so incredible a society could only mean that the pleasures of wealth would be theirs—or if not, that the sons might at least become rabbis or philosophers. But expectations are crushed; and the scarred members of this once hopeful family could blame only themselves, and turn upon each other with such resentment and rage that one

son, Sidney, tries to kill himself—though he fails at that gesture too. The
tailspin of the Baumanns is not exactly toward impoverishment. But they
do suffer disillusionment. "You see," Mrs. Baumann tells Shenandoah's
mother, "This is what we came to America for forty-five years ago, for
this,"[22] that is, for the ashes of defeat.

Schwartz's own life as a writer and critic became a downward trajectory
of promise unfulfilled and talent squandered. For example, he left behind
an unfinished novel, *An American Dream.*[23] (In 1965, Norman Mailer
bestowed that title on a novel he published one year before Schwartz
died.) But Schwartz's own feeling for America had become more upbeat.
In the postwar era, he joined in the general reconciliation of intellectuals
to the American Way of Life, and helped to narrow the critical distance
from mainstream society that he had taken with others who started out in
the 1930's at *Partisan Review.* How far Schwartz was willing to go toward
the embrace of America was revealed in 1958, when he argued that civilized
life was hanging in the balance. The United States had displaced Europe as
"the sanctuary of culture," he proclaimed. "Civilization's very existence depends upon America, upon the actuality of American life, and not the ideals
of the American Dream. To criticize the actuality upon which all hope depends thus becomes a criticism of hope itself."[24] Unfortunately Schwartz's
formulation could be read as a plea to abrogate critical thought, as though
to invoke the right to dissent (or to yield to pessimism) might embolden
the totalitarianism against which hope was presumably pitted.

Certainly others demurred. Two years before Schwartz's address, another
poet published what he labeled "a sort of surrealist anarchist tract" and "a
longish absurd poem on America"—and that subject served also as its title.[25]
Of the literary legacy of Allen Ginsberg, perhaps only three of his poems are
destined to endure; and each deploys only one word in the title. "Howl"
(1955–56) made him notorious. U. S. Customs officials seized *Howl and
Other Poems,* as did the San Francisco police; his father, himself a poet,
also objected to such "vehement, vaporous, vituperations of rebellion. . .
Your attitude is irresponsible. . . It stinks!"[26] Though *Partisan Review*'s John
Hollander extolled the "real talent" and "marvelous ear" that characterized
"Howl," he declared that it was "only fair. . . to remark on the utter lack
of decorum in this dreadful little volume." Decorum was of course the test
that Ginsberg intended to flunk—and even as "Howl" would later be taught
in classrooms, President Reagan's Federal Communications Commission
banned the recitation of Ginsberg's poetry on the radio during daylight
hours.[27] That FCC decision is about right, since the sunny cheerfulness that
the American Way of Life was supposed to project—the hopefulness that
Delmore Schwartz entwined with Americanism—is what Allen Ginsberg
devoted himself to defying.

Mourning—not morning—in America is the theme of "Kaddish" (1959), which made Ginsberg endearing. Three years earlier, the Aramaic prayer for the dead could not be read at the funeral of his mother, because fewer than ten men showed up.[28] Not that the late Naomi Levy Ginsberg had been pious. She had been a Communist, married to a contributor of poetry to *The Masses*; and their older son Eugene was named, as were the call letters of the *Forward*'s Yiddish-language radio station WEVD, after the socialist tribune Eugene V. Debs. Naomi Ginsberg died in the year of the appearance of "America," a poem that is charged with the fiercely leftist politics of Allen Ginsberg's family background. The structure of the poem is indecipherable. But the accusations that he makes are clear: the Cold War showdown is so awful that a nuclear-armed nation should commit a sexual act with itself. The poem also sentimentalizes doomed radicals to the point of perpetrating fuzzy math, asking America when it "will. . . be worthy of your million Trotskyites?" Ginsberg mocks the clichés of Fifties patriotism, while conceding that his own contribution to civic life resembles a *shlemiel's*: "I don't want to join the Army or turn lathes in precision parts factories; I'm nearsighted and psychopathic anyway." But the poet who would soon be photographed wearing an Uncle Sam costume to sell an underground poster wants to retain his membership in society ("It occurs to me that I am America") and proposes instead an enlargement of the definition of responsibility: "America I'm putting my queer shoulder to the wheel."[29]

In complaining that "America I've given you all and now I'm nothing," Ginsberg blended the personal—taking the form of the confessional—with the political. He mixed rage with tenderness, combined anger with humor. "Yiddishe Kopf" (1991) seems to parody the excesses of ethnic affirmation ("I'm Jewish because love my family *matzoh* ball soup"). But Jewish identity is also affiliated with bookishness ("Jewish because reading Dostoevsky at 13 I write poem at restaurant tables Lower East Side, perfect delicatessen intellectual") and with a revulsion to organized religion ("antique Nobodaddy Adonai's mind trap—Oy! Such Meshuggeneh absolutes—!"). How fitting for the poet who found it "intolerable [to be] intolerant"[30] to have been the first Jew to whom Ezra Pound acknowledged the error of his wartime broadcasts from Fascist Italy. "The worst mistake I made was the stupid suburban prejudice of anti-Semitism," Pound told Ginsberg. "All along, that spoiled everything." It took Pound seventy years to "realize. . . that instead of being a lunatic, I was a moron."[31] Ginsberg himself was neither. Though intimate with madmen, he stayed quite sane; and the criticisms that he mounted against stultifying political constraints were free-verse analogues of the conventional views of other public intellectuals. Their criticism of the nation's policies and institutions hardly constituted the defeat of hope (as Schwartz had feared), though the "bop kaballa" that

Ginsberg pumped into the bloodstream of American verse departed dramatically from the optimism of Walt Whitman.

A year after the composition of Ginsberg's "America," a troupe of Broadway dancers put over a song by that title as well. Pretending to be recent migrants from the commonwealth of Puerto Rico, the performers describe an experience that is double-sided; and their quatrains drip with irony: "I like to be in America!/O. K. by me in America!/Everything free in America/For a small fee in America!" The newcomers' belief in material benefits is gently kidded: "I like the shores of America!/Comfort is yours in America!/Knobs on the doors in America,/Wall-to-wall floors in America!" *West Side Story* was, according to one scholar of the genre, "the first Broadway musical to seriously question the universality of the American Dream."[32] This work constituted a plea for tolerance and understanding, an expression of sympathy for new arrivals to New York City, and measured the pointlessness of violence.

Such passions have animated many Jews—and not just the composer Leonard Bernstein, the lyricist Stephen Sondheim, the director and choreographer Jerome Robbins and the librettist Arthur Laurents. Criticism of the bigotry that has scarred the nation's history was integral to the liberalism of the postwar era; and in "America" (one of the two satirical songs in *West Side Story*), Sondheim and Bernstein allow pride to duke it out with disillusionment. Opening on Broadway in the very month that white mobs attacked black children trying to desegregate Central High School in Little Rock, the musical announces that "everything [could be] right in America"—but only "if you're a white in America." To get an apartment with affordable rent meant obeying the injunction to "get rid of your accent." Though *West Side Story* opened in the midst of the celebratory 1950's, there was little politically daring about such a counterpoint; the criticism voiced in Sondheim's "America" was of course far milder than Ginsberg's outrage in his own "America."

But by confronting the serious social problem of juvenile crime, the creators of *West Side Story* testified to the resilience of the genre, which could renew and reinvent itself. Musicals were supposed to produce scores that could float into the atmosphere after the final curtain; but Bernstein's jazzy, nervous rhythms made his score difficult to hum. Without the 1961 film adaptation, Sondheim believed, the music would not have been given a chance to linger, and then to be appreciated. (The Broadway version picked up only two Tony Awards—for Best Choreography and for Best Scenic Design.) Instead of seeing leggy chorines when the curtain went up, audiences were probably a bit startled to see six finger-snapping guys looking like juvenile delinquents, staring at them.[33] *West Side Story* was not a musical *comedy*, but an experimental work in which the curtain that falls after each act coincides with a death. When Sondheim showed his father, a dress manufacturer, the libretto, there was hope that he might be willing to invest in it. Herbert Sondheim was disappointed: "Not many laughs, are there?"[34] What was acceptable in avant-garde poetry in San Francisco found little receptivity, at first, when domesticated for Broadway, where audiences found *West Side Story* too peculiar and pioneering—too searing a portrayal of ethnic maladjustment—to make the show into a big hit.

"America" is also the title of a song that Simon & Garfunkel recorded in 1968. In expressing angst and loneliness, the narrator seems dwarfed by the mysterious vastness that the road opens up: "'Kathy, I'm lost,' I said . . . 'I'm empty and aching and I don't know why.'" In suggesting that the scale of a nation (when it takes four days just to hitchhike from Saginaw to Pittsburgh) dooms the prospect of human intimacy, the song projects the estrangement that so many artists have felt on native grounds. From Richard Avedon's cover portrait for *Bookends* to the printing of the lyrics as though to elevate them into poetry, the album that included "America" brandished a seriousness that spurned the 2 1/2 minutes of radio air-play marking the conventional duration of popular song. Themselves the denizens of an outer borough as well as the beneficiaries of higher education, Paul Simon and Art Garfunkel neither anglicized their names (as had some contemporaries) nor sought to pitch their music to adolescents (however hip). Their "America" does not hint at the passions of the decade—so closely associated with the struggle for racial justice and with the war raging in Vietnam—but does convey a sense of disquietude amid the whimsy.

More than a stimulus to the imagination of those residing here, America has also been the object of fantasy for those who never reached its shores. Consider *Amerika*. It is a first novel that its author never managed to complete, and that he wanted to have burned rather than convert the manuscript into a book. Even the title was provided by a friend, Max Brod, who ignored Franz Kafka's wishes and arranged for the novel to appear posthumously in 1927. The title that Kafka had apparently preferred was *Der Verschollene*: the one who vanished. It nearly did. The original text has in fact disappeared. Its first part, "The Stoker" (*Der Heizer*), was written in 1912; and Kafka was satisfied enough with it to publish it the following year. Rather surprisingly, Rainer Maria Rilke liked "The Stoker" more than either "The Metamorphosis" or "The Penal Colony," which were among the tiny handful of stories that Kafka permitted Brod not to burn. Brod managed to extend *Amerika* to eight chapters.[35]

Susan Sontag once described the United States as "the quintessential Surrealist country"; and there is something surreal about the *Amerika* of Franz Kafka, who had three cousins living in the U. S. but who rarely ever left Prague. The Statue of Liberty that the protagonist, Karl Rossman, sees upon arrival holds up a sword, not a torch. Oklahoma is spelled as "Oklahama."[36] San Francisco is located on the East Coast; and the Brooklyn

Bridge, by spanning the Hudson River, manages to connect Manhattan to Boston. The cartography is cockamamie because Kakfa's America is inspired by fantasy, not certified by Rand-McNally. But what registers with special force is the atmosphere of this fiction: it is not Kafkaesque. Though the fateful "K" shows up at the start of the protagonist's name, his fate is less sinister than what befalls Josef K. or K. Their creator would become famous for his incapacity to enjoy feelings of emancipation or of freedom, writing what became *Amerika* while telling Felice Bauer, who became his fiancée: "I am beyond help." Were their relationship to continue, he feared, "I should deserve to be cursed, were not I not cursed already." But Karl Rossman is given a chance at the redemption that Kafka believed his own circumstances foreclosed. According to him, Karl is "innocent," while Josef K. is "guilty" (though of what remains notoriously elusive).[37] In *Amerika* no trials are conducted in which the crime is unspecified; no tattoos are burned into the arms of the inmates of the distant penal colony; no remote and mysterious authority exists to which any appeal can be directed; no leopards drinking blood must somehow be assuaged and then absorbed into the ceremony.

The prisoner in the penal colony is executed for having fallen asleep at 2 a. m., so that he has failed to salute the captain's door (as was required every hour); the officer's motto is that "guilt is never to be doubted." To Karl Rossman, by contrast, nothing worse happens in America than getting kicked out of jobs. Though a "missing person," he is not a condemned one. *Der Verschollene* could be rendered not only as "The Man Who Vanished" but also as "The Forgotten One," disappearing into the void, as though the New World peels away the core of identity. Karl achieves a certain forgetfulness. His past recedes, and indeed in the course of the novel he even manages to become younger. *Amerika* does not track a protagonist learning from experience, but instead depicts a repudiation of maturation. Karl's identity seems to become discontinuous, as though he were the kid brother of Mary Antin, whose autobiography—published in the very year that Kafka was writing *Amerika*—reveals a yearning for amnesia. "The Wandering Jew in me seeks forgetfulness," she wrote. Rather than remember the days of yore, Antin sought to seize the day, to escape the tug of generations: "The past was only my cradle, and now it cannot hold me, because I am grown too big." Karl is a drifter, an outsider who cannot locate himself within any fixed social coordinates.[38] But though he has lost his way, the bureaucratic system—with its intricate and malevolent labyrinths—would not lose *him*. *Mitteleuropa* traps the typical Kafka protagonist in institutions and in sites that make banality menacing. But the atmosphere in *Amerika* is carnivalesque, not claustrophobic. Unlike Josef K., who is stabbed at the end, Karl is sent off into the void, to vanish. He is on the road. Kafka's *Amerika* is Prague unplugged.

In 1914, while still working on *The Trial*, he wrote what Brod turned into the final chapter of *Amerika*, after which the narrative breaks off. After the chapter that Brod entitled "The Nature Theatre of Oklahoma," Kafka's oeuvre becomes fully Kafkaesque, punctuated by the suffocating sense of enclosure, the inescapable ordeal of injustice, the terror of insecurity. But in the giant Theatre of Oklahoma, Karl is to be engaged in the process of promoting a vast, come-one-come-all venue where bamboozlement and hoopla are sovereign. But before he can be employed, he has to admit that he has no papers. Karl does not know—perhaps its author did not know—that in the U. S. the authorities do not need such papers, and he is hired as an actor anyway.[39] No experience necessary. In contrast to the shadowy and sinuous byways of Prague, the Nature Theatre of Oklahoma is set in the open spaces to which Huckleberry Finn vows to flee in seeking respite from civilization.

(*Terra incognita* to Kafka, Oklahoma was not much more familiar three decades later, when two New Yorkers, Richard Rodgers and Oscar Hammerstein II, decided to write a musical about the achievement of statehood. Rodgers had peeked at a volume of Southwestern songs, but then "closed the book and never looked at it again. If my melodies were going to be authentic," he concluded, "they'd have to be authentic in my own terms." Such was the eclectic hospitality of the Oklahoma legislature, however, that, when it picked an official state song, the work of Woody Guthrie was ignored—even though the great troubadour was born in Okemah, in favor of the rousing finale to Rodgers and Hammerstein's 1943 musical.)[40]

Six decades after Kafka died, the expatriate painter R. J. Kitaj adopted Kafka's spelling for the name of a large canvas. *Amerika* was used, Kitaj announced, in order "to register my American self from afar and in exilic fantasy, to which (fantasy) I feel drawn. Kafka never went to America and *my* Amerika will allow me all the craziness I may need, upon his inspiration." The formal design of this painting is adapted from a landscape that hangs in the National Gallery in London, Velázquez's *Philip IV Hunting Wild Boar*. But Kitaj's subject is the same as George W. Bush's answer to a question about his favorite "cultural experience." The President replied: baseball. Born in Cleveland in 1932, Kitaj began his art studies at the Ruskin School in Oxford in 1958 and remained in England until 1997, when he returned to live in the United States. "For most of my life[,] I've lived thousands of miles away from real baseball," he complained; and he has shown special sympathy for "my poor lost tribe of Cleveland Indians," who last won a pennant in 1954.[41]

Amerika (Baseball) (1983–84) is the fulfillment of Kitaj's enduring desire to paint a large baseball scene that would blend fantasy and verisimilitude. The players are caught in assorted poses on a blue field that could be a lake but is certainly not a diamond. He portrays only a couple of spectators, who inhabit the foreground. It is a field of dreams on which no bases are placed, as though the players were preparing to play on a diamond that is not shown. This painting reflects a search for lost time. Kitaj recalled that "Kafka's crazed, beautiful, unfinished book inspired me, years ago, to look at my exilic self in changeful ways. I would attempt to paint that selfhood, to reconstruct its homeland." Kitaj "decided to paraphrase both Velázquez and Kafka, and so the great fieldscape of the Boar Hunt . . . combined with the Cuckoo Nature-Theatre of Ohio and [the Cooperstown of] upstate New York; the Velázquez setting reminded me of the low hills of home which often framed the playing fields where we toiled at pick-up ball long after dusk . . . The little figures on that broad plain stand for the hundred ways that baseball lives mirror our own, teach me lessons—even *art* ones."[42] In the era of Velázquez, proselytization in behalf of Judaism was both difficult and dangerous. But in the United States, conversion is simply an option. In the last few decades in particular, so many Jews by choice have joined the community that one rabbi calculated that our imports are better than our exports. Two decades ago a major league ballplayer named Bob Tufts converted to Judaism. At the ceremony the rabbi asked him if he wished to signify the sincerity of his new identity by adopting a Jewish name. The ballplayer blurted out: "Sandy Koufax."[43] *Koufax* is the subject and the title of a portrait that Kitaj painted only a year after returning to his homeland.

"I have had a lifelong affair with the idea of America," Ezra B. Slavin pompously asserts in Johanna Kaplan's *O My America!* (1980),[44] a satirical novel that won the National Jewish Book Award for Fiction. Slavin (1908–1972) is a professor of American Studies at a New England college. Smug in his "iconoclasm," he is a familiar specimen of the leftish Jewish New York intellectual (labels that are so frequently stitched together that they could be pronounced as though one word). Kaplan's novel targets the 1960's in an especially acerbic way. But so much about the Jewish experience of the past century is encapsulated in *O My America!* that it ambitiously exposes the lapses and confusions of several generations of Jewish believers in the idea of America.

The title of the novel is plucked from the Nineteenth Elegy of John Donne, who refers to the "new-found-land" of his mistress's body; no actual country is described. Ezra Slavin, a "free-thinker" with a big progressive heart and a clammy love of The People, is not a very keen observer of the actual republic he professes to love. He prefers the comforts of sentiment. Indeed a 1939 essay, which the novel "reprints" in its entirety, evokes "our" America, and promiscuously hails "the real life of a farm community in the prairies, a mining town in the West, and a fishing village on the New England coast." Such places may constitute "a *community*."[45] This rhapsody resembles Alfred Kazin's account of how dissident, often expatriate writers reconciled themselves to the nationalist spirit of the 1930's, largely because ordinary folk showed true grit in battling the Great Depression. "America! America!", the final chapter of Kazin's *On Native Grounds* (1942), tracks how the vision of a plucky, democratic nation, which once paled by comparison to the less philistine culture of the Left Bank, was recovered. The American left had come to appreciate how gallantly The People had faced the crisis of capitalism, and encomia were therefore offered to the simple rustics and villagers of the heartland.

Slavin's crush on America was hardly unique. A year after his "essay" appeared (and two years after Berlin's "God Bless America" was first publicly sung), the greatest radical of the previous half century died in exile; and her wish to be buried in the U. S., alongside the Haymarket martyrs of Chicago, was honored. Emma Goldman had championed a patriotism that "loves America with open eyes." She compared it to "the relation of a man who loves a woman, who is enchanted by her beauty and yet who cannot be blind to her defects." Speaking also for her fellow radicals, the anarchist orator announced that "we love America, we love her riches, we love her mountains and her forests and above all we love the people who have produced her wealth and riches, who have created all her beauty, we love the dreamers and the philosophers and the thinkers who are giving America liberty. But that must not make us blind to the social faults of America."[46] (This speech nevertheless proved unpersuasive when delivered in 1917, in open court. For violating the conscription act, Goldman was sentenced to two years in prison sentence and a $10,000 fine.)

O My America! is less about the progressive infatuation with the New World, however, than about the vicissitudes of the family. When George W. Bush campaigned in Wisconsin in 2000, he declared: "Families is where our nation finds hope, where wings take dream." Perhaps. There is also an underside, which Kaplan traces; the indifference and thoughtlessness and self-indulgence of Ezra Slavin leave his own family in tatters. Neither as a son nor as a husband nor as father does he cultivate the virtues of responsibility or commitment or caring. His first wife is the Polish-born Pearl Milgram, the mother of his first two children. But she drives him away—in part because of what he scorns as "bourgeois domesticity," and in part because of antagonistic values. She had once hoped to live on a kibbutz; such a faith in Zionism Slavin disdains as a "senseless, pathetic obsession with Jews."[47] His second wife is a preacher's daughter from a small town in Wisconsin; his third is a simple, downtrodden Kentuckian three decades his junior. From a mistress between wives #2 and #3, Slavin also fathers two daughters. Kaplan's story is largely energized through the resentment of Merry Slavin, a daughter from his first marriage. She is quite aware of his own incorrigible flight from the accountability of adulthood (which the Yiddish term *mishegoss* might encapsulate).

Her own animus is certainly not remotely as intense—and definitely not as murderous—as the radical Merry in another novel about the 1960's with

"America" inserted into the title, *American Pastoral* (1997). Philip Roth's version adopts the perspective of the baffled father, Seymour "Swede" Levov, who cannot fathom what has become of Merry, a bomb-throwing fanatic. By contrast *O My America!* tells Ezra's story from the angle of Merry Slavin, whose father's fatal heart attack opens the novel. At the memorial service, his son Jonathan unexpectedly announces that he is "going to read the Kaddish," which leads one Upper West Side mourner to whisper to another: "Oh! Allen Ginsberg! What a wonderful *idea*!. . . . I saw him on the street the other day, and I really didn't think he looked at all well."[48] It is instead the traditional prayer, which generates some vexation in that secularist set of attendees. An ancient prayer and faith are further embattled in a society that can produce someone like "Ffrenchy" (Slavin's daughter Francesca Meisel). Born in 1950, she exemplifies the amnesia that diminishes and cramps American culture. When Slavin tries to instruct her about the travails of his own mother in Tsarist Russia, Ffrenchy responds: "Was that because of like Auschwitz?" An exasperated father has to explain that his mother had been born in the 1880's, whereas "*Anne Frank* was because of like Auschwitz. *Like Auschwitz* occurred in the nineteen forties."[49] *O My America!* belongs on the shelf of neo-conservative fiction, and exposes how the acids of assimilation have eroded the moral seriousness to which Judaism lays claim.

A similar criticism of the shallowness of national values is incorporated into Susan Sontag's novel, *In America*, which won the National Book Award in 2000. Her subject is Polish visitors who come ashore during the Centennial celebration of 1876, and who observe the citizens' exuberance as well as its cultural cost, in a nation that "is meant to mean everything." Bogdan, an enterprising vintner who is married to an actress named Maryna, praises the optimism that is so evident, even as the absence of a tragic sensibility puzzles him. One of Bogdan's diary entries notes that "I am bred to a distinctively Polish appreciation of the nobility of failure." That phenomenon is missing here; neither historical interest nor historical wisdom can be discerned. He finds it a "humbling experience to be without a past. Nobody knows, or would care if they did know, who my grandfather was." Replacing such filiopietism is the authority of individualism: "What is paramount in America is the personal calendar, the personal journey. . . *my* life, *my* happiness." Poles are pessimists. They know that the past—with all of its broken promises and crushing defeats—will recur. Americans are optimists, who believe that history can be defied: "Here the present does not reaffirm the past but supersedes and cancels it." Americans therefore strike Bogdan as superficial. But their obliviousness to the inexorable force of history "gives them great strength and self-confidence. They do not feel dwarfed by *anything*." Sontag gives a drunken, garrulous Edwin Booth, cursed by memories of a wife who had gone mad and a brother who had murdered a

President, the last word, however. He proudly tells Maryna of eliminating the twisted finale to the version of *King Lear* to which American audiences had become addicted, in which Cordelia and her father are permitted to survive. Booth knows what the groundlings seem so devoted to denying: happy endings do not exist.[50]

The images of America that this essay has considered range from the affectionate to the furious, from the appreciative to the disenchanted. All reflect a self-conscious effort to define a connection to the larger society. At first, perhaps, an authentic sense of citizenship could not be taken for granted. But just as the naturalization papers were filled out with remarkable speed, the desire for social inclusion quickly surfaced. Already in Abraham Cahan's 1896 novella, *Yekl*, Jake announces: "I am an American feller, a Yankee—that's what I am." In his adopted land, he adds, "a Jew is as good as a Gentile." And when Cahan's David Levinsky is asked: "Are you a Russian?", the response of this successful commercial person testifies to the faith in self-invention: "I used to be. I am an American now." By the half-century mark, the process was completed, as Augie March introduces himself: "I am an American, Chicago-born."[51]

The exact meaning of such a statement could not be stabilized, in a nation in which Jay Gatsby "sprang from a Platonic conception of himself."[52] The varieties of self-fabrication could neither be foreseen nor limited. Among many examples, here is one: Ralph Lauren, a product of the Bronx—and of Yeshiva Rabbi Israel Salanter—somehow projects himself as a Westerner. When Lauren once asked to be cast in a film, a movie director inquired: "Who do you see yourself as?" Lauren replied: Gary Cooper. The director did not agree: "Ralph, you're a short little Jew." Nonplussed, the designer replied: "Not when I'm dressed."[53] Just as cards of identity could seem to be easily shuffled, the premise that Jewish ancestry and American citizenship were seamless has marked this minority's experience in the United States. That particular battle the nativists rather decisively lost.

Zionism has of course has advanced a different sort of claim upon American Jewry. Perhaps that is what a public intellectual, Leon Wieseltier, had in mind when he asserted in 1980: "No country on earth has been better to the Jews than the United States; but it is not our country."[54] Presumably Israel is. But he neglected to mention whose country America is, and that omission suggests what problematizes such an assertion. Is America therefore a country that belongs only to Christians? Or only to Protestants? Even if those Christians are Roman Catholics from Haiti? Even if those Protestants are, say, Methodists who have immigrated from Korea? Or Arabs whose ancestors came from Lebanon? The notion that Jews cannot speak in the first person possessive about America would have surprised those military veterans who had not realized that they had risked their lives for someone's country other than their own.

American history can be told as an impetus toward greater diversity and greater inclusion—to such an extent that descendants of the founding colonists doubted whether America belonged to them. No American historian was more accomplished, or more subtle, than Henry Adams. Yet so estranged did he feel on native grounds, so unwilling was he to absorb the shock of recognizing millions of newcomers—especially the Jews among them, that his friend, Secretary of State John Hay, considered Adams's bigotry "clean daft. The Jews are all the press, all the cabinets, all the gods and all weather. I was amazed to see so sensible a man so wild." Compared to the half-million New Yorkers whom Adams complained were "eating kosher, and saved from the drowning they deserve,"[55] the grandson and great-grandson of Presidents felt like a loser. Even John Adams himself was so dispirited by the democratizing tendencies of the polity, which he blamed for foolishly defying the inevitability of human inequality that he lamented in 1812: "From the year 1761, now more than Fifty years, I have constantly lived in an enemies Country."[56] The shifting, fluid character of national identity can be put more positively, however. It means that Yezierska's narrator was right after all: the republican experiment is far from exhausted, and its wonders and surprises remain to be contemplated and recorded.

NOTES

1. Michael E. Parrish, *Felix Frankfurter and His Times: The Reform Years* (New York, 1982), p. 24; "Migration," in *Encyclopedia Britannica* (Cambridge, 1911), 11th ed., vol. 18, p. 431.

2. Quoted in Victor Greene, *A Singing Ambivalence: American Immigrants Between Old World and New* (Kent, OH, 2004), p. 65.

3. Greene, *Singing Ambivalence*, p. 68.

4. Isaac Bashevis Singer, *A Crown of Feathers and Other Stories* (New York, 1973), p. 103.

5. Henry James, *The American*, ed. James W. Tuttleton (New York, 1978), p. 318; Singer, "The Son from America," p. 107.

6. H. Leyvik, "To America" (1954), in *American Yiddish Poetry: A Bilingual Anthology*, eds. and tr. Benjamin and Barbara Harshav (Berkeley, 1986), pp. 763–69.

7. Anzia Yezierska, "America and I" (1922), in *America and I: Short Stories by American Jewish Women Writers*, ed. Joyce Antler (Boston, 1990), pp. 73, 78; and Madison Grant, *The Passing of the Great Race* (New York, 1916), p. 81.

8. Yezierska, "America and I," p. 81.

9. Quoted in Meryle Secrest, *Being Bernard Berenson: A Biography* (New York, 1979), p. 395; Yezierska, "America and I," p. 82; Carol B. Schoen, *Anzia Yezierska* (Boston, 1982), pp. 55–56; and Sam B. Girgus, *The New Covenant: Jewish Writers and the American Idea* (Chapel Hill, 1984), pp. 108–11.

10. Quoted in Lawrence Bergreen, *As Thousands Cheer: The Life of Irving Berlin* (New York, 1990), pp. 156, 371; and Irving Berlin, "Alexander's Ragtime Band"

(1911), in *Reading Lyrics*, eds. Robert Gottlieb and Robert Kimball (New York, 2000), p. 72.

11. Irving Berlin, "Puttin' on the Ritz" (1928), in *Reading Lyrics*, eds. Gottlieb and Kimball, p. 84; Kathleen E. R. Smith, *God Bless America: Tin Pan Alley Goes to War* (Lexington, KY., 2003), p. 12.

12. Quoted in Bergreen, *As Thousands Cheer*, p. 372.

13. Bergreen, *As Thousands Cheer*, pp. 380–81.

14. Quoted by Jenna Weissman Joselit, "Waving Old Glory is August Tradition at U. S. Synagogues," *Forward* (October 9, 2001), p. 25.

15. Quoted in John Lahr, "Revolutionary Rag," *New Yorker*, p. 75 (March 8, 1999), pp. 77, 83.

16. Benjamin Franklin, "Information to Those Who Would Remove to America" (1782), in *The Political Thought of Benjamin Franklin*, ed. Ralph Ketchum (Indianapolis, 1965), p. 338.

17. Quoted in Marshall Sklare, *America's Jews* (New York, 1971), p. 18.

18. Alfred Kazin, *A Walker in the City* (New York, 1958), p. 56.

19. Quoted in Jonah Raskin, *For the Hell of It: The Life and Times of Abbie Hoffman* (Berkeley, 1996), p. 224.

20. Quoted in James Atlas, *Delmore Schwartz: The Life of an American Poet* (New York, 1977), p. 273.

21. Delmore Schwartz, "A Bitter Farce" (1946), in *The World is a Wedding* (Norfolk,CT, 1948), p. 103.

22. Delmore Schwartz, "America! America!", in *World is a Wedding*, pp. 118, 128.

23. Atlas, *Delmore Schwartz*, p. 347.

24. Delmore Schwartz, "The Present State of Poetry" (1958), in *Selected Essays of Delmore Schwartz*, eds. Donald A. Dike and David H. Zucker (Chicago, 1970), p. 46.

25. Allen Ginsberg to Louis Ginsberg, ca. late March 1956 and April 26, 1956, in Allen and Louis Ginsberg, *Family Business: Selected Letters between a Father and Son*, ed. Michael Schumacher (New York, 2001), pp. 37, 40.

26. Louis Ginsberg to Allen Ginsberg, December 12, 1955, in *Family Business*, p. 32.

27. John Hollander, "Poetry Chronicle," *Partisan Review*, 24 (Spring 1957), pp. 296–97, 298; Mike Zwerin, "The Wave of Poetry Slams: A Rap with Allen Ginsberg," *International Herald Tribune*, November 17, 1993, p. 22.

28. Barry Miles, *Ginsberg: A Biography* (New York, 1989), pp. 10–11, 206–7.

29. Allen Ginsberg, "America" (1956), in *Selected Poems, 1947–1995* (New York, 1996), pp. 62–64.

30. Ginsberg, "America," 62, and "Yiddishe Kopf" (1991), in *Selected Poems*, p. 378.

31. Quoted in Miles, *Ginsberg*, pp. 402, 403.

32. Stephen Sondheim, "America" (1957), in *Reading Lyrics*, p. 587; and John Bush Jones, *Our Musicals, Ourselves: A Social History of the American Musical Theatre* (Hanover, NH, 2003), p. 193.

33. Meryle Secrest, *Stephen Sondheim: A Life* (New York, 1998), pp. 126–27.

34. Secrest, *Stephen Sondheim*, p. 119.

35. Frederick R. Karl, *Franz Kafka: Representative Man* (New York, 1991), pp. 247, 307, 320n, 413, 718.

36. Susan Sontag, *On Photography* (New York, 1979), p. 48; and Karl, *Franz Kafka*, pp. 431, 445n.

37. Quoted in Karl, *Franz Kafka*, pp.320–21, 536.

38. Franz Kafka, *The Penal Colony: Stories and Short Pieces*, tr. Willa and Edwin Muir (New York, 1948), p. 198; Mary Antin, *The Promised Land* (Boston, 1969), pp. xxii, 364; Joyce Antler, *The Journey Home: Jewish Women and the American Century* (New York, 1997), pp. 22–23; Karl, *Franz Kafka*, pp. 106, 443.

39. Karl, *Franz Kafka*, pp. 461, 487, 498.

40. Richard Rodgers, *Musical Stages: An Autobiography* (New York, 1975), pp. 219–20, 229.

41. Quoted in Maureen Dowd, *Bushworld: Enter at Your Own Risk* (New York, 2004), p. 492, and Marco Livingstone, *Kitaj* (London, 1999), p. 39; and Ori Z. Soltes, *Fixing the World: Jewish American Painters in the Twentieth Century* (Hanover NH., 2003), p. 82.

42. Quoted in Livingstone, *Kitaj*, p. 195.

43. Nathan Cobb, "Tribute is in the Cards for Jewish Ballplayers," Boston *Globe*, October 13, 2003, p. D5.

44. Johanna Kaplan, *O My America!* (New York, 1980), p. 11.

45. Kaplan, *O My America!*, pp. 69, 70.

46. Quoted in Richard Drinnon, *Rebel in Paradise: A Biography of Emma Goldman* (Boston, 1961), pp. 193–94.

47. *George W. Bushisms*, ed. Jacob Weisberg (New York, 2001), p. 30; and Kaplan, *O My America!*, p. 91.

48. Kaplan, *O My America!*, pp. 281–82.

49. Kaplan, *O My America!*, pp. 186–87.

50. Susan Sontag, *In America* (New York, 2000), pp. 91, 211, 213, 223, 384; and Joan Acocella, "The Hunger Artist," *New Yorker*, 76 (March 6, 2000), p. 77.

51. Abraham Cahan, *Yekl and The Imported Bridegroom and Other Stories of the New York Ghetto* (New York, 1970), pp. 5, 70, and *The Rise of David Levinsky* (New York, 2001), p. 328; and Saul Bellow, *The Adventures of Augie March* (New York, 1995), p. 5.

52. F. Scott Fitzgerald, *The Great Gatsby* (New York, 1925), p. 99.

53. Quoted in Michael Gross, *Genuine Authentic: The Real Life of Ralph Lauren* (New York, 2003), pp. 350–51.

54. In "Liberalism and the Jews," *Commentary*, vol. 69 (January 1980), p. 80.

55. Quoted in John Higham, *Send These to Me: Jews and Other Immigrants in Urban America* (New York, 1975), p. 183; and Alfred Kazin, "The Jew as Modern American Writer," in *The Commentary Reader*, ed. Norman Podhoretz (New York, 1967), p. xvi.

56. Quoted in Gordon S. Wood, *Creation of the American Republic, 1776–1787* (Chapel Hill, 1969), p. 592.

18

Yiddishkeit and the American Jewish Writer: The Breakthrough Reconsidered

Eugene Goodheart

1953 was a signal year in the history of American literature. With the publication of Saul Bellow's third novel *The Adventures of Augie March*, American Jewish writing took center stage. His first two novels, *Dangling Man* and *The Victim* had been critical successes. *Augie March* was at once a critical success and a bestseller, winning the National Book Award. "I am an American, Chicago born," the hero declares in the opening sentence of the novel. No mention of the fact that he is Jewish, though there is no doubting it as the novel unfolds. The focus on his Americanness and his birth in Chicago dispels any expectation that this may be another novel of a Jewish hero enclosed in a claustral *shtetl* psychology. The echo of Mark Twain's great novel *The Adventures of Huckleberry Finn* in the title suggests that Bellow sees himself in the great tradition of American writing. In tracking William Einhorn, rich, wealthy, crippled, but politically powerful, one of Bellow's larger than life characters, Augie enters him in an "eminent list" of world-historical figures. He imagines one of Einhorn's disciples having to make an important decision and asking himself: "What would Caesar suffer in this case? What would Machiavelli advise or Ulysses do? What would Einhorn think?") Against the philistine democratic view that "the race [the human race] no longer has in any important degree the traits we honor in these fabulous names," Augie insists on his "right to praise Einhorn," an epic character of his time. At the end of the section devoted to this "superior man," Augie finds himself "not in the center of the labyrinth but on a wide boulevard." There are, of course, no boulevards in the *shtetl*. Isn't this the achievement of Bellow—to take the Jew off the side streets and put him on the boulevard of the imagination?

The titles of his first two novels are a measure of the imaginative leap he made in writing *Augie March*. No longer dangling man or victim, Augie in his swagger displays a confidence in his place in American life that verges on bravado. "I go at things as I have taught myself, free style and will make the record in my own way, first to knock, first admitted, sometimes an innocent knock, sometimes a not so innocent." Even anti-Semitism fails to faze the youthful Augie, whose take on it is peculiarly American. "And sometimes we were chased, stoned, bitten and beaten up for Christ-killers...But I never had any special grief from it, or brooded, being by and large too larky and boisterous to take it to heart, and looked at it as needing no more special explanation than the stone-and bat-wars of the street gangs or the swarming on a full evening of parish punks to rip up fences, screech and bawl at girls, and beat up strangers.". How did Bellow manage the leap? Well, there is the matter of genius and temperament that goes beyond explanation. But genius and temperament are not the whole story. There is also the matter of the historical moment, the post World War II period. It is one of the extraordinary facts of our democracy that the military may be in the social sense its most democratic institution. It is the place where men and women of different religious, racial and ethnic backgrounds mix in a condition of equality sometimes under fire, despite the hierarchical structure of the military. Moreover World War II was a war against the most pernicious racism and anti-Semitism in history. During the postwar period America became increasingly hospitable, though not without resistance, to the claims of its minorities to full cultural, social and political enfranchisement. World War II served as a rite of passage for Jews as well as for other ethnic groups. Bellow was a pioneer in literature. Bernard Malamud, Philip Roth and others were soon to follow.

According to an anthology of American-Jewish writing published in the nineteen-sixties, the "breakthrough" meant not that "the Jew has caught up with America, [but rather] that America has at long last caught up with the Jew. His search for identity is its search. Its quest for spiritual meaning is his quest." This is a pleasant fiction, encouraged by the writers themselves. Malamud remarks somewhere that the burden of his work is to show that all men are Jewish. And the narrator of Walker Percy's *The Moviegoer* declares his "Jewishness by instinct. We share the same exile." But the idea that American writing had finally caught up with the Jewish writer ignores creative and historical realities. He had to learn to speak English and he had to learn to speak it artistically. He also had to overcome his immigrant defensiveness and his sometimes blinding fear of the new country. You have only to read much of the Yiddish literature written in America in the early twentieth century to see what was required of Jewish writers to gain entry into the larger world of American letters. Yiddish is the language of despair, the resentful person's imaginative revenge against life. It has unique capacities as a bearer of the experience of suffering. Its words and cadences seem to have evolved for the purpose of conveying the experience of persecution, exclusion and massacre and at the same time redeeming it through humor and irony. Its mood or moods have little in common with the buoyancy of American speech.

I don't mean to dismiss Yiddish literature in America as unworthy. There were Yiddish writers of talent and power. Leyles, Glatshteyn, Halpern, Teller, Heifetz-Tussman, Vaynshteyn and Leyvik, the subjects of Benjamin and Barbara Harshav's superb bilingual anthology of *American Yiddish Poetry.* But in a way their work makes my case. I quote from an English translation of Leyvik's moving poem: "To America," which concludes the anthology. The poem was published in 1954, a year after the publication of *Augie March.*

For forty-one years I have lived within your borders, America
Carrying within me the bounty of your freedom—that freedom,
Sanctified and blessed by the blood of Lincoln's sacrifice
And in the hymns of Walt Whitman. See how strange it is: to this day
I seek an answer to the contradictions, to the unrest of my life,
I wonder, why haven't I sung you, to this day
With joy, with praise, with pure admiration—. . . .
For forty-one years I have lived under your skies
For over thirty years I have been your citizen,
And until now I have not found in me the words, the mode,
For painting my arrival and my rise on your earth
With strokes as broad and revealing as
You are yourself, America.
As soon as speech would shift toward you, I would curb
My words, rein them in with austere restraint,
Bind them in knots of understatement. My whole world and my whole life
I held under secret locks, far from your wide open breadth.
I shall disclose it now: when I got off the ship
Forty-one years ago, and touched your earth—I wanted to
Fall prostrate upon it, kiss it with my lips. Yes, yes, I wanted to, should have,
And I didn't . . . And later on, on your blessed earth
I wrote, in memory of my father's image, songs of guilt and longing.
And I said to that image: accept, though late, the kisses
That I wanted to give—should have given as a child
And ever was ashamed to give you . . .
I tried—and it is clear: the fault is mine, not yours,
That thirty years ago I mourned under your skies
Deep inside me, lamented that I carried my Yiddish song
In fear through your streets and your squares.
Clenched in my teeth, as a forsaken cat might carry
Her kittens, in search of a cellar, a place of rest—
That when I think of my brothers—

Yiddish poets—their destiny
Embraces me like a clamp, I want to pray for them,
For their lot—and then all words grow mute,

Poverty, mourning, fear, the backward elegiac contemplation of the old world left behind—all this continues to frustrate the poet's attempt to embrace and sing America. And as Leyvik makes clear, he speaks for his fellow Yiddish poets. The America of Lincoln and Whitman remained beyond the grasp of the immigrant imagination of the early twentieth century.

It is not that the generation of Bellow, Malamud, Delmore Schwartz and Alfred Kazin sever all connection with the enclosed, past obsessed world of the Yiddish poets. Kazin's wonderful memoir *A Walker in the City* is rooted in that world. But unlike the Yiddish writers, he is American born a native English speaker and he can look beyond the confines of the Brownsville home of his parents to the bridge that will take him into the cosmopolitan America of Manhattan. Kazin and his American born contemporaries need to complete their parents' migration and enter into the mainstream of American life. And yet (here is the important qualification) they do so without divesting themselves of their heritage. Bellow and Kazin retain the Yiddishkeit of their childhood. One can even hear in their prose the inflections of Yiddish. Listen to the opening paragraphs of Kazin's memoir:

> Every time I go back to Brownsville it is as if I have never been away. From the moment I step off the train at Rockaway Avenue and smell the leak out of the men's room, then the pickles from the stand just below the subway steps, an instant rage comes over me, mixed with dread and some unexpected tenderness. It is over ten years since I left to live in "the city"—everything just out of Brownsville was always "the city." Actually, I did not go very far; it was enough that I could leave Brownsville. Yet as I walk those familiarly choked streets at dusk and see the old women sitting in front of the tenements, past and present become each other's faces; I am back where I began.
>
> It is always the old women in their shapeless flowered housedresses and ritual wigs that I see first; they give Brownsville back to me. In their soft dumpy bodies and the unbudging way they occupy the tenement stoops, their hands blankly folded in each other as if they had been sitting on these stoops from the beginning of time, I sense again the old foreboding that all my life would be like this. *Urime Yidn, Alfred, what do you want of us poor Jews?*

Kazin had wanted to write about his journey from Brownsville and his walks around "the city," but found himself instead drawn to the past he had escaped or tried to escape. The return is registered in the language of intense ambivalence: "rage," "dread," and yet an "unexpected tenderness."

Bellow's career oscillates between the present and future-mindedness of his American identity and memories of the Yiddishkeit he imbibed with his mother's milk. For all of the American adventurousness of his novels, *Augie March* and *Henderson the Rain King* in particular, the introspective, self-divided, self-ironical victim's voice recurs in novels such as *Herzog* and *Seize the Day*. The burden of the past persists in Bellow's superb short story "Something to Remember Me By." In his last novel, *Ravelstein*, the narrator Chick (short for boychick) speaks for Bellow himself: "I had a Jewish life to lead in the American language, and that's not a language that's helpful with dark thoughts." Clearly, aging has something to do with this sentiment, but Bellow's residual attachment to Yiddishkeit is a pervasive feature of his work. He was a friend and when I met with him from time to time the first words that this master of the American language utters were in Yiddish. It is as if the language was his comfort zone.

Leaving behind an alcoholic life in New York, Seymour Levin, the hero of Malamud's novel, *A New Life*, makes the trip to the mythical Western town of Marathon, Cascadia to assume a position as instructor of English at Cascadia College. With his wonderful ear for the Yiddish idiom, Malamud recalls the Yiddish immigrant tale. "Bearded, fatigued, lonely, Levin set down a valise and suitcase and looked around in a strange land for welcome." No frontiersman would set down a valise and suitcase, nor would he passively expect a welcome. And yet Levin has already been Americanized in alcoholism. And he strikes the epic American note with a certain self-irony. He tells his new colleague Fabrikant that he left New York, "seeking, you might say, my manifest destiny." Fabrikant replies: "This corner of the country was come upon by explorers searching for the mythical Northwest Passage, and it was opened by traders and trappers in their canoes trying to find the great river of the West, the second Mississippi they had heard of. Then the settlers came, fighting the Indians, clearing the land, and building their homes out of guts and bone. . . . There were great giants in those days. Their descendants are playing a defensive game. Their great fear is that tomorrow will be different from today. I've never seen so many pygmies in my life." Levin is a belated Natty Bumppo.

Yiddish is a dying language, though it has lingered longer than expected. You will know that the disappearance of Yiddish will have occurred when the following joke will cease to be a joke. A lady on the upper East Side of New York gives an elegant dinner party. In ladling out the turtle soup, the butler accidentally spills it on the hostess's dress. She cries out in distress, "oy veh! Whatever that means." Yiddish is a language without a home, homeless even in Israel, the Jewish homeland. Immigrants from other countries may in the passage of time leave their native languages behind, but the languages remain alive and well in the homelands. As the Yiddish poet, Herschel Edelshtein in Cynthia Ozick's remarkable story, "Envy; or, Yiddish in America" puts it: "A language that never had a territory except Jewish mouths and half the Jewish mouths on earth already stopped up with German worms." But that is not the whole story. Even where Jewish mouths are free to speak the language as in America, the language dies because its speakers are also free to enter into a richer language and enjoy its rewards. If, as Bellow's Chick says, the American language is not helpful with dark Jewish thoughts, it has nevertheless absorbed Yiddishisms into its idiom. As a literary language, however, Yiddish has effectively disappeared in America.

The notable exception has been Isaac Bashevis Singer. Singer wrote in Yiddish, but his reputation was made in English. There was a time (I am not sure that the time has past) when more of his books were published in English translation than in the original Yiddish. His appeal has always been greater among English than among Yiddish speakers. How to explain his anomalous place in American literature? Like other Yiddish writers, he wrote mostly about Jewish life in the East European past; it took him a long time to treat the American scene. But all his work was distinguished by a modernist sensibility rare among Yiddish writers of fiction. His work is erotic, ironic, unsentimental, sometimes obscene and without moralizing. It is a sensibility with which most Yiddish readers are uncomfortable. Singer alone of Yiddish writers escaped confinement in Yiddishkeit through translation. This is the happy ending of the Singer story.

But it is not a happy ending in the eyes of the protagonist Edelshtein in Ozick's story. The character of Edelshtein is based on the Yiddish poet Jacob Glatshteyn, who was critical of what he viewed as Singer's unearned success. Singer is portrayed by the character Hershel Ostrover, whom Edelshtein characterizes as a "a humorist, a cheap fast article writer for one of the Yiddish dailies . . . his subject matter insanely sexual, pornographic, paranoid, freakish—men who embraced men, women who caressed women, sodomists of every variety, boys copulating with hens, butchers who drank blood for strength behind the knife." Ostrover, the joker about serious matters, is declared a "modern" and becomes internationally famous through translation. This is the envious vision of the marginal Yiddish poet, destined to oblivion. But Ozick, an American Jewish writer, herself a master of the English language, means us to take Edelshtein's vision of the death of Yiddish with absolute seriousness. "Whoever forgets Yiddish courts amnesia of history." The story can be read as bitter elegy on the death of the language of the diaspora in the diaspora. Her achievement in the story, however, suggests a different and happier outcome at least for the historical moment of the breakthrough. It did not free the Jewish writer from his Yiddish past, but rather allowed him the freedom to carry it into American literature. It is as if the precocious Yiddish capacity for suffering, grievance, pathos and wit has been allowed to penetrate the brittle reserve of WASP culture and transform it into something else.

The breakup or the disintegration of Yiddishkeit in American life has not been without its advantages for the American Jewish writer. It has enabled him or her to look upon experience with a certain detachment and possess it in a new way. There is the often noted parallel between the new creative power of Jewish writers in the nineteen-fifties and that of Southern writers like Faulkner, Flannery O'Connor and William Styron who too found imaginative freedom in the disintegration of the Southern tradition. No longer simply a spokesman for the Jewish people, the Jewish writer is now free to say the unsayable, to express candidly and critically what he or she sees in the life of the Jewish community. Hannah Arendt once spoke of the Jew as Pariah, in one of his roles. The pariah is the outsider to the gentile world, but he may also become the outsider to his own people. Kafka, the classic example of the Jewish writer as outsider, once stated "what do I have in common with the Jewish people? I have nothing in common with myself."

From the very beginning of his career, Philip Roth, a great admirer of Kafka, assumed the role of pariah to his own community. He has given us a satiric view of Jewish family life in *Goodbye Columbus* and other stories and with a kind of comic savagery in *Portnoy's Complaint*, provoking self-proclaimed spokesmen for the Jewish people to denounce him from the pulpit and other venues as a traitor to his people. King Lear may have spoken for Roth's Jewish elders when he said, "how sharper than a serpent's tooth it is to have a thankless child." Even Irving Howe, who began as an admirer of Roth's early stories, took Roth severely to task for what he viewed as his *ressentiment*, impatience with uncertainties and doubts, a thin personal culture and vulgarity. Any writer's work is fair game for criticism. But the charge of ingratitude does not deserve to be taken seriously. As the critic Leslie Fiedler once remarked, the artist bites the hand that feeds him. There is an extremism in Roth's imagination (*Sabbath's Theater*, a novel written under the influence of the anti-Semitic French novelist, Louis Ferdinand Celine is the most extreme example) that may be viewed as an emblem of the freedom of the artist to go wherever the daemon leads. Are the interests of the Jewish community compromised as a result? Not if you consider what that imaginative freedom signifies: the enfranchisement of Jews in American society—as when Jews or blacks can tell jokes about or even against themselves in public. To be able to turn critically upon one's own community and self-critically upon oneself paradoxically reflects confidence, the feeling that one has arrived.

Roth has been seen as part of a troika with Bellow and Malamud, the effect of which is to obscure the significant differences between him and them. Roth is eighteen years Bellow's junior, born of American born parents. Yiddish words and phrases appear in his work, but they do not resonate with a knowledge of the language, which Bellow, Kazin, Isaac Rosenfeld, Delmore Schwartz and Ozick fully possess. (Malamud is an exceptional case, because though he did not really know Yiddish, he had an extraordinary empathy for its inflections, its cadences, its tonality.) The spirit of Roth's work is rebellion. Much has or had been made of his language, its profanity and obscenity, its obsessive sexuality intended as a force to break through the inhibitions and prohibitions that afflict him and his fictional surrogates. Recall the shock of the title of the excerpt of *Portnoy* that appeared before the publication of the novel, "Whacking Off." The shock has worn off and we now see more clearly the elegance, force and wit of his style and can appreciate his deadly ear for the way people speak. From the beginning of his career one of its principal targets has been alrightnik suburbia. The stories in *Goodbye Columbus* and the novel *American Pastoral* are exemplary instances. It was the Jewish community of suburbia that was most offended by Roth's work. He had come from that community and he had turned against it. In the story, "Eli the Fanatic," it is the Jewish community led by the lawyer Eli Peck that invokes the zoning laws to drive out the Hasidic synagogue. Yiddishkeit in the form of the rabbi Tzuref, a play on tzures, is the return of the repressed that threatens the complacency of the assimilated Jews of suburbia and possesses Eli himself. Who then is the traitor to the community, Roth or the community itself?

Roth's imagination continues to be obsessed with contending versions of Jewish identity. In *The Counterlife* and *Operation Shylock*, he dramatizes the opposing claims of secularism and religious orthodoxy and of life in the diaspora and life in Israel with the freedom of the novelist, who does not have to take sides. Haunting the conflicts is the inescapable memory of the Holocaust. Of course, the return to Yiddishkeit is impossible for Roth or any second or third generation American Jewish writer. Roth's brilliant and prolific career, still very much in flight, is a search for personal identity. Or is it an escape from personal identity? In *The Counterlife* and *Operation Shylock*, the rootless self (whether Nathaniel Zuckerman or a character named Philip Roth) splits and imagines alternative counter-lives. . He has become a virtuoso of self-multiplication. Roth's alter ego Nathan Zuckerman speaks of having "no self. What I have instead is a variety of impersonations that I can do, and not only of myself—a troupe of players that I have internalized, a permanent company of actors that I can call upon when a self is required, an ever-evolving stock of pieces and parts that forms my repertoire."

Without rootedness in the immigrant cultures, personal identity in America becomes fluid, if not vacuous, with little prospect of its ever achieving stability. One name for it is personal freedom, another is what one critic has called the American uncertainty of who or what one is. We might think of unhypenated American identity in terms of mobility, changefulness, fluidity, waking up one morning with the idea of who you are and what you want to be, and another morning with another idea, never quite settling down, postponing adult responsibility into middle age. This is one version of our vaunted American freedom, and it doesn't always make for happiness, or for that matter, freedom. Increasingly the unhyphenated American has little or nothing to fall back on—in the family, in the ethnic tradition.

What is striking is that there is little sense of liberation and pleasure in Roth's rebellion. He wrote an autobiography, *The Facts*, in which he presents himself without fictional disguise. In an inspired afterword, he has the characters of his fictional surrogate Nathan Zuckerman and his English wife Maria render judgment on their author. "I don't mean that he [Roth] is presenting a deceptive image to make himself look terrific, because on the whole, for me, it's rather the other way. He looks to be awfully narrow and driven, and my God, so pleasureless." The judgment (really a self-judgment) is meant to apply to Roth himself, not to his characters, who are at least allowed to explode against the conventions. But pleasurelessness is defining of the characters as well. If I had to name the dominant emotions of his work, it would be *angst* and rage, not sexual passion. Here is a sample of what I mean from *American Pastoral*. The setting of the novel is suburban New Jersey in the late nineteen sixties. The protagonist, Swede Levov, an affluent glove manufacturer, married to an American beauty and father to a daughter who joins the radical underground of bomb throwers, wreaking havoc on her life and the lives of her parents. In a splendid passage, Swede explains the glove making process to a messenger from his fugitive daughter. In the course of the explanation, he becomes suddenly possessed by the enormity of what has befallen him and the account of the glove making turns into an incantation of grief, unbroken by punctuation, with echoes of the book of Job.

> This is called a polishing machine and this is called a stretcher and you are called honey and I am called Daddy this is called mourning this is called hell, pure hell, and you have to have strong ties to be able to stick it out, this is called trying-to-go-as though nothing as happened and this is called paying-the-full- price but-in God's-name-for-what, this is called wanting-to-be-dead-and-wanting-to-find-her-and-to-kill-her-and-to-save-her-from-whatever-she-is-going-through-whatever-on-earth-she-may-be-at-this-moment, this unbridled out-pouring is called blotting-out-everything and *it does not work, I am half-insane, the shattering force of that bomb is too great.*

Here Roth, the *enfant terrible* (there is no Yiddish phrase for it) assumes the role of Lear in a prose of grief and rage.

In speaking of 1953 as the breakthrough year for American Jewish writing, one risks obscuring its achievements before Bellow's arrival. The fact is that there was extraordinary work done earlier by writers such as Abraham Cahan, author of *The Rise of David Levinsky* as well as founding editor of

The Jewish Daily Forward, Henry Roth, author of *Call It Sleep* (a modern classic with Joycean affinities) and Daniel Fuchs's remarkable trilogy of Jewish life in Brooklyn: *Summer in Williamsburg, Homage to Blenholt* and *Low Company*. (Fuchs's novels were critical successes, but not life sustaining, so he went to Hollywood to write screenplays and in the course of his career won an Academy Award for *Love Me or Leave Me*.) The effect of the breakthrough was to retrieve these novels from obscurity. Credit for the recovery of these writers goes to the American Jewish critics Irving Howe, Alfred Kazin and Leslie Fiedler. The achievements of Bellow, Malamud and Roth were in a sense prepared for by these writers, but it would be a diminishment, indeed a travesty, to see their works simply as preludes rather than extraordinary achievements in their own right.

The career of Daniel Fuchs should remind us that Jews were a powerful presence in American culture decades before the literary breakthrough. John Updike's Jewish protagonist, the novelist Henry Bech regards "the mutually profitable romance between Jewish Hollywood and bohunk America, conducted almost entirely in the dark, a tapping of messages through the wall of the San Gabriel range" as "one of history's great love stories." He goes on to pay tribute to Fuchs, "his favorite Jewish writer…who turned his back on his three beautiful Brooklyn novels and went in to the desert to write scripts for Doris Day." But Bech or Updike fails to reveal the nature of that marriage. Jewish screen writers, directors and producers created the collective fantasy life of Americans, but without revealing their Jewish identity in their work. The novelist of Brooklyn had to pass, artistically speaking, in order to succeed. The appearance of an identifiable Jew on the screen was a rarity. Occasionally, a screen writer may have slipped in a message to the folks back home in Brooklyn. It was in the thirties or the forties of the last century that my father recalled seeing a Western film in which the Indian Chief was addressed as Chief *Potch in Tuches*.

If you want a vision of what non-Jewish Jewish Hollywood was like read Leslie Epstein's novels *Pandemonium* and *San Remo Drive*. *San Remo Drive*, his "novel from memory," contains an early comic scene that is emblematic of the way Jewish identity was refracted through the anxiety of concealment. Lotte, the mother of Richard the novel's protagonist, exposes the vicissitudes of the family name Jacobi, after her disturbed son Barton, Richard's brother, refuses to eat non-kosher meat. So René, Lotte's lover (a Frenchman, not a Jew) mistakenly believes. "Perhaps he is a true Jacobi, eh?" said René with a belly laugh. "Ha! Ha! He must not eat what is forbidden." But Bartie confounds René by denying that his name is Jacobi. "My name is Barton Wilson." Lotte explains defensively to René that it "is only a phase," that Barton is passing through. But René wonders whether Barton is ashamed of his name. Lotte responds somewhat irrelevantly that her deceased husband Norman may have not been a religious man, he may have laughed at "the rabbis," but he was "proud of his people." René expresses disdain for changing names. Lotte reminds him that she changed her name to Jacobi and that names were changed on Ellis Island, and Richard, witness to the scene, recalls with laughter that the family name originally was *Ochsenschwantz* "oxtail." In the Hollywood novels of Leslie Epstein, son and nephew of Philip and Julius, screen writers most famous for *Casablanca*, the Jew comes out of the closet. Epstein has written the classic American novel of the Holocaust, *King of the Jews*, and he has created in Goldkorn of *The Goldkorn Tales* one of the most effervescent and memorable Jewish characters in fiction. Unlike the writers of the breakthrough, he is a latecomer, I am tempted to say, a convert, with the passion of a convert, to Jewish experience.

The generation of Bellow, Malamud and Kazin had its feet planted in two worlds. The English critic Matthew Arnold once spoke of the modern poet (that is, the modern poet of the nineteenth-century, his century) as existing between two worlds, "one dead, and the other powerless to be born." The Bellow generation, in contrast, was between two worlds both very much alive in their imaginations. Thorstein Veblen's shrewd comment about the secular Jew in the diaspora comes to mind. According to Veblen, he is a hybrid who brings the mental energy of the Jewish tradition to modern life. "It is by loss of allegiances," Veblen writes, "or at best by a divided allegiance to the people of his origin, that he finds himself in the vanguard of modern inquiry." Veblen here has in mind scholarship and the sciences, but it is no stretch to read his statement as a gloss on the American Jewish literary imagination.

What was distinctive about American Jewish writers, and why did they come to occupy center stage in the fifties and the decades that follow? It was their European past that they brought into the literature, and not simply the past of the ghetto and the Pale of Settlement and the Hebrew bible. It was also the past and present of the great European writers who informed their imaginations: Flaubert, Tolstoy, Dostoevsky, Proust, Mann and Kafka. To become American writers they had to come into possession of the American literary tradition of Emerson, Thoreau, Twain, James and Melville. One of the most extraordinary works of American literary history is Alfred Kazin's *On Native Grounds*, written when he was only in his twenties. To succeed as a cohort of writers something else was needed, a sophisticated and persuasive critical community that would promote their writing. The critics in that community, or family, as Norman Podhoretz has characterized them, came to be called the New York intellectuals. Bellow, Roth, Malamud, Isaac Rosenfeld, Cynthia Ozick found their champions in Philip Rahv, Alfred Kazin and Irving Howe. (Howe, I should repeat, was an early champion of Roth.). The organs of the community were Partisan Review and Commentary. It underestimates the importance of their criticism to see it simply as vehicles of support and publicity. Criticism at its best circulates ideas that nourish the imagination.

Why is America different? This is the question assigned by the conference. Can a similar story be told about Jewish writers in Europe or in other parts of the world? I think not. Two of the greatest writers of twentieth-century Europe were Jewish: the Frenchman Proust and the Czech writer in German, Kafka. Isaac Babel comes to mind in Soviet Russia. There are also important Jewish writers of lesser distinction, among them Arthur Schnitzler and Franz Werfel. The works of Kafka and Babel are marked by Jewish themes and a Jewish sensibility. But unlike their American counterparts most of these were fully assimilated into the national cultures. Moreover, though German, Russian and Polish contributed to the formation of the Yiddish language, Yiddishkeit flourished as a separate culture. The relationship between Yiddish and the national languages was in a sense the reverse of what it came to be in America, where Jewish writers were able to bring the Yiddish sensibility into the American language and literature. In short, what we don't have is the phenomenon of a Jewish cohort of writers in France or Germany or any other country in the diaspora establishing itself as a presence, indeed as a dominant presence as is the case in America.

The American difference has to do with the particular character of its democracy. America is a young country, a new nation without a feudal past. The weight of its literary tradition is light compared to the weight of tradition in European societies. What Walter Jackson Bate has called the burden of the past or what Harold Bloom has called the anxiety of influence is not so great in America as it is in Europe. America is culturally an open and porous nation composed of immigrants in which its character is still being defined. Unlike every other country in the world, America in its ideal definition is not racially or ethnically marked. (Note that I am speaking of its ideal definition, not its actual history, which *is* racially marked by the experience of slavery.) One way to think about America is to think about it through the poetry of Whitman, who I believe has no analogue in any other society. America may be the only country in the world that is not only a nation, but also an idea. It is in its ideal conception the exemplary nation welcoming immigrants from other countries, fleeing from persecution and poverty.

In time the American-Jewish hybrid that Veblen speaks of may disappear in assimilation. Increasingly, the writer will become, indeed may have already become, the American writer of Jewish extraction rather than the American Jewish writer. Most writers of Jewish extraction, I believe, prefer to think of themselves as American writers or perhaps simply as writers. There is the suggestion of parochialism in the hyphenation. He or she will share with non Jewish writers the Jewish inflection that has already entered permanently into the literature. If the writer maintains an attachment to the

Jewish past, it will be archeological, the well known phenomenon of the skipped generation, the grandchild who is curious about his grandparents mysterious past. We have an extraordinary example in Jonathan Safran Foer's recent novel *Everything Is Illuminated* in which the young author, still in his twenties, becomes the protagonist, who seeks to discover the mystery of his grandfather's fate during the Holocaust. The archeological interest may wane and wax, depending upon historical circumstances. I am not a prophet, so I can't predict the Jewish future in America. History is filled with ironic reversals, for good or ill. A resurgence of anti-Semitism might be one such reversal. (Not an outlandish possibility, given the insurgence of political Islam, hostility to Israel and its potential in the Christian Right.) I suppose the revitalization of religious Judaism could become an inspiration for a continuing American Jewish literature, though in its present form its power derives from the decline of the tradition. The current trend is a secular one of attenuation and assimilation. Should this be an occasion for regret or celebration?

We have cause to celebrate. After centuries of exclusion, persecution and massacre, the Jews of America have achieved full citizenship. Yiddishkeit has left its traces in American culture—in cinema, musical theater and literature, but as a culture it has passed into history, a cause for regret. The real measure of its achievement in American literature is in the work of Bellow, Malamud, Henry Roth, Kazin, among others, all writers on the cusp, who possessed Yiddishkeit at or before the moment of its decline. Their work is richly marked by "a divided allegiance" to the world of their mothers and fathers and to the promise of America.

19

Cinema as a Lens on America's Jews

Eric A. Goldman

A close study of films that portray the American Jewish experience provides an unusual insight into the changing condition of the American Jew over the last century. Since the beginning of filmmaking in America, Jews were active producers of movies and the works they produced about the Jewish experience should be seen as important historical texts that carry a great deal of information. The films that these Jewish moviemakers created not only touched on the Jewish condition but largely reflected their own self-image. By better understanding why the film was made and how it reflects on the time in which it was made, we gain a unique lens on a changing American Jewry.

In the course of my paper, I screened examples from a variety of films made during various moments of the twentieth century. Pen, paper and the laptop do not easily lend themselves to a clear enunciation of what film images can convey. Examples of films can run the gamut from early American pictures like *His People* (1926) and *The Jazz Singer* (1927) to *Gentleman's Agreement* and *Crossfire* (1947) into the 1990's with Barry Levinson's *Avalon* (1990) and *Liberty Heights* (1999). Examination of even newer films like *Meet the Parents* (2000), *Keeping the Faith* (2002), *Meet the Fockers* (2004) and *Everything is Illuminated* (2005) shed a great deal of light on the situation of American Jews into the Twenty-first century. To illustrate my point, I will turn to two film segments screened in my presentation.

Gentleman's Agreement, as one of the more important films of the late 1940's, sheds a great deal of light on the situation of Jews during those important years. We see this not only by the visuals that director Elia Kazan brings to the screen, but by the fact that the Jewish establishment of the time was wary and worried about the release of a film that would tackle anti-Semitism. Even the Jewish film company heads put pressure on Twentieth Century-Fox studio mogul Darryl F. Zanuck, one of the few non-Jewish heads of a studio at the time, trying to persuade him to drop the project. Many Jews simply were not comfortable enough as Jews and were concerned that such a film would help spur anti-Semitism rather than combat it. They were wrong.

In the film, Philip Schuyler Green (played by Gregory Peck) is a non-Jewish writer who is doing investigative reporting for New York-based "Smith's Weekly." His assignment is to write a series about anti-Semitism and he pretends to be Jewish so he can experience anti-Semitism firsthand. He realizes, after several overtures, that he gets a different response when he uses the name Green than he does as Greenberg. Then, in the scene I screened, Philip Green goes to New Hampshire with a confirmed reservation in hand for a stay at the Flume Inn.

The scene opens with a lone car pulling into what the book's author Laura Z. Hobson described as the "long crescent that was the approach" to the Flume Inn. The birds are chirping, the weather appears to be glorious. People are sitting on lounge chairs; others go by in their tennis outfits or

Figure 19.1.   Avalon (1990). Directed by Barry Levinson. Shown: Elijah Wood (first row center), Elizabeth Perkins, Aidan Quinn, Joan Plowright, Armin Mueller-Stahl (all behind Wood). "The Family in Avalon."

Credit: TriStar Pictures/Photofest © TriStar Pictures.

Figure 19.2.   Gentleman's Agreement (1947). Directed by Elia Kazan. Shown from left: Gregory Peck, Ray Roberts. © Twentieth Century Fox. "Green confronts the manager."
Credit: Twentieth Century Fox Film Corp./Photofest.

on horseback. Philip Green from New York City, the *outsider* arriving in the restricted upper class world of this New England White Mountains resort turns up in a lone car that makes its way around the crescent. Into the hotel, through wide open doors, enters Mr. Green carrying a suitcase ready to check in.

As Elia Kazan lays out the sequence, he is at once giving us a visual understanding of the Jewish world of the immediate post-World War II period. We have just transitioned from the New York kitchen of this "pretend" Jew, Philip Green. Now he finds himself in the open spaces of New England's gentry. Around the driveway, a single automobile brings our New York City *outsider* into a world not yet ready to receive his *kind*. "I have a reservation for. . . ." begins Green, as he arrives at the hotel desk. "Ah yes," responds the desk clerk, as he places a registration card out on the desk in front of Phil Green. "Oh, one more thing—is this hotel restricted?" asks Green. Herein begins a dialogue between Green, the clerk and eventually the hotel manager. "Well, I'd hardly say it's restricted," replies the clerk. "Then it's not restricted?" At this point, the clerk excuses himself and walks into the manager's office. After a few moments, the inn manager comes out and asks, "May I inquire. Are you—that is, do you follow the Hebrew religion

Figure 19.3. Liberty Heights (1999). Directed by Barry Levinson. Shown from left: Ben Foster, Bebe Neuwirth, Joe Mantegna, Adrien Brody. "Family at Rosh Hashanah."
Credit: Warner Bros./Photofest. © Warner Bros.

yourself, or is it that you just want to make sure?" "I've asked a simple question; I'd like to have a simple answer," asks a more vocal and militant Green. "Well you see we do have a high class clientele, and naturally. . . ." Green interrupts him, "Then you do restrict your guests to gentiles?" "Well, I wouldn't say that, Mr. Green." The manager reaches over to the Rolodex in which all reservations are kept and gives it a twirl. "But in any event, there seems to be some mistake because we don't have a free room in the entire hotel." The Rolodex turns like a revolving door and the Jew's visit to this restricted world is about to end. The image is most clear. The wide open doors were only how things appeared, not how they really were. The revolving door would have been a more appropriate image reflecting the reality of the times. "If you'd like, I could fix you up at the Brewster Hotel, near the station." The back and forth with Green continues until finally the hotel manager has had enough. "Don't raise your voice to me, Mr. Green. You speak a little more quietly please!" In the background, we see an elderly, "more refined" couple looking on, clearly annoyed by the "loud" altercation that is taking place a few yards away. Finally, the manager hits the bell, signaling the end of the conversation. Before you know it, he retreats to his private room, the door slams shut behind him, Green looking down for his bags, sees a bellman carrying them out of the lobby to the outside. Phil Green has come through open doors, but in reality they were revolving doors, with his stay in the lobby only a brief one. These were the revolving doors of that day. No sooner is he in than he is back outside.

This powerful scene is highly representative of the situation of the post-War American Jew. A war against prejudice and hatred had been won by the Allies. Liberty, religious freedom and an end to bigotry were to be the byproducts of that victory. The Flume Inn doors were, as Hobson describes them, "opened heavily," as were America's doors of "opportunity" now ostensibly wide open to its Jews; so it seemed. Jews had fought in the war, served their country admirably and expected to reap the benefit. When Phil Green walked into that hotel lobby, there were no signs decreeing that Jews were prohibited. No guard stood at the entrance and eyeballed each guest who entered. In truth, had Green simply gone to the desk and picked up his room key, he would have had a comfortable night's stay. This "don't ask, don't tell" understanding made it possible for the 1940s Jew to go through the door. Making it possible was that Phil Green's name was Green, not Greenberg or Greenfield. "You keep your voice down!" was just one retort that said it all, contempt for Jews that very much continued to be a part of America through the Forties. Even after the war, Green, the *outsider*, was able to just about go anywhere to share in what America had to offer: affluence, an airy and bright openness and the best that money could buy. Yet, once it was obvious who he was, it became clear that he was not welcome, as seen when the manager hits the bell and slams the door. Kazan's long shot of the car driving down the crescent at the beginning of the sequence symbolized that seeming openness. In contrast, Green's startled look when he sees the bellman carrying out his bag from the spacious lobby is all the more powerful. The message: "Sorry! Although it may appear that everyone is welcome, that reception does not hold for Jews. It's okay to look but keep it brief!"

In 1947, the question of anti-Semitism was still a very delicate one. The Jews in America were experiencing an "era of good feeling," able to advance socially, culturally and economically. Judaism was more and more seen as one of America's three major religions. Yet the massive anti-Semitism of the 1930's and World War II were still very much in memory, leaving Jews with great discomfort. Most Jews seemed to feel that anti-Semitism was rampant and even growing. Certainly, many communities had "gentleman's agreements" to restrict entry to clubs, neighborhoods and a variety of professions. At this time, most Jews were not ready to take on the fight to change this. In light of this, it is not surprising that leaders in the established Jewish community went so far as to try and keep this film from being made. Contrary to what they expected, this and *Crossfire*, another film made about anti-Semitism that year, were shown in studies (conducted by agencies like the Anti Defamation League of B'nai B'rith) to have helped lower the rate of anti-Semitism over the next several years. *Gentleman's Agreement* went on to garner the Academy Award® for Best Motion Picture of 1947.

Another film screened was Barry Levinson's highly acclaimed 1990 *Avalon*. Levinson, who is both writer and director of this film, is a master of the mise-en-scène, a visual representation of ideas and themes, as well as the positioning and editing of those scenes. Levinson's visual punctuation of this film is quite powerful and very Jewish. A close reading of the film text from just one selected sequence in the movie again sheds light on how cinema can provide a distinctive understanding of the American Jewish experience.

The first scene in this sequence has Sam Krichinsky and his wife Eva, foreign-born patriarch and matriarch of a Baltimore family, going to the train station to meet Eva's brother, whom she has never met. The setting is shortly after World War II and Simka, his wife Gittle and their daughter Elka are arriving in Baltimore by train. All three are survivors of the Shoah.

In cinema, careful attention needs to be given not only to the dialogue but also to the choice of image. The first shots are of the train's arrival and of the steamy and ghostlike Baltimore train station. The platform seems almost devoid of people and, with Randy Newman's music as backdrop, this eerie station is visually reminiscent of the steamy train station scenes in films set during the war. Such a scene, with its peculiar music and the train's arrival, brings to mind Europe and the deportations of Jews to the concentration camps. But this is Baltimore: we are in America, and this train is bringing family together, not drawing family apart; it is somehow what America is all about. In the next scene, the elders are sitting with Simka and Gittle in a drawing room, speaking largely in Polish but also some Yiddish. Levinson purposely does not subtitle the dialogue, leaving those of us unable to understand not knowing what is going on. At one point, we hear a word that resembles "concentration"; the survivors must be sharing their stories. Through this device, we are made to understand that these were the stories not immediately passed on by most survivors to the next generation, like Ann and Dottie in the kitchen. Ann and Dottie's generation (like that of Levinson's parents) was often left ignorant and did not know what happened. As the two women prepare the turkey, they continue trying to grapple with the extent of the horror, while at the same time preparing the Thanksgiving meal.

> I'm not sure she was in a camp. Her husband might have died in the war," Ann tells Dottie. "No, I didn't get that," Dottie responds, and they go back and forth. "It must be. The child couldn't have been born in a concentration camp. I got that they met in a refugee camp and her husband had died. But the refugee camp is really recently and the kid is like. . . six. . . . No. We'll have to ask later.

In Levinson's original screenplay, Ann and Dottie are placing dishes on the holiday table while they are chatting. In the actual film, he transitions from the drawing room to the kitchen where the women are preparing dinner. They are basting a turkey. We watch through a close-up as the women place the turkey into the oven, all the while talking about the Holocaust and Simka's family. The close-up of the oven doors being closed proves to be an incredibly powerful visual relating to the crematoria and the death camps.

In this scene, we are awaiting the beginning of a feast that is particular to Americans, yet has no real meaning to the older immigrant generation about to sit at the table. "The Pilgrims, whoever they were," reflects how the holiday means nothing to Sam and Eva, but what Simka is relating has everyone on the edge of his or her seat. In contrast, Ann and Dottie know very well why they are preparing turkey, but have little comprehension of the events that affected Simka and his family. Meanwhile, the turkey, the American feast, is waiting for the oven, while the women grapple for an understanding of the concentration camps, the ovens. In Europe, ovens were used one way; in America, ovens are just for preparing food.

We then find ourselves in the basement with the next generation, the children. There is a close-up of a German fighter plane, complete with swastika. The kids decide to create what they call a "cliff-hanger" (a reference to a movie seen earlier by the children) and go about setting the plane on fire. All the youngsters scream with great delight, but for Elka, now separated and sitting apart on the steps, the screams are representative of something entirely different, as Levinson shows us a close-up of the swastika in flames. It is another interesting visual twist that Levinson uses to show the spatial separation of Elka from the rest of the children, in which we have a foreshadowing that she and her new immigrant parents will never fully be accepted by the extended family.

Levinson then presents us with the Thanksgiving dinner scene. As mentioned before, the meaning of the holiday is somehow lost on the older generation, except that they know that this is a time for everyone to gather. In many Jewish families, Thanksgiving and Passover are the two times in the year when extended families meet. Passover has no place in this film, but the Fourth of July and Thanksgiving, American holidays with no religious connections, are very much present. The Fourth of July represents a beginning for this family; Thanksgiving is characterized by recurring family get-togethers that erode with change and the passage of time. This particular year, the pressures of the moment somehow keep the family from waiting for older brother Gabriel, as had always been done in years past, and they proceed to begin eating without him. The seemingly innocuous act of cutting the Thanksgiving turkey without waiting for Gabriel has dire consequences, and it will be the beginning of the demise of this extended family. "You started without me?!! You cut the turkey without me?!! Come on; we're going. . . . They start without us, we leave. . . . Your own flesh and blood, and you couldn't wait?!! You cut the turkey?!!" In a curious twist, Thanksgiving, which unites the Krichinskys with millions of Americans who celebrate the same feast, is the holiday that marks the beginning of the dissolution of this Jewish family.

Significantly, turkey on this American holiday, with its connection to a different starting point in early America, plays this vital a role. The visual image of turkey represents America as much as it does Thanksgiving, a time for the coming together of family. When Mr. Plowman, who has never met a Jew before, finally accedes and invites his daughter's Jewish boyfriend home in *The Young Lions* (1958), he invites him for turkey. Yet, in *Avalon*, Levinson merges the American visual of the turkey with the close-up of the oven, with all that it connotes. He converts a Jewish visual of the steamy train of death into an American one of survival and reunion. Finally, with a close-up on the knife and turkey, we observe as the bird is carved. With the premature slicing of the turkey there is a symbolic connection to tradition and, in this case, the breaking of tradition. Had Sam and Jules only waited for Gabriel's arrival, as they had done countless times before, the family's tradition of not starting dinner before everyone arrives would have been sustained. In Judaism, it is with the slicing by a knife at a circumcision, *the brit-mila*, that tradition dating back to Abraham is maintained. Circumcision represents the induction into the Jewish family. But on this Thanksgiving, tradition is broken by the slice of a knife. Gabriel's abrupt departure upon seeing that the family started eating without him marks the breakup of the family.

In the final scene of the sequence, we see an extended shot of Gabriel and his wife driving off, never to return to the neighborhood. As the car recedes into the distance, ending the sequence, we see an image in sharp contrast to the opening scene, where we had seen a train bringing family together. In a visual afterthought, the scene is dramatically broken with the scream of Elka, as she awakens from a nightmare prompted by the "cliff-hanger." In a very real way, Levinson, in the course of a sequence lasting only eight minutes, captures an important snapshot of American Jewish life in the post-World War II period.

These and so many other American films with strong Jewish content or characters provide us with a deep grasp of the time in which they were made and a unique look at the Jewish experience which they portray. Cinema can serve as a wonderful reading on the values, concerns and issues of the day. *Gentleman's Agreement* is not just a movie about anti-Semitism and *Avalon* is not just a film about the immigrant experience and the changing American landscape. *Gentleman's Agreement* gives us insight into how fragile the Jew was at World War II's conclusion and *Avalon* provides insight, through the 1990s lens of an American storyteller, into the upwardly-mobile Jewish family. They, like so many other American film narratives are rich as document and artifact. Movies can provide a great deal of understanding into how American Jews related to their place in America. Film is one of many creative expressions that make America different! Jews have dominated the film industry and their occasional flirtation with Jewish material reflects on how they feel as Jews. American cinema provides an appreciation of not only who we were but who we are.

20

What Makes America Different: Jewish Artists and Their Concerns in the Twentieth Century

Ori Z. Soltes

With the reconfiguration of the Western Christian world by the end of the eighteenth century by way of a series of political, technological, scientific and conceptual revolutions, for the first time since the late fourth-century era of Theodosius Jews found it possible to enter the socio-economic and cultural mainstream. Among the varied consequences of this development is not only that Jews were increasingly present within the visual arts, but that the themes and subjects that they began to take on began to carry them in directions theretofore unimaginable. That a German Jewish painter like Mauritzy Gottlieb should depict Jewish scenes such as "Sabbath Afternoon" or even that a Lithuanian Jewish sculptor like Marc Antokolski should produce charming and sympathetic genre figures such as "Jewish Tailor," is not so surprising in this expansive atmosphere. Overt Jewish subjects for an increasingly successful Jewish middle-class clientele were part of a world of changing possibilities.

More provocative were those occasional works depicting Jesus. None startled the still mostly Christian art-viewing public and community of critics more than those by the American Jewish sculptor Moses Jacob Ezekiel (1844–1917). One of these is a bronze torso in which we see the beginnings of the extended arms of the Crucified Christ, the Crown of Thorns jammed onto his head. A second work, in marble, depicts Christ laid out in the tomb as if in peaceful sleep rather than death. A Jewish prayer shawl, a *tallit*, is wrapped around his head [fig 20.1]. Ezekiel's contemporaries were surprised both that a Jew would depict Jesus and that the image was so sensitive and sympathetic. For Ezekiel, Jesus is no longer a symbol of Christianity and its antagonistic relationship with Judaism since the second century.

Figure 20.1.   Moses Jacob Ezekiel, "Christ in the Tomb", ca 1895.

Nor is the image similar to the thousands of Christian portrayals of the long-suffering, self-sacrificing Savior. He is simply a quiet symbol of noble, peaceful possibilities. Christians can view him through religious eyes but both Jews and Christians can view him through secular humanist eyes.

The question of where, as a Jewish artist, one might fit into Western art, which has been essentially Christian art for seventeen centuries is addressed by Ezekiel by engaging the most familiar of Christian subjects from a new perspective. It is the kind of perspective that few European Jewish artists would have dared or desired to produce at that time.[1] Growing up in parts of America (Richmond, Baltimore and Cincinnati) which felt replete with goodwill between Christians and Jews, in which the artist counted luminaries such as Robert E. Lee among his personal friends, Ezekiel could approach such a subject with the same comfort and confidence that he applied to his relief sculpture, "Israel". It was this earlier work that yielded the artist the Rome Prize from the Berlin Academy of Fine Arts in 1873, and brought him to Europe for what ended up being most of the rest of his life. In "Israel", in which a muscular allegorical figure likens the Jewish people in its suffering to Christ on the Cross, we recognize the pained Jewish issue boldly emerged from where it lay hidden beneath Ezekiel's American confidence.

The artistic legacy of Emancipation arrives through Ezekiel into the twentieth century, with its question of where Jewish artists fit into Western art.[2]

In America, these issues would be intermittently interwoven with a second question, for immigrant artists—not for Ezekiel, who was born in the United States and whose last forty years were spent mostly living and working in Rome, but for all of those unlike him who traveled in the opposite direction—of where and how to fit into America. But even with a doubling of the artistic question, there rapidly developed here a comfort in focusing on social, political, historical and religious issues that one can hardly find or imagine finding anywhere else in the work of Jewish artists. *Comfort* with socio-political commentary which is more intense among American than among non-American Jewish artists has often been wedded—consciously or not—to a sense of Jewish *obligation* to comment and question. It is linked to the rabbinic concept of *tikkun olam*—"repairing the world"—which derives from its particularly strong articulation in the sixteenth-century school of kabbalistic thinking associated with Rabbi Isaac Luria of Tsfat.

By the 1920s and 1930s subtle angles of approach to contemporary issues by means of comments and questions, articulated through re-visioned Christian symbols, were becoming increasingly visible, most particularly in the Social Realism of Ben Shahn, who traced his socio-political concerns all the way back to the Biblical prophets. Hence his interest in the miscarriage of justice that led to the deaths of the Italian-American immigrants, Sacco and Vanzetti. He viewed the event as a contemporary equivalent of the Crucifixion of Jesus in the Roman Judaea of two millennia ago, and he used Christian symbols in the paintings he focused on it.[3] In the centerpiece of his series on that subject, "The Passion of Sacco and Vanzetti" (1932–3), white lilies held by two members of the Lowell Committee—whose upper-crust WASP members sent the two anarchist immigrants to their deaths—refer in traditional visual terms to the purity of the Virgin Mary [fig 20.2]. Here it becomes a sarcastic comment on the impurity of those holding the lilies, underscoring the moral bankruptcy of the Committee's bluebloods who claimed to be saving America from the satanic evils of unwashed, unlettered immigrant anarchists—but who martyred two Christ-like innocents.

The sense of art as commenting on the ills of the world and, by causing the viewer to consider them, helping to correct those ills, is a theme that has engaged many Jewish American artists since that era, including Raphael Soyer and Jack Levine, each differently following the sort of Social Realist course exemplified by Shahn. Soyer's brooding, lonely dark-eyed figures—whether his immigrant parents (1933), struggling to adjust to the New World, or children on a New York City street (1952)—are seeped in existential isolation. Levine's imagery is often politically charged. Works like "Feast of Pure Reason" (1937) shimmer with a gauze-like light that illuminates the overly well-fed look of the officials whose job it is to protect the People, but who have grown fat leeching them [fig 20.3]. Levine's "Gangster's Funeral" bursts with allusiveness to the hypocrisy of those whose economic well-being is

**Figure 20.2. Ben Shahn, "The Passion of Sacco and Vanzetti"
(Detail), 1932–3.**

Figure 20.3. Jack Levine, "The Feast of Pure Reason", 1937.

derived from nefarious means: we can have little doubt that among the pious, self-possessed mourners is the gangster's own murderer. And the body of the dead man is placed with perhaps another irony in mind: we see it from the difficult perspectival angle of head to foot, precisely the opposite angle with which Andrea Mantegna presented his innovative "Dead Christ", feet toward the viewer, in 1504 or so.[4]

Toward the other end of the century, Joyce Ellen Weinstein taught for years in a mostly African American high school, where any number of the pupils to whom she became emotionally connected did not make it through school alive. They have been abandoned by an America whose educational system is increasingly bifurcated between those who have and those who don't. Weinstein began a series that memorialized *The Bold Dead Boys*, in 1988, continuing to work on it through the mid-1990s. Sixteen portraits and eight smaller details were done with charcoal on paper and dripping red oil paint. The colors of death and blood, which are the colors of purgatory[5]—but leading to no salvation—offer Malcolm, Kevin, Robert and the others. Their names and dates of births and deaths—none older than 21 years—tell a poignant story requiring no further words [fig 20.4].

Figure 20.4.   Joyce Ellen Weinstein, "The Bold Dead Boys", 1988–91.

The blood of these young men cries out, but the society from which they have been written out is deaf to such cries.

Differently, the work of Marilyn Cohen addresses both the idea of immigration to America and the notion of both Jewish and American social action. In one remarkable series of collage-paintings—*Where Did They Go When They Came to America?* (1989–94)—she presents the stories of one Jewish family in each of the 50 states. Based on oral histories and images in old photographs, these reflect more than a century of everyday life and shared experiences. Cohen's work is both historical document and aesthetic tour-de-force. One would hardly imagine that it is collage, so delicate are the gradations of chiaroscuro and color range. Figures famous and obscure, wealthy and impoverished, learned and untaught peer out of the many-faceted mirror she holds up to the lives of Jews in this brave new world.

"Aloha Gothic", for instance, depicts Nachman ben Joseph Usheroff, who migrated from Tsarist Russia to Harbin, China in 1905, where he worked on the trans-Siberian railway. In 1928 he sailed for Hawaii, where his wife and daughter were able to join him two years later—as part of the *Chinese* immigrant quota. We see the happy couple—in a pose echoing Grant Wood's famous "American Gothic"—among the flowering trees and the red-and-white-American-flag-striped awning of their Oahu home. There, on that edge of America, the strapping blacksmith made ironworks for the Dole Pineapple Company and the Royal Hawaiian hotel and for the Oahu prison—and for the *mikvah* (ritual bath) in his backyard.[6] [fig 20.5]

Figure 20.5. Marilyn Cohen, "Aloha Gothic," (from *Where Did They Go When They Came to America*), 1993.

Cohen has also focused, as a separate matter, on the disenfranchisement of women in America. In a second series completed in 1997 called *Teach Me the Songs My Mothers Sang*, the artist depicts an array of women who have defined myriad aspects of the American past. Eighteen of them, each in her own frame, have had an impact on aspects of twentieth-century life not often associated with women—like aviation and baseball—and often obscured by the shadows of male counterparts. One might say that "Annette Retablo: Our Lady of the Convoy" combines aspects of both of Cohen's series. Raised on a dairy farm begun by her parents in upstate New York, which she and her husband eventually took over, Annette volunteered to help out on a humanitarian mission to Central America in 1989. That put the 72–year-old Jewish grandmother behind the wheel of a 14–year-old Mercedes bus which, at a dusty, heat-filled 16–hour-a-day pace, carried medicines and vitamins, toothbrushes and blankets, diapers and soap, into the unpredictable landscapes of Mexico and Guatemala, Honduras, El Salvador and Nicaragua, to women and children in refugee camps and union halls, in orphanages and corn fields. We see her as a *santera*, a *Central American Gothic*: an icon clothed in the blood red of passionate involvement, surrounded by the attributes of the worlds whose borders she has traversed, surmounted by an angel-held banner.

Within this context of social concern, the subject of the Holocaust has evolved as one of the most frequent reference points for Jewish American artists, especially in the last quarter of the twentieth century. From Ben Zion's series, *de Profundis* (1943) and Leon Golub's "Charnel House" (1946) to Marty Kalb's *They No Longer Cry* series (1993), scores of Jewish artists have responded to the event in a manner representational enough for there to be no question as to the horror which has inspired them. Others, like survivor Kitty Klaidman, have produced work which falls on the border between the representational and the abstract, so that it is the titles and/or the viewer's awareness of this period in her life which clarify and classify the subject. In her 1992 *Abstracting Memory* series, she has reduced the joists and beams of an attic space to a Chromaticist exploration of verticals, horizontals and diagonals filled in with flattened pigment [fig 20.6]. The attic was the space in which she, as a three-year-old, together with her brother and parents, began to be hidden for two years by a brave Slovakian family. She began to wrestle that subject onto the canvas only after a 44–year hiatus—the last decades of it spent in America, where she married and raised her own children—that ended with a trip back to Slovakia and to the farmhouse where she and her memories were hidden.[7]

Differently, Samuel Bak addresses the matter of the Holocaust by means of a rich vocabulary of figurative and representational Jewish symbols. He was born in 1933, six years old when World War II began, and not much older when it arrived into the Lithuania of his childhood, the childhood left buried in the ashes of Vilnius. In Bak's *"Otiyot"* ("Letters"), the Ten Commandments disintegrate in mid-air, as they float in their stony weight. The letters, symbols of the commandments, peel off the crumbling surfaces and float upward—we are reminded of the Hassidic story of the righteous illiterate, who simply recited the letters of the alphabet which, floating to-

Figure 20.6.   Kitty Klaidman, "The Past Purged: Abstracting Memory IV", 1992.

ward heaven, were gathered by God and formed into words of prayer. But we wonder if the Gatherer is still there—or if what is absent is our memory of how to adhere to the Commandments. The sixth letter, "*vav*," is the only one not fully visible. Its prominence is found both in its absence and its accentuation by means of its replacement with the number six—which is also the number of points on the Star of David, and the number of Jewish millions killed in the conflagration beginning by the time the artist was six years old, and the number of the disintegrating commandment "Thou shall not murder."

The Star of David also rises repeatedly from rough-hewn, barren and empty landscapes, or floats like numberless paper kites in skies crowded with purple and gold light—or, in "Alone III", is shaped as a cracked and ruined island surrounded by a vast night-lit sea. The symbol which, in the twentieth century, has become universally recognized as representing Judaism, reaches out in the six directions—east, west, north, south, up and down—for help, for humanity, for contact, for Covenant. And the spaces around it respond with an infinite silence, recalling Balaam's prophecy (in *Numbers* 23:9) that the Israelites would dwell alone [fig 20.7]. It turns on its ear the phrase of John Donne that "No man is an island," for in the vast, stormy seas of history and of the Holocaust Jews have been all too often precisely that.

Figure 20.7.   Samuel Bak, "Alone III", 1994.

But if Bak's work reflects on Jewish aloneness wherever he works—including America—Jacques Lifschitz arrived to America as a Holocaust-era refugee and saw this country as an island, in the positive sense: of salvation within the churning seas of European anti-Semitism. His sculpture, "Prometheus Strangling the Vulture" synthesizes two ideas. The Greek myth of Prometheus, bringer of fire to humanity, tortured by Zeus by being tied to a rock in the Caucasus Mountains as Zeus' eagle daily devours his ever-reborn liver, is recast as if he is Jacob Wrestling the Angel—only the angel has become a bird of prey and the bird is being strangled. The visual *midrash* is intended as a symbol of reason and justice—personified by the United States—destroying the fascism rampant in Europe, of which the vulture is a manifestation [fig 20.8]. Lifschitz, born, like Bak and Marc Antokolski, in Lithuania, was continuously astonished by the possibilities offered to him in America as an artist who was overtly Jewish—from a commission to sculpt an image of the Virgin and Child to a model for the Gate of the Roofless Church, for the sprawling religiously pluralistic sculpture garden in New Harmony, Indiana in which artists of diverse backgrounds were invited to express themselves.[8]

Klaidman and Bak share in common the fact of having survived the Holocaust and eventually, by way of Israel and at least one European country, immigrated to America. But focus on the Holocaust by Jewish artists born

Figure 20.8.   Jacques Lifschitz, "Prometheus Strangling the Vulture", 1949 version.

in the United States, who were not themselves its direct victims has, in the last two decades, expanded exponentially. Among these are children of survivors, such as Kity Klaidman's daughter, Elyse. I have noticed a tendency in such "second-generation" artists toward a much more strident style than that of the "first generation". Kitty's work offers the assuagement of pain; Elyse's the release of anger. Each speaks a very different dialect of the visual language addressing the ineffable. But the need to comment and respond extends beyond those with any personal connection to the Catastrophe: there seems to have arrived a time, by the mid-1970s, for a range of reasons, when Jewish artists of all sorts began to feel that imperative to bear witness to not having forgotten.[9] In works like Judy Herzl's "Forest of Witnesses" and "I Question" (1990), leaves and the trees from which they have been stripped and the forest from which the trees come are multiply evocative of the Holocaust. They call out regarding those marched into the woods to be executed without human witnesses. But the trees themselves in those many woods across Europe *were* the witnesses, standing silently, passively—as silent and passive as so many humans beyond those forests were. Forests were also redemptive witnesses, as they *hid* those fleeing from or fighting against the Nazis. Forests are also the setting for diverse questions, such as: if a tree—or a dead body—falls in the woods and there *is* no human witness, does it make a sound?

For Alan Berliner, it is not trees, but stones. His video installation, "Gathering Stones," projects sequences of delicate portrait photos from the archives of the JDC (which organization relocated refugees after the war, among other things) onto the open "pages" of a large "album". The album is made from a bed of stones placed in a shallow pool of water: two large fields of small black pebbles against which five (the number is the number of books of the Torah) smaller rectangles of white stones are placed. The haunting effect is as if the faces are made up of tiny pieces—or leaves, in fact, which is the illusion the stones offer to the eye—intact and yet broken (a paradox expressed again and again in work by Jewish artists) by myriad tiny cracks and crevices. The entirety trembles with the gentle if inevitable agitation of the water. The pebbles also evoke the centuries' old Jewish tradition of leaving tiny stones on the grave before leaving a cemetery as a concrete symbol of having *been* there, of marking remembrance and continuity, with the individual who has died and with the sweep of history and culture of which s/he is part—of connecting past to present, individual to community and dead to living.

Various Jewish American artists have shaped particular images as symbols of the Holocaust. For Ohio-born and raised R.B. Kitaj—for whom early in his career, the baseball field was the symbol of the America and its innocence of Jewish history which he shared, before he immigrated, for thirty years, to England and before he became aware, by the late 1960s, of the Holocaust and Jewish history and traditions—the crematorium chimney became a recurrent motif in the 1980s: for him it is *the* Jewish symbol. Others have found resonance in other images. Railroad tracks are an obvious example: leading, ladder-like upward, to evoke Jacob's Dream—but to nowhere except the oblivion beyond the canvas, as in work by Alice Lok Cahana, a Hungarian survivor who ended up in Houston, Texas—or converging to a vanishing point deep within the picture plane.[10] Suitcases, particularly piled up alongside attenuated figures, are a Holocaust symbol in the hands of a sculptor like Michael Katz. They connote the Bakian Jewish experience of *aloneness*—waiting, suitcase in hand on the railroad platform to the concentration camp—but joined to the universal idea of the loneliness experienced by *any* traveler in an alien setting.[11]

Judy Chicago's enormous *Holocaust Project* is a vast enterprise which seeks new methodological ground by combining photography by her husband Donald Woodman with her painting and drawing—ironically enough, the material that could most effectively sustain this combination, photo linen, was available only from Germany—together with an eighteen-foot tapestry and stained-glass work. The 3,000 square-foot result is a compendium of darkness and hope. An array of details from the Holocaust with both larger Jewish issues and larger human issues offers "a prism though which Donald and I view universal issues—memory, vulnerability, power and victimization—in the history of Western civilization." It includes among those details elements habitually ignored, such as the fate not only of gay men but of lesbians, about which there is virtually no information (and no specific Nazi legislation, since the Nazis assumed that women lacked any sex drive of any sort).

It includes among those issues the map of twentieth-century genocides that garland the globe and Auschwitz's child, Hiroshima, because of which the threat of nuclear annihilation hovers like an SS officer's truncheon over us all. It includes among its significances both those actively engaged in torturing and destroying others and those passively indifferent. In manipulating two media in combination in order to produce its powerful imagery, its dominating parts play on the question of the power of manipulation, and on the border between the issues of truth and the details of fact. In what might be called the conceptually seminal image from the series, "Four Questions," each triangularly faceted edge thrusts out at the viewer, asking unanswerable questions regarding God's presence or absence and the term "humanity" as it applies to the human role, active and passive, in the Catastrophe [fig 20.9]. The "Four Questions" turn on its edge the line between photography and painting as they turn on its head the issue of continuity to which the phrase "Four Questions" traditionally alludes. For these would be the questions asked by the youngest child at the Passover Seder table for which the answers are the narrative that shapes the Seder, the *Haggadah.* If the theme of the Seder is God's redemptive power, the turn of the Four Questions toward the Holocaust induces us to wonder where that redemptive right arm and outstretched hand were half a century ago, in particular when the youngest and oldest children alike were being ground up by the Nazi machine?[12]

Dorit Cypis' photographs offer analogous visual questions, but directed at humans, not at God. Her *Aesthetic Lessons* series is a group of abstract plays with line and form, and dark/light contrasts. Slowly we realize that these are piles of hair and eye-glasses, suffused with a familiar horror. They can only be piles gathered, stored and half a century later displayed in the Nazi extermination camps. Cypis' *Hybrid Eyes* series is an eerie and fascinating play on re-visioning familiar elements—what could be more familiar to

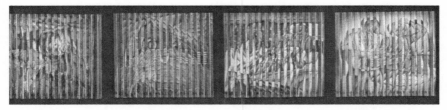

Figure 20.9. Judy Chicago, Study #3 for "Four Questions" (from *The Holocaust Project*), 1992.

our eyes than *eyes*?—in unfamiliar combinations (one blue, one brown, for instance) that have as their visual purpose to make us look and look again, to question whether our first vision was true or false. In the context of the experiments with eyes, as with other body parts, in the Nazi camps, these enormous off-eyes are more *disturbing* than merely disturbing.

Julie Dermansky and Georg Steinboeck disturb us from a different angle. A series of video monitors captures the constant movement of eating. Close-up images of people stuffing their faces—in the "Auschwitz Museum Café"—stuff our eyes. "An Australian woman caught me taking a photo of her and her children eating lunch. She asked me 'we seem rather gauche eating here?,' answering her own question by asking it. She hadn't thought about what it meant to be eating lunch at Auschwitz," where people were systematically starved to death and then placed in ovens. The banalization and profanation of memory itself, that most sacred and extraordinary of human qualities, the transgression of the sharp edge between different forms of horror, confront us.

Steinboeck and Dermansky also underscore the sense of broad possibility that is particularly endemic to America: for she is an American Jew and he is an Austrian Christian, and their marital and artistic collaboration reflects arrangements not impossible, but less likely in other parts of the world. Within the pan-human implications of the Holocaust there is an array of obviously narrower parallel concerns for particular groups like Jews and Gypsies on the one hand, Germans and Austrians on the other—and more recently, from yet other angles, the Swiss and others who have felt compelled to review their role in the Nazi-directed drama of half a century ago. The connective range of victim to victimizer and the perception of these two categories, far from offering black and white is minutely striated with grays.[13]

Grays carry forward from one era and its different places to other eras and their own places. The concern for the universal has led many Jewish American artists to use the Holocaust as a stepping-off point for a broad visual discussion of human violence and brutality. This is part of what Judy Chicago's *Holocaust Project* does. And so Seattle-based Selma Waldman's feverish drawings extend in subject matter from Terezin to pre-Mandala South Africa to the Israel-Palestine relationship. Waldman's work also reminds us that the Jewish art which addresses the Holocaust tends to address its subject from an entirely human, rather than Divine, perspective: it reflects on what *humans* have wrought against humans; it dwells on the specifics of an extraordinary human experience derived from twisting human creativity into the most perverse of destructive shapes.[14]

These sorts of aspects of Holocaust-response, while more pronounced in America than elsewhere are not unique to the United States. But the art that reflects the coming of age of American-sourced painting shortly after the Holocaust is. For contrary to general critical assumption, the Abstract Expressionists who dominated the New York art scene by the end of the 1940s, whose visual muscularity was putting America on the map of art history, were not merely focused on aesthetics. The Chromaticists among them were perhaps not by coincidence, mainly Jews. Mark Rothko, Barnett Newman and Adolph Gottlieb and their peers engaged in long-night discussions asking what, if anything, their art had to do with their Judaism, and how their art might be an instrument of response to the Holocaust.[15] Their large, unframed canvases became part of the answer. The Actionist works of non-Jewish Expressionists like Pollock and De Kooning may be seen to reflect the explosion of the world expressed by the cataclysms of the first half of the century, culminating with World War II and the bombing of Hiroshima and Nagasaki. But the works of Rothko, Newman and Gottlieb put the world *back together*. One's eye is drawn toward the *center* of a Rothko or a Newman; chaotic forms are framed in a unifying white in Gottlieb's canonical works of that period. Of the three it was primarily Barnett Newman who wrote on the results of their gathering in each others' studios to debate and discuss art issues, including references to the sixteenth-century kabbalist, Isaac Luria; Newman also often offered titles suggesting his beyond-mere-aesthetics agenda. They suggest the Lurianic goal of *tikkun olam* by putting it back together on the canvas.

In Newman's "zip" paintings, a central element emerges from behind the larger fields of color that flank it, which are being driven apart by it (as when, in *Genesis*, the ordering process leads from light to the separation of the waters above from those below by a firmament). But the central element also draws the viewer's eye *toward* it, thus functioning to restore order symbolically by reunifying the world blown apart by the events of mid-century. Some works, particularly the *Covenant* series, allude specifically by title to the agreement between God and the Israelites at Sinai. The Covenant carries with it promise and responsibility for those who practice the moral behavior set forth by the Covenantal text (the Torah). Such works express the hope for the restoration of moral order in a moral covenant of humans with humans.

There are further layers to consider in Newman's work. His "The Name II" (1950) adds to the matter of unifying the canvas as a symbolic statement of fixing the world a double theological issue of which the first part echoes certain Jewish art historical concerns and the second particular post-Holocaust Jewish and Christian concerns [fig 20.10]. The painting in question is all white, which is to say that it offers both the absence and the totality of color—since white appears absolutely devoid of color but both chemically and as a symbol of light contains all the colors within it. The image is thus an image of nothing and everything in the coloristic terms which are endemic to traditional painting. A careful look reveals that the

Figure 20.10.   Barnett Newman, "The Name II", 1950.

canvas is divided into three parts by a pair of barely visible vertical lines. As such, it may be construed as a triptych, that most traditional of Western—Christian—forms of visual self-expression throughout the centuries. In traditional Christian terms, the triptych form symbolizes the Trinity, and the center is typically occupied by a Crucified Christ, flanked by the two crucified thieves or by the Virgin and John the Evangelist; or the center might be occupied by or a Virgin and Child, flanked by saints in a transhistorical *sacra conversazione*. In short, images of God and Its concomitants are the visual subject matter offered to the viewer. But the Jewish view of God is that It is invisible and therefore cannot be portrayed. If this last statement raises the old issue of how a Jew might represent God through the visual medium that has been so essential an instrument in the hands of religions from time immemorial, the conflict between Christian and Jewish views obviously focuses that question of where a Jewish artist might fit in to Western art which has been essentially Christian art for so long.

Newman seems both to have asked and to have answered both questions. He has appropriated a classic Christian form of visual self-expression but, in furthering a course pioneered by Ezekiel and furthered by Marc Chagall and others, radically transformed the substantive elements that fill out that form. His triptych is filled with the image of the imageless God, for he has offered both the absence of color and the totality of color; like the Jewish concept of God, the colors on the canvas are invisible and yet present. God is simultaneously absent and present on the canvas. The name of the painting confirms this as part of the artist's intention. For everyone conversant with traditional Judaism knows that one never uses the word "God" in contexts other than prayer, and that the circumlocution customarily used is *HaShem*—a Hebrew phrase that translates as "The Name." Newman has portrayed the God verbally referred to by traditional Jews only through circumlocution by means of visual circumlocution.

The painting also offers a response to the question raised by Jewish and Christian theologians regarding where God was during the Holocaust. How could an all-powerful, all-loving God have been present and yet silent in the midst of those horrors? The answer is paradoxical: God was both present and absent—as human action was both moral and immoral. The question of how to be a Jewish artist in a world of essentially Christian art is wedded to the question of how Jews and Christians can understand the matter of God in the context of the massacre of Jews by Christians carried to its apogee—in visually abstract and thus secular terms. The notion of restoring— re-ordering, re-creating—the world is embedded in the whiteness as a cognate to light. For that is the element called into existence by God at the outset of the world as an instrument with which to begin ordering empty and chaotic pre-order.[16]

The symbolic language invented by the Chromaticist Abstract Expressionists continues the dialogue between human and divine realms of earlier eras, but along non-traditional and non-figurative as well as secular lines, and this is particularly evident in the work of Jewish Expressionists wrestling with the question of where their art might fit into a world grounded in traditions that are both figurative and Christian. This notion takes nothing away from their accomplishment in pure aesthetic, color-and-shape terms. If, as has often been observed, there is something intrinsically American about the brash, frameless canvasses of Abstract Expressionism, then there is something both Jewish and American about the work of the Chromaticists.[17] Moreover, this combination of socio-political with aesthetic concerns continues as art history moves forward into the 1960s and beyond. One fascinating instance of this is Morris Louis' painting. Concerning the first group of his "canonical" works, the *Veils II* series with its unbearably rich yet delicate overlapping pigments, (1958–59), it has been asserted that they offer a mystical quality.[18] If one recognizes that Louis, up again and again to New York City from Baltimore, sat in on and cannot but have been fascinated by the kinds of issues with which Newman and the other Chromaticists were wrestling in the aftermath of the Holocaust and Hiroshima, (and experimented with his own version of Abstract Expressionism in the three years just before the *Veils II* paintings), then it seems reasonable to suppose that some of the issues raised in such discussions were lurking within the artist's unconscious, if not his conscious mind, as he painted in isolation. Veils of color might be merely veils of color, but they might *also* relate to the Jewish mystical notion of the veils that ultimate remain, however infinitesimally thin, between God and the Jewish mystic seeking union with the hiddenmost God.[19]

In his *Unfurleds* series, (1960–61), Louis obtains a translucence analogous to that in the *Veils* by allowing the pigment to soak directly into the unprimed canvas. Except that in the *Unfurleds* paintings, the pigment flows down along the sides of the canvas, leaving a vast, open space as the center [fig 20.11]. That center is not merely unpainted, it is, in being unprimed, as empty as a stretch of canvas could possibly be. In art historical terms, the space that is traditionally positive is here negative; the outer edge which would frame the subject is all there is of the painted area that one might call a subject in traditional terms. Perhaps there is more than meets (or eludes) the eye here, though, for in traditional art, leading back to the beginnings of painting and sculpture and forward to the sweep of Western, Christian painting, that central area might be expected to depict and/or address Divinity and Its concomitants. In Louis's *Unfurleds* series that space is devoid of subject and even of color (yet with a colorless color that is actually the

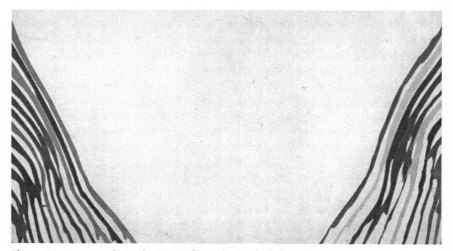

Figure 20.11.   Morris Louis, "Mu" (from the *Unfurleds series*), 1961.

totality of color, as we have noted in the context of Barnett Newman's work).

So here, too, a Jewish American artist seems to be addressing that ultimate question of where he fits into Western art by depicting that which cannot be depicted in Jewish terms precisely through the paradox of its depictablity/non-depictability. Louis' canvases re-order the universe in microcosmic terms, and they comment on the absence of the Supreme Orderer when humans were so overwhelmingly destructive of one another in the generation preceding these works. The tail end of that era initiated the one in which his paintings were actually created, an era of atomic experimentation and nuclear terror within the reshaped context of a cold war. The dripping downward of the side pigments contradicts that explosive potentiality, even as it records it. For the dripping down and in, which the mind recognizes upon careful scrutiny, runs contrary to the sense that the eye and emotions receive, of the upward, outward thrust of those irregular arms of pigment—presents itself as if from a blast the inner flash of which is blindingly white. God is present and absent. The atomic potential of human scientific enterprise can lead to fragmentation or unity, in works that, like God Itself, are rife with paradox.

We might re-angle the discussion ever so slightly to remind ourselves that throughout most of human history the artist is both the analogue of the priest and prophet in being inspired—in-spirited—to create what s/he does and the emulator of Divinity in creating on the microcosmic scale (in this case, the canvas) as God does on the macrocosmic scale. In which case the unprimed central visual stretch of Morris Louis' *Unfurled* paintings becomes not merely a vacuum. On the assumption that, under normal painting conditions what will follow on the canvas is priming and then painting on that surface—creating, i.e. shaping an image in the empty, unprimed and unpainted space—we might also understand these works to offer the nothingness that precedes the order of creation. Or otherwise understood: the nuclear, Cold War reality of the Kennedy-Krushchev-Cuban missile crisis era offers an analogy to the sort of chaos to which the world was reduced in the era of Noah and the Flood, and we are still awaiting the following moment of re-order. Is it mere coincidence that the colorful side elements of the *Unfurls* bear a strong resemblance to rainbows?

In short: a kind of secular *messianism*, a reflection not of the world as it is but as it could become if we actively work to repair it is reflected in such abstract works typically touted as pure formal, non-narrative aesthetic exercises. Yet they also further the notion of a social significance to art—an idea that was articulated first by the St. Thomas-born (New World-born) French Impressionist Jewish painter Pissarro[20] and brought to its figurative apogee in the Social Realist styles of Americans like Ben Shahn and Jack Levine, whose work would later be upstaged by Abstract Expressionism.

One of the most noteworthy features of all of this is the increasingly prominent role played by women artists in the visual expression of American Jews, particularly in the last third of the twentieth century and the beginning of the twenty-first. Many of them combine questions of Jewish and/or American artistic identity with that of female identity within both the artistic and the Jewish worlds. Susan Schwalb's *Creation* series in the 1990s furthered the Jewish identity question shaped through addressing Christian symbols in a manner reminiscent of Barnett Newman. Her series is comprised of triptychs redefined in Jewish terms: the general terms of non-figuration and the specific historical terms of the most famous of medieval Jewish illuminated manuscripts, the *Sarajevo Haggadah*. Her technique revives the Renaissance penchant for silverpoint and copperpoint and weds it to the medieval use of gold leaf—but in completely abstract compositions inspired by the opening images in that fourteenth-century manuscript.

Creation has been re-visioned in the abstract geometry of the circle (its universal symbolism that of perfection, since it is without beginning and without end). "I am obsessed by the extraordinarily tenuous line of silver point; it has been my primary medium since 1974. I use thousands of fine lines to obtain a luminous surface in each picture. . . . When I first came across the *Sarajevo Haggadah* I was powerfully stirred to find images of arc and circle. . . . Unlike familiar Christian portrayals of the creation, the image of God is not represented. But sun, moon and earth are clearly rendered by circular forms . . ." she wrote in 1993.[21] In many of the works in Schwalb's series six small circles and a significantly larger seventh circle swirl in silverpoint against an earth-brown and/or a dark or light (night or day) sky-blue background, the whole edged by a white gold leaf frame.

Certain of these add to the arc-circle configuration a downward-pointing triangle with vertical line from mid-base to apex. This symbol of femaleness is traceable to Neolithic art [fig 20.12]. The role of female artistic creatrix so long suppressed is restored in the very textures of the silverpoint surface she works. Thousands of fine lines engender an active energy—flesh-like, water-like, sky-like—within the static confines of the framing forms. The watery, wave-like lines of the silverpoint surface within the tumescent frame suggest the amniotic fluid of the womb which connects the birth of humans to the birth of fine art and the birth of the universe. The question of artistic creativity is synthesized to that of female creativity. By implication the suppression of female artistic creativity by a male-dominated world is an analogue of the act of ignoring Jewish visual artistic creativity by an art world that is uncomfortable with the word "Jewish"—even if it has come to be dominated as much by Jews as by non-Jews.

In a manner both apposite and completely different, Susan Ressler has also re-visioned the triptych form in her *Missed Representations* series. "Ex-

Figure 20.12. Susan Schwalb, "Beginnings" (from the *Creation* series), 1988.

pulsion" offers a small triptych the middle panel of which is a detail from the early fifteenth-century Florentine Massaccio's "Expulsion". Adam and Eve are leaving the Garden of Eden in anguish, conveyed by their sucked-in stomach muscles and the expression in the deep, dark eyes of Eve—who is perceived as the primary perpetrator of the Expulsion-inducing crime, in the Judaeo-Christiano-Islamic tradition. But Eve's primary role is most strenuously emphasized, almost as much as the quality of the sin is, by the Christian branch of that Abrahamic tree.[22]

Ressler has flanked this with two images of contemporary models in bathing suits (whose body language echoes that of Massaccio's Eve)—one with a design offering a snake (Satan personified) slithering around her torso. The models are all but unidentifiable as *people*: they are advertising armatures for the bathing suits and/or enticing sexual objects. So an icon from western and the (Judaeo)-Christian theological tradition (Massaccio's painting) within a Christianate theologico-aesthetic structure (the weight accorded to sexuality in the context of the Expulsion, as well as the triptych form) is synthesized to an icon from the modern visual world (bathing suit advertisements) and the art historical pattern of objectifying women.

The co-existence of positive and negative, particularly where women are concerned, is hauntingly addressed in Shari Rothfarb's video installation,

"Water Rites". The artist projects twenty-seven comments regarding the significance of the *mikvah*—the pool of ritual purification into which Jewish
women have immersed themselves for scores of generations, most often
before the Sabbath and after menses (again, then, part of the intention is
to reflect on the supposition that menstrual blood is *unclean*)—into a tiled,
mikvah-like pool of water. The quotes are not just commentaries, but narratives, including one which speaks of a group of women who insisted to
their Nazi executioners that they be allowed to immerse themselves properly, cleansing themselves before being shot to death. Landscapes of lush
and provocative imagery form a backdrop for the speakers of the words,
"transgressing the boundaries of time and space to reflect the many different experiences and points of view about Mikvah"—including footage of
ancient and modern *mikvaot* from Masada, Jerusalem and the Galilee.[23] In
a unique combination of word and image, stasis and motion, stillness and
dynamism, Rothfarb's work suggests a range of understandings, from oner-
ous to uplifting, of this aspect of Jewish tradition.

From a related but different angle, Devorah Neumark's work focuses
on the two edges of Jewish married life—wedding and divorce—with
irony and wit. *"Harrei At Mutteret . . ."*—"Behold you are released . .
." are words of divorce, echoing the words spoken by the groom, as
he places a ring around the bride's finger: *"Harrei At Mikoodeshet [lee]"*
("Behold you are sanctified [unto me] . . . "). Neumark's installation follows women through the passage between marriage and non-marriage,
a metaphor for the passage between entitlement and non-entitlement.
Framed transparencies of historic illustrations by unknown (presumably
Jewish) and well-known artists (not Jewish, like Rembrandt; and Jewish,
like Moritz Oppenheim) depict the joy of the Jewish wedding. There are
ten of these photo boxes, as if we are observing a women's *minyan;* each
is surmounted by a wine goblet. The breaking of the wineglass at the
culmination of the Jewish wedding ceremony (wine being the most traditional of Jewish symbols of joy) is intended to recall, even in the midst
of happiness, the destruction of the Temple. Seven of the goblets (the
number of blessings recited at the wedding, and the number of times the
bride walks around the groom) are inscribed with the Hebrew words of
release. Scores of goblets complete the installation, stacked and pulling
from the wall in a semicircle. The shattered forms of some recalls simultaneously the relative ease of divorce in Judaism (when compared to the
Christian tradition), and yet its difficulty, indeed impossibility if the husband should not desire it. While a wife can, under defined conditions,
demand a divorce, the husband may refuse. If Judaism is a historically
marginalized minority within Christendom, women are a historically
limited majority within Judaism, particularly as defined by the beginning
and even more so the ending of a marriage.

Such commentaries are rich with paradox and as narrow as Judaism at its narrowest and as broad as humanity at its broadest. Helene Aylon's "The Book That Would Not Close" re-visions the beginning point of Judaism in the five books that anchor her installation—the five individuated books of the Torah, textual foundation of Judaism. But in *her* texts she has singled out and deleted or highlighted passages that reflect a traditional negativity toward women. In this the artist highlights her own struggle (she comes from an Orthodox background) to reconcile her religious and gender identities as she reshapes what is traditionally understood to be the word of God into a more female-inclusive form. Can God have uttered the words which she has excised, or do they derive from God's male conduits and interpreters? One might argue—the title of a second installation, "The Liberation of God" does so explicitly—that she frees the Deity Itself from the male-oriented bonds that have traditionally constrained It. If we are to move forward, we must reform as much as conserve, as Judaism has repeatedly done throughout its history. Otherwise we may *further* marginalize the female half of the Jewish world, and thereby render the task of continuity that much more challenged—and, as Aylon has commented, make a posthumous victory for Hitler that much easier.

So Jewish American women artists in the last generation have turned inward toward Judaism and not just outward toward the larger Christian and/or American world to ask about and define themselves. If traditional Judaism does not include me in a *minyan*, does not permit me to read from the Torah, does not expect me to recite the mourner's prayer daily for my deceased father, then how do I fit myself in, when these are such essential elements of Judaism? But interestingly—and perhaps only conceivable in America—reflection on the place of those on the margins of Judaism within its traditional structures is not only a concern of Jewish *women* artists. Geoff Laurence's triptych, *"T'fillin"*—"Phylacteries"—breaks the body of a woman into three discontinuous parts, around each of which is wrapped the leather thong of the phylactery box, which a pious Jewish male wraps around his arm and forehead for the daily morning prayer, literally fulfilling the Torah injunction to "bind it for a sign upon thy hand and place it as a frontlet between thine eyes" [fig 20.13]. Those prayers include words thanking God "that He did not make me a woman." The generalized issue of women as commodities (bodies made of parts—see Ressler, above—without minds, much less souls, within them) and the specifics of woman-exclusion or even negativity toward women in specific corners of Jewish ritual are intriguingly interwoven with the suggestion of contemporary sexual mores: the nipple ring reinforces the notion that the leather thongs play a role in sexual bondage here, which then becomes a pun regarding gender bondage and "binding it . . . upon thy hand" in traditional Jewish settings. Which are the ties that bind and which are those that bound?[24]

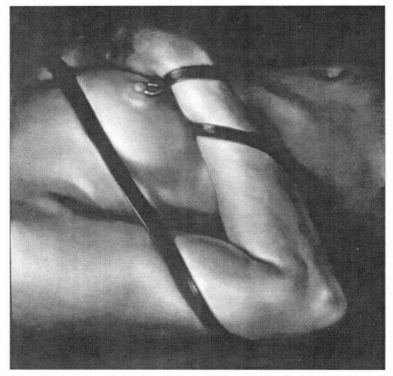

Figure 20.13.   Geoff Laurence, "T'Fillin" triptych (detail), 1999.

On the other hand, the past century has yielded an impressive array of Jewish artists focused affirmingly on the richly textured texts that form the backbone of the Jewish tradition. From Ben-Zion to Jacques Lifschitz and Jack Levine, artists in the first half of the century found material to wrestle with in the narratives within the Torah and prophetic books. In the last generation the focus on biblical subject matter has expanded exponentially, far more so in America than anywhere else except, perhaps, Israel. Like Lifschitz, many of these contemporary Jewish American artists interweave a biblical moment with social or political commentary. Certainly no subject is more worthy of wrestling with than the passage in *Genesis* 22 relating the offering of Isaac by Abraham to God, since at one and the same time it offers the ultimate paradigm of faith in God and of the complexity of parent-child relations—and by implication, husband-wife relations, since Sara is never informed of the *akeda*, and afterwards, Abraham never sees her again alive, as if he cannot face her with what he (almost) did. Carol Barsha's 1997 "The Love that Binds" is one among many works that have addressed this subject in the last generation. Hers is a triptych, in each section of which a different body part, "floating in a limbo of love and oblivion" against a barely cloudy blue sky is loosely encircled (more than really *bound*) by a blood-red cord.[25]

That is: her Isaac is caught between realms in the sense of being *tied* by this process to the God with which his father heretofore has had a special relationship—having become the next in the line of prophetic intermediaries between human and Divine realms—and therefore hovers between heaven and earth. But his hovering is also born both of the *oblivion* of *meaninglessness* (complete unreason—i.e., the irrational act of his father who, suddenly one morning, wakes him up before dawn and leads him on a nightmare journey which culminates with his being bound by that father who then stands above him with an upraised knife); and it is born of *love* in the most ambiguous of ways: his father's love for God, his own love for his father—and in the end, with both his redemption and his consequent initiation into the immortality-giving Covenant, his father's love for him. Isaac (as the Everychild—who is any of us at one time or another) floats ambiguously in the watery skies, only parts of him—only parts of the story—visible to us, who can only speculate on what he truly feels, as indeed, all of the *midrashim* and the interpretations through the various traditions are speculations on the whole, based on a few choice parts. The rope looped around those visible limbs is the color not only of blood, of sacrifice, but of passion and love.

Differently, Ruth Weissberg's "Passing Over" (1991–2) explores a biblical theme by combination of a wall drawing and a sand and steel construction that pushes deep into the viewer's space as it puns on the notion of transcending a simple delineation of time [fig 20.14]. The enormous installation simultaneously refers to that passage in *Genesis* that records Jacob's dream of the ladder between heaven and earth and that, in *Exodus*, describing Jacob's descendants passing dry-shod through the Sea of Reeds from Egypt to the wilderness of Sinai—and perhaps that in *Joshua* describing the grandchildren of those descendants who pass from the wilderness over the Jordan River into the Promised Land. For the long (35′) scroll offers a drawing that can be seen as Sinai in its mountainous central shape, or as simply the heights bordering the Jordan valley; one accesses the drawing past a steel archway and ladder-like form and a sea of sand that spreads from the wall along the floor toward the base of the ladder. The work plays on the etymology of "Hebrew" as one who passes from place to place—and thus both on the diaspora of the Jewish descendants of Jacob's descendants and on the keeping of festivals like Passover which, throughout the year, connect far-flung Jews from one century and continent to another. In pushing into our space, the ladder literally connects the interconnected biblical moments and places to us.

On the other hand, Katherine Kahn's "Cain and Abel: Assassination of Rabin" offers an overt connection between the first biblical act of murder

Figure 20.14.   Ruth Weisberg, "Passing Over" (front view), 1991–2.

(and its ramifications for the endless future of human history) and the first murder of an Israeli leader by an Israeli who believed that he was acting in God's name, as a biblical prophet would. The huge (80″w x 66″h) charcoal drawing offers the assassin on the right, seen twice simultaneously—as if the man who pulls the trigger is inhabited by some other—and to the left, the victim, shown in four poses simultaneously, as he is shot and collapses, stage by slowly crumpling stage, to the ground. The four stages might be viewed in symbolic terms: four is the number of letters in both the Hebrew name of Yitzhak (Rabin's first name, and the name of the patriarch who links the covenant of Abraham with that of Jacob-Israel) and the name of God; as six "figures" may be said to encompass both sides of the overall image, then we recognize in that number the number of points on the Star of David, the number of millions destroyed by the Nazis who imagined themselves doing God's work, and the number of the days of Creation without the paradise-related, redemptive Sabbath seventh.

The *mystical* possibilities that such numerological play suggests have also, not surprisingly, been explored by a growing array of Jewish American artists in the last twenty-five years or so. Marilyn Banner's *Soul Ladders* series accomplishes two antithetical ends simultaneously. They surround the viewer, suspended between floor and ceiling—as between heaven and earth—by structures that allude both to Jacob's dream of a ladder connecting the two realms and to the ladder of the *spherot*, that quintessential kabbalistic image that articulates the paradoxic notion of God's simultaneously transcendent, inaccessible distance from us and achievable, infinite proximity to us. And in being made up of the flotsam and jetsam of everyday elements, from old family photographs to animal skins, the ladders underscore the idea of mysticism as a borer through paradox, to bring the infinitely hidden God near to the mystic—at the same time they address the question of God's presence/absence during traumas, most particularly the trauma of the Holocaust, for many of the old photographs are of family members who perished in that traumatic event.

Jane Logemann's work is completely different. It is layered with text: rows of letters and words over which subtle pigments are washed. They may be viewed as abstractions (particularly if one doesn't read the Hebrew, Arabic, Japanese, Russian and other writing systems that she uses), while at the same time they may be read (literally) in terms of their content and message [fig 20.15]. The word has become the image: the ongoing repetition of a word, run together so that its beginning and end points are not apparent suggests that it is the letters and not the words that are repeated endlessly. This in turn suggests the patterns of sound-and-syllable repetition prescribed for the Jewish mystic in some kabbalistic systems. The *sense* of the words is lost within the patterns that carry the mystic toward union with the realm of *non*-sense. But the ongoing rhythmic patterns also recall contemporary music (Philip Glass, for instance), ancient Byzantine mosaics, Islamic art and some of the painting of Sol Lewitt—thus embedding specific Jewish concerns within universal ones.

Archie Rand's varied work does not fit into a particular box of Jewishness. His painting consistently expresses the conviction that art can be con-

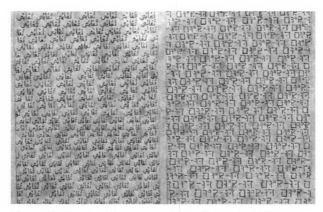

Figure 20.15.   Jane Logemann, "Co-existence", 1993.

temporary—even abstract—and yet bear overtly Jewish content. One of the frequent features of his work is text—as the ultimate Jewish "tradition"— but invariably superimposed over visual elements that would be more likely otherwise to invoke Chromaticist Abstract Expressionism. As both a painter and an art historian he is acutely conscious of the underlying secu- larized spirituality of modernist greats like Cezanne, Picasso, Pollock and Rothko, and is wont to push the interpretational edge of interface between their work and more overt religious concerns—and then to do the same to his own work: as a Jew in the arts community and an artist in the Jewish community. From his overrunning the walls of the B'nai Yosef synagogue, in Brooklyn, (1974–77) with murals that in their totality recall the mid- third-century synagogue at Dura Europus, to his 1994 series of paintings, *The Eighteen: Blessings at the Heart of Jewish Worship*, Rand synthesizes the oldest of Jewish visual imagery with features customarily thought to eschew religious connection. After the B'nai Yosef murals he commented, in 1986: "my fear of having my Jewishness crawl recognizably into my exhibition work was abating. It was replaced with teasing delves into what was for me daredevil Jewish iconography mixed up, uninvited, with my more tradi- tional secular attempts."[26] Rothko and Pollock share conceptual space with Nachmanides. Moreover, his striding back and forth between cartoon-like elements and "fine art" elements, and his application of cartoon elements to the most serious of subjects—often exhaustive series focused on those subjects—wryly pushes the Warholian pop art message to the outer edge of its envelope.

With *The Eighteen* . . . one can observe four distinct elements that, in each of the panels, offer an extremely effective synthesis of visual thinking [fig 20.16]. The general tenor is that of a color field painting, but within it symbols significant to Jewish visual history, such as the seven-branched candelabrum or the early synagogue's Syrian gable share the foreground with multicultural elements that range from Ionic/Aeolic column capitals to the infinitizing Islamic patterning that at one and the same time con- notes God (the Infinite) and ourselves (the infinitely small over and against the monumental space filled by the pattern). The center, mid-ground area offers the sweep of the Hebrew benediction; text and image thus interplay in eighteen particular forms that not only refer to those benedictions, but pun on the number eighteen as representing life.[27]

Rand has gone one further step in his most recent body of work, *The Nineteen Diaspora Paintings*, in which he reverts to a comic-book style, but with a deliberately Mannerist emphasis on dramatic angles of perspective, strident and jarring colors and extreme light/shadow contrasts. And he has synthesized passages from the Hebrew Bible to passages from the same eighteen benedictions of the earlier series (because there are really nineteen "themes" embedded in the "Eighteen Benedictions"). "I asked myself 'what

Figure 20.16. Archie Rand, "Number Fifteen" from *The Eighteen*, 1994.

does it *mean* to identify as *Jewish* now? Here?' . . . I thought a lot about Arnold Schoenberg evaluating his experience and finally *having* to write *Moses and Aaron* . . . I wrote (painted) a Jewish 'opera.' I quoted nineteen blocks of Scriptural fragments, each of which addresses a pivotal point in the story of the Jewish people. These 'highlights' were re-arranged to tell a story, in a restructured order, about the rise of Israel, its internal dissolution and exile—with the last pictures reflecting on the hope of continuance. The featured sentences were picked to correspond respectively with the theme of each prayer in the *Amidah* service . . . I wanted to make an art that was not *about being Jewish* but that *was Jewish.*"[28]

Other examples abound of the endless variation of ways in which Jewish American artists have come, particularly in the last generation, to wrestle with or express their Jewish identity while addressing the larger concerns sometimes as Americans but always as artists. Tobi Kahn (no relation to Katherine Kahn) is the quintessence of this in a manner somehow diametrically opposite to that of Rand. Recognized in a 1985 Guggenheim Museum exhibition as one of nine young artists representing "New Horizons in American Art," Kahn stands simultaneously on several borders that make limiting the sense of his work an impossibility. On the one hand his paintings—landscape-like abstractions, which in their luminous spiritual quality evoke Mark Rothko and in their biomorphic qualities recall Arthur Dove and Georgia O'Keefe—are richly sculptural. On the other hand, he does Jewish ceremonial objects, albeit with a newness of style and method that recalls his paintings and sculptures. The fact that ritual objects are among his work reminds us that in that arena of visual self-expression, the free-flowing style of America has offered a most natural context for "New Horizons" in Judaica made by a growing array of Jewish artists/craftspeople. If the Jewish painters and sculptors of the late nineteenth- and early twentieth-century *Ecole de Paris* offered an outburst of Jewish visual creativity after centuries of visual self-suppression, the Judaica artists of the United States have, in the past half-century, offered an outburst of creativity after centuries of guild-restrictions and inhibitions.

From Ludwig Wolpert's innovative designs for Sabbath candlesticks in the 1950s to Jennifer Karotkin's Havdalah Set, 1995, with its floral, vegetal and fruit of the vine elements to Cynthia Schleimlein's *"Zoe:* Hanukah Lamp" to Robert Lipnick's colorful ceramic pieces (laden with a consistent vocabulary of symbols and intended, as he once put it, to fill in the lacuna left by all of the Judaica destroyed by the Nazis) to Tobi Kahn's innovative series of ceremonial objects, collectively entitled *Avoda*, the line has become increasingly blurred between Judaica and sculptural art.[29] As with most of Kahn's works, Schleimlein's Hanukah lamp has a *name*, suggesting it as a sculpture and not merely a ceremonial object. *Zoe* in Greek means "life" and the flames in her piece rise from a pool of oil held by what offer the simultaneous appearance of wings and upstretched arms holding an offering bowl [fig 20.17]. The offering is light itself, and the dedication (which is what "Hanukah" means) and commitment to God that the effort of the Maccabees symbolized. It is this that we celebrate every December—or should—rather than the array of gifts that have become the American Jewish parallel to the Christmas celebration.

But American Judaica has innovated in the last twenty years in another way: it has created an entirely new object and object-idea with the Miriam's Cup that now graces the Passover Seder table of many households, that, filled with fresh water, rather than wine, both restores Miriam to a role of prominence in the Passover narrative and specifically alludes to the tradition that where she was among the wandering Israelites, wells of water seemed to appear almost miraculously, to slake the thirst of those exiles. Among the myriad such works that have taken shape, Linda Gissen's 1997 "Miriam Cup" offers a bronze, Giacometi-like figure as the stem which then appears to hold the goblet itself: a glass form upon which the artist has depicted the Israelite women in bright colors dancing as they danced and rejoiced, led by Miriam, in praises of God after their successful passage

Figure 20.17. Cynthia Schleimlein, "Zoe" (Hanukah Lamp), 1997.

through the Sea of Reeds. Tobi Kahn's Miriam's Cups are, as so often in his Judaica, emphatically sculptural.

And as for his sculptures, whole groups of them—the "Shrines," in which carved pieces of wood, cast in bronze, are placed within architectural settings—suggest liturgical art without being liturgical art. He has been creating these for years, in all sizes; they simultaneously evoke Greco-Roman aedicula (temple-like grave markers, with the deceased shown in relief within the frame of the "temple"), Christian reliquaries and—not least of all—the *mishkan* itself in the Jewish tradition [fig 20.18]. Inspired by diverse art historical elements they in turn bridge those elements to each other and to abstract contemporary art. That is: his Judaism and his art are subtly inter-woven strands in one tapestry. More than this, all of his works (and not just his ceremonial objects) have names, made up, (sometimes but not always of Hebrew elements) which evoke but don't quite land on recognizable subjects. Thus they demand thoughtful participation from the viewer to "read" them: "Look and look again. Tranquility grows disturbing; tension gives way to serenity. The poetry of color and the severity of form convey the seduction of memory, which alchemizes unconscious daily life into lyrical and awe-filled landscapes of the mind," he wrote in 1993.[30]

The matter of identity diversity within and expressed by stylistic or media diversity is well illustrated, too, by the work of Rose-Lynn Fisher, who works as a painter in a manner that often combines different media as well as figurative with abstract elements and whose fascination with "otherness"

Figure 20.18.   Tobi Kahn, Installation of Three Works from *The Shrine Series*, 1985.

in time, space, experience and *being* places her constantly on the boundary between the selves which define her—artist, woman, Jew, American, Los Angelina. On the border separating and uniting these identities she asks where, precisely, her place *is*, while allowing the uneasily answered question to contour her work, rather than to paralyze her convictions. "The metaphor of threshold is the thread of constancy in my work. As a point of entry and departure between the known and the unknown, a threshold is the internal structure of spatial, temporal and spiritual transition . . . Here the sacred meets the mundane, the absurd joins the poignant . . . a vanishing point becomes visible . . . Patterns in perspective create distance; patterns in time create tradition. . ."[31]

Her work plays with Renaissance imagery and the Albertian discussion of how to produce the illusion that, when one looks at a painting one looks through a window into space filled by volumetric figures and objects, rather than at lines and colors on a flat surface. Again and again her landscapes become topsy-turvy exercises in rectilinear perspectival geometries. "Key" (1995), for example, offers a hilly realm of Rubik's cube-like patterns across which four figures move, like a series of odd pilgrims—the first, who leads them, is a plump baby (a small Eros—a little child who leads them?); the last is a figure dressed in monk's garb (celibacy?); and in between are two figures who, together with the outer two complete four stages of life—four generations. They move at a slight diagonal from the lower right of the picture frame, toward a scintillating ember just below the horizon. The orange glow offers the only color in what is otherwise black-brown highlighted by gray—as if the whole were part of an old manuscript in which the once-black ink has become brown with age. The dark sky, too, offers a faint glowing, just above the point where the bright light within the womb of earth glimmers. The four seek the Light. The search carries them—four males—toward the life that swells within the topsy-turvy mother earthscape, its inner geometries human-made, just below the threatening, sheltering sky. Which key is it that they seek? Immortality? Goodness? Identity? At the very least the key near the horizon threshold is one of paradox.

Fisher's work as a photographer has taken her to diverse places on the external and internal edges of time and space. While visiting Israel several times since 1991, she turned to the relentless austerity of the Negev desert, the timeless quality of which served as a boundless spiritual centering point for re-locating in herself a sense of home by virtue of that *Homeland* (as she named the series of photographs that resulted): what defines "home" and "homeland" for one with the varied layers of identity of which she is conscious? That identity includes an imprecisely but distinctly articulated Judaism and in turn connection to a people whose historical condition has been one of homelessness and fixation on a homeland of the distant past and the messianic future. In photographing the remnant of Morocco's

Jewish community, in its Berber villages on the edge of the Sahara desert—
particularly its elders and its children—she has explored memory and loss,
as she has recorded one among the myriad ebb-and-flow phases of Jewish history. In photographing the tombs of Moroccan Jewish holy men
venerated by both Jews and Muslims, and in living and photographing in
a Belgian Catholic community, she has addressed the boundary between
humanity and divinity as it is approached in common across the diverse
borders of faith.

One of the ways in which Arlene Becker's photography connects individual to individual and group to group is by observing the common ground
of *disconnection* upon which we often stand. In a work like "Black Guy and
White Guy" she has contrived two opposite figures—Black/White, Young/
Old, without hat or glasses/with hat and glasses, with hands hidden/with
hands revealed—who share the isolation in which each sits at the same kind
of table eating the same kind of food. Indeed the food is emphasized by
the only particle of color in the image, that of Ronald McDonald's orange
clown-hair. The context of this scene is the ultimate *gastronomic* American
icon. It has become the symbol of America across the planet, even as the
issue of the intermingling and separation of races also symbolizes America.
Perhaps not surprisingly, other Becker images play on the idea of American icons, such as the double-exposed repetition of James Dean imagery
(an *infinitizing* repetition that therefore pours us into the timeless infinite
realm of the Other into which traditional Icons are the windows). This is
the reverence of "James All Over Again". Her "Elvis in Jerusalem" turns *that*
American icon toward the Holy Land (Land of Grace)—where, indeed, on
the edge of Jerusalem, the Holy City, a foodstop/gas station offers the largest, most diverse collection of Elvis memorabilia outside of Graceland.[32]

Judy Moore-Kraishnan connects the edges of realities identical to or parallel to those which draw the focus of Becker, by visual mergence, ". . . like
chamber music in which two or more instruments combine to produce a
wholeness not apparent in the individual voices... Blending images taken at
different times is a way of bringing time into an otherwise static medium."[33]
One angle of overlap between place and tradition emerges from the
photographer's "Daibutsu and Temple Mount" [fig 20.19]. The southwest
corner of the Temple Mount wall—a central focus of archaeologists for the
past hundred and fifty years, seeking the layered history of the Sacred City
and its peoples—rises, its edge like a pyramidal point, through and above
the head of the Buddha. The two images soak through each other. The
viewer is reminded of the enormous attraction Buddhism has come to hold
in the late twentieth century for (particularly American) Jews, an astounding number of whom have embraced Buddhism while remaining Jewish.
(Since Buddhism offers no God, but the model of the Buddha as one who
has achieved enlightenment, there is no necessary contradiction in this. It

Figure 20.19. Judy Moore-Kraichnan, "Daibutsu and Temple Mount", 2000.

is possible—to come full circle back to the beginning of this essay—to be defined as a Jew by religion or culture and a Buddhist by conviction). The image also suggests the question: are we at the edge of a new synthesis, another corner in the turns and twists of the spiritual history of Judaism?

Where do we most effectively fit in? Is our view affected by where we come from? By the place we call home and how we define home? These are ongoing questions for a dispersed people. The edge between past and future and between Old World and New World is the point from which questions of belonging are raised by and for emigrants/immigrants of all times and circumstances. But few groups have endured so consistent a condition of that blurry-edged *betweenness* as have Jews.

At the end of the twentieth century, with the opening up and then tearing down of the Iron Curtain, once again a substantial number of Jews poured onto these shores. Among the most famous arrivals are the painters and performance artists Vitaly Komar and Alexander Melamid. Refugees from the former Soviet Union, Komar and Melamid went first to Israel, where in

1978, in Jerusalem, they erected a red metal tower, surmounted by the five-pointed Red Star, which they labelled the "Temple for the Third Exodus". Within it they placed an old Russian suitcase—one of the suitcases in which they had carried their belongings in their exodus from the Soviet Union—and set it on fire. This "sacrifice of the Russian suitcase" was followed by the destruction of the Temple itself, crushing it into a small box-like shape upon which the star sits, the only obviously intelligible fragment left. The remains of both Temple and sacrifice rest in vitrines. The Soviet Union has itself become a piece of past history, fit for a museum.

The artists prepared a pair of fragmentary gravestones, in Hebrew, inscribed with their own names, deceased as Soviet citizens. They wrote a three page text—"The Book of the Komar and the Melamid"—in Hebrew, and inserted it in a copy of the Hebrew Bible, between the books of Prophets and Sacred writings. There is a pun: "Komer" means "priest"; "Melamid" means "teacher" in Hebrew. The transition in Judaean history between leadership by prophets and priests and that by scribes and scholars—teachers—begins after the return from Babylonian exile. The artists' arrival to Israel echoes such a return from exile, even as it echoes the earlier Exodus of the Israelites from Egypt: layers of echoes make up the history of which they are an integral part. Indeed, having moved on to America Komar and Melamid have further considered that history and their part within it, as the range of their projects has continued to expand. They have carried the ashes of the past with them, and so it cannot be forgotten. "The Remains of the Temple" is a crushed compendium of the identity that they took with them from Russia to Israel and to the United States. But what *is* that identity? Jewish artists in the former Soviet Union were, since 1934, subject to a peculiarly difficult struggle with identity.[34] *All* artists desirous of expressing their inner aesthetic selves while surviving *as artists* by towing the Party line were aesthetic *marranos*—Crypto-artists—creating official art publicly, but creating unofficial art, the art of protest, hidden behind closed doors, for a small loyal following. For Jewish artists who were part of the unofficial art scene, the world often had three, not two simultaneous conditions: that of operating within its outer, official elements; that of being part of unofficial art circles; and that of being Jewish within both official and unofficial non-Jewish reality.

The complexity of the Jewish three-world Crypto-artistic condition could not simply be left behind upon arriving into the United States. On the contrary, whereas *there* such artists were viewed as *Jews*, not *Russians*—and they certainly did not think of themselves as *Soviets*—*here* they are viewed as *Russians*. *There*, they had strong support from a very small but close circle; *here* the art world is too big to be interested in any but the lionized few. What identity should they embrace once they are here, but not yet American—and how long does it take to *become* American—but also no longer either part of the Soviet scene or part of the protest scene, since emigration and/or *perestroika* eliminated many of the specifics against which they had formerly protested?

Komar and Melamid are an exception to this troubled rule. While still in the Soviet Union, they were known for their 1972 creation of *SotsArt*, an allusion to American Pop Art and a satire of socialist (*Sots*) propaganda and its art. And they have been successful almost since their arrival in America, capturing the interest of the art public with their clever visual commentaries on icons of Soviet history *and* Euro-American history and art history. They refer to this work as "Anarchistic Synthesism." In recent years they who visually toppled the sacred trinity of Marx, Lenin and Stalin again and again in their paintings, have incorporated into their artistic experimentation the images of those images as they have been toppled by the fists of *glasnost*. In 1995 they began collaboration with an elephant, Renee, in the Toledo, Ohio, zoo, and since then with other elephants: teaching them to paint and exhibiting their work.

The edge between human and animal creativity reached a particularly ironic apogee when Komar and Melamid were invited to *represent Russia* at the 1999 Venice Biennale, and they exhibited works by three elephant artists. Perhaps not by coincidence, during this same recent period, they have also redefined themselves—not as Russians or Soviets or Americans or any narrow national or ethnic box into which others might place them. "We realized that we are, when all is said and done, Jews, as we migrate from one place to another and take root in one culture after another. The cosmopolitan tendencies of which our grandfathers would have been accused *defines* us, in the most positive and dynamic way!"[35] The pieces of their identity would not fit easily into a burnt suitcase or onto an elephant-sized canvas. It has exploded in fact: their most recently completed large project was an exploration of the relationship between the Star of David and other visual forms, ranging from the Ouroboros to the broken cross—the swastika. Called *Symbols of the Big Bang*, the exhibition wrestled with the origins and changing meanings of familiar symbols and the synthesis of one visual idea to another. But its centering point was the artists' interest in reflecting on their identity by way of visual reflections that form an edge between the national/ethnic and the universal.[36]

Spiritual syntheses have been part of Judaism's entire history. When are new syntheses a fad and when do they offer the extending of another limb on the extended family tree? How do we understand the distinction, for Jews, between religious and cultural and political syntheses? No synthesis has been more profound and covered more completely by all three aspects of Judaism than that shaped by the long history of the Sephardic Dispersion extending from Spain and Portugal in the fifteenth century to various other parts of Europe and America into the twentieth century. In 1992, the quincentennial of the expulsion of Jews from Spain and of the first voyage of Columbus sparked a bonfire of interest in and research into the history of interface between the world of Jews and the world of Native Americans, since both were so strongly and unhappily affected by the events of 1492. One particularly interesting interface which such research has argued is this: when the Inquisition arrived in Mexico in the late sixteenth century, many of those who, having re-opened their lives as Jews once they left Spain or Portugal, now ran the risk of trial and torture as heretics and went back into hiding in two ways. They fled to the furthest available corner of Mexico—New Mexico, which one day would become part of the United States—and they hid their Judaism behind the same sort of veil of Catholicism that had obscured the faith of their ancestors of a few generations earlier. They became Crypto-Jews, and their own descendants would only recover their identity with some clarity in the late twentieth century. Some of the "proofs" for generations of hidden Judaism are customs—like removing a goblet and candlesticks from a cupboard on Friday evening, filling the goblet with wine and kindling the candles and not replacing them in their secret storage until Saturday night—and celebrations, like the feast of St Esther (heroine of that eponymous biblical book who was, in a distinct sense, the first Crypto-Jew). So, too, gravestones, marked not only with symbols that might be construed as both Jewish and Christian (like the Cross and the Star of David) but inscriptions in both Latin and Hebrew.

Cary Herz' 1994 photographs of such gravestones are part of the record of a particular Jewish edge—between being hidden and being revealed as a Jew, in this case visually marked on the marker of the edge between life and death. Her series, *Crypto-Jewish Burial Sites* is a visual parable of the struggle for and against self-assertion that has marked Judaism historically and is present among even the most apparently free-to-express-its identity Jewish community the diaspora has ever known, the American Jewish community. The details of this particular narrative within the larger Jewish story are more complex, still. In the bare decade since the "discovery" of New Mexico's Crypto-Jews, at least one scholar has argued that these are, in fact *false* Crypto-Jews—crypto-Crypto-Jews—who took on the guise of Crypto-Judaism at the end of the nineteenth and beginning of the twentieth century (for reasons that fall outside this discussion).[37] A gravestone bearing the first five commandments of the Decalogue was probably removed at some point from a synagogue where the other half of the stone may still be seen, rather than created originally as a gravestone. So the question is whether the juxtaposition of its primary Hebraic-Jewish contents with its secondary Catholic contents is accidental or intentional and connected to what larger cultural-religious-political context.

Whether such images represent true Crypto-Jews, descended from refugees from Spain, or whether they reflect a more recent form of false Crypto-

Judaism, they signify the boundary between individual and group and the edge between true and false knowledge of one's roots, as well as between memory and forgetting. For the artist, ". . . this photographic essay has redirected me back to my own spiritual center and my Judaism. It has connected me with my own past."[38] If the question of identity posed by these images and their argued context may never be answered to everyone's satisfaction, then her work is simply like so many other definitional questions pertaining to Judaism: without resolution. But whatever the true identity of those covered by such tombstones, the fact of the tombstones had an important impact on the artist who photographed them.

The American condition, with its alternation between competing senses of itself as melting pot and as tapestry of interwoven threads, offers syncretistic twists and turns that are all but unimaginable in the Old Worlds from which those who have become Americans derived, except under the duress of "forced" identity transformation. Synthesis and the re-shaping of identity category are particularly well echoed in the life and work of George Wardlaw. His "Exodus II: Warning Signs"—one side swarms with locusts to the careful eye—is simultaneously a large, black aluminum step-pyramid and a stylized representation of the mountain which Moses ascended [fig 20.20]. It evokes both the Egypt whence the Israelites fled and the place in the wilderness where they were reformed into a covenantal people before completing the return to the Promised Land. It thus recalls the synthesis of the *ethnicity* of Moses—the Israelite raised in the ultimate Egyptian household—and the *spirituality* of Jethro, his Midianite father-in-law, who joined the covenantal community when he heard about "all the goodness that God had done for Israel" (Exodus 18:1–12). It is part of a series of fourteen large sculptures and over a hundred paintings which "[helped me] to better understand some facets of Jewish history and identity, and to reaffirm my own . . . And foremost, I wanted to make work that had a religious theme but that manifested itself primarily in spiritual presence and awareness, work that might cut across diverse religious boundaries and reveal a common spiritual concern and work that crossed contemporary art with cultural history".[39] The edges between the realities of servitude and freedom, wilderness and homeland, covenantal obligation and covenantal promise, ethnic and spiritual identity, reflect those of Wardlaw's own life. Brought up Baptist in a small southern town he was eventually inspired, in part by contact with the Judaism of one of his key mentors, Jack Tworkov, to convert to Judaism many years ago. So, among other things, his large sculptures are part of the large unanswerable question of how to define "Jewish" art with regard to the identity of the artist.

The Jewish experience is broad and filled with positive and dynamic concerns and diverse participation in the world. In America in the last 120 years or so that experience has been richer and more complicated than

Figure 20.20.   George Wardlaw, "Exodus II: Warning Signs", 1989–92.

ever before, and for the first time in more than a millennium and a half
Jews have indulged the urge to express that experience in stunningly varied
visual terms. We might turn the screw of this narrative in two last antithetical directions. The first, pulling from the textual aspects of the work of any
number of the artists we have discussed, is toward that long-time designation of Jews not as a people of visual images but as the People of the
Book—a turn of phrase coined by Muhammad in the early seventh century.
The second pulls completely away, not only from textual reference points
but from any apparent reference to Judaism at all—for that form of visual
self-expression has also been available to Jewish artists in America.

Thus one sees the screw of textuality twisted a final turn in the work of
Diane Samuels. Her 1993–99 "Letter Liturgy (For Leon)" reflects on an old
Hassidic story regarding what God accepts as piety: not book-learned knowledge of the prayer book or the Torah, but the purity of the heart's intention,
symbolized by the illiterate Jewish peasant who cannot read the prayers
but keeps reciting the Hebrew alphabet, allowing God to combine the letters into words. [40] Samuels plays on the very abstract arbitrariness of letters
as symbols that, in combination, represent words and ideas [fig 20.21].

Figure 20.21. Diane Samuels, "Letter Liturgy (For Leon)", 1993–99.

Are the "letters" in her "book" *letters?* If not, *is* this a book? More importantly, can *non*-letters form the words which comprise prayers? Do prayers
require well-wrought words or, for a textual people like Jews, well-shaped
letters? With what instruments—words? melodies? gestures? images?—
does one most effectively address God? Is God listening and looking—and
interested—anymore?

Mel Alexenberg's work asserts emphatically "yes" to the last of these
questions. Alexenberg is an Orthodox Jew; his work repeatedly and overtly
draws from the Jewish tradition and/or his thinking about it. His visual
textuality is both self-conscious and self-reflective: his texts comment on
the images in which they are imbedded. The very method of much of that
work, computer generation, he regards as inherently Jewish. For the circular, rather than linear structure characteristic of computers and their chips
is analogous to the circularity that is at the heart of Jewish, as opposed to
Greek-based Western, thinking. The Torah is a double scroll; it is read from
beginning to end and again from beginning to end *ad infinitum* (which
is to say there is no ending to its study); its primary forum of study and
discussion, the *midrash,* is circular in the very pattern of its discussions. As
for content, Alexenberg often uses the images of angels (which he com-
puter-generates) based on those in Rembrandt's version of Jacob's Dream,
superimposed over or in conjunction with banal advertisements for food.
His intention is to suggest art as a connector between heaven (angels) and
earth (food), by way of word-plays in Hebrew (for the root of all three
words—food, art and angel—is the same in Hebrew).[41] Frequently, lest the
message be missed, he expresses this idea through quotes from the biblical
and/or the rabbinic traditions and/or of his own devising.

The opposite of such Jewishly-laden sensibilities is found in the paintings of Helen Frankenthaler. Whereas the artists who most directly inspired
her, the Abstract Expressionists, were, as I have argued above, as seriously
engaged in socio-political commentary (with, on the part of the major
Chromaticists, a significant Jewish component), as in pure exercises in new
aesthetic thinking; and where so many other Jewish American artists have
either overtly embedded or unconsciously embedded but later recognized
the embedment of varied Jewish questions within their work; she has
argued emphatically that there is not a scintilla of Jewish *anything* in her
paintings.[42] Certainly, her most famous, classic canvas, "Mountains and
Sea" (1952), can be seen as combining the influence of both the Actionist
and the Chromaticist Abstract Expressionists, just as methodologically (the
allowing of pigment to soak into an unprimed canvas) it may be seen to
have inspired Morris Louis. But the case for any sort of "Jewish agenda"
such as I have also argued undergirds Louis' work, cannot be found in that
magnificent painting. But that is also as it should be. For the freedom to
create without *any* conscious—or perhaps even unconscious—reference

whatsoever to one's ethnic or religious or racial background is also part of what made America different, for Jews as for other groups.

NOTES

1. The most notable exception, interestingly enough, is a Christ sculpted by Antokolski—the last place from which one might have expected such an image is Eastern Europe. Antokolski's "Christ Before Pilate" is a brooding image, similar in feel to other brooding works, such as "Ivan the Terrible".

2. I am distinguishing the artistic legacy from the more general legacy of how to define Jews and Judaism in a post-Emancipation world and all of the complications growing out of that problem of definition.

3. See Ben Shahn, *The Shape of Content* (Cambridge, MA., 1957) and Frances K. Pohl, *Ben Shahn*, (San Francisco, 1993) especially p. 12.

4. For more on Shahn, Soyer and Levine, see Ori Z Soltes, *Fixing the World: American Jewish Painters in the Twentieth Century* (Hanover, NH., 2003), Part One. Mantegna's little gem was found in his studio at his death in 1505, so we might assume that it was painted within the year or two prior to his death.

5. Black and Red in combination are those colors in Christian Renaissance art symbolism.

6. For more on Cohen see Ori Z. Soltes, *Jewish Artists on the Edge*, (Santa Fe, NM., 2005; this is a reprint of the catalogue of the exhibition by that name, curated by Soltes in 1999–2000), p. 69; Soltes, *Fixing the World*, pp. 115–16; and the catalogue of the exhibition curated by Soltes, *Marilyn Cohen: Where Did They Go When They Came to America?* (Washington, DC., 1994).

7. In the context of "Holocaust" art, for more on Ben-Zion, see Tabitha Shalem and Ori Z Soltes, *Ben-Zion: In search of Oneself* (exhibition catalogue at the B'nai B'rith Klutznick National Jewish Museum, 1997). For more on Leon Golub see Matthew Baigell, *Jewish-American Artists and the Holocaust*, (New Brunswick, 1997), 46–8); and Soltes, *Fixing the World*, pp. 78–80. For more on Kitty Klaidman see Soltes, *Fixing the World*, p. 103–104 and Soltes, *Intimations of Immortality: The Paintings of Kitty Klaidman and Elyse Klaidman* (exhibition catalogue at the B'nai B'rith Klutznick National Jewish Museum, Washington D.C., 1994).

8. For more details, see Soltes, *Fixing the World*, Introduction.

9. In over-simplified, rapid succession: the growing array of reasons for overall "Holocaust consciousness" begins with the Eichmann trial in 1961, followed by the sense of abandonment by the world of Israel prior to the June, 1967 war, a sense repeated even more intensely before and in the first week in particular of the Yom Kippur war of October, 1973, and culminates with the emergence, during the Carter administration, of a plan to build a Holocaust Memorial or Museum in 1977 (which, in the end, became both).

10. For more on Cahana, see *From Ashes to the Rainbow: A Tribute to Raoul Wallenberg, Works by Alice Lok Cahana* (catalogue of the exhibition of that name curated by Barbara Gilbert at Hebrew Union College Skirball Museum, Los Angeles, CA,1986).

11. For more on Michael Katz' "Luggage People" see Soltes, *The Contents of History: Works by Janis Goodman and Michael Katz* (exhibition catalogue at the B'nai B'rith Klutznick National Jewish Museum, 1995) pp. 2–15.

12. For more analysis of the *Holocaust Project*, see Soltes, *The Ashen Rainbow: The Arts and the Holocaust.* (2007). The project itself was reproduced in book form—the quotes from Judy Chicago come from that source—as *Holocaust Project: From Darkness into Light* (New York, 1993).

13. For more on Cypis and on Dermansky and Steinboeck see Soltes, *Edge*, pp. 80–81.

14. For more on Waldman's works see Soltes *Fixing the World*, pp. 107–108 and Soltes, "From Here to There: Eight Jewish Artists from the Pacific Northwest" (exhibition essay from the B'nai B'rith Klutznick National Jewish Museum, Washington, D.C., 1995).

15. See further discussion of this in Soltes, *Fixing the World*, pp. 61–70 and footnotes Part II, ms. #7–10.

16. See Gen 1:3–4: "And God said 'Let there be light' and there was light. And God saw the light, that it was good; and God divided the light from the darkness . . ." Note both that the pre-light state of things is *tohu vavohu* which translates "unshaped, empty *isness*" and that the word "chaos" (*khaos*) as it is used in Hesiod's Greek creation text probably derives from *khasko/khaino/khasmao/khasmaomai*, different forms of a verb meaning "to gape/yawn," and thus refers also to a yawning empty *no-thing-ness*.

17. See, for example, Barbara Rose, *American Art Since 1900: A Critical History.* (New York, 1973), chapters 6–8; and Dore Ashton, *The New York School: A Cultural Reckoning.* (New York: Penguin Books, 1979) especially chapters 9–11; on the Americanism of the Abstract Expressionists in general. But neither of these extremely insightful works recognizes the "Jewish content" in the Chromaticists for which I have been arguing since 1983.

18. See for example Stuart Preston, "Sculpture and Paint," *The New York Times*, 26 April 1959, p. X17.

19. I find it difficult to imagine that, were Louis a Catholic, the same critics who are blind to or deny any Jewish influence in his work would not jump to see the influence of his Catholic upbringing in his "mystical" abstractions.

20. Not incidentally, perhaps, the lone Jew among the founding fathers of Impressionism. In his letters to his son Lucien, Pissarro talked of the obligation of artists like them to share with the world at large the improved results such as advances in optics were giving to their art. Camille Pissarro, *Lettres a son Fils Lucien*, ed. John Rewald (Paris, 1980).

21. Quoted in Soltes, *Everyman A Hero: The Saving of Bulgarian Jewry/Susan Schwalb: The Creation Series* (exhibition catalogue at the B'nai B'rith Klutznick National Jewish Museum, Washington, D.C., 1993).

22. While all three Abrahamic faiths traditionally look unhappily at Eve and her guiding Adam to eat of the forbidden fruit, Christianity alone articulates this as *The Original Sin*—so egregious that only a unique act of Divine intervention can assuage it. Both Islam and Judaism place more emphasis on human action with regard to post-mortem rewards and punishments. Islam is closer to Christianity than Judaism in its view.

23. Rothfarb is quoted from her artist's statement in Soltes, *Edge*, pp. 76–77.

24. Laurence's background offers yet another twist to the issue of Jewish identity. He grew up virtually commanded by his father—who had, as Laurence's mother had, escaped the Holocaust with deep scars—to forget that he was Jewish. ". . . whilst constantly lecturing [me] from the age of four about the horrors of what he and others went through, [he] was vehemently anti-Semitic and refused to answer the obvious questions that occurred to me about his background . . . I was told not to emulate 'Jewish' traits. My father even went so far as to banish garlic from the kitchen because he said it 'smelled of ghetto cookery.'" (This from his artist's statement for *Edge*, pp. 78–79). Laurence's address of Jewish subjects reflects a rebellion against the identity strictures under which he, albeit male, grew up with regard to participation in any aspects of Jewish life. For more on Laurence, see also Soltes, *Fixing the World*, 123–5 and Soltes, *Ashen Rainbow*, pp. 162–163.

25. The quote is from a letter from Barsha to the author in 1997.

26. Rand is quoted in Zelda Shluker, "Too Jewish to be Hip?" *Hadassah Magazine*, vol. 79, no. 12 (1996).

27. Because the numerical value of the two letters that comprise the Hebrew word for "life" is eighteen.

28. The quotations are all from a letter to the author from Archie Rand (April 3, 2003), although the order of his comments has been re-arranged to allow the sequence of ideas to come through in spite of the imposed lacunae. One of the issues raised by Rand was the *pleasantly surprising* fact that the (Jewish) owner of a large commercial gallery (The Bernice Steinbaum Gallery) proposed to the artist that he do "a full-blown Jewish show at her Miami exhibition space." So there may be progress here and there not only where Jewish self-conception and art might coincide for artists but for those who promote and discuss their work.

29. Lipnick's comment came in a conversation with the author in 1996. His repeating symbols—images adorning his various work—include Elijahs' goblets and chairs, doves of peace, Egyptian pyramids, ancient Israelite pottery and a small white house with red roof that represents the Midwestern home in which he grew up, among others.

30. For more on Tobi Kahn, see the catalogue of the exhibition curated by Peter Selz, *Tobi Kahn: Metamorphoses* (Lee, MA., 1997) where this statement is quoted, and the catalogue of the exhibition curated by Mark Andrew White, *Tobi Kahn: Correspondence*, (Wichita, 2001).

31. From the artist's statement in Soltes, *Edge*, pp. 66–67.

32. These images and further discussion may be found in Soltes, *Edge*, p. 7.

33. From the artist's statement in Soltes, *Edge*, p. 72.

34. This is the year in which Stalin decreed that the only acceptable form of visual self-expression in the Soviet Union would henceforth be Soviet Socialist Realist art.

35. This statement was made to the author by Vitaly Komar, in late 1999, when discussing the *Edge* exhibition.

36. For more detail on this project see Soltes, "Komar and Melamid, Jewish Questions and Art," in *Komar and Melamid: Symbols of the Big Bang* (exhibition catalogue at Yeshiva University Museum, 2002). The catalogue also contains an excellent short piece by Anthony Julius and an interview with Komar. As of this writing, with the completion of this series of four paintings and scores of drawings,

and after decades of collaborative work, the two artists have decided to go their separate artistic ways.

37. See Judith Neulander, "The Ecumenical Esther: Queen and Saint in Three Western Belief Systems," in *Esther through the Ages* eds., S.W. Crawford and L.J. Greenspoon (Sheffield, 2004).

38. From Herz' artist's statement for and quoted in Soltes, *Edge*, p. 73.

39. From Wardlaw's artist's statement for and quoted in Soltes, *Edge*, pp. 73–74.

40. Alternate versions offer the simple and pious man explaining to the *rebbe* what his methodology of praying is or the *rebbe* reassuring the simple and pious man that, if he continues to recite the Hebrew alphabet with strong and pure intention, God will know how to formulate the letters into prayers. A third version offers the simple and pious man explaining to the great mystic and scholar, Isaac Luria, that this is how he prays, when Luria asks how and why his prayers are so effective.

41. For more on Alexenberg see Soltes, *Tradition and Transformation: A History of Jewish Art and Architecture* (Video series; Cleveland, OH: Electric Shadows Corp, 1984–90), segment 13b; Soltes, *Mosaic*, (exhibition catalogue at the B'nai B'rith Klutznick National Jewish Museum, Washington, D.C., 1994) p. 4; and Soltes, *Fixing the World*, pp. 131–132.

42. In personal communication to the author, in which she refused to allow her work to be shown in *Fixing the World*, since she did not want to be labeled a Jewish American painter.

21

Studies in Hysteria, or Jewish Comedy from Shtetlakh to Shticklakh

Mark Shechner

AUTHOR'S NOTE

This essay was originally written for oral presentation, to be accompanied by excerpts of recorded song and video. The video portions can't be reproduced at all, and while some spoken routines and song lyrics have been transcribed here, they can't even begin to suggest the furor and comic vitality of the songs as actually sung. At the end of the paper I'll append a discography for those readers who wish to track down this music and comedy for themselves.

–M.S.

The subject of this talk, Jewish comedy, is so vast that nothing less than an Encyclopedia Judeo-Comica will suffice to cover it, and so I think it best to ease my way into the labyrinth by saying a few words about myself and how I became interested in Jewish comedy to begin with. It was the late 1950s. I was in college and living with a group of other young men around my age in Berkeley California. To be explicit, we were in a Jewish fraternity and these were my fraternity brothers, my fraters. (Why fraters? Why not chaverim? Well, chaverim was not then an option, and our charter existed within the Greek system. But I will tell you that that was as close as I will ever come to kibbutz life, and I didn't have to clear the desert or kill a single chicken.) We were all of about the same generation. Our parents were almost all American born, many of our grandparents, maybe most, were from the Old Country, which means that we grew up hearing some Yiddish. We were all Bar Mitzvahed and could pass the physical: we tested positive for

Jewishness. As for Yiddish, some might have spoken it—I can't say—but we all spoke a language that was English in syntax and vocabulary but had been rubbed with a Yiddish garlic that had been handed down to us with the stewed chickens and rock hard knishes of our childhoods. Yiddish was so much the undertone of our English: its lilt and cadence, its chutzpah and complaint. The language we spoke could be called irony. We spoke irony to each other, day and night. You've seen the movie *Animal House*? This was the Jewish version of it: *Irony House*. I've never been around so many funny people at one time in my life. *Saturday Night Live* was *Sesame Street* compared to this group. It started as Monday Morning Live and ran 24/7. I single out this moment, not because it was the first time I ever experienced comedy, but the first time that I understood it to be something larger than what I heard on radio or saw on TV. It came into view rather as a kind of inherited behavior that was as natural to us as flying south in the winter is to geese.

This was the late 1950s in the San Francisco Bay area, and while hippies did not officially exist for another decade, there were beatniks everywhere, and some of the fraters were themselves from San Francisco, where they absorbed beat culture just by going out for a bagel. Literally. Was not one of the great hangouts on upper Grant Avenue in San Francisco's North Beach named the Coexistence Bagel Shop? (I've sometimes wondered if there was an actual owner named Max Coexistence? I mean, might that not be a reasonable translation of "shalom"?) I may have been a college fraternity boy, but I had fraters who grew beards, wore berets, played bongos, smoked weed, and listened to Charlie Parker and Thelonious Monk records deep into the night. Boys though we were, we were calling each other "man." Some Jews recite the Shema; these Jews said "Bird Lives." Allen Ginsberg sound-alikes and sometimes look-alikes, they were the best minds of my generation; they were my chaverim of Birdland.

Comedy was normal to our culture. In the late 1950s the clubs around the Bay area became home to a particular breed of comics whose sensibilities were keyed to jazz and bebop. Lenny Bruce was the most famous, but there were also Mort Sahl and Shelley Berman, and satire was rampant on the radio with the likes of Stan Freberg doing send-ups of popular tunes and Tom Lehrer singing songs about Poisoning Pigeons in the Park and Wernher Von Braun. ("Once the rockets are up, who cares where they come down? That's not my department," says Wernher Von Braun.)

A friend came into my room one night with a record titled *Interviews of Our Time* and played for me comedy monologues and dialogues that were unlike anything else I had heard before: a prison movie parody titled "Father Flotsky's Triumph," another about religion as big business titled "Religions Incorporated," and an interview with one Shorty Petterstein, a jazz musician. This was nothing like what I had been seeing on television.

It is impossible to capture the full flavor of this in print, the credulous inter-rogator trying to get radio chat out of the stoned and distracted musician, but a portion of it went like this.

> "Ladies and Gentlemen, we'd like you to meet Shorty Petterstein, who is one of the up and coming jazz, uh, French trump- trumpeters, do they call 'em Oscar?"
>
> "No, man, I blow, um, French horn, man. I blow French horn, man."
>
> "Would you get a little, just a, a little closer to the microphone?"
>
> "French horn man."
>
> "A little closer, Osc."
>
> "Uh, huh. French horn, man."
>
> "French horn. And what do they call you, a French hornist?"
>
> "Like, you know, I blow horn, man."
>
> "Would you speak up a little bit Osc?"
>
> "I blow horn, man."
>
> Asked how he would compare his kind of music with art, he answers, "Art blows the most."[1]

The album was by Lenny Bruce, a Jewish hipster whose mother was a nightclub stripper and who was himself a heroin addict. To us this comedy was fresh, hilarious, and very very hip, and it spoke to us through synapses we didn't even know we had. It was a new world just opening up for me, for all of us, and my fraters and I spent hours together improvising our own inner Shorty Pettersteins and interviewing each other.

It was also the first and last time I ever envisioned for myself a possible career as a comic. I'm sure you've all had the experience of being funnier while in the company of funny people and then having your timing and inventiveness dry up once you've left that company. I've been in academic life now for some forty years as a grad student and a professor, and while that can sharpen your sense of the absurd, you can well imagine the havoc it plays with your imagination, your boldness, and your delivery. I used to do routines; now I just do conferences. That is, if I'm lucky. Mainly I do memos.

Forgive this personal detour, but I want at the start to place myself in relation to the comedy I'll be talking about and the people with whom I first encountered it as an attitude, a perception, a vision of life itself. I'll be talking about performances, but comedy is no more a creation of the stage or record studio than singing is: it is first and foremost an ancient form of global positioning satellite, a way of locating yourself in the world, or maybe taking advantage of a place that's already been assigned to you. The great comedians, I came to understand, were us, only smarter, faster, crazier, and more desperate, but us all the same. The brother of one of my friends actually had a successful stage and screen career, some of it in comedy, and while I was envious of that career, I was not surprised. I'd have been surprised had he become a streets and sanitation worker. Comedy is what you made with that particular underdog's anxiety and shrewdness about the world. You performed, but the performance was something that welled up in you, unbidden and urgent: a return of the repressed, if you like, from a collective unconscious. What the great Jewish comics of the mid 20th century—the Sid Caesars, the Marx Brothers, the Woody Allens, the Jackie Masons, the Henny Youngmans, the Milton Berles[2]—were doing on stage or film was being themselves just as surely as the Italian crooners of the day—the Frank Sinatras, Perry Comos, Dean Martins, Vic Damones, Frankie Laines—were being themselves. Just as "That's Amore" was as Italian as pasta e fagioli, "Duck Soup" was as Jewish as matzo brei. It was applied Yiddishkeit, actually, because despite its being English, Yiddish was so clearly the language that held the copyrights on it. No Italian, no Dean Martin. No Yiddish, no Groucho Marx.

It is not that Yiddish is in itself a comic language any more than English is, but for reasons that were built into the life of Jewish diaspora culture in Europe, it gave itself to comic use, and the Jewish comics pressed it into service as the language of parodies and punch lines. I'll get back to this in a bit, but just now let me step back in time from the Beat era to the Borscht years and do a couple of splendid little Yiddish-English routines for you. One is the famous Barton Brothers mock advertisement for Joe and Paul's clothing store on Yiddish radio in the 1949. With the rollicking Klezmer background and the nasal voices that belonged to nobody on earth save the children of Yiddish speaking Jews, the Barton Brothers keened and mugged their way through a parody of a real clothing store commercial that appeared regularly on radio station WEBD. It began with a quick froelich overture that slows to a world-weary niggun of lamentation: "Yoi boi yubba boi Yubba boi boi o-boi, WBVD, Hey! Ba-ba-re-bop. Yoi boi yubba boi Yubba boi boi a-boi, WBVD, oi send me sister. Yoi boi yubba bubba bubba boi, yoi boi yubba bubba bubba boi, every Sunday morning over WBVD." (That hey ba-ba-re-bop was a nice witty wink at xylophone master Lionel Hampton.) Then racing ahead on the wings of a syncopated klezmer beat:

> *Joe un Paul s'a fargenign*
> *Joe un Paul's, men ken a bargn krign.*
> *A sut, a koyt, a gabardine.*
> *Brengt arayn dayn klaynem zin.*
> *[Spoken] Cut, speech [and then a pitchman's huckstering voice]*
> *A gite fri morgn aykh, mayne libe radio tsuherers.*
> *Mir brengn yetsts a program fun Joe un Paul's vos hobn dray stores.*
> *Der ersther stor is located in Stanton and Delancey in donton Manhatan.*
> *Di tsvayte stor is located in Hunts Poynt, Sudern Bulevard in der Bronx.*
> *Un der driter stor is lokated in Pitkin Avenyu, Brwonsvil, Bruklin.*[3]

The casual play of two fraternal languages (Yiddish and English both being Germanic languages), the supersonic patter, the irreverent sex (see the complete text in the footnotes), the sheer exuberant merriment of it makes "Joe un Paul" available even to those whose Yiddish is shaky.

And so long as we are speaking of Yiddish and parody, this is a good moment to bring in that most popular of the modern Yiddish, or Yinglish, parodists who worked right up through the 1960s, Mickey Katz, a clarinetist whose trademark was to take a popular American tune and pickle it in a brine of Yiddish until it came out as steamed brisket of its former self. To be sure, Katz first learned his chops playing with Spike Jones, the musical farce-meister of the 1940s, but when he left Spike Jones to create his own musical hit parade ("hit" here as in whack), Katz had a secret weapon that was unavailable to Jones: Borsht Belt slapstick. Here is one of my very favorites among his parodies, "Geshray Fun Der Vilde Katchke," his send-up of Frankie Laine's stirring 1950s homage to seasonal waterfowl migration, "Cry of the Wild Goose." (Katchke is Yiddish for duck or goose.) To the racing beat of the klezmer sound and the honking of a hunter's duck call, Katz sings:

> *Ikh vil geyn vu di katchke geyt*
> *Un I wanna dray vi a katchke drayt*
> *Vayld goose brekh a fus*
> *Geshtopte haldz*
> *A maykhl in baykhl*
> *[untranslated] in shmaltz*
> *Yesterday I went to the butcher shop*
> *To buy two chicken and a couple of chops*
> *The butcher said that "We got katchke today,"*
> *Di katchke huyd im and he gave a geshray.*
>
> *I wanna go where di vilde goose goes*
> *'Cause I know more than di vilde goose knows,*
> *Mayn kop tsekvetcht un mayn pipek tsedrikt.*
> *It won't be long I'll be opgeflikt.*
>
> *The butcher said that it weighed ten pounds*
> *Oy, it's a beautiful katchke lady a magnificent gans*
> *Six dollars a metsiya*
> *Lady you'll buy it*
> *Di katchke cried "rakhmones" I dunwan a levaye.*[4]

Other songs in the Katz songbook included "Noshville Katz," "Comin' Round the Katzkills," "Borscht Riders In The Sky" ("An old cowpunch went out to lunch beyond the pearly gates"), and "Herring Boats," a spoof of Teresa Brewer's "Shrimp Boats." To remember the lame originals is to understand what sitting katchkes they were for Yiddish parody. Didn't the

American payola boat have it coming? Parody is an art that reveals the true state of affairs; what could you do about the American hit parade of the 1950s but laugh it off? Anyone remember Stan Freberg's rendition of Harry Belafonte's Day-O?[5]

I've only quoted Lenny Bruce, the Barton Brothers, and Mickey Katz—a mismatched trio if ever there was one—but it is plain what their routines have in common. They are burlesques, parodies, comic demolitions of something that could be made to sound ridiculous, whether it was so or not. And parody is what we practiced in Irony House. Had they known how their tuition was being used, our mothers might have marched up University Avenue en masse with cooking spoons raised high and ordered us back to our homework. But interviewing each other deep into the night using anything for a microphone: a fork, a shoe, a slide rule, a rolled up term paper, was also our inheritance from them. Comedy was in our blood like a mutant gene, and it was the likes of Freberg, Bruce, Sahl, Berman, Lehrer, along with so many others, that was setting that blood on high boil.

And besides, once I got the idea that parody and send-up were what the great comics did because it was bred in the bone, I began to find it all around me: it had always been there, and we had been taking it in with bubba's horse radish. Jews engaged in parody because, well, it is what they did—what we did. We couldn't help it. The American contribution to that comedy may have been the show business career, but what we brought to the stage was very Old World.

Of course, in starting as I have with my two years in Irony House, I've done an end run around past some earlier and wonderful years of the parodist's art. In my childhood, the king of send-up was Sid Caesar, who brought the art of burlesque to heights it had scarcely known before and, at least on television, has hardly known since. *Your Show of Shows* went on the air in 1950 and was immediately a great hit due to Caesar's genius and the great staff of writers and comics he assembled around him: Mel Tolkin, Woody Allen, Mel Brooks, Carl Reiner, Howard Morris, Imogene Coca, and Neil Simon. The interview was a staple of his performance, and some of his most brilliant routines were the interviews he gave to Reiner as a shabby European professor just off the plane: Professor Sigmund von Sedative, the great expert on sleep, Professor Hokus von Pokus, the magician, and Ludwig von Fossil, archaeology professor. But many of Caesar's most inspired skits were beyond prose transcription: they were either pantomimes he performed with Imogene Coca or Nanette Fabray or withering doubletalk spoofs in mock German or French or Italian with Reiner, who proved to be as gifted a shpritz artist as Caesar himself. I have seen few things in my life more comically ingenious than a parody done by Caesar, Reiner and Coca of Vittorio De Sica's film "The Bicycle Thief." Since none of it can be reproduced in prose, all I can do is urge readers of this essay to spend the money to buy one or more of the available DVD's that have been made of *Your Show of Shows* and discover this virtuosity for themselves.[6] They could make any language sound as glib as Delancey Street haggling, though to the best of my knowledge they never did Yiddish routines as such. It was Italian, French, and German accelerated into Yiddish overdrive that they pioneered: the result was hilarious no matter what was said.

The question I was asked to address in this essay is "What is so special and different about Jewish comedy in America that distinguishes it from Jewish comedy in the Old World?" How are the great Jewish comics of America different from their counterparts in Poland, Galicia, the Pale of Settlement? You can bet that there were as many comedians in the old Pogrom Belt, that stretched from the Black Sea to the Baltic and from Poland to the Pale of Settlement, as ever there were in the Borscht Belt of upstate New York. But getting at their comedy is difficult now since so much of it was spontaneous performance that left no documents behind. You can't go to YIVO and look it up.

We can be fairly certain that Jews did not become suddenly funny at Ellis Island. "Your name from now on is Goldstein, and you are free to knock 'em dead." Jews were knockin' 'em dead right along in Minsk and Pinsk and Łodz and a thousand tragic little shtetlakh where they were as riotously funny as they were pitifully poor. Didn't Minsk have its Dovid Rickelsman, with more insults than a katchke has feathers? Didn't Pinsk have a Jacob Maza (Jackie Mason), reeling off jokes in an accent so thick that even the Pinskers could scarcely understand him? Didn't Odessa give rise to a hundred Sid Caesars doing boffo Ukrainian, Russian, and German doubletalk? Sending up Dr. Casmir von Cossack? Dr. Kishmir von Tukhas? Didn't a ghetto full of Grouchos roll their eyes and their cigars and crack one-liners faster than most of us can say "duck soup"? Of course they did. As surely as every teppel (pot) had its hen, every family had its Henny. Art critic Harold Rosenberg once said of the Jews that throughout our history we specialized in the mass production of intellectuals. But why not also the mass production of wits, kibitzers, punsters, tummlers, mimics, wedding jesters, fools, and story tellers beyond number?

When Sigmund Freud wrote his famous book *Jokes and Their Relation to the Unconscious,* who was he was talking about? The stony-faced burghers of Vienna, with their stiff collars and icy manners? I don't think so. He was talking about his patients. They cracked him up with their insane dreams and infantile demands and secret repressions. And their grievances. It had to be a riot listening to them. "Let me tell you this one about that momser my father, the *farbissiner paskudyak* (bitter schmuck), leeches should drink him dry. *Zol er krenken un gedenken* (Let him get sick and remember). Let me tell you about my Cousin Emma and her nasal reflex neurosis. Her nose is driving her nuts." Kvetch, kvetch, kvetch. Joke, joke, joke. Jackie Mason said of Jewish theater-goers, "They can't even enjoy a show if it's good. If it's good it leaves them with nothing to talk about. A Jew could never enjoy a show if it's good. They can only enjoy a show if it stinks. If it stinks are they happy. You know who stunk yesterday, boy, did he stink. You think he stunk, I saw a show that really stunk, boy. They see four shows that stunk, they walk out happy, they stunk, they all stunk. You walked out, I didn't even walk in."[7] Where do you think they learned that? At mamele's knee, where else? You think Freud didn't stifle a laugh at the hearty kvetching? "Papa, that shmendrick, that shtick drek, boy did he stink. Mamele? That kurve, she stunk too, but she was some dish. And the things papa did to her, don't ask. Every Shabbes by us was a primal scene, believe me. *Ich hub 'im in drerd* (I'll see him in the grave). All his teeth should fall out except one to make him suffer." It's what kept Freud going back to the office every day. The jokes, they founded an entire psychoanalytic empire that persists to this day. Before the Ritz Brothers, Al, Jimmy, and Harry, the Three Stooges, Curly, Larry, and Moe, or the Marx Brothers, Groucho, Chico, and Harpo, there were the Unconscious Brothers: Rat Man, Wolf Man, and Schreber. Freud must have run right over to Otto Rank's house to tell him the latest. (Jung he didn't tell. He had no sense of humor.) What did he tell Rank? What else? "My patients are completely meshugah." Only he probably said "hysterisch," hysterical. Here's a joke about Jewish mothers told by Henny Youngman at the usual warp speed. "Miami Beach, the little Jewish grand-mother is supposed to take care of the Jewish grandson by the water. She turns her head away. A wave washes the kid way out. They call the lifeguard, the helicopter, the police. They finally grab the little kid; they bring him in. They pump him out for an hour. The kid starts to breathe again. The grandmother says, 'He had a hat.'"[8]

And the patients, didn't they have stories of their own to tell about crazy Professor Sigmund von Meshuganeh, that alter kokher with his stale breath and farshtunkener cigar and his oral this and anal that? Didn't it all sound like Professor von Sedative to them? In 1895 Freud published his famous early book *Studies in Hysteria*, prophetically predicting the Marx brothers three decades later and Sid Caesar and Milton Berle two decades after that. Woody Allen, anyone? Hysteria was their calling card, and they didn't need to be cured of it. (Hysteria, the story goes, was so named by Hippocrates in 400 B.C. When unsatisfied with the body's desire to have children, the womb wandered through it like a restless animal.) Some of them indeed did give a backhand thanks to their analysts who had given them finally permission to be themselves. But then, to be yourself, how simple was that? As Jackie Mason tells us. "The great trick is to know who you are. Most people don't know. Thanks God I know. I didn't always know. I'm not ashamed to admit it. There was a time I didn't know who I was. I went to a psychiatrist. I did. He took a look at me. Right away he said this is not you.

I said this is not me then who is it? He said I don't know either. I said then what do I need you for? He said to find out who you are. He said together we're going to look for the real you. I said if I don't know who I am then how do I know who to look for? And even if I find me, how do I know if its me? Besides, if I want to find me why do I need him? I can look myself. Or I can take my friends. I know where I was. . . ."[9]

Could Philip Roth have written *Portnoy's Complaint* without the weekly challenge of eliciting a smile from the stone-faced Spielvogel with tales of the family that had to sound more or less like a Jackie Mason monologue? I doubt it. These comedians may have all undergone analysis at one time or another—it is certainly one way of unearthing the material of no respect they shared in common—but on stage they turn the audience into their therapists and come to us for treatment. And we pay them to listen in on their tsuris, their wandering uteruses or wandering spirits or minds. They confess to us and suddenly we all feel better. We give front row absolution.

And now, back to the Old World. What we know about comedy there is more by inference than evidence. After all, it was an oral tradition. We know for certain that it existed and was as widespread as poverty. And we know that our grandparents and great grandparents never unveiled their talents or performed their comedy for anyone but each other. The Poles, the Russians, the Ukrainians, the Czechs, the Germans undoubtedly suspected that these crafty, secretive Jews behind their beards and caftans and low mutterings were poking fun at them behind their backs—and they were right—but it was always in Yiddish and it wasn't on stage or radio or TV. It was all a private vaudevillsky. Before television, before e-mail, before the weblog, the peddlers carried comedy around in their heads from town to town. Every day was Purim. Joking in Yiddish was the Purim Shpiel of daily existence, the great Yiddish oral counter torah. And let's not forget the badkhen himself, the wedding jester, whose job it was to make jokes at the expense of everyone at a wedding party. Being anti-social was part of the social ritual. Aren't Jackie Mason, Jack E. Leonard, and Don Rickles our own cherished badkhenim of Shtickland, our Gaons of Vegas?

The comedy too had extra dimensions. I don't want to get too trendy here by trying to bring Jewish comedy, send-up, and burlesque in under the gigantic tent of midrash, but what the hell. I mean, wasn't it? Isn't comedy finally commentary? Comedy may be the property of all cultures but didn't we have a flying start at it by being born to commentary? Where is it written that commentary should be conducted without mirth? Wasn't it midrash by other means? Midrash for the masses? Listen to Jackie Mason sometime and listen closely to the accent and the rhythm, not to mention the tormented logic. A rabbi's son and himself a rabbi for a portion of his life, Mason does routines that verge on what shtetl comedy must have sounded like: Talmudic disputation—pilpul—in a minor key. Here is how Mason's routine about the psychoanalyst and "finding his real self" continues.

"I can take my friends; we know where I was; and besides, what if I find the real me and I find that he's worse than me. Why do I need him? I don't make enough for myself, why do I need a partner? Ten years ago I'd have been happy to look for anybody. Now I'm doing good; why should I look for him? If he needs help, let him look for me.

He said, The search for the real you will have to continue. That will be one hundred dollars.

I said to myself, If this is not the real me, why should I give him the hundred dollars. I'll look for the real me, let him give him the hundred dollars. What if I find the real me and he doesn't think it's worth a hundred dollars. For all I know, the real me might be going to a different psychiatrist altogether. He might even be a psychiatrist himself.

I said, Wouldn't it be funny if you were the real me and you owe me a hundred dollars? I said, I'll tell you what. I'll charge you fifty dollars, we'll call it even."

What is Mason here but comedy's own "ba'al pilpul" or master of ingenious disputation? Mason comes later in the line of American Jewish comics, and yet there is something in his delivery that takes us farther into Eastern Europe and to the very deep roots of Jewish comedy.

Here is something that Saul Bellow and Isaac Rosenfeld wrote as a lark in Yiddish in the 1940s that has stayed with me as an instance of the comic impulse of a very high order. You'll recognize this right away.

> *Nu-zhe, kum-zhe, ikh un du*
> *Ven der ovnt shteyt unter dem himl*
> *Vi a leymener goylem af tishebov.*
> *Lomir geyn gikh, durkh geselekh vos dreyen zikh*
> *Vi di bord bay dem rov.*
> *Oyf der vant*
> *fun dem kosheren restorant*
> *Hengt a shmutsiker betgevant*
> *Un vantsn tantsn karahod. Es geht a geroykh*
> *fun gefilte fish un nase zokn.*
> *Oy, Bashe, freg nit keyn kashe, a dayge dir!*
> *Lomir oyfenen di tir.*
> *In tsimer vu di vayber zenen*
> *Redt men fun Karl Marx un Lenin.*
> *Ikh ver alt, ikh ver alt*
> *Un der pupik vert mir kalt.*
> *Zol ikh oyskemen di hor,*
> *Meg ikh oyfesen a flom?*
> *Ikh vel onton vayse hoysn*
> *Un shpatsirn by dem yom.*

Ikh vel hern di yom-moyden zingen khad gadyo.
Ikh vel zey entfern, Borekh-abo.

Roughly translated, the parody sounds something like this:

Nu, let us go, you and I,
When the evening stands beneath the sky
Like a lame golem on Tisha b'av.
Let us go, through streets that twist themselves
Like the rabbi's beard.
On the window
Of the kosher restaurant,
Hangs a dirty bedbug
And bedbugs dance in circles. There is a stink
Of gefilte fish and wet socks.
Oy, Bashe, don't ask questions, why bother?
Let me open the door.
In the room where the women walk
They speak of Karl Marx and Lenin.
I grow old, I grow old,
And my navel grows cold.
Shall I comb out my hair,
May I eat a prune?
I shall put on white pants
And walk by the sea.
I shall hear the sea-maidens sing Chad Gadya.
I shall answer them: "Baruch Abba."

You needn't know much Yiddish to know that this is a send-up or a take-down of T.S. Eliot's "The Love Song of J. Alfred Prufrock" and it is T.S. Eliot's nerves that have been projected on a Yiddish screen. After "Ich ver alt, ich ver alt, un der pupik vert me kalt," what is left of poor J. Alfred but a pair of rolled trousers? I don't have to tell you that this little bit of parody is midrash of a very high order; Eliot isn't just being burlesqued but also being translated and critiqued. Yiddish overdrive has driven Poor Eliot right down a wormhole into the borscht dimension. And because it is a bit of private fun, it also gives us a look behind the scenes at what naturally went on in the Old World and the New whenever kibitzers got together and felt playful: there goes Eliot, there goes Italian opera or modern Italian film, French new wave cinema, German U-boat movies, psychoanalysis, prison movies, anything at all with the slightest pretension to high culture and high art. Sure it's shtick, but it reveals something of the high modernist vamping of J. Alfred himself: the wasteland blues that singles him out as yet another of modernism's pale neurasthenics.

But seriously folks, I can't imagine a transliteration of Eliot in French or German capable of this kind of comic domestication. A bedbug hanging

in the boulangerie? The rathskeller? French and German are elevating languages and are just not geared for the crisp deflation of "Ikh ver alt, ikh ver
alt, un der pupik vert mir kalt." Yiddish evolved in the Old Country without
a pressing need for a vocabulary of idealization. Hebrew and Aramaic fairly
monopolized the task of providing the Jews with idealizing and spiritual-
izing concepts and thereby of satisfying the portions of Jewish culture that
traded in ennoblement—in *Edelkeit*. The Yiddish Jew is the historical Jew;
the Hebrew Jew the transhistorical, the transcendent Jew. With the Hebrew
and Aramaic dominion over higher worlds established, Yiddish was free to
evolve as a language of the household and the street, remarkably free from
high purpose and platitude. It specialized in a de-elevation that, for want of
better terms, we sometimes call vulgarity but is something very different. It
is, to take a phrase from Saul Bellow's *Herzog, transcendence downward*: the
ennoblement of the ordinary.

Another of the wonderful interviews on the first Lenny Bruce album was
with one Dr. Sholem Stein, a "well-known Hebrew scholar from the City
College of New York" and an expert on the origins of calypso. (Bruce was
not actually on this track: the interview was conducted by Henry Jacobs
with Woodrow Leafer as Sholem Stein.) Asked if there had once been a
significant Hebraic influence in that music of the West Indies, Dr. Stein
replies, "That's very true Mr. Jacobs. You know, uh, the, uh, story of the
wandering Jew, and we find the Hebraic characters of world history scat-
tered all over even in such far away places, as in Nassau and the Bahamas.
. . ." Commenting on a calypso song about tomatoes and bananas, he in-
forms us confidently that tomatoes and plantains represent "the cosmos."
Asked about the situation in Palestine, he responds, "The general picture
in Palestine is very menacing. It is fraught with great danger for the entire
world. Do you realize that Israel is the pivot point of the Near East, and if
that falls, the British Empire, the Suez Canal, consequently the Panama Canal, in fact all canals, uh, international trade will be effected, and the British
pound sterling will go down, that will bring the value of gold up, and the
ratio will be thrown off balance to create reflections even in the ruble, the
yen." With calypso playing in the background Dr. Stein winds up pitching
his forthcoming book, *Bahama Mama*, his "penetrating analysis" of West
Indian music and the Mishnah. Roll over Belafonte, tell calypso the news.

Here is the essential point to be made. Irony and its attendant variants,
from satire to send-up to invective, was nothing less than a staple of Old
World Jewish life. There is no way to understand it in America unless it
came by boat from Galicia. It was the property of an entire community
that was required to live by perception and wit, by keen observation and
skilled mimicry. The Old World Jews had a national gift for parody and
ridicule; it grew out of necessity. The imitation of another's dialect may
have been shtick in America, but it was survival in Galicia. You needed

perfect pitch for accent, nuance, and inflection. It is not at all far-fetched to think that irony was nothing less than the secret language of the Jewish people, and though it was a secret held in common, nobody was in on the secret but themselves. What was secret in Poland was public in America: as Irving Howe put it, the ghetto became a stage. What does Woody Allen say of Groucho: "He reminded me of every uncle I knew at every bar mitzvah and wedding. He was the wise-cracking uncle. If you are going to do comedy, they were unsentimental, they were anarchic, they were original and surreal and hilarious." Who did you suppose Mel Brook's 2,000–year-old man was, after all? It was Uncle Abe, Uncle Ike, Uncle Jake. We are now celebrating 350 prosperous and secure years in America, but who can forget those 2000 miserable years on the road? The 2,000-year-old man— that's us

And speaking of two millennia on the road, one of my favorite bits is from an American novelist who learned his lines from the great comics so very well: Philip Roth. It is from a Roth story titled "On the Air" and is about the real 2000–year-old man, a small-time hustler and pitchman named Milton Lippman, whose voice keens with the desperate wisdom that comes of 2000 years working bum territories: Egypt, Spain, the Pale of Settlement, New Jersey. He is trying to package a radio program to be called "The Jewish Answer Man" and has it in mind that Albert Einstein would make a terrific answer man for the call-in show. So, of course, he writes to Einstein.

> Dear Mr. Einstein:
>   I can understand how busy you must be thinking, and appreciate that you did not answer my letter suggesting that I try to get you on a radio program that would make "The Answer Man" look like the joke it is. Will you reconsider, if the silence means no? I realize that one of the reasons you don't wear a tie or even bother to comb your hair is because you are as busy as you are, thinking new things. Well, don't think that you would have to change your ways once you become a radio personality. Your hair is a great gimmick, and I wouldn't change it for a second. It's a great trademark. Without disrespect, it sticks in your mind the way Harpo Marx's does. Which is excellent. (Now I wonder if you even have the time to know who The Marx Brothers are? They are four zany Jewish brothers, and you happen to look a little like one of them. You might get a kick out of catching one of their movies. Probably they don't even show movies in Princeton, but maybe you could get somebody to drive you out of town. You can get the entire plot in about a minute, but the resemblance between you and Harpo and his hair and yours, might reassure you that you are a fine personality in terms of show business just as you are.)[10]

When you are dealing with Roth, a writer as conscious of his tradition as he is skilled at it, you have an eerie sense of watching a performance of comedy that is also a commentary, a form of shtick that some of my colleagues at the university would be quick to call metashtick. Maybe it is, but then as Groucho Marx might say, I never met a shtick I didn't like.

Meanwhile, back to America, which, after all, enabled this transformation of irony from secret language to colossal industry, from the language of peddlers and pariahs to the routines of prime time and Broadway. It goes without saying that it was made possible by an environment of freedom and safety, where anti-Semitism had dwindled to a shell of its old self—where Americans put themselves on a low-pogrom diet and practiced anti-Semitism lite: "Feels great, less killing." Philip Roth's fearful vision of *The Plot Against America* notwithstanding, America had other minorities to persecute, and the Jews, kept out of the country clubs, founded an empire of their own on stage and screen, not to mention in American music. When the Jews entered show business, at first in the touring shows of vaudeville, they found a nation within a nation ready to absorb their talents and their neuroses and teach them the tools of the trade. Indeed, show business really proved to be a counterlife, as so much that was prohibited outside of it became mandatory inside. The great teachers were the likes of Charlie Chaplin, Buster Keaton, Stan Laurel and Oliver Hardy, the great farceurs, the native surrealists, the American shtickmeisters, and unlike the country clubs, the board rooms, and the English departments, vaudeville welcomed the Jews because showbiz was a republic unto itself with its own immigration laws: the only passport you needed was your talent. Think of vaudeville as the Ellis Island of entertainment, the gateway to the great Republic of Shtick, and it was this republic, not America as such, to which the Jewish comics assimilated. And particularly in the days when corking up in blackface was in vogue, who could make out the sharp Levantine profiles beneath the greasepaint? Weber and Fields, two Jews, were interchangeable with Abbott and Costello who were interchangeable with Gallagher and Shean. Jew, Irish, Italian, Yankee—what did it matter so long as you had a straight man? And what was America to them anyway?

Abel Meeropol, a Jewish schoolteacher from New York, who would be known to history as the man who adopted the sons of Julius and Ethel Rosenberg, had a second life as a song writer under the name of Lewis Allen. Under this nom de plume he is best known as the author of Billie Holiday's great song "Strange Fruit." But he also wrote a love song to America, "The House I Live In," that was sung by Frank Sinatra in a film short in 1945 and whose last line went, "And especially the people, that's America to me." But what was America to the comedians: especially the people or especially the paid clientele? As a comic you lived in New York or Hollywood, later in Las Vegas—the great cities of Shtickland. It was America yes, but an America of your own making where you could be perfectly at ease. There you were at home.

NOTES

This essay would not have been possible without lots of help. The book I've kept at my side throughout is Lawrence Epstein, *The Haunted Smile: The Story of Jewish Comedians in America* (New York: Public Affairs, 2001). Other excellent sources of information have been essays in the magazine *Judaism* by the late Irv Saposnik, one of the original scholars of Yiddish music and theater. See in particular his "'Joe and Paul' and other Yiddish-American Varieties," *Judaism*, Fall, 2000, and "Jolson, Judy, and Jewish Memory," *Judaism*, Fall 2001. Both are available on-line through the free magazine database *Findarticles* at http://www.findarticles.com.

I could not have managed this labor of transliterating and translating Yiddish songs without considerable help, and I want to thank in particular Professor Anita Norich of the University of Michigan. The work of rendering a fast-paced and street-vernacular Yiddish of sixty something years ago into prose is not simple, and I'm grateful to my colleague for her efforts.

1. The album *Interviews of Our Time* is currently available in CD form in *The Lenny Bruce Originals, Vol. 1* (Fantasy—FCD-60–023). The interview with Shorty Petterstein actually does not involve Lenny Bruce himself, but rather is an interview by Henry Jacobs with a faux hipster who is probably the disk jockey Woodrow (Woody) Leafer. But Bruce was the maestro of the entire record, and it has to be considered his particular brand of bop language that is being exposed.

2. The roll call of names from the golden era of comedy is virtually endless, but here is a representative list. Woody Allen (Alan Stewart Konigsberg), Morey Amsterdam, Roseanne Barr, Belle Barth, Jack Benny (Benjamin Kubelsky), Milton Berle (Milton Berlinger), Shelly Berman, Joey Bishop, David Brenner, Mel Brooks (Melvin Kaminsky), Lenny Bruce (Leonard Schneider), Fanny Brice, George Burns (Nathan Birnbaum), Red Buttons (Aaron Chwatt), Myron Cohen, Billy Crystal, Rodney Dangerfield (Jacob Cohen), Shecky Green, Buddy Hackett (Leonard Hacker), Goldie Hawn, Danny Kaye (David Daniel Kaminsky), Robert Klein, Paul Krassner (editor for years of the periodical of social satire *The Realist*), Jack E. Leonard (Leonard Lebitsky), Tom Lehrer, Sam Levenson, Jerry Lewis (Jerome Leivitch), the Marx Brothers, Jackie Mason (Yacov Moshe Maza), Bette Midler, Carl Reiner, the Ritz Brothers, Gilda Radner, Joan Rivers, Mort Sahl, Soupy Sales (Milton Supman), Jerry Seinfeld, Sophie Tucker, Gene Wilder (Jerome Silberman), and Henny Youngman. An encyclopedia entry could be composed out of names alone.

3. The entire "Joe un Paul," as nearly as they could get it goes as follows.
    Joe un Paul s'a fargenign
    Joe un Paul's, men ken a bargn krign.
    A sut, a koyt, a gabardine.
    Brengt arayn dayn klaynem zin.
    Cut, speech [and then a pitchman's huckstering voice]
    A gite fri morgn aykh, mayne libe radio tsuherers.
    Mir brengn yetsts a program fun Joe un Paul's vos hobn dray stores.
    Der ersther stor is located in Stanton and Delancey in donton Manhatan.
    Di tsvayte stor is located in Hunts Poynt, Sudern Bulevard in der Bronx.
    Un der driter stor is lokated in Pitkin Avenyu, Brwonsvil, Bruklin.

Hot ir a bar mitsve yingele vos darf hobn a slak-suit, a two-tone, a reversible slicker,
a herringbone, a djaket, a por hoyzn, a Miami charvette, a Bronx sharpie, a Bruklin
droop. Brengt im arayn tsi.
Joe un Paul s'a fargenign . . . .
Mames, hot ir a yungere boy in der heym, a yor fertsn, fuftsn yor alt, vos s'glaykht
im tsu zeyen a burlesk show. Er koyft shoyn French postel karts. Er kimt ahaym, gayt
arayn in der bat-rum, makht tsi di tir un makht awww, ahwww. Mames, tit mir a
toyve un git dem boy a por tuler un shikt im arayn tsu kokay-Djeni (Cockeyed Jenny).
Un a'tomer vayst ir nisht vi dos iz, iz fraygt ayer man. Er ken shoyn dos plats zeyer git.

The translation is as follows:

Joe and Paul's is a pleasure
Joe and Paul's, you can get a bargain:
A suit, a coat, a gabardine
Bring in your small son.
Good morning to you, my dear radio listeners.
We are now bringing you a program from Joe and Paul's who have three stores.
The first store is located in Stanton and Delancey in downtown Manhattan.
The second store is located in Hunts Pt., Southern Blvd, in the Bronx. And the
third store is located in Pitkin Ave., Brownsville, Brooklyn.
Do you have a bar mitzvah-age boy who needs a slack suit, a two-tone, a re-
versible slicker, a herringbone, a jacket, a pair of pants, a Miami charvette, a
Bronx sharpie, a Brooklyn droop. Bring him around.
Mothers, do you have a young boy at home, around 14–15 years old, who
likes to see burlesque. He's already buying French post cards. He comes home,
goes into the bathroom, closes the door, and goes ahwww, ahwww. Mothers,
do me a favor and give that boy a few dollars and send him to Cockeyed Jennie. And if you don't know where that is, then ask your husband. He knows
that place really well.

There are many sources for this popular routine, but one that puts it in the best
historical context is *Music From The Yiddish Radio Project*, Shanachie Records.

4. Mickey Katz's "Geshray Fun Der Vilde Katchke" goes something like this.

Ikh vil geyn vu di katchke geyt
Un I wanna dray vi a katchke drayt
Vayld goose brekh a fus
Geshtopte haldz
A maykhl in baykhl
[unknown word] in shmaltz
Yesterday I went to the butchershop
To buy two chicken and a couple of chops
The butcher said that "We got katchke today,"
Di katchke huyd im and he gave a geshray.
I wanna go where di vilde goose goes
'Cause I know more than di vilde goose knows,
Mayn kop tsekvetcht un mayn pipek tsedrikt.
It won't be long I'll be opgeflikt.
The butcher said that it weighed ten pounds
Oy, it's a beautiful katchke lady a magnificent gans

Six dollars a metsiya
Lady you'll buy it
Di katchke cried "rakhmones" I dunwan a levaye
Ikh muz geyn vu di vayld goose muz
Before der shoykhet khapt arup mayn noz
Vayl goos bruder goos [untranslated]
Bald I gonna lay vi a toyte katchke
Let me fly, let me fly, let me fly avek
Oy s'iz shoyn farfaln
It ain't no use
D'butcher er farkeyft mir
I'm a cooked goose
I've got to be brave
[unknown words]
Goodbye little chicken don't forget to say Kaddish
I can't go where the vilde goose goes
"Cause I must go where the schakhet goes
I'll be opgezalts, I'll be in a top.
A make oyfn butcher, zol im shtinkn fun kop.

A plausible translation might be this:

I want to go where the duck goes,
And I wanna spin/turn like a duck spins/turns.
Wild goose, break a leg
Stuffed throat,
A delicacy in your belly
And a [untranslated] in shmaltz
Yesterday I went to the butchershop
To buy to chicken and a couple of chops
The butcher said that "We got katchke (goose) today,"
The goose heard him and he gave out a cry.
I want to go where the wild goose goes,
'Cause I know more than a wild goose knows,
My head squeezed and my bellybutton turned around
It won't be long, I'll be de-feathered.
The butcher said that it weighed ten pounds
Oy, it's a beautiful goose lady a magnificent goose
Six dollars a bargain
Lady you'll buy it
The duck cried "have pity" I don't want a funeral.
I must go where the wild goose must
Before the butcher snatches off my nose.
Wild goose brother goose [untranslated]
Soon I'm gonna lay like a dead duck
Let me fly, let me fly, let me fly away
Oh, all is already lost
It ain't no use
The butcher is selling me

I'm a cooked goose
I've got to be brave
[untranslated]
Goodbye little chicken don't forget to say Kaddish
I can't go where the vilde goose goes
"Cause I must go where the schakhet (kosher butcher) goes
I'll be salted, I'll be in a pot.
A plague on the butcher, he should stink from his head.

5. Freberg's "Banana Boat Song" is available on many of his compilations, but see *Stan Freberg—Greatest Hits* [Curb Records].

6. There is so much Caesar now available on DVD to choose from that it is hard to go wrong, but the largest selection of routines from *Your Show of Shows* is *Sid Caesar Collection: Fan Favorites—3 Volume Gift Boxed Set* and *The Buried Treasures: The Lost Episodes from the Sid Caesar Collection*. These are most easily available at Amazon.com. See also his books: *Where Have I Been?: An Autobiography*. By Sid Caesar with Bill Davidson (New York: Crown Publishers, 1982), and *Caesar's Hours: My Life in Comedy, With Love and Laughter*, by Sid Caesar and Eddy Friedfeld (New York: Public Affairs, 2003).

7. For this and other routines, see Jackie Mason, *The World According to Me*. Mason is also available on DVD in the *Jackie Mason Comedy Trilogy*.

8. For this and other routines, see Henny Youngman, *The Best and the Worst of Henny Youngman* (Collectables Records), but available like all other CDs and DVDs used to prepare this talk, from Amazon.com This may be an old joke; I've seen it credited to Myron Cohen. But if it is an oldie it is a goodie, and Youngman's pacing and delivery are priceless.

9. See Mason above.

10. Philip Roth, "On the Air," *New American Review* 10, August, 1970.

22

The Transformation of Traditional Jewish Music in Jewish America

Hankus Netsky

Recent years have witnessed the emergence of a robust literature on American Jewish musical culture in the guise of articles and books about contributions Jewish performers and composers have made to American music. Writers and academics including Kenneth Kanter, Jack Gottlieb, Jeffrey Melnick, and Stephen Whitfield have actively sought to broaden the definition of Jewish music to include a startling number of musical styles, including everything from Richard Rogers' musicals and Carole King's pop songs to Bee Gees disco and Beastie Boys' hip-hop. Such an approach has hardly been limited to academia, as one will quickly discern by browsing such popular internet-websites as "Heebmagazine.com" or "Jewsrock.org."

In *A Right to Sing the Blues*, Melnick examines the two way street of African American and Jewish creativity in American popular music, arguing that Jewish composers and publishers such as Irving Berlin, George Gershwin Harold Arlen, Al Jolson, and the Witmark brothers (publishing company) "established Jewish agility at expressing and disseminating Black sounds and themes as a product of Jewish suffering and as a variant of Jewish cultural nationalism.[1]"

He also mentions the Jewish overtones he hears in the output of Tin Pan Alley composers, a theme first explored by Kenneth Kanter in *The Jews of Tin Pan Alley*, and echoed by Jack Gottlieb in his ambitious coffee-table volume, *Funny, It Doesn't Sound Jewish*. A cantor and Yiddish music aficionado, Gottlieb attempts to document what he hears as direct connections to Yiddish song and Hebrew prayers in many Tin Pan Alley classics. To his ear, Berlin's "Blue Skies" includes a thinly disguised version of the popular Hassidic dance tune *Reb Dovidl* (Rabbi David), Gershwin's "Summertime" echoes *Rozhinkes Mit Mandlen* (Raisins and Almonds), and the traditional eastern European melody for the Passover Seder's four questions provides a template for an interlude in Gershwin's "Bess, You is My Woman." A relentless peruser of American popular song, Gottlieb also unmasks "Jewish" melodic content ("signifiers") in the popular works of Leonard Bernstein, Marc Blitzstein, and Harold Arlen.[2]

Gottlieb presents an interesting thesis, and one that is somehow not all that surprising: Since composers create in a subconscious state, why wouldn't their music carry the stamp of their own cultural background, whether they want it to or not? And yet his book begs a more important question (putting aside the perennial debate over whether melodies that "sound" Jewish[3] are indeed "Jewish"): Whether such subconscious allusions to Jewish folksong actually signify intent on the part of composers to invoke "Jewishness," a question he wisely leaves unanswered. As Mark Slobin has pointed out, when Tin Pan Alley composers consciously touched on their Jewish roots, they generally did it to poke fun at their co-religionists.[4] In the world of American popular music, for a Jew to "sound" Jewish was usually to parody his or her roots. A popular music composer who wanted to succeed in America generally tried his or her best to write what others were writing, music based on Irish, British, or African-American models.

One thing we do know about the "Jewish" composers mentioned above is that they were not actually all that well attuned to their ancestral religious heritage. Kenneth Kanter points this out in his preface to "The Jews of Tin Pan Alley":

> The Men and women of Tin Pan Alley were highly assimilated Jews, or tried to be. They belonged to, or were not far from, a generation of immigrants who wanted nothing better than to be "Americanized." Although few, if any, rejected their Jewish heritage, few vociferously espoused it. They were primarily "life-cycle" Jews—Bar Mitzvahs, confirmations, weddings, and funerals provided as much Jewish identity as they desired.[5]

From Melnick, we find out that most of them had little connection to anything culturally Jewish:

> While several important Tin Pan Alley composers had cantorial roots in their families there is only meager evidence that any of the young Jews learned important musical lessons from the cantors. Berlin achieved his musical education on the streets and in the rathskellers, while Arlen's most influential teachers were other Jewish composers and straight-ahead jazz bands.[6]

Kanter, Melnick, Gottlieb, and Whitfield all do make the point that Jewish composers were thoroughly integrated into and, indeed, central to America's entertainment industry. Of course, such immersion in the musical cultures of host countries has been typical of Jews worldwide for many years. Algerians, Moroccans and Tunisians have all held Jewish oud and kanun players in high esteem, and Polish and Russian Jewish popular songwriters wielded influence in their home countries not unlike that of their counterparts on Tin Pan Alley.

Interesting as the aforementioned studies might be, one might want to keep in mind that the recent spate of interest in high-profile assimilated Jewish American composers doesn't actually make such individuals particularly significant within the world of Jewish creative arts, especially if that world is perceived in the more traditional sense, as a hedge against assimilation. While their work can give us insights into patterns of immigrant adaptation and Jewish business practices, psychology, and sociology, one can easily argue that their relevance to Jewish culture begins and ends there. The amount of Jewish content one actually finds in their music might best be compared to the trace quantities of peanuts found in snack foods made on certain machinery.

Moreover, regardless of whether or not one believes pop and Rock'n'roll songs penned by Jewish composers are "Jewish music," it is abundantly clear that such compositions only represent, at best, one side of the Jewish cultural coin. An alternative story can be told by examining the work of those whose creative output actively dovetailed with eastern European Jewish musical traditions that evolved over the course of many centuries: cantorials, wedding dances, Hassidic melodies and Yiddish folk songs. Such genres provided the basis for Jewish theatre, popular, instrumental, and art song traditions, forms that began to germinate in Europe and continued to evolve in America at the hands of certain resourceful, creative, and culturally committed individuals.

Unfortunately, the work of those whose musical creativity nested in such traditions has largely been ignored by Jewish historians and most Jewish musicologists.[7] The few authors who have written about Jewish music have generally focused only on certain formal aspects of religious and art music traditions, dismissing popular and folk culture as unworthy of study. The lack of interest in the culture of immigrants among historians is actually not unique to those emanating from Jewish ethnicity. As ethnomusicologist Victor Greene has pointed out, American immigration historians have generally lagged behind their colleagues in related fields, such as ethnomusicology, anthropology, and folklore, in exploiting the ethnic aesthetic expressed through popular arts.[8] Anthropologist Margie McClean has argued that more comprehensive study of popular culture is necessary since such expression "presents the essence of a group's culture. As symbolic expressions of identity, they touch directly on a group's most deeply-held values . . ., reinforce a feeling of belonging . . ., and define the communities for others and themselves . . ."[9] Greene adds that,

"If (one's) goal is to monitor and asses the process of cultural assimilation among immigrants, then a more sophisticated exploitation of previously neglected sources, particularly the folk and popular arts, is essential. Reviewing the expressive culture among immigrants would certainly enhance an understanding of both the nature of ethnic cohesion and the variety of personal ties, even while they changed over time." [10]

It is through precisely such material that one learns the true story of Jewish adjustment to life in the New World. Mark Slobin has observed that early immigrant composers found common ground with their new American neighbors as they created Yiddish songs extolling family ties and romance, lamenting various kinds of conflict, empathizing with the plight of orphans, taking stock of marriage, and chronicling contemporary events. Such individuals also created popular song genres unique to the Jewish community that included folksong and folk dance arrangements, songs that parodied certain Jewish stereotypes, songs with staunchly Zionist themes, and songs that emphasized traditional religious observance. [11]

As the decades went by, Yiddish-American songwriters connected with their immigrant audience by writing songs about America as a land of opportunity, or its flip side, the land of the sweat shop. Others expressed nostalgia for European homelands, or composed melodramatic songs that dramatized the kinds of scandals that went along with adjustment to new lifestyles and mores. Traditional-style dance-songs quickly became standard-fare at family celebrations, and mixed-language songs poked fun at the difficulty immigrants had in adjusting to their new surroundings. Yiddish popular music constitutes a significant body of work that reveals a great deal about American Jewish history in the immigrant era and in the decades that followed it. It is perhaps time to accord the composers of these works their rightful place in Jewish cultural history.

Consider the case of Vilna-born Joseph Rumshinsky (1879–1956), who, by 1935, had composed over eighty Yiddish operettas containing almost four hundred songs. [12] Rumshinsky had abandoned his early religious training and his position in a synagogue choir to take a job as composer and music director in a theatre at age sixteen. Arriving in America in 1907, he found himself in an ideal position to set the standard for American Yiddish popular music.

Arguably as talented as any Broadway composer of his day, Rumshinsky had the ability to adapt his style to the popular trends of the time, while always keeping in mind the particular aesthetic sensibilities of his Jewish audience. *Mamenyu* (Dear Mother), his 1911 elegy to the victims of the Triangle Shirtwaist Factory fire, is as much a traditional prayer as it is a song, while *Dos Tsigayner Meydl* (The Gypsy Girl) weaves its seamy tale of exotic seductive power by syncopating the scale musicians call "Jewish Minor." [13] Equally comfortable writing songs with titles such as "In Mexico," In Harem" or *In Chulem Land* ("In Dreamland), his early love songs such as *Dos Lid Der Lib* ("The Song of Love") took their inspiration from Victor Herbert and the European music hall, but later on in his career, Rumshinsky turned back to the Yiddish folksong of his youth to concoct a truly remarkable hybrid Jewish-American popular style, crafting such love songs as, *Sheyn Vi Di L'vone* (Beautiful as the Moon) and *In Mayn Oygn Bistu Sheyn* (In My Eyes You Are Lovely).

Rumshinsky set the stage for other composers with solid Jewish musical backgrounds to carefully play to the divided sensibilities of their audience. Alexander Olshanetsky's traditional-sounding melodies unwind sensuously over tango and bolero rhythms (*Ikh Hob Dikh Tzufil Lib* {"I Love You Much Too Much"} and *Shiroh Adoshem Shir Khadash* {"Sing Unto the Lord a New Song"} respectively), invoking exotic middle-eastern tonalities, while Abe Ellstein and Sholom Secunda found a way to launch the "Jewish minor" into jazzier territory with Yiddish American classics including Abi *Gezunt* ("If You've Got Your Health") and *Bei Mir Bistu Sheyn* ("To Me, You're Beautiful").

Of course, it wasn't only composers who needed to adapt their styles to American tastes. European-born Yiddish actors also needed to find their American personas. None did it more gracefully than Seymour Rechtzeit (1911–2002) the son of a cantor from Lodz, who came to America as a *vunderkhazn* (boy wonder-cantor), first appearing with cantor Mordechai Hershman in a command performance for President Calvin Coolidge, and later apprenticing with superstar Yossele Rosenblatt on the Keith vaudeville circuit. Soon enough, he found his way into the Yiddish theatre, as a protégé of Boris Tomashevsky. But by the late 1930s, popular composer and radio music director Sam Medoff (otherwise known as "Dick Manning") had taken him under his wing, turning him into the "Yiddish Frank Sinatra," although the actual prototype for his new style was one of Medoff's other clients, Perry Como.[14]

Theatrical transformations were many and varied. Menashe Skulnik, once a romantic lead in Warsaw's theatres became the ultimate *shlemiel* on the American Yiddish stage, while Michal Michelesco an extraordinarily handsome matinee idol and a peerless tenor, became the Yiddish Nelson Eddy playing opposite Bella Meisels, his Jewish Jeannette MacDonald. Peysekhe Burstein, "Der Vilner Komiker" (the comedian from Vilna) became the embodiment of Odessa's sailors, while American-born Molly Picon, the "Jewish Fanny Brice" simultaneously channeled both Charlie Chaplin and Mary Pickford in her endearing comedic persona.

Although the American cantor's inability to resist the lure of popular music provided the dramatic plot-line for the world's first talking picture,[15] one can hardly claim that the choice between a career as religious officiate and Jazz or opera singer was always so cut and dry. Within America's cantorial realm we find such individuals such as Yossele Rosenblatt, a mega-star who created an entire genre of cantorial "parlor songs" suitable for his Vaudeville touring shows. Leybele Waldman earned his reputation as a radio cantor, as did Freydele Oysher and *Sheyndele di khazinte*, women whose singing talents were not welcome in the synagogues of their time. Jan Peerce and Richard Tucker, amply gifted tenors found themselves poised to take advantage of the blessings of a country that allowed them dual identity as operatic doyens and cantorial stars.

One singer who truly pushed cantorial music's stylistic envelope into new territory was Moyshe Oysher (1907–1958), the charismatic Bessarabian born Yiddish movie star whose flamboyant lifestyle challenged the boundaries of traditional Judaism as much as his gypsy-like cascades and jazzy flourishes stretched the limits of Jewish musical improvisation. Beginning his career as an actor in Rumania at age six, Oysher rose to fame in the American Jewish community for his role in Yiddish films, including *Yankel Der Shmid* (The Singing Blacksmith). A popular musical duet incorporated into that film, "Hassidic in America" (featuring his wife at the time, Florence Weiss), showed just how astute Oysher was in mingling Hassdic chant with the popular scat-singing craze of the day. His late 1940s recording of *Amar, Amar* ("Thus Said Rabbi Elazar"), with musical direction by the aforementioned Sam Medoff, offered a prototype for languid cantorial improvisation over a driving rhythm, a path largely ignored until the Middle Eastern World Beat revolution of the 1990s, and his recording of *Halevai* ("It Should Only Happen") set the pace for modern Yiddish swing. Along with his sister Freydele, his niece Marilyn Michaels and his other protégées, the Barry (Bagelman) Sisters, Oysher showed the world that Jewish music could indeed breathe with a truly modern American spirit.

Even the St. Petersburg Jewish Art Music tradition took a new turn in America at the hands of Lazar Weiner (1897–1982), a pianist and composer from Kiev who dedicated his life in America to Jewish vocal and choral music. Encouraged by Jewish music pioneer Joel Engel, Weiner learned every nuance of Jewish traditional and European concert music. He wrote numerous Yiddish Cantatas and even translated European masterworks into Yiddish. His settings of poems by such trailblazing New York writers as Jacob Glatstein, Jacob Rolnick, and H. Leivick stand out as uniquely American artistic statements in a culture almost exclusively dominated by commercial creations.

As for Jewish-American instrumental style, hardly anyone would ever admit to being a *klezmer* on this side of the Atlantic, but the children of *klezmers* abounded and profoundly changed the traditional music they played. The European Jewish wedding ritual, with its *badkhonim* (wedding poets) and religious customs enjoyed only very temporary success on this side of the Atlantic. The children of immigrants turned American Jewish weddings into more orderly affairs, thanks to the American-style masters of ceremonies and dance leaders, who invented new rituals that doubled as photo-opportunities worthy of political press-conferences.

America's cities served as grand gathering places for musicians from diverse regions of Europe, becoming laboratories that produced distinctive regional klezmer repertoires and styles. Particular Russian sher medleys became codified through-composed compositions, while the Romanian *bulgar* emerged as the dance of choice for proud European Jewish immigrants. Virtuoso clarinetists such as Naftule Brandwein, Shloimke Beckerman and especially Dave Tarras became prolific composers and made iconic recordings that captured the lively ethnic spirit of 1920s and 30s American Jewish weddings for all time.

Klezmer/jazz hybrids gave instrumentalists a chance to test the crossover market. Lieutenant Joseph Frankel's "Yiddish Blues" led the way in 1918, followed closely by the 1921 recording, "Lena, the Queen of Palesteena," J. Russell Robinson's reworking of a popular Greek *bulgar* (Greek-Jewish dance). Through it, Robinson sought to reconcile his Jewish lineage with the jazz he pioneered with the "Original Dixieland Jazz Band." Such hybrids continued to gain momentum throughout the 1930s, providing an opening for Jewish culture on the popular main stage.

The movement was in full steam by the time of Benny Goodman's landmark 1938 Carnegie Hall concert when Ziggy Elman (indeed, the son of a *klezmer*) blew his famous Jewish dance chorus on Sholem Secunda's Yiddish crossover hit, *"Bei Mir Bistu Shein."* Adapting the sound of his father's Jewish clarinet to the trumpet, Elman had spawned a style that made the Jewish *krekhts* (literally "groan") an indispensable part of the jazz vocabulary, influencing everyone from Roy Eldridge to Clark Terry. Soon Artie Shaw was sparring with Goodman, not only over who could swing more, but also over who could sound more Jewish.[16] The creative atmosphere of the era that followed paved the way for such innovators as Sammy Musiker, Jewish clarinetist par-excellence and jazz tenor star with the Gene Krupa band who, in his arrangements of old-fashioned Jewish wedding repertoire, replaced static klezmer harmonies with modern chromatic underpinnings and introduced syncopation and big-band ensemble writing, even in settings created for his father-in law, traditional klezmer icon Dave Tarras. By the late 1950s, vibraphonist Terry Gibbs, son of New York Jewish bandleader and radio host Abe Gubenko, was fusing klezmer with bebop, pairing musicians from both worlds (including clarinetist Ray Musiker and pianist Alice Coltrane) to create his L.P., *Jewish Melodies in Jazztime.*

One should not overlook the fact that non-Jewish performers also showed the way toward innovation while "legitimizing" Jewish culture for the Jews themselves. It was Thomas "Fats" Waller's Russian Fantasy that most brilliantly merged the "Jewish minor" sound with the frenetic stomps of the

1920s, and it took Cab Calloway (in at least eight recordings with Jewish subtexts) to turn the cantor into a truly "hep" cat.[17] The Andrews Sisters put *"Bay Mir Bistu Sheyn"* on the charts; when they did (in 1938), it became the top-selling song of the year and the biggest song-hit the country had ever known. And the trend didn't stop there; by the post-war era, Jewish music had entered the repertoires of Connie Francis (Tzena, Tzena), Tom Jones (My Yiddishe Mama), Johnny Mathis, (Eli, Eli), Ray Charles (Where Can I Go?), Ertha Kit (Rumania Rumania), and Perry Como (Kol Nidre), just to name a few mainstream entertainers. Like Judaism itself, Jewish music had become a normal fact of American life.

In the world of Jewish music education, the 1950s were a time of serious transformation. The destruction of the eastern European Jewish community gave American Jews a profound reason to mourn, but the emergence of the State of Israel created an opportunity for them to re-invent their identity in dramatic ways. Musical traditions that had been the culmination of a thousand years of European Jewish civilization were quickly abandoned to make way for new ones that were being generated as quickly as the younger generation could take them in. In his preface to *The Songs We Sing*, a landmark songbook, published in 1950 by the Conservative movement, editor Harry Coopersmith announced the new agenda:

> The rise of the Nationalist Movement, culminating, at long last, in the establishment of the State of Israel, the upsurge of religious feeling, especially during the war years, an awakened concern on the part of educators and parents for the development of an integrated Jewish personality through a curriculum providing for emotional as well as intellectual growth—these are the forces most responsible for this renewed outpouring of a rich and variegated folk and art song.[18]

His impressive volume (containing over 260 songs) was indeed variegated with regard to English and Hebrew material, including contributions from such composers as Leonard Bernstein, Isidore Freed, Herbert Fromm and Judith Kaplan Eisenstein, and arrangements by Darius Milhaud and Kurt Weill. But the only section containing any Yiddish songs, under the caption "Hebrew and Yiddish," contained seventeen songs in Hebrew and only two in Yiddish, *Rozhinkes Mit Mandlen* (Raisins and Almonds) and *Oyfn Pripetshik* ("By The Fireplace"). Musically, American Jews were making a conscious effort to move on from their immigrant roots.

Hebrew took over as the proud and exotic language of the future, while Yiddish became the sentimental and funny language of the past. This was no problem for musician/satirist Mickey Katz, who knew, for example, that cowboys would be a lot funnier if they could sing in Yiddish. Spurred on by the comedic success of the Barton Brothers (see Mark Schechner's article in this volume), he impressed an RCA record executive by hamming it up in Yiddish in the recording studio at his final Spike Jones recording session. The result was his 1947 recording of *Heym Afn Range* (Home on the Range), which sold 150,000 copies in less than six months. Soon he was taking on every other possible target in popular music, including opera ("The Barber of Shlemiel," "Carmen Katz"), Rock'n'roll ("K'nock Around the Clock"), and American novelty ("The Flying Purple Kishke Eater"). Accompanied by a band that included the finest studio musicians of his time, including trombonist Si Zentner, drummer Sammy Weiss, and trumpeters Manny Klein and Ziggy Elman, Katz hired Hollywood arranger Nat Farber, music director for both Dinah Shore and Carol Burnett, to create a hybrid klezmer sound that proved to be enduring as both music and comedy.

The 1960s successor to Katz's musical and comedic legacy may well have been Alan Sherman, the Los Angeles-based folksinger/parodist whose New York-style Jewish mother loomed large both in his psyche and in his songs. He used *"Hava Nagila,"* with its incessantly increasing tempi to weave a tale of American upward mobility and *"Frere Jacques"* to frame a love letter in Brooklynese. In his setting of an Irish Jig, "Shake Hands With Your Uncle Max," the Jewish subtext bubbles over, as Sherman strings together a list of names of relatives and family friends that speaks volumes about the humor of Jewish ethnicity in the face of 1960s assimilation:

> Meet Marowitz, Barowitz, Handleman, Shandleman,
> Sperber and Gerber and Steiner and Stone;
> Moscowitz, Lupowitz,[19] Aarons and Behrens and
> Kleinman and Feinman and Friedman and Cohn;
> Smalowitz, Swalowitz, Teitlebaum, Mandlebaum,
> Levin, Levinsky, Levine and Levi;
> Brumberger, Shlumberger, Minkus and Pinkus and
> Stein with an "ei" and Styne with a "y." [20]

Of course, Sherman's success would hardly have been possible without the emergence in the previous decade of Theodore Bikel, who used the guitar he brought from Israel to earn traditional Yiddish folksong a place at the table in the American and international folk music revivals. Bikel's performing persona also arguably enabled the transformation of the most conservative of all Jewish traditions, that of the Hasidim. Heirs to dynasties that had held court in Eastern Europe for hundreds of years, their *rebes* (leaders) had been dramatically rescued from the encroaching fires of Poland, Hungary, Rumania, and Galicia's ghettos during World War 11 and brought to Brooklyn and other urban centers. Satmars, Bobovers, Skoliners, and others sought to hold firmly on to their traditional modes of expression while taking great pains to isolate themselves from the decadence of American culture.

Such complacency was not the path of Shlomo Carlebach (1925–1994), the rabbi who, with his populist approach, brought Hassidism and its music to the hippie generation. Emanating from a long line of German Orthodox rabbis and cantors, Carlebach began his career as an outreach emissary for the Lubavitch movement from 1951 until 1955, eventually splitting with the Hassidic movement's leadership over the issue of inclusion of women in prayer (ironically, later on, the open flirtatiousness he exhibited throughout his career was often cited as a sore point by women). After three years on his own, he took up his most important outreach tool, the guitar, and recorded his first album of new compositions in 1959. A breakthrough appearance at the Berkeley Folk Festival in 1966 led him to create the "House of Love and Prayer," arguably the first "New Age" synagogue, in San Francisco and, later, the Carlebach Shul in New York City.

His open friendship with practitioners of various Eastern religions and his free attitudes toward love and spirituality drew in both observant and non-observant followers all over the world (and drew the scorn of others), laying the groundwork for a network of "Holy Brothers" who embraced "Carlebach Judaism" as a viable pathway to contemporary enlightenment. But it was his elegantly grounded infectious traditional melodies, often accompanied by legions of busily strumming folk guitarists that gave Hassidic chant a truly American form, transforming the face of Jewish prayer melodies, dominating Israel's Hassidic festivals and Americas Jewish youth movements and summer camps, and continuing to have an impact far beyond the fringe status of his Rabbinical court.

American Hassidic communities have continued to spawn new hybrid versions of their traditions at the hands of rock crossover artists, including Mordechai Ben-David (son of Hassidic cantor David Verdeger), Avraham Freed and, most notably, the Piamenta Brothers, who bring the wailing spirit of Jimi Hendrix to bear while promulgating their Lubavitcher legacy. Meanwhile, As Steven Cohen and Arnold Eisen point out in *The Jew Within*, the radical democratization of traditional customs and observances at the hands of such figures as Carlebach and Zalman Schachter made Hassidic expression (once the object of endless parody) the new "authentic Judaism, the real thing, as opposed to the ersatz varieties of Judaism born of the other survival strategies employed to navigate modernity."[21] Furthermore, "more and more Jews during the past few decades, opposing efforts to diminish, downplay, and minimize ethnically based differences, have come to see Jewish ethnic distinctiveness in a new and more positive light.[22]

In this last quote, Cohen and Eisen touch upon the ethnic pride stirred up by the 1960s African-American roots phenomenon and the romanticization of eastern European Jewish traditions, most profoundly symbolized by "Fiddler on the Roof." A combination of all of these developments has created several generations of overtly "Jewish" creative artists, unwilling to live under the assimilationist guise of their precursors. One can count among them many of the current leaders of the klezmer revival (a much-discussed international phenomenon), a slew of excellent young cantors, Yiddish vocalists and cabaret performers, and, most recently, a "post klezmer" movement. These young performers mine the riches of Europe and America's Jewish cultural heritage with great irreverence and unapologetic Jewish pride, inventing such forms as Yiddish hip hop and performance art, and entertaining each other by organizing festivals of Ivy-league collegiate klezmer, Jewish *acapella*, and Knitting Factory/John Zorn-affiliated "Radical Jewish Culture."

The entire atmosphere in which American Jewish culture functions today is one where third generation American Jews see their musical expression as part of a larger whole, part of a folk, improvisational and world music scene, no longer confining itself within a "musical shtetl." As such it is a bona fide "heritage" music that has taken its place alongside so many other revivified treasures, including New Orleans jazz, gospel, bluegrass, and Irish ceili. [23] One can find all kinds of examples in the mix, from Andy Statman, whose immersion in klezmer eventually led him toward an observant lifestyle, to Anthony Coleman, whose fascination with traditional Jewish "signifiers" leads him to compose and perform some of the most powerful music of today.

In an article reflecting on the klezmer revival, contemporary klezmer violinist Alicia Svigals articulates the idea that the current creative generation of Jewish artists considers it a top priority to advocate "for the seriousness the Yiddish heritage," asserting that their output must be compatible with the values of "high Jewish self esteem" and should point the way toward a "Jewish way to become more American."[24] Downtown Jewish music scene guru and Klezmatics founding member Frank London sums up the approaches he sees around him in the following way:

> For some musicians it's an outgrowth of their secular, cultural Jewish identity, while for others it's an expression of Jewish spirituality. Some people draw pride, as I do, in the secular, social activist Yiddish song tradition, while others are drawn to mystical, trance-inducing Hasidic *nigunim*. Some look for that nostalgic, warm feeling, while others look for answers as large as the Holocaust, or why Yiddish culture dies, or why it was killed off.[25]

Many of those involved in the current creative Jewish music scene see their "in your face" Jewish identities as a blatant and provocative challenge to the bland complacency of their own assimilated upper middle-class American Jewish upbringings. Radical Jewish Culture Guru John Zorn expresses his Jewish connection this way:

> How do I come to my Jewishness? I was raised in a completely secular environment; it was an environment of total alienation and denial when it came to matters Jewish. My parents were brutal when it came to eliminating the past. I came to Jewishness by walking down very different paths...I actually came to it

when I was living in Japan. There it was impossible to blend in, and I learned to value my position as "Other."[26]

For many years Zorn has flaunted traditional religious symbolism in his work, calling his recording label "Tzaddik" (the Hassidic term for a mystical religious scholar) and wearing a *tallis* as a performance outfit. He, more than any other individual has encouraged those who partake in what he has dubbed "Radical Jewish Culture" to draw on any and all possible facets of Jewish Cultural expression, be it American popular music by Jewish composers or Moroccan religious chant. One of his latest releases (a session led by Frank London), *khazones* (cantorials), features a prominent Conservative cantor, Jack Mendelsohn, jamming freely with some of the downtown scene's most creative and innovative musicians, including pianist Anthony Coleman and percussionist Gerald Cleaver.

Montreal-based Hip-hop artist Josh Dolgin (a.k.a. DJSocalled), a contemporary Hip-hop artist, felt that in order to stay true to the essence of hip-hop culture, which prides itself on "authentic" self-expression, he had no choice but to immerse himself in klezmer and cantorial traditions. In recent years he has taken to deriving his "beats" and "samples" from old Yiddish and klezmer recording.[27]

If hip-hop artists are ready to explore and sample old Yiddish recordings, can the Jewish academy be far behind? Only time will tell. But one thing's for certain: For those who take the trouble to explore the riches of America's Jewish heritage there is indeed plenty of music out there—much of which is close to a hundred years old! All one needs is access, something finally becoming easier in this age of digital transfers and file sharing. If Jewish institutions don't take on the preservation of such materials, individuals are likely to continue taking up the slack. The transformation of Jewish culture continues in America and, who knows; perhaps, the best is yet to come.

NOTES

1. Jeffrey Melnick, *A Right to Sing the Blues* (Cambridge, MA., 1999), p. 12.
2. Gottlieb also comments on "Jewish melodic content" in compositions by many non-Jews whom he claims were influenced by Jews, including Cole Porter and New Orleans blues man Spencer Williams.
3. The question of whether the melodies he selects actually "sound" Jewish is a debatable point in its own right—the minor mode, for example, is characteristic of a large number of central and eastern European musical traditions.
4. Mark Slobin, *Tenement Songs* (Urbana, 1982), p. 190.
5. Kenneth Aaron Kanter, The Jews on Tin Pan Alley (New York, 1982), p. x.
6. Melnick, *A Right to Sing the Blues*, p. 170.
7. Writers from the fields of ethnomusicology and folklore, including Moshe Beregovski, Chane Mlotek, Ruth Rubin, and Mark Slobin, and one musicologist,

Irene Heskes, have written extensively about Jewish popular music and folklore. Their work has been supplemented in recent years by the work of a younger group of scholars, mostly specializing in klezmer, including Walter Zev Feldman, Joel Rubin, James Loeffler, Tamar Barzell, Henry Sapoznik, Michael Alpert, Joshua Horowitz, Yale Strom, and myself.

8. Victor R. Greene, *A Singing Ambivalence, American Immigrants Between Old World and New, 1830–1930* (Kent, OH., 2004), p. xvii.

9. Margie McClain, *A Feeling for Life: Cultural Identity, Continuity, and the Arts* (Chicago, 1988), p. 12.

10. Greene, *A Singing Ambivalence*, p. 74.

11. Mark Slobin, *Tenement Songs* (Urbana, 1982), pp. 119–163.

12. Society of Jewish Composers, *Works as of July 1ˢᵗ, 1935* (New York, 1935).

13. I am referring here to a scale with a lowered third, a raised forth, and a lowered sixth degree.

14. Hankus Netsky, interview with Seymour Rechtzeit, New York, 1999.

15. "The Jazz Singer," starring Al Jolson, opened in 1927.

16. In A 1939 radio aircheck of "The Chant," Shaw quotes three "Jewish" melodies, *Yossel, Yossel, Bay Mir Bistu Sheyn*, and a Russian *kamarinska*.

17. A similar situation occurred during the klezmer revival era, when clarinetist Don Byron (an African American) became one of the key innovators. Much has been written about how his embracing of klezmer helped legitimize the genre.

18. Harry Coopersmith, *The Songs We Sing* (New York, 1950).

19. The reference here to Moscowitz and Lupowitz would have been an in-joke for fellow New Yorkers who frequented the *Rumenishe Kretchme* (Rumanian Tavern), a restaurant operated by famed Romanian tsimblist (hammered dulcimer player) Joseph Moscowitz and his partner a Mr. Lupowitz on the Lower East Side of Manhattan for many years.

20. Alan Sherman, *Shake Hands With Your Uncle Max*, from "The Best of Alan Sherman" (Rhino Records, Los Angeles, 1998).

21. Steven M. Cohen and Arnold M. Eisen, *The Jew Within: Self, Family, and Community in America* (Bloomington: Indiana University Press, 2000), p. 106.

22. Cohen and Eisen, *The Jew Within*, 107.

23. Barbara Kirshenblatt-Gimblett has defined "heritage" as "a mode of cultural production that gives the disappearing and gone a second life as an exhibit of itself." From "Theorizing Heritage," Ethomusicals vol. 30, no. 1, pp. 36-43 (Bloomington, 1994).

24. Alicia Svigals, "Why We Do This Anyway," in *American Klezmer* ed. Mark Slobin (Berkeley, 2002), p. 219.

25. Frank London, quoted in Marcus Gammel, Migration and Identity Politics in New York's Jewish Downtown Scene (Unpublished manuscript, 1999), p. 3.

26. John Zorn, quoted in Gammel (op. cit.).

27. Dolgin discussed his approach during a panel discussion that took place at Hebrew College's "Festival of Secular Jewish Culture," June 2005, Newton, MA.

23

America: Memories of Doubts and Hope

Elie Wiesel

We know very little about what is needed to create a religion. The first moments of the birth of any religion are always shrouded in secrecy. The origins remain nebulous, and that may be true also of the birth of a community. How is a community conceived? By whom? For what reason? What factors are necessary for a community to be born? In America we know that anyone who has studied American history or watched Hollywood films recognizes that normally a man, a family, a group of companions started on a journey on horses or on foot, ate and slept at certain places, and then under a tent they dreamt about the next day. And then another person came, another family, and all of a sudden there was a church—not yet a synagogue—and a community was born! With a shop, a bar . . . but we Jews are an abnormal people. When we do things, we do them differently. How did we go into that journey? Usually, we were condemned or elected to be an abnormal people. The decision to leave was a collective one. It came either as a punishment to go into exile, or as a reward to come back to Zion. Jewish history is such, that whenever you touch it, you enter historiosophy.

And then we speak about the event that occurred 350 years ago. Of course we realize that this new beginning was the start of a remarkable chapter of Jewish history that is life in America. And we shall see its trials and tribulations, its constant desire to undertake a quasi-prophetic mission to spread dreams of messianic waiting by establishing a poorly defined Diaspora with new horizons, a chapter filled with human anxiety and Jewish hope, inspiring moral commitment, and occasional moral disappointment. All this is what we are going to explore.

Now look. What happened? Twenty-three Jews came to what is now New York. And look what they have accomplished! In 350 years—what are 350 years!—in the history of the Jewish people. A history of 3500 years—two hundred, three hundred fifty, it's nothing; it's a blink of an eye. And yet, they who came from Recife in Brazil—and they came not because they wanted to, but because they were expelled when the Portuguese reconquered the country and brought with it the Inquisition. And you know, they came, of course, by boat. Everything that happened to them we shall see later on…the marvelous story that they developed. How they arrived . . . and they were caught by pirates. The pirates needed money. Then a French ship, the St. Catherine, freed them and rowed them to New Amsterdam. Peter Stuyvesant did not want to keep them. In fact, he wanted them to be deported as soon as possible. He was anti-Semitically inclined. But he was overruled by a powerful Dutch company in Amsterdam.

But it all began with a simple story. A fairytale of an extraordinary man passionately involved with maps and oceans, drawn to far away lands unknown to him and to his contemporaries. Correction, it all began on September 7, 1654 . . . with a dramatic story about a mistaken destination willed by destiny. A secret dream, perhaps, rooted in melancholy events in the history of an ancient people too long dispersed—and too often oppressed—eternally longing for a homeland. Was it nothing but an overwhelming desire by a sea-intoxicated traveler to find a refuge for future multitudes of uprooted men and women, unwanted by nations and persecuted by religious communities in most areas of the planet? Need I name the hero of our story Christopher Columbus? Who hasn't heard of his exploits? Who hasn't admired his audacity and imaginative powers? If we are here on this soil, on this blessed country, it is thanks to his vision of worlds waiting to be visited and his decision to go and return with exalting discoveries. Was he simply a professional sailor and explorer? He was more than that. He was a loyal servant of the devout King Ferdinand and Queen Isabella of Spain who risked his life for the honor and glory of their country! Is that the only reason for his leaving behind his family and friends so as to lead his expedition to the uncharted territories of his exalted fantasy. Who was he? In numerable stories and legends circulated about him, what it is clear is that had he not discovered America, Jews would not have gone to Brazil and from there—350 years ago—to New Amsterdam. And we would not have celebrated their arrival.

Naturally, we shall discuss his far-reaching impact on our lives now . . . and on Jewish history in general and perhaps even on general history. But for the moment let's stop at just one episode, or more precisely, on one aspect of his departure. The date, according to the Jewish calendar, remains beyond dispute. It happened on the 9th day of Av 1492, when Spanish Jews were ordered by the Church-dominated royal court to convert to Christianity or go into exile. When the last of them left the country, they crossed Columbus on his way to board Santa Maria. Was this simply a coincidence? In Jewish history, there are no coincidences, only encounters. And they became almost preordained, if at the moment they seemed deprived of meaning, they receive meaning later. And what is it? Remember, Columbus's aim was not to reach America, but India. Why? According to one theory, he, the son of *marranos*, or so it is claimed, had heard of a Jewish state, created by the lost ten tribes that existed and flourished somewhere in India. So, he wanted to go there and restore a link between them and their brethren still enduring exile.

I like that theory. In fact, it was Columbus himself who admitted that the goal of his project had some Jewish connection. He wrote to King Ferdinand and Queen Isabella—and I quote him—"Having expelled the Jews from your dominions, your Highness has ordered me to proceed with sufficient armament to the region of India." But is it not to them, but to another Marrano, Louis de Santagel, that he first communicated the result of his historic endeavor which was privately financed by descendants of Jewish converts to Christianity. Strange as it may sound, Columbus's intuition about the Jewish Kingdom in India rooted in bits of information was far from erroneous. There was a kind of Jewish kingdom in Cochin, in southern India, for a thousand years. And most of its remnants—when I was in India, I learned—made *aliyah* in the 1950's.

But Columbus disembarked not in India—he disembarked in the Caribbean. And thanks to him, exiled Jews from Spain and Portugal would later be able to find a haven in Brazil, which was then occupied by Portugal. And the first Jew to arrive in Boston came in 1649. We know his name: Solomon Franko. He didn't stay long. He was chased away from Boston. The first Jews to land as a group upon American soil arrived in New Amsterdam, as I said, in September 1654 –twenty-three adults and children.

Thus began a new chapter in Jewish history, both similar to and different from others, fascinating on more than one level. It contains major elements of what scholars call "The Mystery of Jewish Survival."

For historians, the first arrival of Jewish refugees to America's shores is a fiesta. No allegory, no fantasy, no imagination—only facts and memories. Everything has been recorded: where they came from, why they stopped here, the first marriage, the first child, the first rabbi, the first synagogue— we know so much about them that we could see ourselves as their contemporaries. And therefore, when we speak about them, we know what we are talking about.

Obsessed with memory, the Jewish people have kept alive, always, episodes and events that mark the beginnings of many of their communities in Diaspora. The story of the first is in scripture. It began with Joseph who found himself a refugee in Egypt followed by his family. Others were to experience a similar fate with less success. In Babylon, Rome, the Rhine provinces, Poland, Russia, Spain, France, Greece, and North Africa. We know the geopolitical and geo-religious conditions of migratory destination. We know by whom they've been deported and where and how they rebuilt their communal life. How they succeeded, suffered and endured.

Like Jacob's children in Egypt, the few, in many places, became many. They multiplied and prospered enabling some of their great men and women to occupy high positions in the world of finance, culture, politics and medicine. Until another enemy arose who wanted them totally assimilated or entirely absent so as to put an end to their singular, religious, or ethnic aspirations. Such enemies isolated them in ghettos, burned them as heretics, and/or condemned them to further exile and misery. With emphasis on detail, Jewish chroniclers felt it important to note that in 1654 Solomon Peterson was the first Jew to marry a Christian in New Amsterdam, now New York. That Asher Levy was a ritual butcher—a *shochet*—"excused from killing hogs because of his religion."

In 1655, three Jews bought the first Jewish burial place in the first Jewish cemetery. The Lopez family was the first to acquire social prominence in the early seventies. It is found that Aaron Lopez, a former *marrano*—who escaped from Portugal to Newport, had he remarried according to the law of Moses and of Israel—was praised by Doctor Ezra Stiles, later the president of Yale, as the most universally beloved of any man he ever knew. And Aaron Lopez continued his benefactions to his family, the Jewish nation and the entire community. Lopez made President Stiles meet a renowned Jewish scholar and Kabbalist, Rabbi H'iam Mitcha Habigal. Stiles was so impressed with the rabbi that he placed his portrait in the Yale gallery of important spiritual figures.

We learn how the community grew larger and larger. In colonial times, it numbered around one thousand to fifteen hundred members. Right away, its internal problems manifested themselves: how to observe *Kashrut*, how to arrange communal services on the Sabbath and holidays, how to behave towards renegades, how to attract rabbis and teachers and cantors. The first fifty-two page Sephardic prayer book for Yom Kippur and Rosh Hashanah was printed in 1751.

The rift between Ashkenazim and Sephardim could not be ignored. Complaints of discrimination were leveled on both sides. Which tradition should we follow—mind you, that is not new. We always had it. We had it even in my town—in my little town. There were always quarrels among the members of the community, what to include in the liturgy. And they would fight! Finally they went to an authority, and they asked, "What should we do?" And he said, "Follow your tradition!" And they said, "This is our tradition . . . to fight!"

In 1718 Yiddish or German speaking Ashkenazim became the majority, but the services were conducted according to the Sephardic ritual. In New

York's *Shearith Israel* it remains Sephardic to this day. In 1730, the first official synagogue was opened in New York thanks to a fundraising campaign among wealthy Jews in London, Amsterdam, Barbados, and other states. Fundraising is not a new phenomenon. In 1758, the beautiful synagogue was erected in Newport, Road Island. It still functions as a historical landmark.

Very fast for those times, a hundred years or so later, Jews became a factor in public affairs. Jewish life in America reminds some researchers of the highest form of symbiosis that was attained during the Golden Age in Spain and the Weimar Republic in Germany. Who hasn't learned that both ended in tragedy? And who hasn't had the conviction that, in this respect, the story of Jews in America has been and will remain different from the two others?

Almost from the outset, numerous immigrants found this country special. Named only in 1912 "The New World," it became what some called "The Land of Promise." And others, in Yiddish, "The Goldene Medina"— "The Land of Gold." And also, in literature, *galut shalhesit*: "An Exile of Grace and Compassion."

But politically and economically, the community resembled others in quasi-similar situations. It took sides. To solve the so-called Jewish question, some chose to let their Jewishness vanish while others believed in deepening it. Some prestigious families totally disappeared from Jewish history books. Others remained as inspiring mentors and benefactors in our chronicles. During the revolution, as always, Jews could be found in both camps. Some were for, others were against. Haym Solomon helped the revolutionary cause. Others in New York and Newport remained loyal to the mother country. The same conflict arose during the Civil War. In the North, Jews opposed slavery with all their heart. The humanism in biblical law favoring the stranger, the first law, literally, after the Ten Commandments is indeed about slavery, encourages Jews to oppose such bondage. Slavery is forbidden. It is not only forbidden to own slaves, it is forbidden to be a slave. And we are told the slave who chooses to remain a slave has to be punished because I am free, and I chose my freedom. But I cannot choose not to be free. A slave who wants to remain a slave, therefore, must be punished. And therefore, of course, we oppose slavery and the existence of slaves.

However, we must say that there were Jews in the South who were—they were a small minority but they were—slave owners and slave merchants. In the halls of Congress, the voice of Judah Benjamin was heard supporting the legality of slavery. There were rabbis who preached the virtues of abolition but others whose sermons praised the institution of slavery.

However, the real debate took place around the problem of excessive integration bordering on assimilation. With the growth of the Jewish population, two million at the beginning of the twentieth century, and its achievements in various fields of finance and culture, social success turned into a threat. What if the price for the sense of security would be too high? For it would be at the expense of Jewish identity. And what if the Jewish tradition would be the first victim of freedom accorded to Jews? Remember emancipation caused similar problems in Eastern Europe later on. In Eastern Europe where Jews profited, benefited from their newly acquired rights, they used those rights not to build more Yeshivot, but to enroll in colleges.

In 1839 Lazarus Cohen, a Jewish educator in Germany, entrusted the Jewish emigrants from his city going to America with the following message: "Friends, you are traveling to a land of freedom. There you will have the opportunity to live without compulsory Jewish education. Resist and withstand this tempting freedom. And do not turn away from the religion of our fathers. Do not throw away your sacred faith for quickly-lost earthly pleasures, for your faith brings you consolation and quiet in this life and will bring you certain happiness in the life hereafter. Do not tear yourself away from the laws in which your fathers and mothers searched for assurance and found it. The promise to remain good Jews *must* not ever and *should* never be broken during this trip—not in your life at home, nor when you go to sleep, nor when you rise again, nor in the education of your children."

The fears included in this letter were well-founded. In the colonial period, ten to fifteen percent of American Jews intermarried. Granted, hundred of synagogues were open in the coming decades. Everywhere, people quoted George Washington's superb letter to the Newport synagogue in which he pledged that his government would give bigotry no sanction and persecution no assistance.

Later, when General Uylsses Grant ordered all Jews expelled from the Army, his order was revoked by Lincoln. But with the years passing, the religion lost ground among the young. The conflict between generations erupted mostly in the first part of the twentieth century when children of Eastern European immigrants chose to rebel against their parents' ties to their religious pasts and opted for anarchists' theories: nihilism, socialism, secular Zionism, communism and atheism. Those were the years when the then anti-religious *Daily Forward*—that changed later on when I worked for it—published articles and ads appealing to its Jewish readers to abandon Yom Kippur services and replace them with festive dinners and balls. Those were the years when a warning by a Lithuanian sage did not sound out of place. "In America," he said, "Kosher food is not to be found anywhere. In America, even the stones are impure for consumption." Little did he know that one day we would have hundreds of kosher restaurants in New York and Boston and throughout the country. In other words, in some ultra religious circles, people believed that to emigrate to America meant to stop being Jewish.

Almost a century ago, in 1907, Israel Friedlander, Professor of Bible at the Jewish Theological Seminary, delivered an address whose pessimism reflected such fears. The lecture was called, "The Problem of Judaism in America" and insisted on the possibility that the benefits of freedom for Jews could bring about their dejudaization. He was mainly concerned with the absence of great minds in this community. He said, "In times gone by, Italy presented one of the finest and brightest faces of Jewish culture. Only two generations ago, it was able to produce a personality so profoundly and so genuinely Jewish as Shmuel David Luzzatto and to present American Jewry in our own generation with a man like Sabbatto Morais. Now the tone of Judaism in Italy is utterly stagnant."

"In France," he continued, "centuries ago Talmudic Judaism found its most brilliant exponents. Today, Judaism is but a lifeless and unsuccessful imitation of French Catholicism." Likewise, he went on, "in Germany, we stumble on all sides against indifference and apostasy." And what about America? His diagnosis is sad. "The condition here," he declared, "is scarcely different." He admits that there was a tremendous growth of American Judaism with its ever-increasing number of congregations and institutions. But these, he said, ". . . did not represent an organic growth from within but the result of great minds that came from the ghettos."

In general terms, he believed that American Jews were blind to the fact that the open door shown to the Jews was the dusk of Judaism: "That the nearer the problem of Jewry reaches a solution, the more complicated and the more dangerous becomes the problem of Judaism. That the more emancipated and prosperous and successful the Jews become, the more impoverished, defenseless, and threatened becomes Judaism. The only reason, and the only foundation, of their resistance."

Was he right? Certain facts may prove his point. Little or nothing remained from Alexandria's great schools of Talmud. Has Christianity survived because it adjusted to modernity, whereas Judaism survived because it didn't? But what about the times and places where Jews did adjust? Among the first to convert in medieval Catholic Spain were small communities, and their spiritual leaders, rabbis, who led their communities to conversion. What place do they occupy in Jewish history? Which of Moses Mendelssohn's—the great philosopher, the author of the *Biur*—which of his descendants remain Jewish? Can Jewish culture be severed from Jewish tradition like Shimon Dubnov—the greatest of the Jewish historians and my favorite-believed.

Friedlander believed in the spiritual and cultural power of the Jewish people, but not in its political influence. In spite of his pessimism, he predicted that America would become world Jewry's most vibrant center. And together with Ahad Ha-Am, Friedlander and Dubnov were cultural Zionists; both died tragically. Friedlander was murdered in 1920 while on a humanitarian mission in the Ukraine. Dubnov perished in 1941 in the Riga ghetto, murdered by a Gestapo officer who was his former student in Germany—of this maybe we shall talk another time, because he deserves a full lecture . . . a great historian who ended his life in the ghetto. And we know, from chronicles and witnesses, that he kept on writing his last volume of Jewish history, the greatest—really the greatest, better than Graetz—and his writings vanished. And I am convinced that they were buried somewhere near where he lived in the ghetto. And one day, my dream is to take a group of students, perhaps, and go to Riga and start digging.

Could the secular culture of Jews save them from enemies determined to lead them to destruction? The answer is clear: it did not. Could Jewish culture save them? Could Jewish culture be saved? Will it be? By whom?

In the introduction to his remarkable study on American Judaism on the 350th anniversary of the arrival of Jews to America, the young historian, the brilliant Jonathan Sarna—the son of the great scholar Nachum Sarna—tells of his own experience as he first became interested in American Jewish life and its history. I quote him, "I mentioned my interest", he said, at a distinguished rabbinical seminary, "and the scholar with whom I was speaking was absolutely appalled. 'American Jewish history,'" he growled, "'I can tell you all that you need to know about American Jewish history. The Jews came to America. They abandoned their faith. They began to live like Gentiles. After a generation or two, they intermarried and disappeared! That is American Jewish history. All the rest is commentary. Don't waste your time. Go and study Talmud.'"

Obviously, the distinguished scholar was unaware of the extraordinary growth of Talmudic schools that began to flourish in post-war America. Some speak of a true Jewish renaissance in the field of learning and culture. In literature and music, science and art, politics and academia, Jews have had an impact on the general environment which is disproportionate to the demographic situation which is ours. Others go as far as maintaining that since antiquity, there were never as many Jewish schools, with their teachers and students as there are now in the United States. Until the 1950s, Jews encountered great, and often scandalous, obstacles in their effort to be admitted to the best universities in the country. Professors and chair holders in Jewish studies were rare. Today, few academic institutions do not offer courses and programs in Jewish history, literature, and religion. Everywhere classes on Holocaust-related subjects are overcrowded. Israel, Yiddish literature, and medieval poetry have never attracted as many students.

In the larger context, even before World War II, American Jews did not fail their people. A strange visionary, Mordechai Noah, writer and diplomat, gathered a rally in 1824 in Buffalo and proclaimed the establishment of a city of refuge for homeless Jewish refugees. It didn't take off. His residents converted to Christianity, but to me, the idea sounds exciting. When the

Damascus blood libel inflicted fear and suffering on the Jewish community in Syria and its neighbors, the Jewish community here in America mobilized all its efforts to prevail upon the national leadership in Washington to come to the defense of the Syrian Jews.

The same may be said about the reaction to the violence occurring in the land of Israel between World War I and World War II. When in the thirties Arabs staged murderous pogroms in Palestine, twenty-five thousand Jews filled Madison Square Garden offering their solidarity with their victimized brethren. The Balfour Declaration, issued by the British Foreign Secretary in 1917, promising a homeland for the Jewish people, galvanized American Jewry. To be Jewish was no longer an obstacle to success. Literature and music welcomed Jews with honors. Felix Frankfurter was a respected member of the Supreme Court, Bernard Baruch had great success on Wall Street, Henry Morgenthau served in presidential cabinets.

Pluralism was not an empty word, nor was equality. Was there no discrimination? There was. Shameful racial discrimination towards black people. Religious and ethnic disrespect for minorities, excluding them from clubs, hotels, and apartment buildings. But compared to what my generation, had to endure in Europe, America was a paradise.

When I arrived in the United States in 1956, I was surprised to find a vibrant Jewish atmosphere. Religious in Brooklyn, cultural in Manhattan—I thought I understood why George Washington called America the Promised Land for the Jews. Four Yiddish daily newspapers, several Yiddish weeklies, monthlies magazines, a number of Yiddish theaters proved the vitality of a culture that was near extinction in Europe. Yiddish humor had made its way to Hollywood and the Borscht-bell and Broadway. Yiddish poets were admired, writers applauded. After all, Saul Bellow and Philip Roth and Malamud—wherever you turn, you find Jewish names on the summit of literary creativity. The *Forward*—where I worked together with Isaac Bashevis Singer—was the largest daily, and the communist *Freiheit* was the smallest. The *Forward* was more Jewish than socialist and the *Freiheit* more communist than Jewish. When the bloody Arab hate pogroms erupted in Palestine, the communist *Freiheit* condemned first the Arab hooligans and their British supporters. Shortly afterwards, ordered by Stalin, it changed its attitude both in tone and content. And now its headline banner accused the Zionist fascist who provoked the Arab uprising!

It took many events, many years, for the Jewish communist writers to show their disappointment in Stalin's anti-Semitism and to accept the idea that Jewish solidarity is an essential trait of Jewish identity and Jewish survival. A Jew alone must not be left alone.

When Jews were expelled from Spain and Portugal, they were received with open arms by their co-religionists in Greece and Morocco. When Jews were targeted in the smallest village in Europe, their fear was felt by Jews in Chicago and Boston. So has it always been, in our land of freedom, of social justice, which was meant to be the world capital of human compassion. And the question of course is it is still so today?

My question is, would it father vicious anti-semitism, would such prejudice be as popular today as it was in the 1930s? Would Charles Lindbergh, the all-American hero, have dared to be so openly anti-Semitic now as he was then? Remember, in spite of his pro-Hitler views and anti-Semitic statements, Charles Lindbergh was sent by President Truman on a mission to postwar occupied Germany. Lindbergh was made a General by President Eisenhower. Lindbergh was invited to the White House more than once by President Nixon. Have we forgotten who that man was? That he was decorated by Hitler, by Himmler, by Goering? And he was *openly* pro-Nazi!

After the last sixty-odd years, American Jewry feels that this could never happen now. We feel that Jewish life must now be centered, must center its activity, must organize its defining identity around two major themes: the Holocaust, the darkest moment in Jewish history; and Israel, the most luminous. In other words, the Jew feels himself or herself Jewish by linking their faith to the memory of the dead in Europe and to the hope of the living in Israel. Let's admit it.

In general terms, many Jews in the ghettos, rightly or not, had the painful feeling that American Jews, especially on leadership levels, had let them down. It began with the sad story of the *St. Louis*. More than a thousand Jewish refugees were aboard the ship. They had visas to Cuba but were not allowed to disembark. So, the ship was sent back to Germany. The captain, a good person—a Gentile captain of the ship, a German—knew what the refugees knew, what was awaiting them in Germany. After all, the event occurred only several months after *Kristallnacht*. And he, therefore, encouraged them to do everything they could to disembark in America. The ship spent days and nights not far from American shores, but Roosevelt refused. And to this day, I don't understand why. He was supposed to be a father figure to American Jewry and to me.

Believe me, in my little town, I did not know the name of Ben Gurion, hardly heard of Herzl. I lived in a Yeshiva world. But I knew the name of Franklin Delano Roosevelt as a friend of the Jewish people. We said prayers for him . . . and he refused a thousand men and women and children . . . sending them back to Germany.

Had the Jews in America tried? Had they done enough to make Roosevelt change his attitude? I don't know. Had they tried hard enough? I don't know! There are so many things I don't know.

I, at times, am moved to despair. It is because of what came later. And I say this with anguish and sorrow. And I repeat what I must have stated more than once—namely, that I do not consider myself a judge, but only a witness. I try to refrain from passing judgment on others. I do not believe that Jewish leaders in the early forties were insensitive to Jewish suffering and indifferent to what was happening over there under the silent heavens of Auschwitz. Did they know? And if they did, could they have done more to move the Allies to save the Jews from unspeakable horrors and death?

Historians disagree on the answers, but I read and reread letters written in the ghettos. And what I find in them is heartbreaking. I read and reread the pathetic appeals of the commander and chief of the Warsaw Ghetto Uprising to Jewish leaders in London and in America urging them to declare mass demonstrations and hunger strikes. All political and tactical explanations considered, why was so little done? The fact is that nothing was even tried.

I have asked five American presidents and countless senators and representatives and generals why the Allies did not bomb Birkenau, why they did not bomb the railways leading to Birkenau. And they had no answer. But in truth, the same question could also have been addressed with equal poignancy to Jewish leaders of the time.

I have been tormented by this unanswerable question for many years, but particularly this year which marks the sixtieth anniversary of the extermination of Hungarian Jewry which, I will repeat in my last breath, could have been saved. In fact, of all the large Jewish communities in German-occupied Europe, it alone could have been saved . . . and it wasn't. It could have been saved because it was the last. Because it began days before D-day and lasted for weeks after D-day. Hitler had lost the war already. The whole world knew it. The German nation knew it! The end was near. Allied aircrafts dominated the skies. There was little to stop them from bombing weapons, factories, and railways while ten thousand Jews—men, women, children—were gassed and burned daily in Birkenau alone. Had the railways been destroyed, it would have at least slowed down the process and told Berlin that somebody cared. Why weren't they? Again, I do not accuse, indict, or condemn anyone. But my questions remain. Questions . . .

That also applies, on a quite different level, to what I used to feel about official Jewish passivity towards Russian Jewry in the early years of our battle for their freedom. I visited the Soviet Union in 1965 and brought back a personal report on its Jews. I described their fear, but also their courageous struggle for hope. I told the tale of young Jews who in the thousands on Simchat Torah gathered in front of the great synagogue of St. Petersburg to express their allegiance with fervor and song to the Jewish people and its destiny. I called my book *The Jews of Silence*, but it was misunderstood and surely misinterpreted. I did not say that they, the Russian Jews, were the Jews of silence, but that *we* were the Jews of silence.

My main directed criticism was at our leadership. As always, it was impossible to move its members to action. I remember my late friend, Abraham Joshua Heschel and I would go from conference to conference, from convention to convention, trying to make people aware of what was happening in the Soviet Union without success. Most leaders had other priorities and many excuses for not doing anything. Who came to our demonstrations? Teenagers, thank God for them! At best, their parents brought them by car at our gathering and left. In truth, the situation changed, and when it changed it was thanks to the children. At one point, they prevailed upon their parents, saying that your generation did not do enough for European Jews when they needed you. Let's not repeat their moral mistakes and their historical failures, because then we too shall be criticized.

In the final analysis, the renaissance of Russian Jewry will remain one of the most spectacular triumphs in the history of the Jewish people in the twentieth century. Logically, Russian Jews should have vanished from the stage but they did not. In Israel, they now play central roles in politics, in the arts, and sciences—a million Russian Jews live now in Israel. When I think of them, I feel so proud, so rewarded. Never would I have believed—and I was then in Russia, that meant a lot—that I would see that miracle. And the truth is, it is thanks to Israel that they had the desire to leave, the desire to be Jewish, and to continue history—our story—to the end of times.

And, in conclusion, this brings us to the second element, Israel, that is motivating Jewish existence in America today. How is one to measure a community's commitment to its own passion for a land and a people on the other side of borders and oceans? How is one to explain that the majority of American Jews have not even visited Israel? How do they manage to resist, to relinquish their curiosity just to see what the Jewish state, the dream of their parents and grandparents, looks like! Just to feel what a Jew feels when he or she walks in the all-Jewish quarter of Jerusalem filled with prayers from the time of David and Jeremiah.

Not so long ago, some leaders in Israel felt what Jews in the ghetto had felt, that they were let down by American Jews. It happened after the Sinai-Suez campaign in 1956. It was a military triumph and a political defeat, there was no reason for Israel to join the colonial powers, really, for its monetary gain. The Eisenhower administration applied inordinate pressure on Israel to give back the Sinai-Suez to Egypt. The Russians threatened nuclear weapons. Ben Gurion was convinced that American Jews would rally behind Israel, but they did not. His pleas to some of them went unheeded. Their response was polite, but negative. Were they afraid of being accused of double loyalty? Whatever the reason, they must have felt humbled by the test. Their failure was also his defeat. It hurt him as much as the first. Guy de Rothschild presented him with a stunning proposal: to dissolve the Zionist movement altogether. Who needs it, he said! Since it proved to be disloyal and useless. And replace it simply with a worldwide network of associations of friends of Israel. It was an outburst of anger and bitterness on his part, and nothing came of it—thank God.

What is the situation of Jews today in America? Is it still a different country? Things are different, of course. Things are different. Times have changed. American Jews are no longer afraid to speak up against the administration's policy in the Middle East, even when it's unfair to the Jewish state. What you mentioned, about the uniqueness of American Jewish history, Dr. Katz, is true: I always thought about it. I even spoke to President Reagan, with whom I had very warm relations, about it. I would not have been able to do what I have done in any other country, only in America . . . could a refugee Jew, such as myself, who came to America stateless—who came here and worked, first, as a journalist—I didn't come as a refugee, I came here as a journalist and by accident I stayed—have gone to the White House and speak as I did, with utter frankness, without any fear, to the president of the United States? I belong to a tradition that compels me to speak truth to power, and the expression caught on. Now there are books called *Speaking Truth to Power*.

Demographically, of course, there is a problem which we hear about—the birthrate being what it is—American Jewry is getting smaller in number but not necessarily weaker in influence. We have learned lessons from our forefathers who arrived to settle here 350 years ago, the most important one being that the Jews' principle obligation in society is to remain Jewish, which also entails helping other communities, other minorities, working for human rights, working for the happiness of others, for their welfare. The place of a Jew in history is measured by his or her place in Jewish history. That is what we must learn. Our priorities must be Jewish but without, at one and the same time, ceasing to be universal. In other words, they are to be inclusive, not exclusive. I don't believe in triumphalism. I don't believe in ghettoism. We are who we are. But because we are part of the human family, we *must* look around us. And if people suffer, we must help them. If people are being massacred in Africa, we must help them. In Sudan, we must help them. In Rwanda, we must help those who are still there. We must. We must do it simply because we are not only Jews, we are human. We are part of humanity.

And so, to help another person or another community of persons is an ethical commandment, but not if it means that I must give up my Jewishness in order to attain this end. It is the Jew in me that is universal. To relinquish the one or the other is nothing but a mutilating, self-defeating exercise. And this joint commitment has been tried in other countries and societies, but never as fruitfully as here in America.

Now, as 350 years ago, young Jewish students are eager to learn where they come from and for what purpose. They discover the beauty and the magic and enrichment one finds in learning. How did the late Louie Finkerstein put it, "Every people has its aristocracy." We Jews have ours. Our aristocrat is the scholar. The respect that we pay the scholar is unique.

And so with all the challenges still before us, and with all the occasional setbacks and disappointments that we may encounter in attempting to affirm the creative ingredients of our Jewishness as a factor in Jewish history, I think of America and the Jew in America with less apprehension than hope.

Anti-Semitism comes and goes and comes again. It disturbs and frightens me, but it puzzles me even more. It is the oldest group hatred from antiquity to have survived antiquity. When, and by what means, will it disappear? Whatever may we do to change people's image of us? It must, and will not, alter the image of ourselves. The fact is that if Auschwitz did not cure the world of anti-Semitism, what can? And what will? I know, and we all know, that much is still to be done to justify the hope of our ancestors.

What about tomorrow—how are we to anticipate America's Jewish evolution? Naturally I am not speaking about the next 350 years. Instead I would suggest that we explore a simple question which, these days, does contain a certain urgency. Where, and at what pace, is Jewish history in general—and in America in particular—going? How are we to measure its direction? Is it still going uphill? Will it be defined by the challenging embodiment of its promise or its fears of unthinkable threats and perils which are not only addressed at us but also targeted at the whole world . . . the whole world? Will America replace Eastern Europe with its new forms of what used to be the Kingdom of the shtetl? In other words, I am not speaking about tomorrow, but the day after . . .

I know, the pessimists among us love to quote statistics. It seems that we are losing ground. Intermarriage, especially in small, urban areas, is slow, yet unstoppable; assimilation; general negligence in matters of education . . . astonishingly few Jews are therefore really motivated to take on their destiny and continue to be Leaders with moral concepts. When I came to America, we had here six million Jews. Have we lost a million? That's what I hear. Some insensitive theoreticians go as far as calling the process a new Holocaust—which I resent—implying that there will be time when we shall become less than a minority.

Well, I don't agree with such a pessimistic outlook. I distrust and dislike statistics. I admit it. Also, Jewish tradition negates both the necessity and the validity of statistics. Jews simply refuse to believe in numbers. If we were to rely on their logic, our people would have long ago vanished from the surface of history. We did not lack opportunities: at times through conversion, at other times confronted by oppressive elites, seemingly abandoned by the God of Abraham, Isaac, and Jacob . . . vanquished by armies of gigantic empires, exiled to the far corners of the Earth. In terms of pure logic, we could have gone under more than once—wasn't that the message sent to us by history? Go away, people of Israel! We don't want your gifts nor your poisons. Go! Disappear! Slowly, very slowly or dramatically at your own pace or at ours . . . but go!

A Chinese scholar heard from a visitor that the Jewish people numbered only fourteen million. He is supposed to have exclaimed, "What? In my land that figure is accepted as an accountant's mistake! Only three million in Israel? Give them a hotel!"

But we are still here in the midst of history—but how did we manage? My late teacher and friend, who I remember everyday when I open the Talmud, Saul Leiberman, once gave me the following explanation -and this is, of course, our conclusion:

It happened during the week preceding the Six Day War of 1967. The worldwide Jewish community lived in anguish. Personally, as a correspondent at the United Nations, I was desperate. I listened to the Arab delegates speaking freely about their resolve to throw all the Israelis into the sea. I believe that it could very well happen. In France, the great philosopher Raymon Aron published a front-page editorial in the *Le Figaro* saying, "I do not wish to survive Israel." Some of us, many of us, shared his feeling. I went then to Israel. Single. I had nobody. I went during the war thinking that I will be there when it happens. I confess: I sinned. I sinned because I didn't have the faith in the Israeli Army which I should have had. I really believed that the world was already preparing their eulogies.

Well, in this context the only one who was optimistic was Leiberman. And his optimism disturbed me. I asked him, "How do you manage to look so cheerful? Aren't you worried?" Listen to his answer.

He said, "The master of the universe is like a banker. When the bank invests too much in an enterprise, it can no longer let it go bankrupt. God has, for such a long time, invested so much in the Jewish people, that he can no longer withdraw from it! That is the reason for my faith," he said.

Well, I know nothing about banking, but I know something about history. That, shall I say, is the reason for my faith too—my faith for America, for Israel, for America's Jews. Granted, we know that occasionally outside or internal pressure proved to be powerful . . . that there were Jewish communities that dissolved themselves. But not here. Most communities were endowed with what the philosophers called *emunah*; we call it faith, awareness, commitment, memory, conscientiousness...a desire to stay above ground alive and creative like an open hand.

Paul Celan, the great poet who died—or rather committed suicide—in one of his poems said a handshake is a poem. And we can be that handshake. That's why I believe that wherever we are, we look at others—friends and allies, contemporaries—and we share their destiny as they share ours. And we are all possessed by an irresistible urge to invoke hope even when it seems frail, even when, at times, there is none.

And that is the story of Christopher Columbus's coming here . . .

Breinigsville, PA USA
18 October 2010
247557BV00002B/1/P